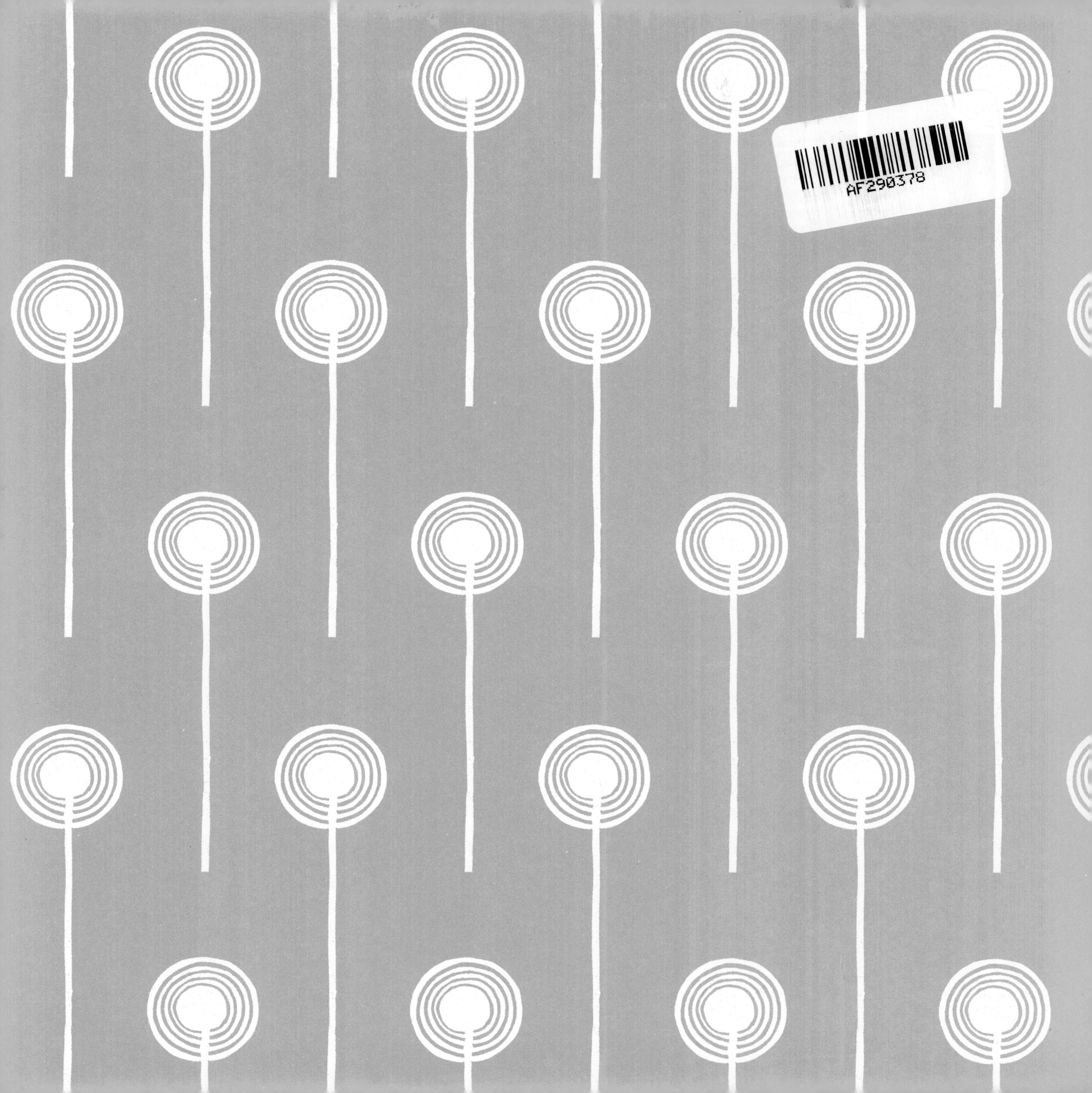

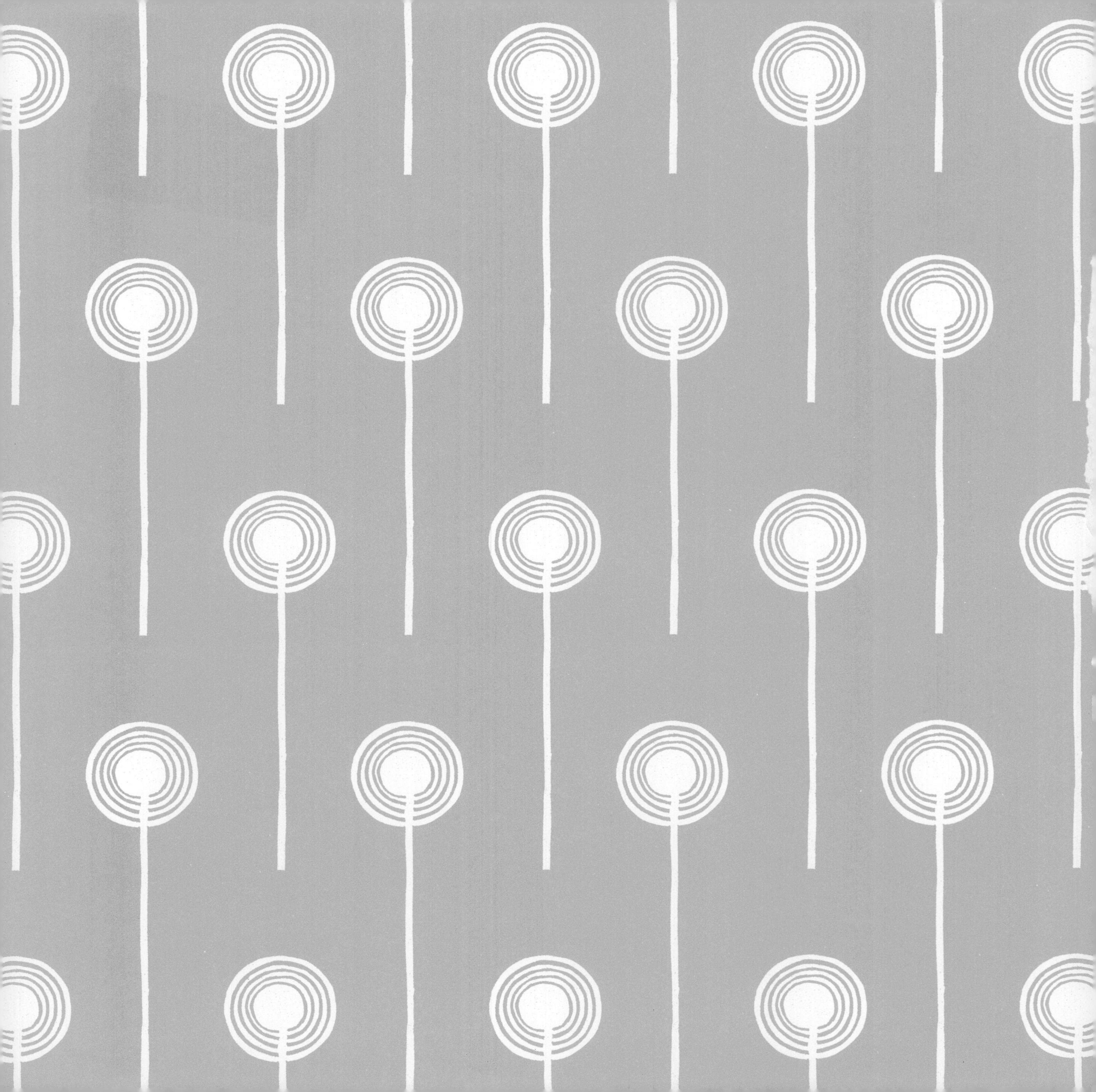

Angie Lewin
Plants and Places

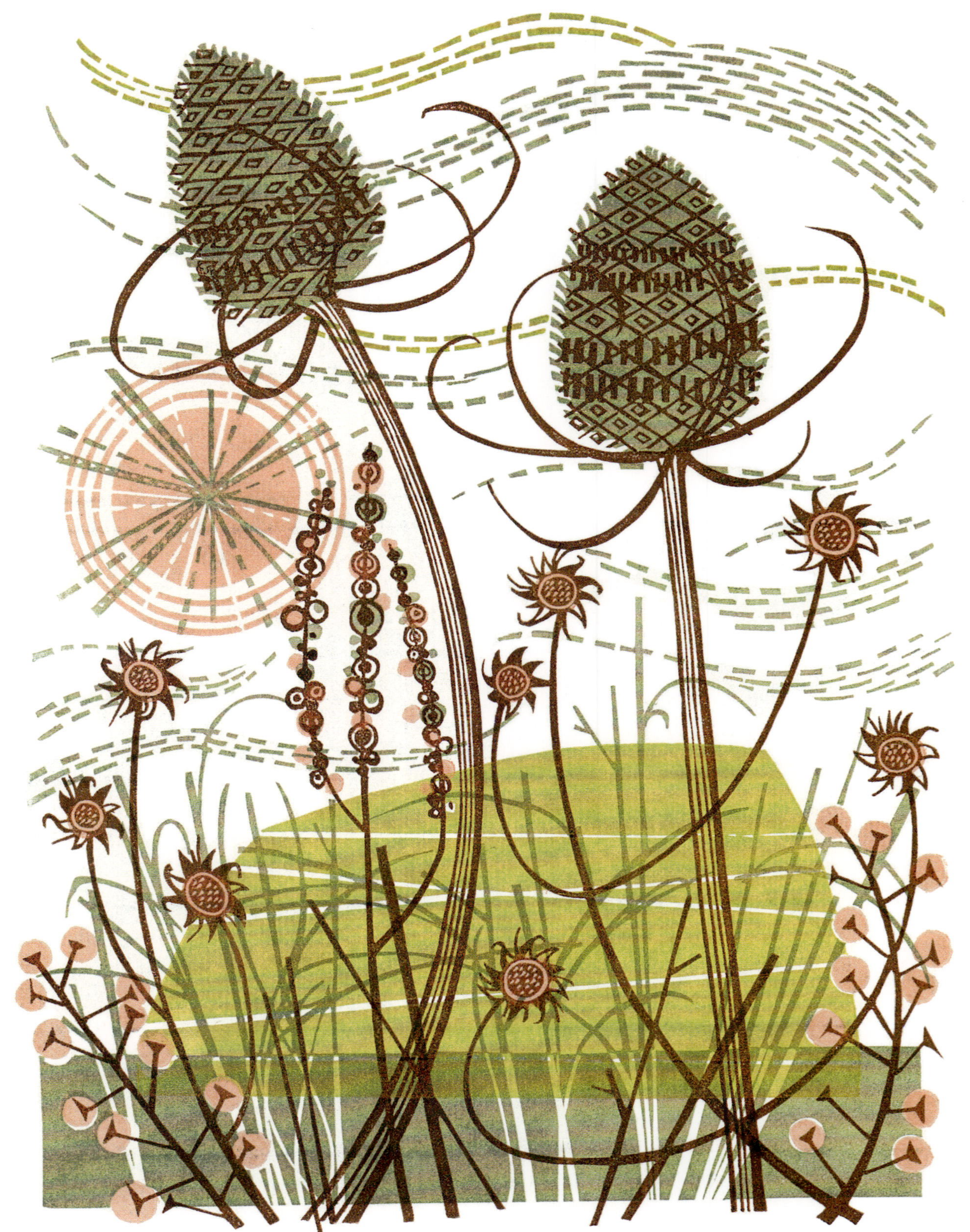

Angie Lewin

Plants and Places

Text by *Leslie Geddes-Brown*

MERRELL
LONDON · NEW YORK

First published 2010 by

Merrell Publishers Limited
81 Southwark Street
London SE1 0HX

merrellpublishers.com

British Library Cataloguing-in-Publication Data:
Angie Lewin : plants and places.
1. Lewin, Angie. 2. Nature in art.
I. Title II. Geddes-Brown, Leslie.
769.9′2-dc22

ISBN 978-1-8589-4536-1

Produced by Merrell Publishers Limited
Designed by Nicola Bailey
Project-managed by Marion Moisy

Printed and bound in China

ANGIE LEWIN, a member of the Royal Society of Painter-
Printmakers and the Society of Wood Engravers, has
exhibited her work around the United Kingdom. With her
husband, Simon, she runs St Jude's in Norfolk, producing
a range of printed fabrics. For further information, visit
angielewin.co.uk.

LESLIE GEDDES-BROWN is a leading writer on gardening and
interior design. Her books include Merrell's *Garden Wisdom*
(2009), which features illustrations by Angie Lewin.

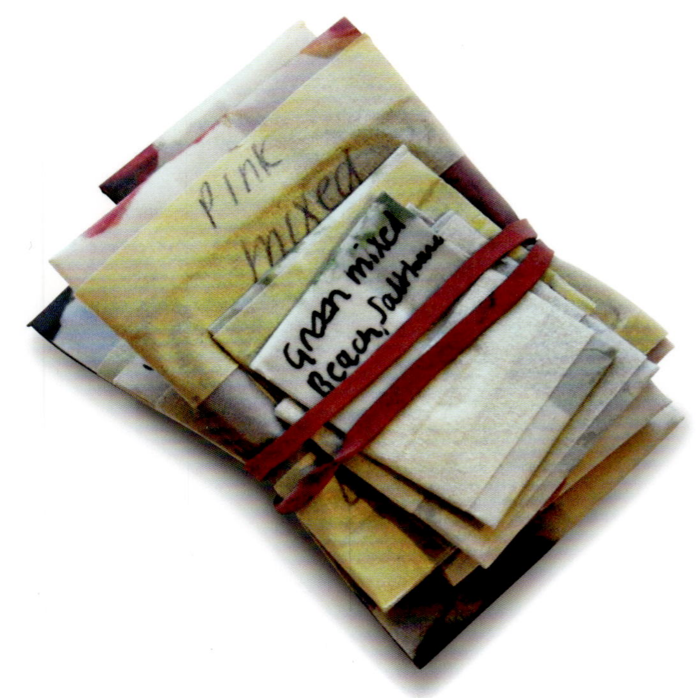

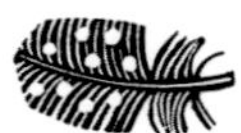

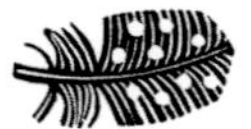

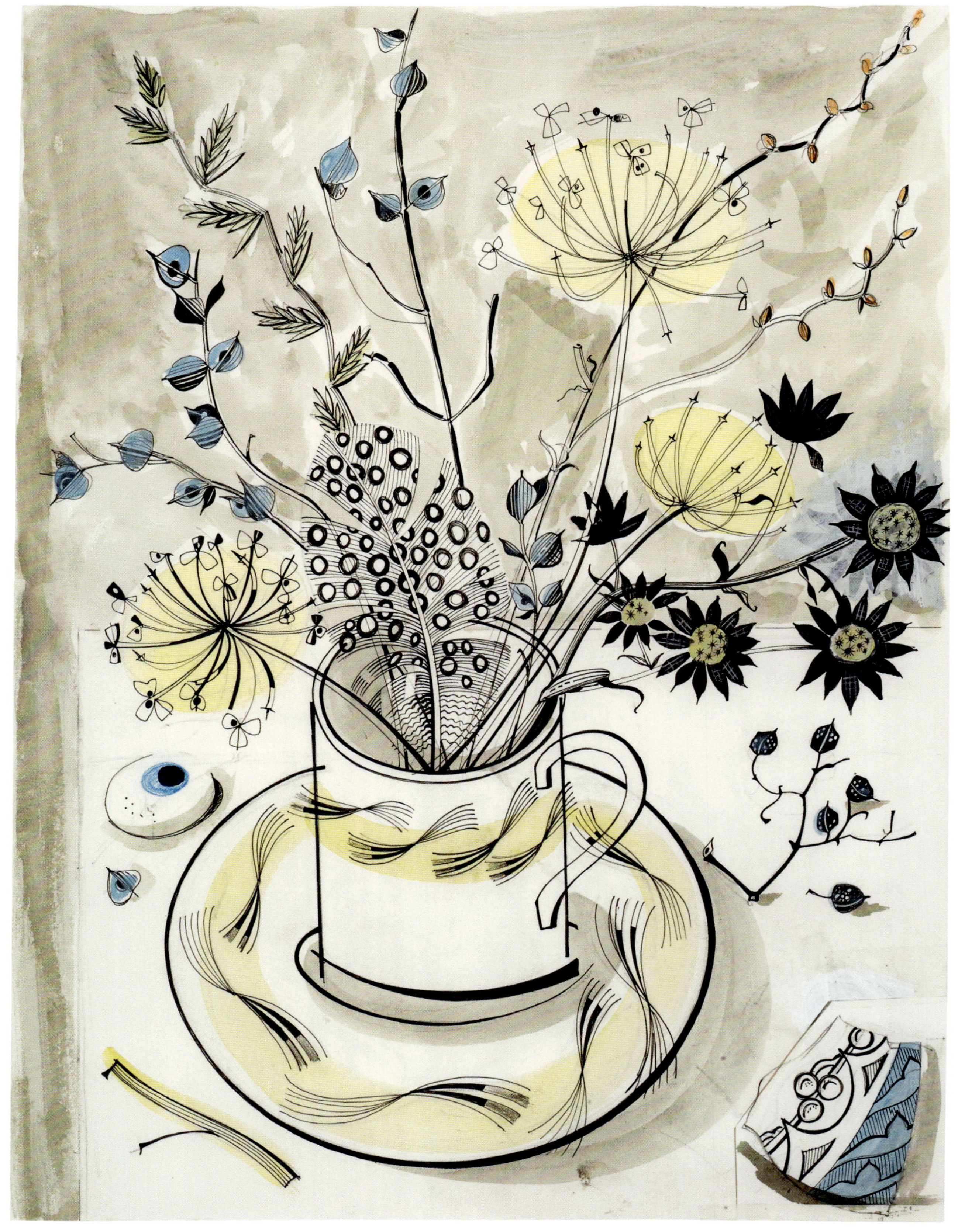

Preface

Angie Lewin

When I look through my sketchbooks and prints, I find a record of past travels, places and plant studies. Sketchy watercolours remind me of chilly autumn days by the river or on a windswept shingle beach; flicking through my pencil sketches with scribbled colour notes of common sorrel and plantain, I remember that they were made quickly by a hill track, the sketchbook's pages taped down against the wind. The sketches contrast with more detailed coloured drawings of teasels, achillea and globe thistles made in my Norfolk garden on a summer's day. These studies give me the information I need for a print. Certain plants I'm very familiar with, and I draw them in the different habitats in which they grow.

I focus on insignificant plants that are often considered to be weeds. Their structure is as interesting as that of exotic specimens in a botanic garden. I try to find how best to depict a plant's structure and character, not with botanical accuracy but by capturing its distinctive characteristics. For this reason, scale is not important. I rarely draw plants in flower, but instead look at the framework of stems and the shapes of seed heads and buds. I'll concentrate on the features that I see as unique, such as the way purple gradually colours the green flower heads of *Allium sphaerocephalon* as they come into bloom from the top buds downwards.

Certain plants to me are symbolic of the landscapes in which they are found: horned poppies on a Norfolk shingle bank, ramsons in deciduous woodland, and valerian by a Scottish river. I'm attracted to sweeping, often desolate places: north Norfolk clifftops, salt marshes and beaches, Highland rivers, hill lochs and west-coast seascapes. What captures my attention is the way a plant's growth is determined by its environment, and its survival against adversity. The stark skeletal outlines of alexanders on a clifftop against the expanse of gunmetal sea inspired my early prints when I first lived on the North Sea coast, perhaps because I am influenced by Alan Reynolds's

paintings — his dark silhouettes of plants
showing spikes, spines and twisting stems
against receding landscapes.

When I'm walking in the mountains of
Scotland or on an exposed East Anglian beach,
the limitless views draw my attention to native
plants at my feet. I get down to ground level,
where I concentrate on a small patch of earth
crammed with interlocking plant forms. As
I draw the indistinguishable mass of growth,
I gradually unravel the structure of individual
plants and explore the patterns made by their
relationships with one another. I'll take a stalk
of grass, a piece of dried, rust-red bracken, a
certain pebble or a twist of bladderwrack to
draw in the studio for future still lifes. The larger
landscape gives a sense of the habitat that shaped
these plants.

In the studio, I surround myself with these
sketches and collections gathered from the wild,
and these are the starting point for my next
print or fabric design. Each one leads naturally
on to the next. My inspiration has and always
will come from the seemingly infinite variety
of plants and an intimate knowledge of how
they grow together.

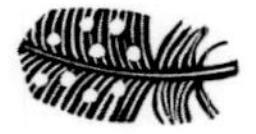

*'I collect ceramics by Eric
Ravilious, including his
coronation mugs (left and
right on the shelf). I used a
coffee cup decorated with his
"Garden" design from 1938
in my drawing on page 6, a
preparatory drawing for my
linocut* The Moonlit Cup
(see page 167).'

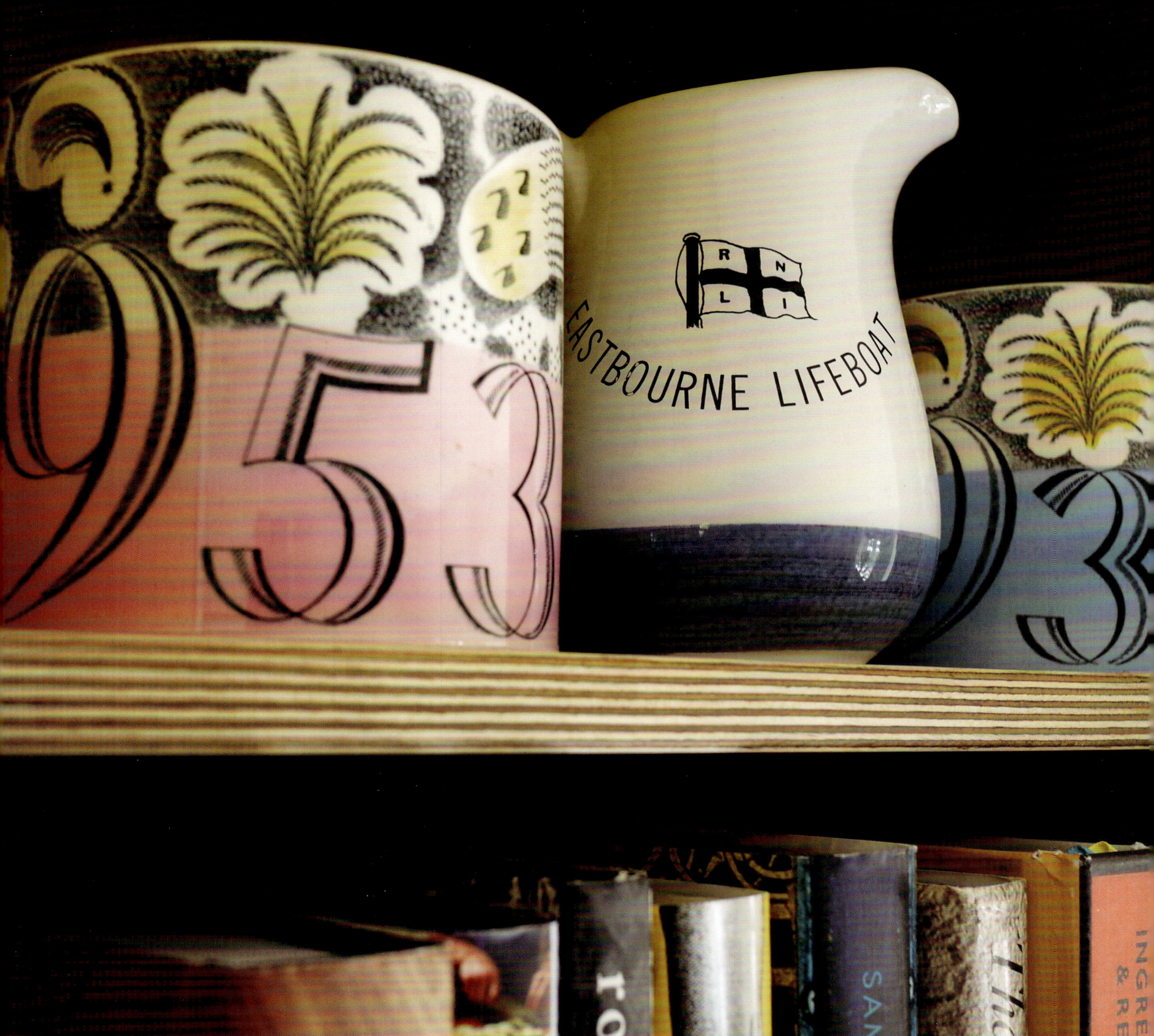
953
RNLI
EASTBOURNE LIFEBOAT
93
roast
SAM & S
INGREDIENTS
& RECIPES

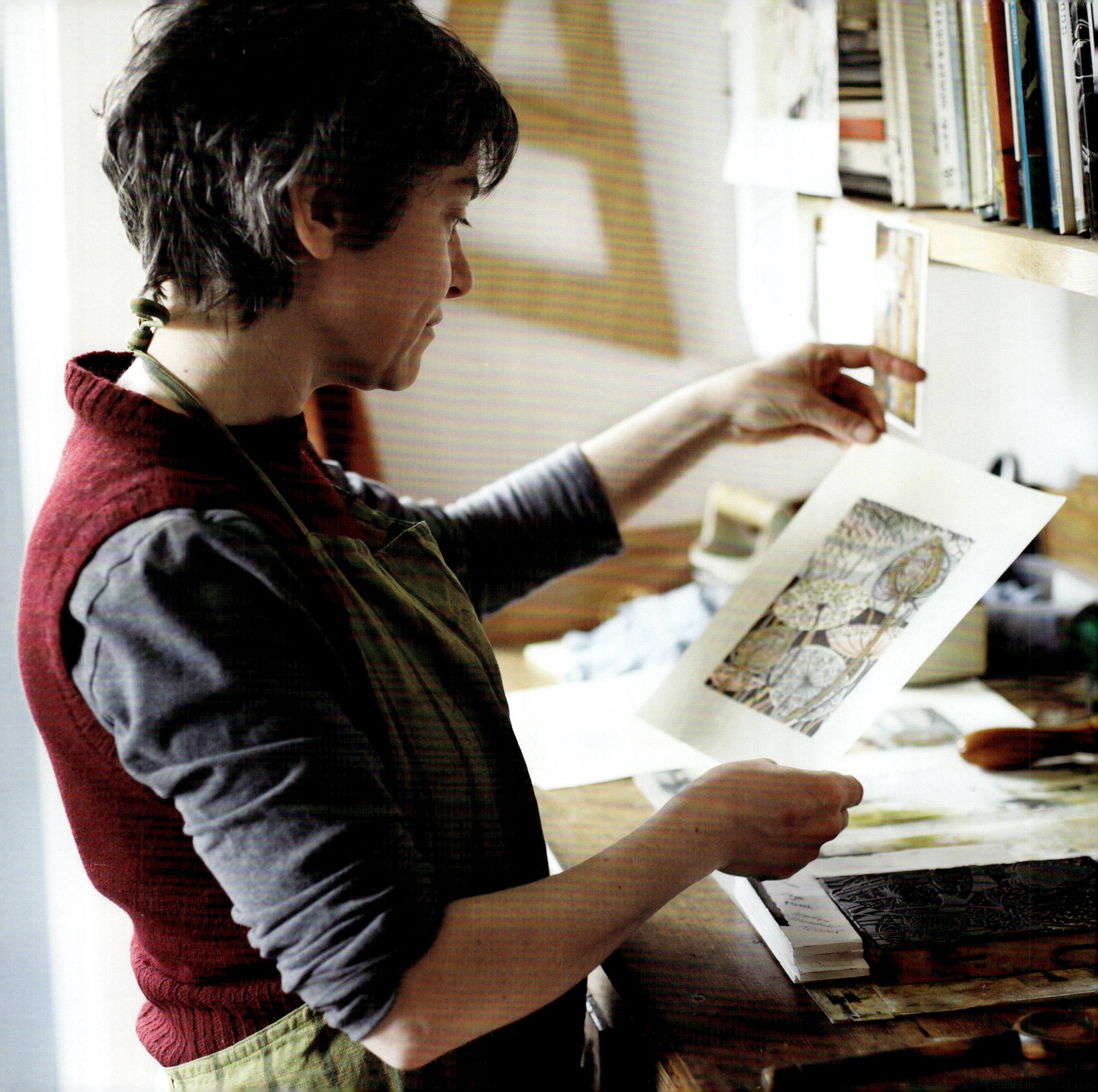

Introduction

Leslie Geddes-Brown

Angie Lewin's world is a universe in miniature. The grasses and seed heads that inhabit her prints may be tiny, unconsidered trifles that most of us would pass by, but she sees them differently, romantically, as part of the natural world. Lewin explains: 'I often sit on the ground when I'm out sketching, which means I'm close up and focusing on the plants, and the landscape is viewed through their layered and interlocking shapes. I might include insect eggs or blotches on buds and leaves.'

Tiny, natural and evocative details are what make Lewin's prints, whether wood engravings, linocuts, screenprints or lithographs, so full of vigour and beauty. Endlessly repeated, the wild flowers and grasses crowd into her fabrics; they appear in her collages made of old paper and print cut-outs; and, in botanical detail, they fill her sketchbooks.

In 1503, Albrecht Dürer had the same idea. His watercolour and gouache painting *The Large Turf* looks in exquisite detail at what is less than a square metre (11 sq. ft) of earth, filled with coltsfoot, plantain, herbs and grasses, their sculptural seed heads graphically drawn in shades of green against a neutral sky. Their entangled roots sink into muddy, marshy soil. The artist must, like Lewin, have crouched down to within inches of this little bit of earth, which teems with everyday natural life. The painting, roughly 40.5 × 30 cm (16 × 12 in.), could have been executed yesterday, so timeless is its appeal. This applies to Lewin's work as well: it may be in the modern idiom, but the plant life is wild and eternal.

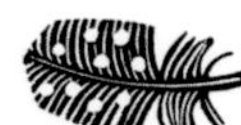

Lewin originally studied sculpture at London's Central School of Art and Design (now Central Saint Martins), but soon found herself inspired by printmaking, prompting a transfer to the fine-art printmaking degree. This was followed by a year's postgraduate study of printmaking at Camberwell School of Art and Crafts (now Camberwell College of Arts). She then took a course in garden design at Capel Manor College, which awakened a great interest in plants and their diversity, growth and structure, and the study of plants and her sketchbooks of them provided the impetus for change. Having worked in illustration, Lewin returned

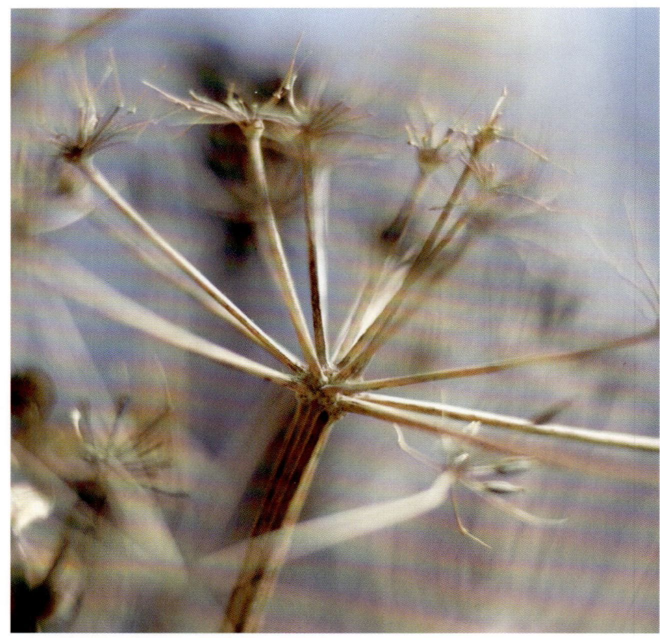

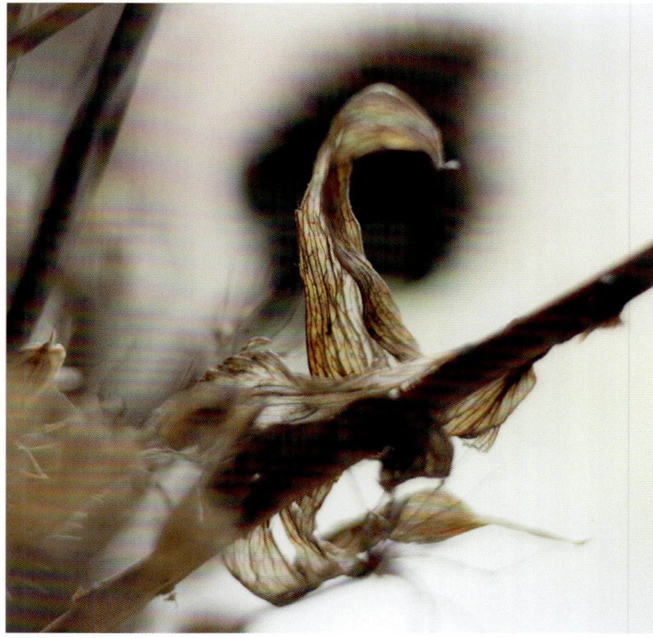

Seed heads from a Norfolk garden.

to printmaking, with a very clear and definite voice: 'I became fascinated by the structure of plants, especially those that had finished flowering.'

This elaborate vision in miniature is found in the works of many wood engravers – Thomas Bewick and Samuel Palmer spring to mind – because it is a precise and detailed art. Lewin also gets inspiration from such mid-twentieth-century artists and designers as Graham Sutherland, Edward Bawden, Eric Ravilious, Peggy Angus and Enid Marx. With its semi-abstract, stylized use of natural forms, Lewin's work is reminiscent of this period. She and her husband, Simon, also collect furniture and fabrics of the 1950s, typified by the 1951 Festival of Britain style, so the period is deeply engrained in her mind. A further explanation for her craftsmanship and attention to detail must be that both her father and grandfather were blacksmiths; in her grandfather's case, for a travelling circus – a startling and telling history.

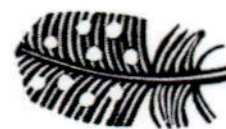

Nature, seen through the Lewin lens, is surprising. On the one hand there is the formality and symmetry of the seed heads, leaves and buds when seen in close-up (look at a dandelion clock to see symmetry in action). But these are at odds with the lack of symmetry found in a meadow or a wood, where order cannot be imposed. Lewin carefully counterbalances these conflicting elements.

Lewin's whole working life is a balance between her meticulous prints and an acute observation of nature seen on long walks in both Norfolk and Scotland, where she spends much of her time. She explains: 'These are my main sources of information, as I divide my time between the two and can work in both places. However, when I travel I'm fascinated by the native plants and by spotting plants there that are either native to Britain or garden plants in different environments and light – alliums and euphorbia seen on a mountain walk in southern Spain, for instance.' A trip to Spain led to a lithograph, *Alliums and Fennel* (see page 127), in which the dish-shaped, flat-topped fennel heads mingle with the globes of the alliums, each flower within the dozens that make up the alliums' globes being drawn in careful detail. In the background there is the suggestion of a mountain, and white clouds drift in the sky. Mountains and other landscapes are often suggested in the most abstract terms as a backdrop to her prints.

Lewin says that a passage in Robert Macfarlane's *The Wild Places* (2007), in which the author is in the Burren, in western Ireland, with the writer and environmentalist Roger Deakin, describes her feelings exactly:

We reached a large gryke running north to south. We lay belly-down on the limestone and peered over its edge. And found ourselves looking into a jungle. Tiny groves of ferns, mosses and flowers were there in the crevasse – hundreds of plants, just in the few yards we could see, thriving in the shelter of the gryke: cranesbills, plantains, avens, ferns, many more I could not identify, growing opportunistically on

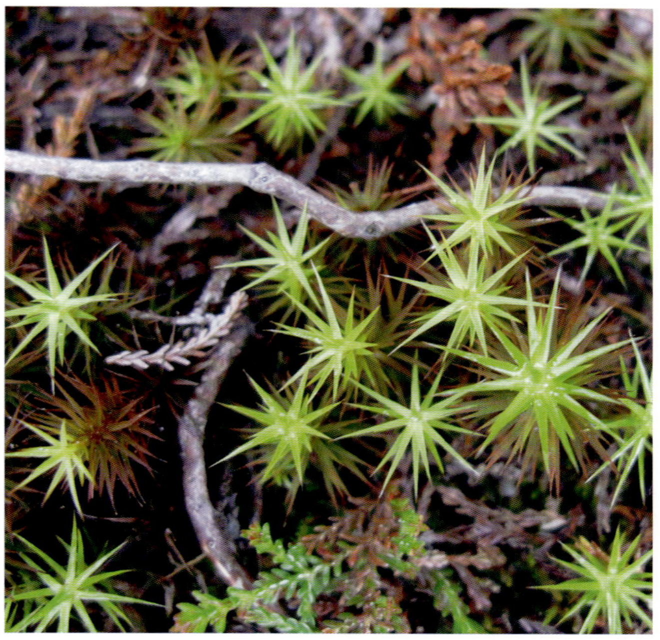

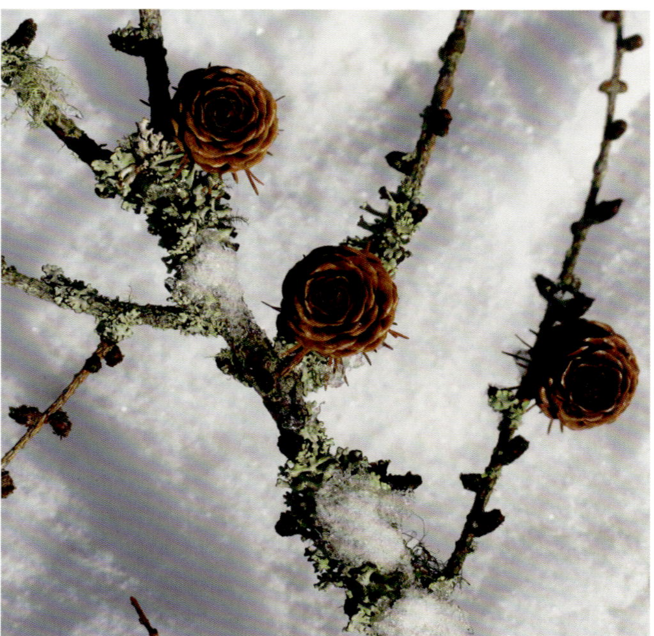

Plants in a Scottish woodland.

wind-blown soil. The plants thronged every available niche, embracing one another in indistinguishability. Even on this winter day, the sense of life was immense. What the gryke would look like in the blossom month of May I could not imagine. This, Roger suddenly said as we lay there looking down on it, is a wild place. It is as beautiful and complex, perhaps more so, than any glen or bay or peak. Miniature, yes, but fabulously wild.

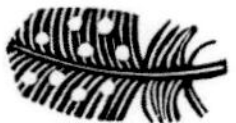

Lewin walks the paths of Norfolk and Scotland with regularity, so that:

The seasonal changes in the landscape and in individual plants are noticeable to me. I'm interested in the habits of plants, how some stems are rigid and upright, as with valerian, whereas scabious stems twist; in the pattern created by the spacing of leaves on a stem or forming a basal rosette. I'm fascinated by the variation within a plant family – for example, the fine seed heads of Queen Anne's lace, the more robust seed heads and the rounder and flatter seeds of alexanders compared with the sharp, long seeds of sweet cicely.

The growth of a plant is influenced by its environment. I am drawn to plants that are shaped by adverse weather conditions: the horned poppies growing out of the shingle bank at Salthouse, as seen in *The Beach, Salthouse* [see page 57]; a twisted rowan growing out of a rock on the west coast of Skye; a plantain growing in gravel by a cottage wall in Findhorn village or alexanders on Norfolk clifftops. I rarely draw plants in flower; instead I focus on the structure of stem, leaf, pods and berries. I wouldn't draw a peony, for example.

Like all the best artists, Lewin has an unmistakable style that has developed over the years while remaining basically unchanged. Her cottage in Norfolk, set between common land and fields at the edge of a small village, has a garden full of seed heads and spiky-leaved plants, and her studio is arranged with more, along with other inspirational objects she has picked up on her walks.

Many of Lewin's works are titled with the places that inspired them: for example, *Rain, Harris*; *Scarista*; and *Birches, Ballindalloch* (see pages 31, 49 and 72–73). Other titles refer to the plants pictured: *Ivy*; *Ramsons*; *Yellow Rattle*; and *Shepherd's Purse* (see pages 79, 83, 116–17 and 155). The works might be wood engravings, linocuts, lithographs, screenprints or collages.

Outsiders (such as me), when visiting Lewin, feel envious of her ability to spot beauty in the discarded, the throwaway, the weeds. Through her work, it is possible to look at a guineafowl's spotted feather, or a grey pebble band-ringed with white quartz, and see its qualities. Why has it never struck us before?

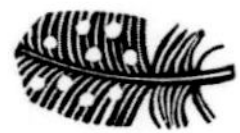

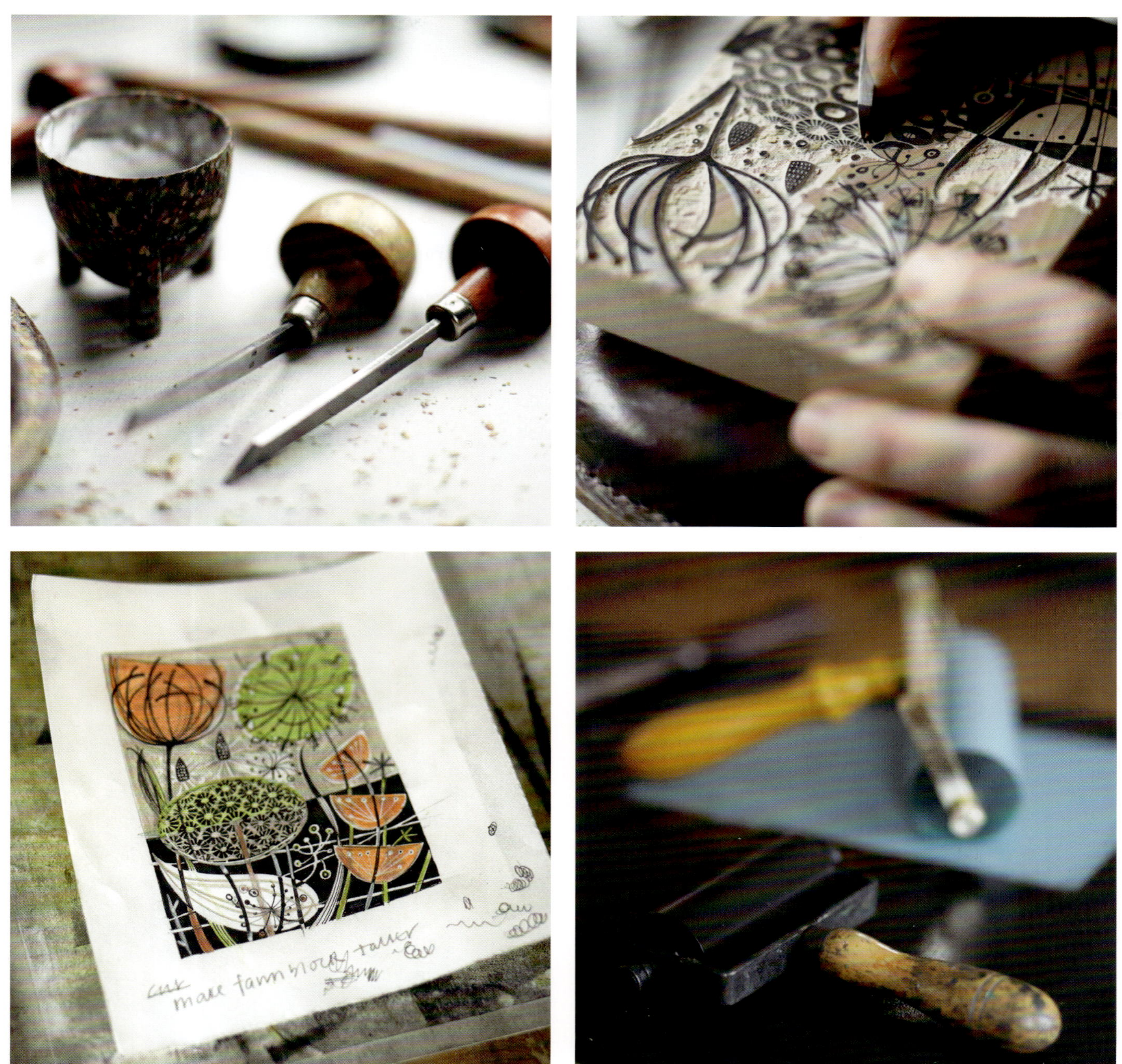

Angie Lewin working on the wood engraving Meadow's Edge; *the print is reproduced on page 145.*

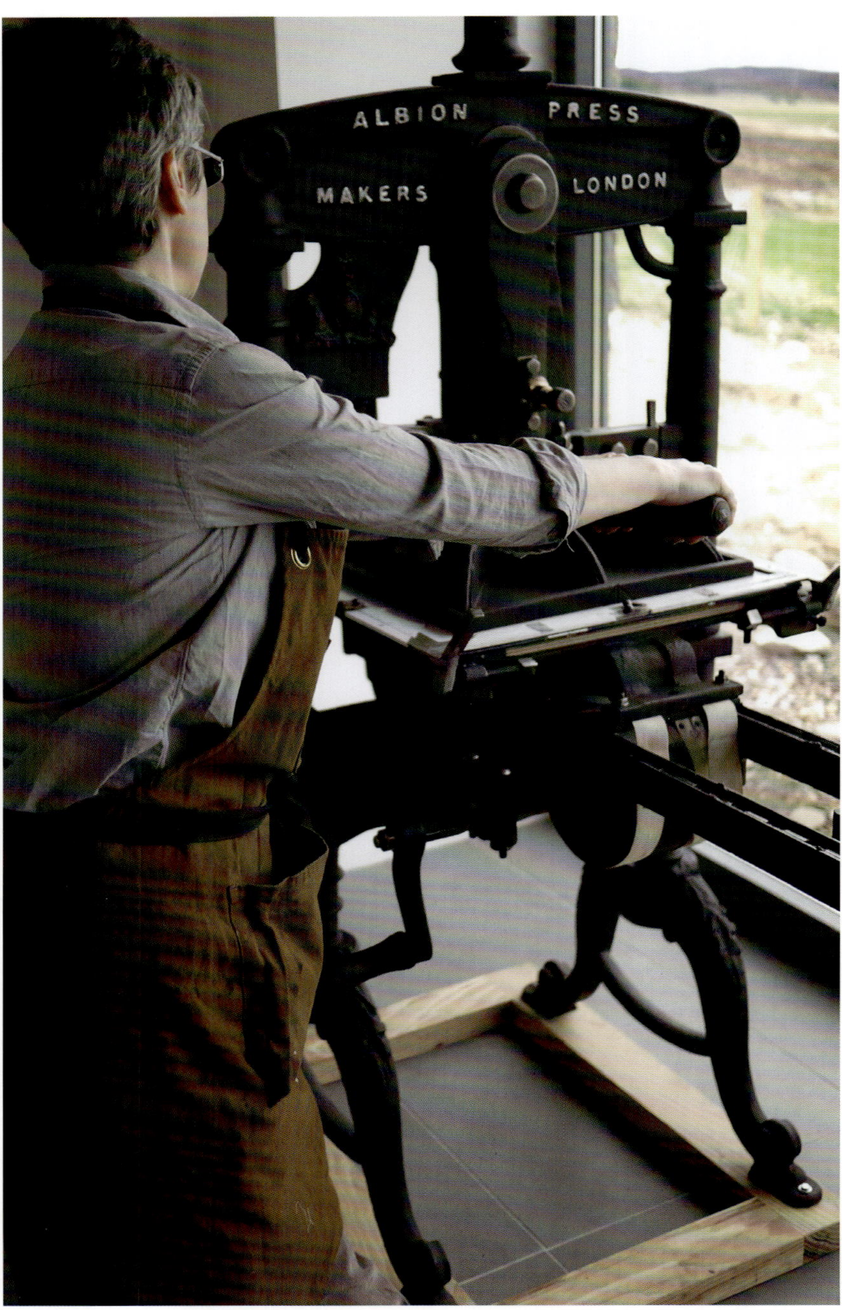

Lewin's late nineteenth-century Albion printing press is now in her Scottish studio.

Lewin's Norfolk studio is a small outhouse reached through the garden of her cottage. It is here that she draws and paints, and prints her wood engravings and linocuts. The studio is immaculately tidy and organized, with a hulking hydraulic press for the printing, over the top of which are racks for hanging the prints to dry after each colour is printed on the special Japanese paper she uses. There's a workbench where the colours are burnished (that is, an olive-wood salad spoon is rubbed on to the back of the paper placed over the wood or lino block) so the paper takes up the ink. Originally, Lewin used an old wooden spoon that had belonged to her mother, but, when that collapsed, she found the present round-bowled version.

The route from sketching or photographing those horned poppies or dandelions is a long and complicated one that characterizes the meticulous art of wood engraving and linocut. First Lewin does the sketch from the living plants on one of her walks, then she returns to the studio to look at various sketchbooks: 'I get the design firm in my mind', she says. This design will eventually appear as a charming, though sketchy, watercolour the exact size of the future print. The watercolour then becomes the guide to making however many blocks are needed to complete the print – generally no more than four or five, one for each colour used on the print. Lewin explains:

As a printmaker I develop drawings and paintings into a composition for a print. A different block, plate or screen (depending on the print process) will be made for each colour and so I naturally break the image down into as few colours as will work. More often than not a print is most successful when fewer colours are used; it has more clarity and impact. Drawing is important to me, and my prints most often have a strong graphic block that holds the image together.

Lewin's wood-engraving blocks are made from the end grains of the densest woods available, which tend to come from such slow-growing bushes or trees as box, holly, pear or lemonwood (which has no connection with a lemon tree). In Lewin's studio is a lemonwood block that is as glassily smooth and unblemished as marble. Engraving blocks are small, and larger examples are made up of two or more blocks joined together. This, in turn, dictates the size of the finished print. When the complete edition has been printed, the engraved block is planed level and the surface smoothed again, enabling the block to be reused for a new image. Lewin does, however, save the blocks of some of her favourite prints.

There are sensual pleasures in the process, Lewin finds: 'I love the perfection of a beautifully crafted new wood-engraving block, unwrapping it from its brown paper packaging, engraving with sharp tools that cut such fine lines through the wood so smoothly. Most of my tools I've had since college.'

Woodblock printing goes back thousands of years to ancient China, and, over the long centuries, specialized tools have evolved to cut exactly the shape or line needed. A scorper, square- or round-ended, is used to clear broad areas; the spitsticker cuts curved lines; and the bullsticker does curved lines and stabbing marks. Gravers or burins are used for cutting straight lines and diamond-shaped pocking marks; tint tools are very slightly tapered and cut straight lines of equal proportions. And then there are chisels, which are small versions of those a carpenter would use. Linocuts have a whole set of their own tools, including knives and v-shaped and u-shaped gouges.

Lewin's tools, whether for lino or wood, have rounded wooden handles like mushrooms with one flat side, and fit comfortably in the palm of the hand. Lewin loves these details, as she confides:

There's a craft to printmaking and a series of processes that must be worked through. I enjoy these constraints. I enjoy seeing the transformation from drawn line on paper to the cutting of a line in lino or wood and then the crisp line printed on paper; the challenge of positive and negative shapes and working with the image reversed. I print linocuts and wood engravings on to Japanese papers, which readily absorb the ink. The ink doesn't sit on the surface.

The Japanese papers – seikishu, shoji and yumayami – are fine yet strong. Seikishu and shoji are a soft white, with visible watermarks, and yumayami is pale beige.

It might seem, from the outside, that the printmaker's art is rather repetitive. Far from it, says Lewin: 'There's always a great sense of anticipation when taking the first proof from a new block.' In common with most printmakers, she is never quite sure how the detailed cutting and designing will actually look as a print, and that adds to the excitement: 'The satisfaction of creating a multiple image draws me to printmaking – each hand-printed image has very subtle variations. Hanging prints to dry in the rack or laying out small engravings row on row to dry emphasizes these tiny differences. However, I produce only small editions. I'm eager to move on to develop my other sketches into the next print.'

Lewin also works in lithography and screenprinting, both processes she carries out at editioning studios, where skilled printers help her to create limited-edition prints. 'My lithographs are printed at the Curwen Studio near Cambridge', she explains. 'I enjoy the collaboration with the printers there as it's a huge contrast to working alone in my studio. In the case of screenprints, too, I work with an editioning studio, Jealous in north London.'

Of course, wood engravings, linocuts, lithographs and screenprints are made using different techniques (see pages 19–20). I asked Lewin how she decides which technique to use for which designs. She responded:

If I want areas of flat colour, that generally suggests a linocut or screenprint. Screenprints allow me to work on a larger scale than I can print on my relief press; the papers on which they are printed have far more body and less delicacy than the Japanese papers I use for wood engraving. Lithography enables me to create a print that retains the quality of the drawn line, wash or collage. No cutting is involved in lithography and screenprinting, giving the works a different quality. Wood engravings are always quite small, because of the limited size of the block; thanks to the tools used to cut, they allow for graphic, detailed work that can be quite intricate.

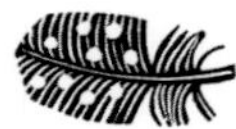

If you are lucky enough to own an Angie Lewin print or collage, or simply spend some time studying the illustrations in this book, you will get endless satisfaction. At a superficial level, these are delightful prints in subtle colours, fit for any wall. But look deeper and a whole, tiny world emerges: nature, where even the most microscopic insect or seed is a marvel of complexity; where a miniscule crevice is as dense as the rainforest. You may find that your whole outlook on the universe, on beauty or on creation is altered – which is quite something to say about a printmaker.

WOOD ENGRAVING is the process
whereby the image is cut into the end
grain of the wood (that is, cut across
the growth rings), so the tool never has
to cut against the grain. (Woodcuts, on
the other hand, use the side grain of
generally softer, faster-growing woods,
allowing for larger, less finely cut blocks.)
While the block is being cut, it rests on
a small, heavy leather sandbag and is
swivelled around to guide the tool (see
page 142). Ink is then rolled on to the
uncut raised area, from which a print is
taken (see page 156). The image on the
right is a detail from the wood engraving
Mug with Feathers (see page 183).

LINOCUT, like wood engraving, is
a type of relief printmaking in which
areas are gouged out, in this case of
linoleum, and the ink is rolled on to
the raised surface. As with her wood
engravings, Lewin then prints either by
hand or with a press: 'I either hand-
burnish using my wooden spoon or
use a press on to fine Japanese papers.
I print with oil-based inks in transparent
colours, often with a more detailed
graphic block in a stronger colour.'
The image on the right is a detail from
the linocut *Black Island* (see page 29).

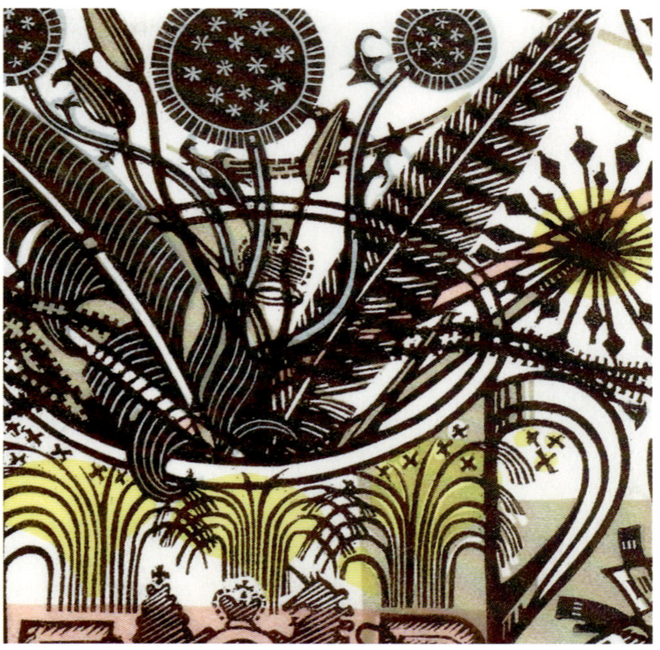

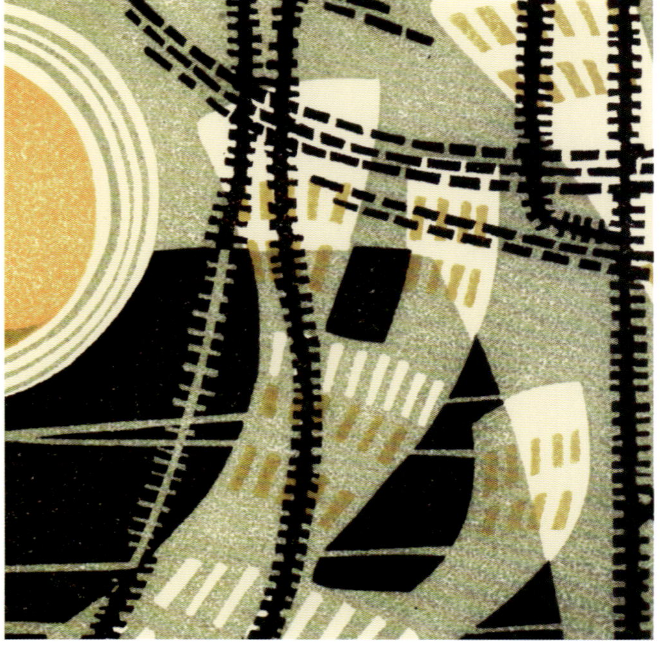

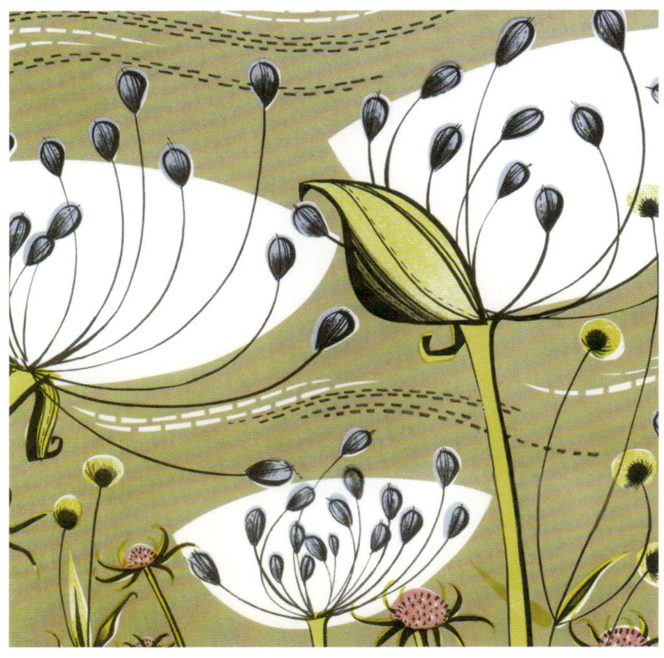

LITHOGRAPHY involves drawing or painting directly on to a smooth limestone slab or a zinc plate (see page 174). The oil-based crayon drawing and ink washes will keep their qualities when the stone or plate is processed. Alternatively, the image can be drawn on to a thick, transparent film (Trugrain), which has a similar grain to the zinc plate; this image is then exposed by ultraviolet light on to a sensitized printing plate. In each case, the printing plate is rolled with oil-based ink that adheres only to the drawn image. The image on the left is a detail of the lithograph *Agapanthus* (see page 123).

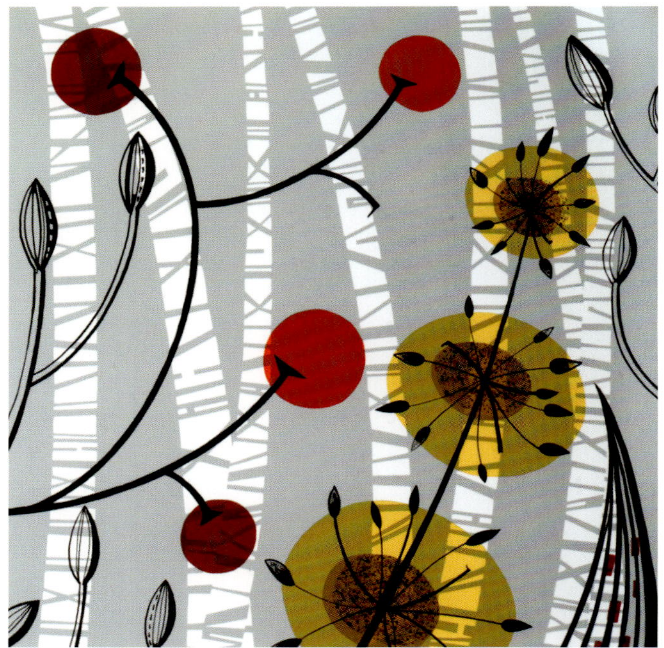

SCREENPRINTING (also known as silkscreening) uses woven polyester mesh in rectangular frames. Areas of the mesh are treated with a compound that blocks the flow of the ink. Lewin makes an image on clear film with black ink and red light-resistant film (see page 84). This image is exposed on to the screens, one for each colour in the finished print. The ink is then forced through the remaining open mesh with a rubber squeegee, on to paper. The image on the left is a detail of the screenprint *Birches, Ballindalloch* (see pages 72–73).

COLLAGE is the making of pictures by
sticking paper and other materials on
to a background. Lewin uses discarded
proofs of her prints, which she overprints
with another layer of colour and pattern,
and also cuts and prints new elements
for a collage. She says: 'I use patterns
from the inside of envelopes and other
patterned papers. One of my favourite
collages (*Applecross*; see page 192) was
created using a small, weathered piece
of 1950s Formica that I found on a beach
as the base for a collage of thin Japanese
papers. Japanese papers are great to
work with because, as I create layers in
the collage, the colours show through
but are muted, and so one gets a sense
of depth and of the layers of plant forms.'
The collage on the right is *Coast*.

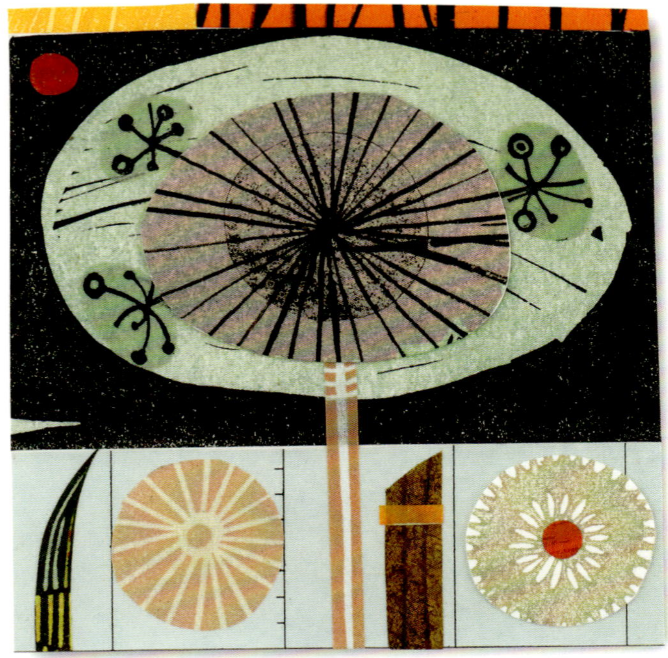

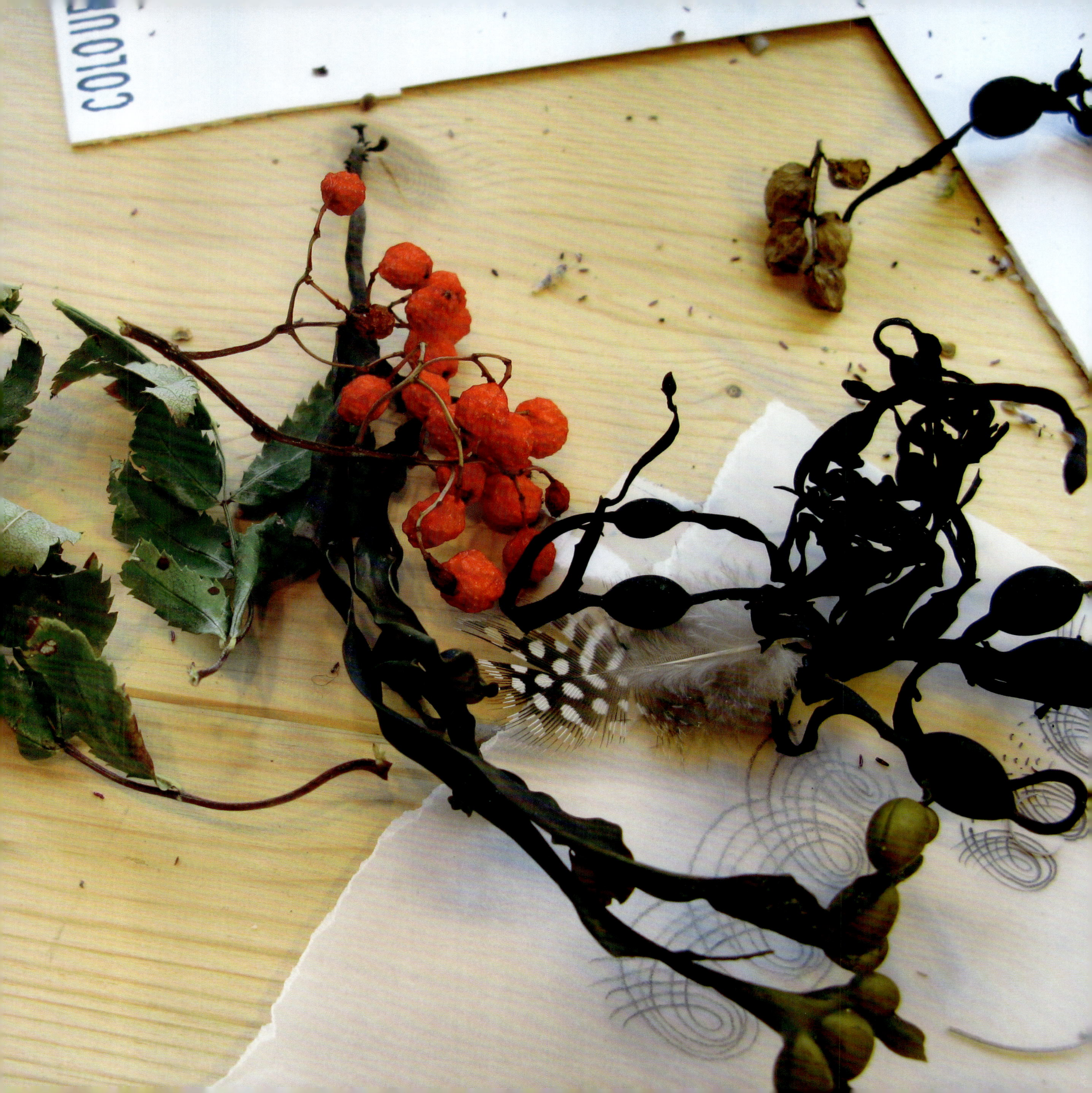
COLOU

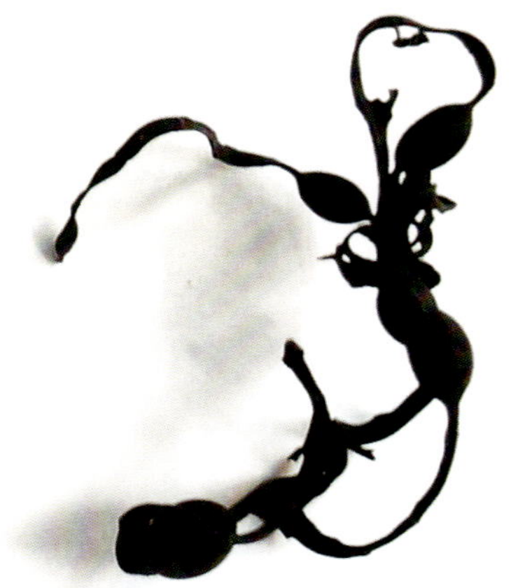
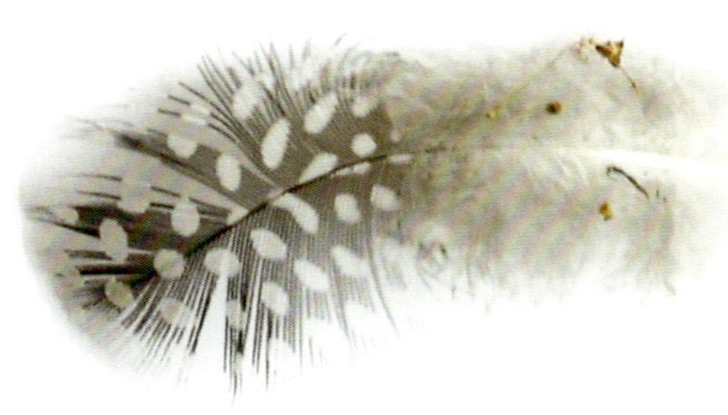
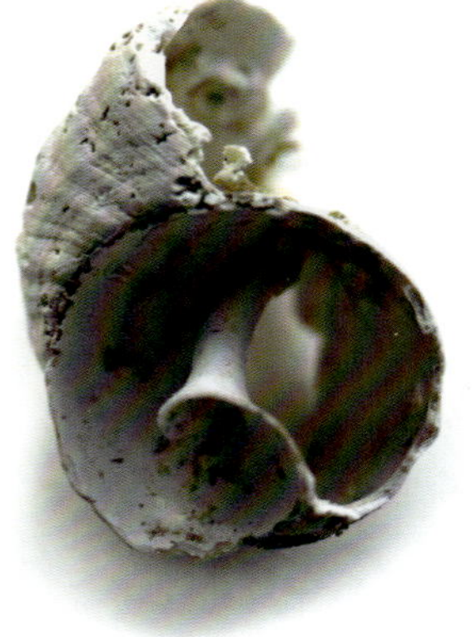

Coast

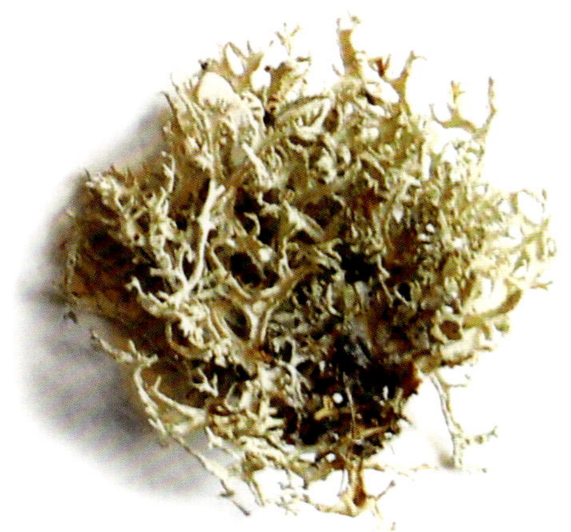
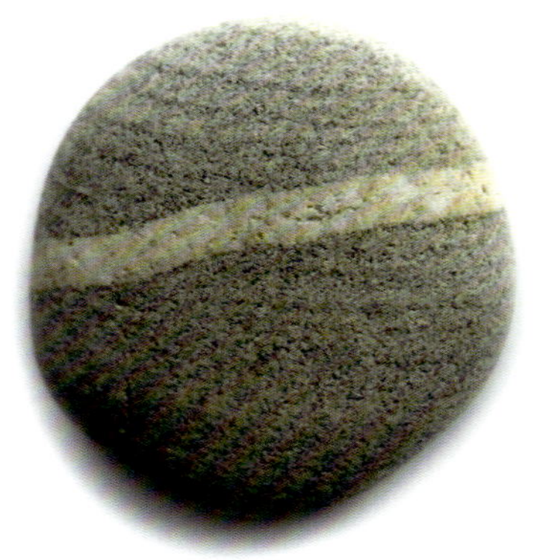
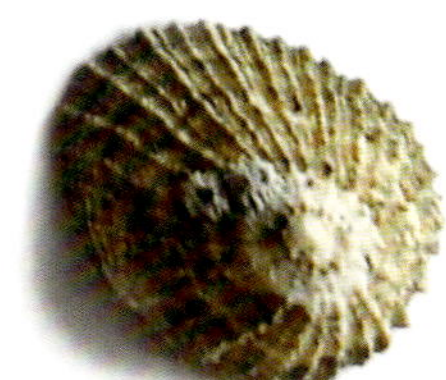

Angie Lewin is drawn to wild stretches of coast and shingle beaches where native wild flowers and plants can thrive. From her home in north Norfolk, she often walks along the cliffs and pebble strands that characterize the area. 'Walking on the salt marshes at Morston [the inspiration behind *Winter Creek*; see page 27] you can see across "the pit", where boats are moored, to the long shingle bank of Blakeney Point. I love the bleak, exposed nature of this coastline, especially in winter', Lewin says.

This sense of coastal wildness is communicated in the linocut *The Beach, Salthouse* (see page 57), in which the sinister seed heads of horned poppies writhe against the sky, their pods like toothed monsters. In this work, as in many others in this series (such as *Salthouse*; see page 53), the pebbles and flints, striated and pockmarked, ground the plants and the prints. The only hint of man-made objects are the fine lines that cross some clifftop prints horizontally. They might be the lines of fences, but the backgrounds and skies of these prints remain enigmatic.

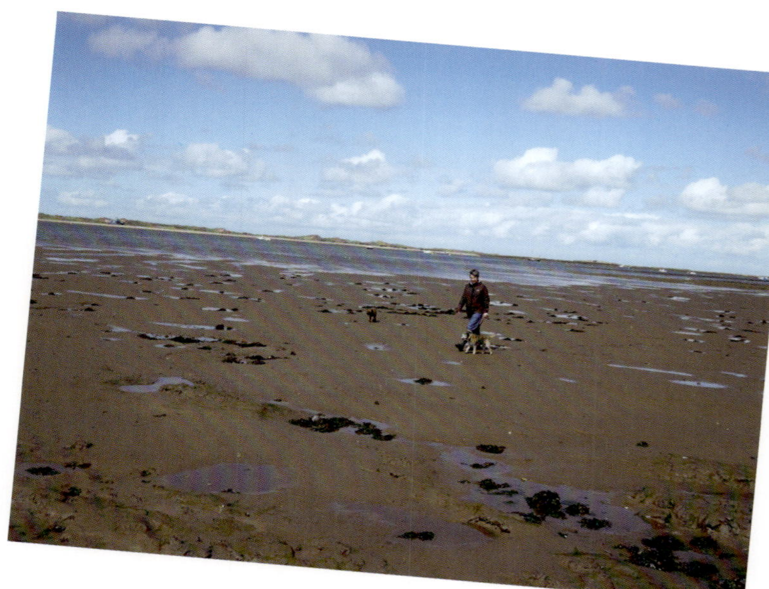
Beach at Morston, Norfolk.

Lewin also revels in the fierceness of the elements, as seen, for instance, in the prints inspired by her visits to the west of Scotland. This part of Britain is indented with sea-lochs and sounds, filled with islands large and small, and is subject to spells of some of the most extreme weather in the country.

In the linocut *Rain, Harris* (see page 31), a storm's ferocity is evoked by slashes of rain slanting at forty-five degrees and skeins of dotted lines for

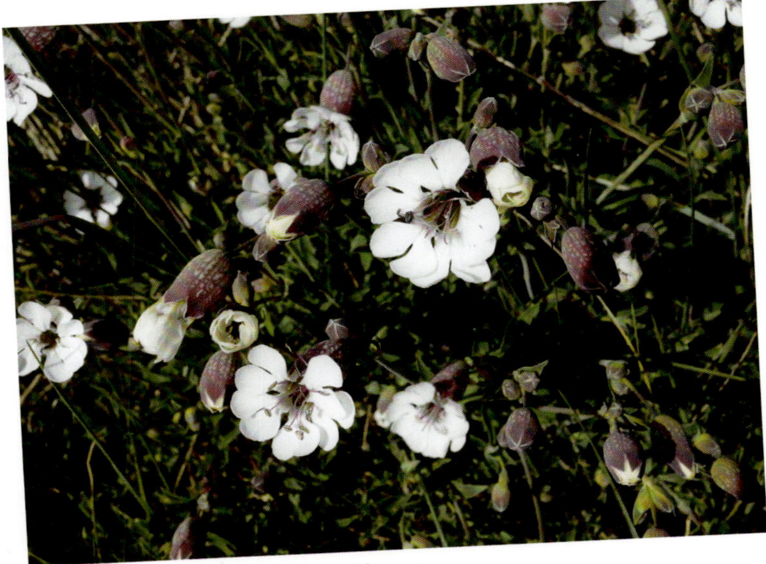
Sea campion on salt marshes at Morston.

the wind; the background is of muted greys and black. At the more abstract end of the artist's work is *Black Island* (see page 29), with its baleful shades of egg-yolk yellow and an ominous, stormy green. *Skye to Harris* (see page 29), a tiny (4.4 × 8 cm/1¼ × 3⅛ in.) but menacing wood engraving, is about as abstract as Lewin gets: a dark and threatening black shape is accompanied by furious wind patterns in the dull khaki sky above and in the muted blue-green that represents the sea below, and a group of concentric circles patterns the black rock.

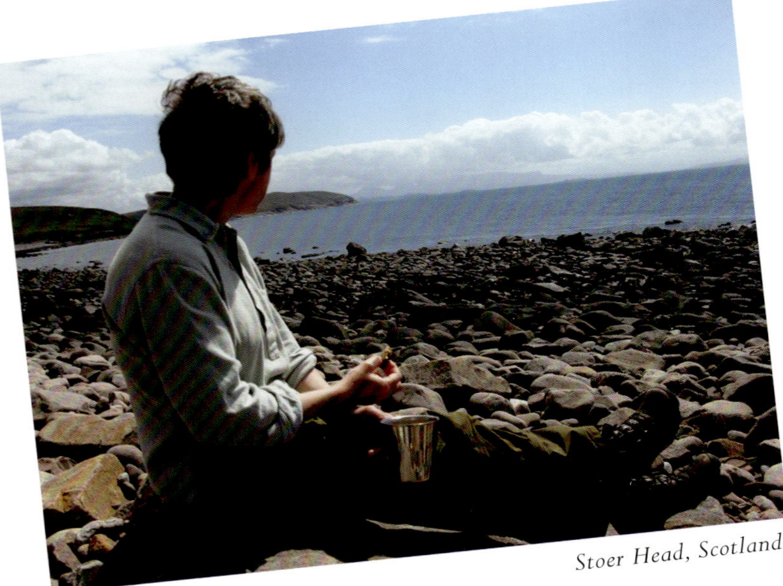
Stoer Head, Scotland.

There are some fine days, too: *Scarista* (see page 49) has the plants of the machair (low-lying land formed from sand and shell fragments deposited by the wind) set before a steep black mountain, and *Island with Teasels* (see page 2) seems sunny, if windy.

Whatever the location and the weather, plants are usually at the forefront of Lewin's work, and one of her favourites is alexanders, with its umbrella-like groupings of flowers and seed heads. The plant features in many of her prints, both as a wide cup shape and as swirling groups of seeds. It is often contrasted with sea plantain (as in *Clifftop*, page 42), the elongated heads of which are shaped like old-fashioned microphones. Its broad leaves, familiar to though unloved by most gardeners, provide further variation.

These coastal plants and 'found objects' from the beaches she loves are a constant presence in all Lewin's works.

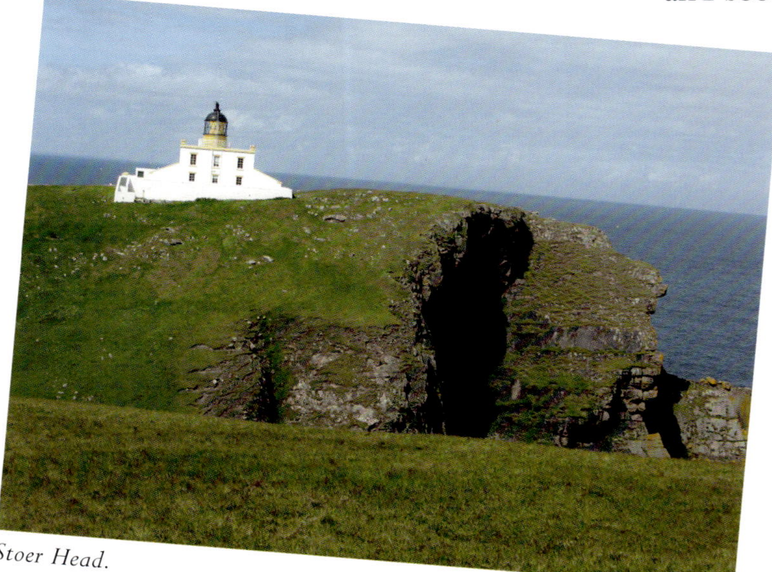
Stoer Head.

'While I was walking on the Norfolk
salt marshes, my eye was drawn to a
tideline of dried seaweed and feathers
that snaked through the sea lavender.'

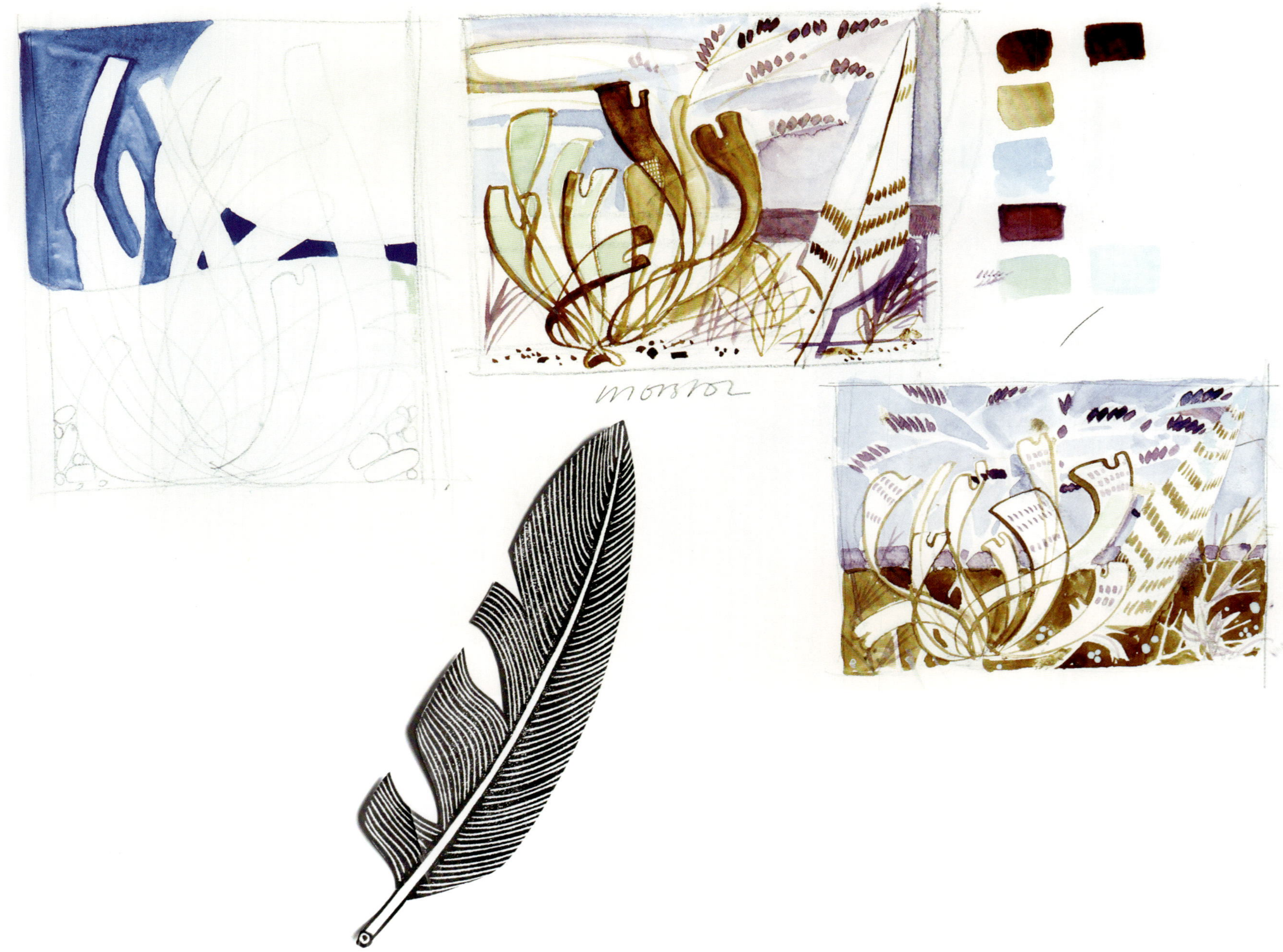

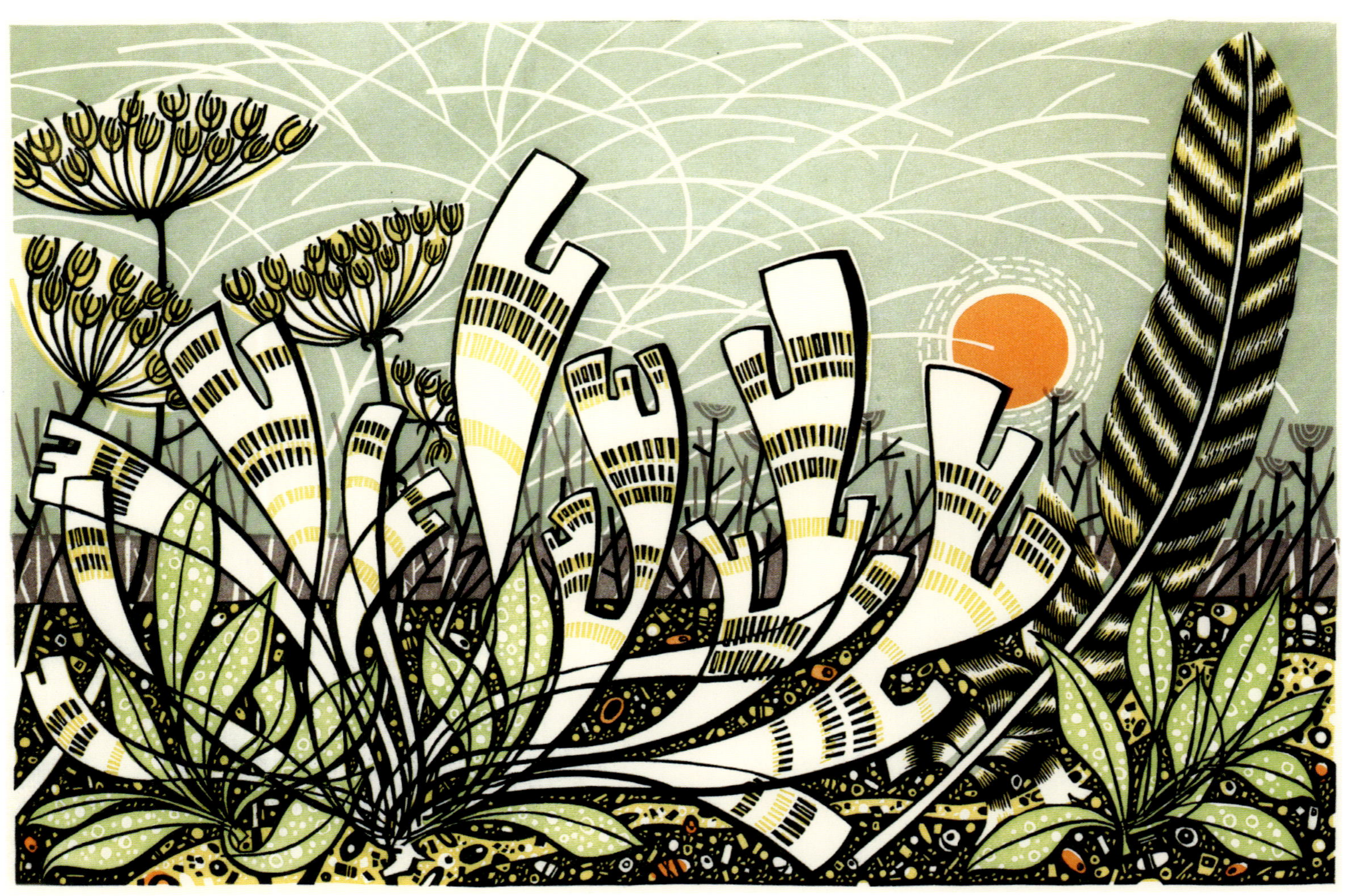

Winter Creek

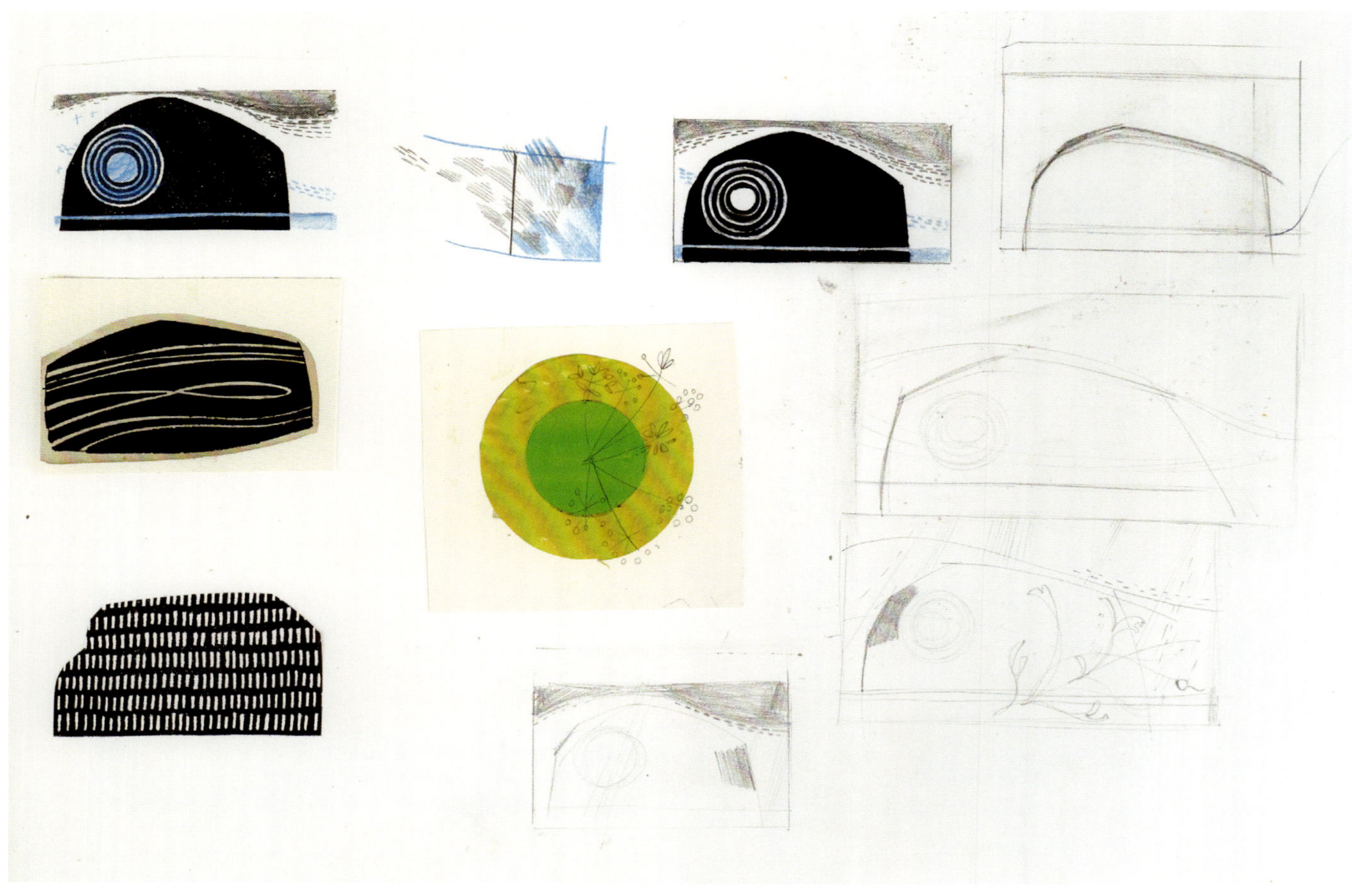

'A ferry trip I took from Uig to Tarbert,
which passed by dark, rocky islands,
inspired Skye to Harris.'

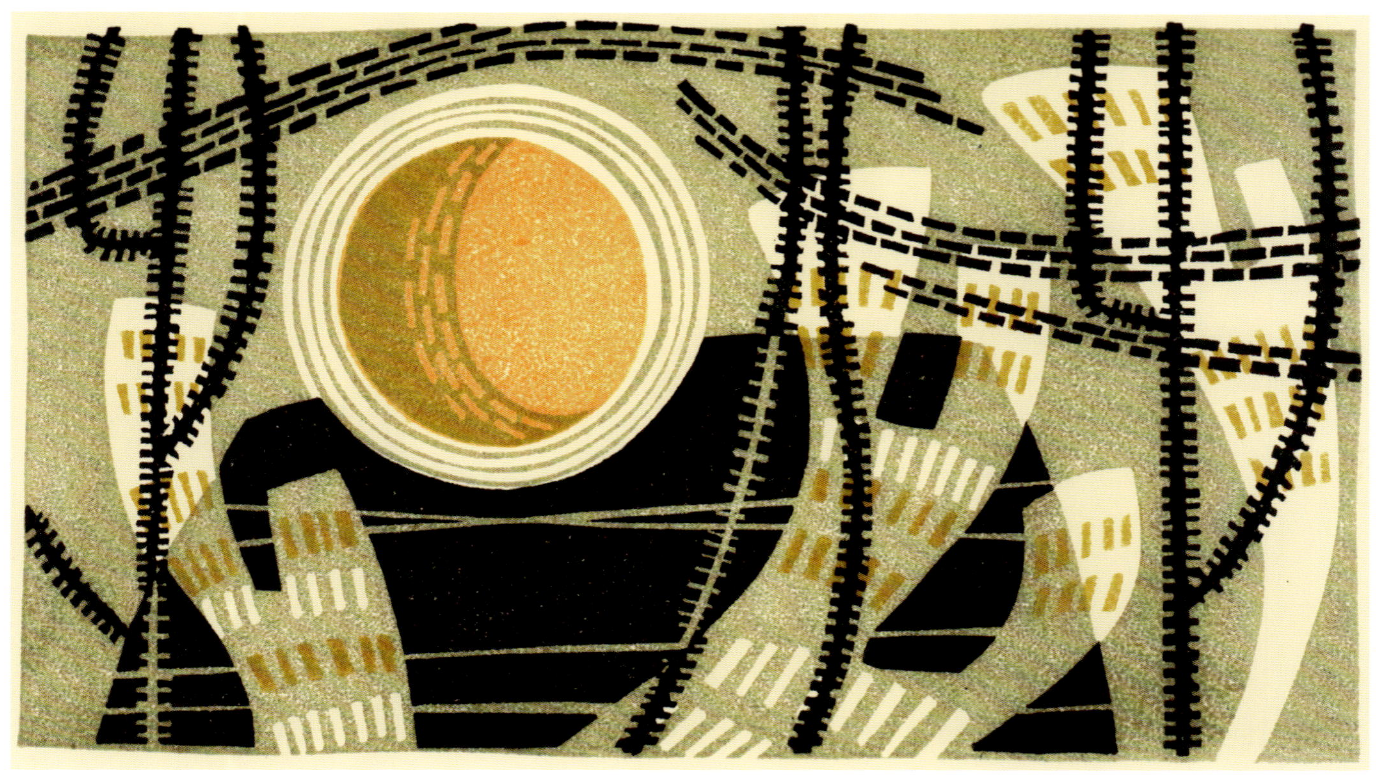

Black Island

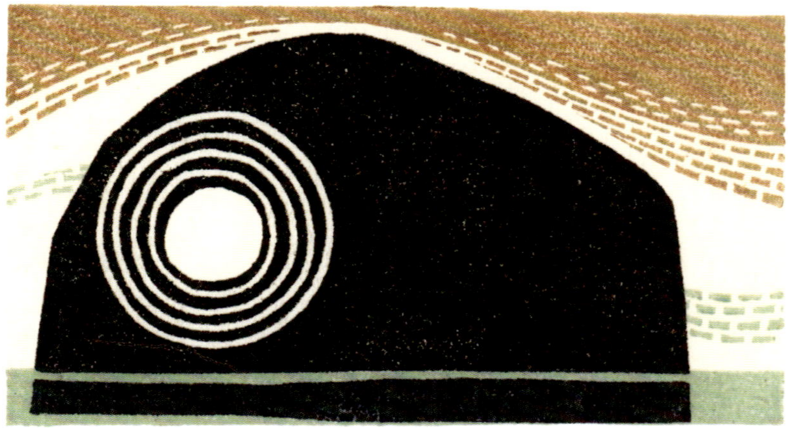

Skye to Harris

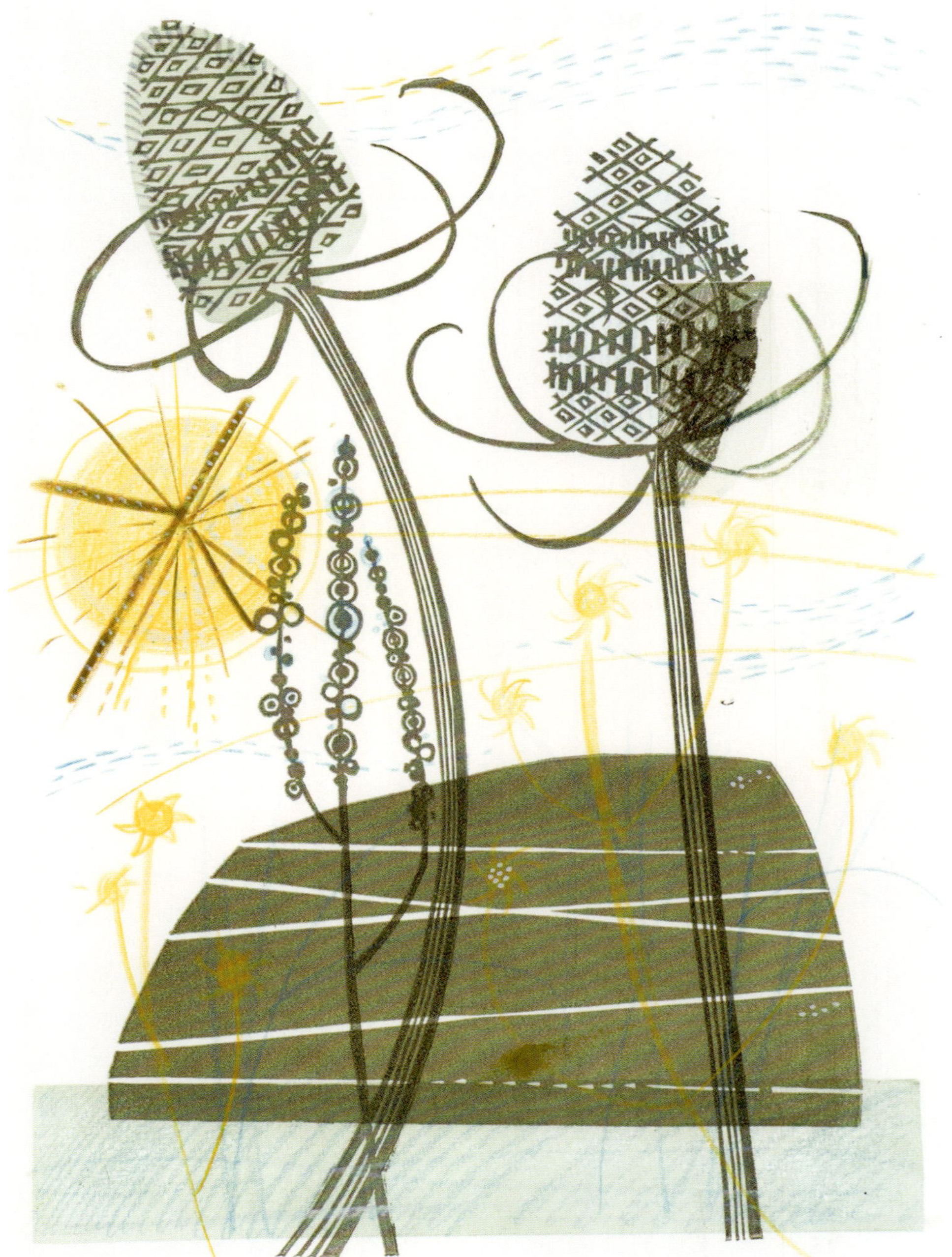

'This working proof of Island with Teasels *(see page 2)* has collage and pencil additions. The image is based on a view I had from a beach on the west coast of Scotland.'

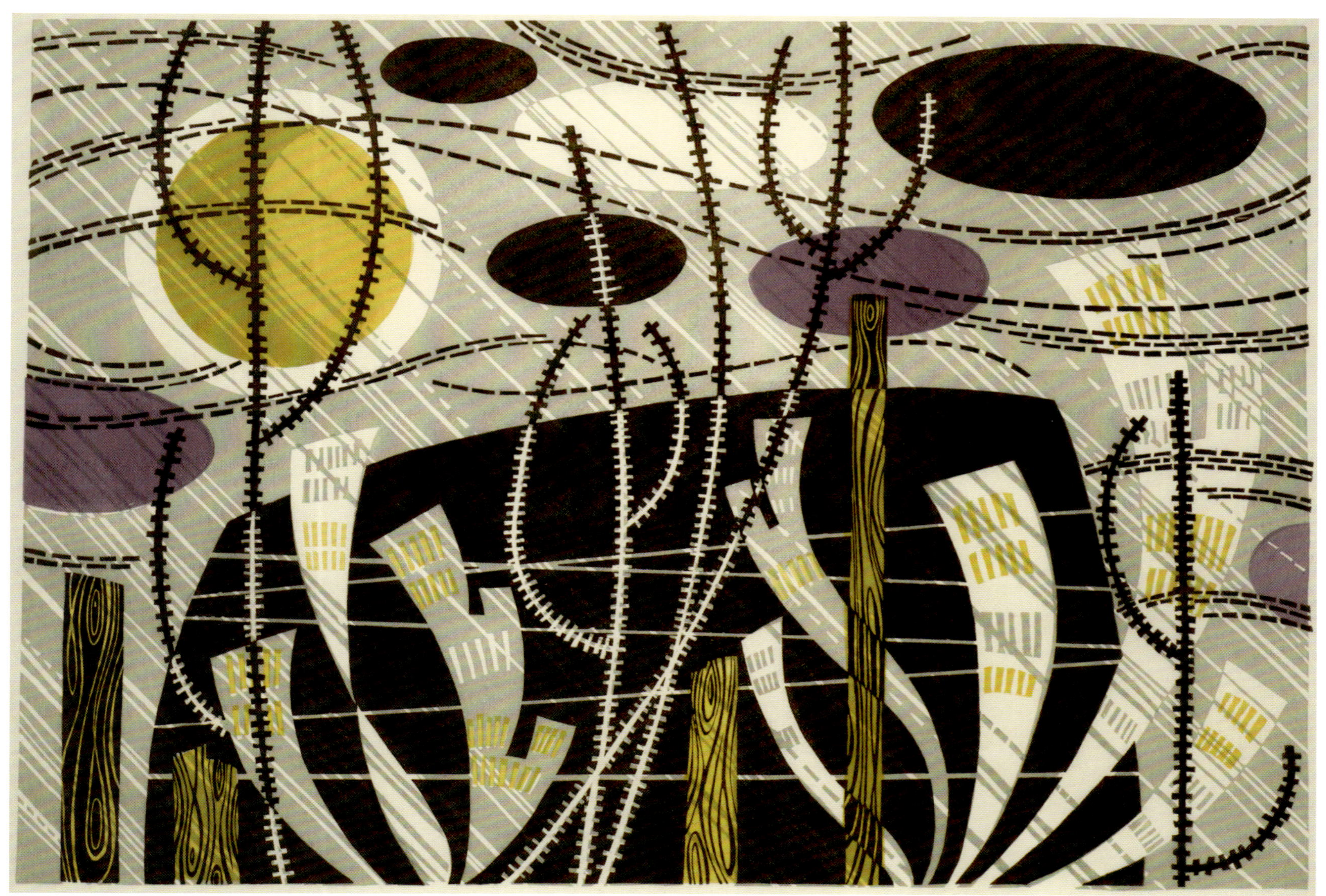

Rain, Harris

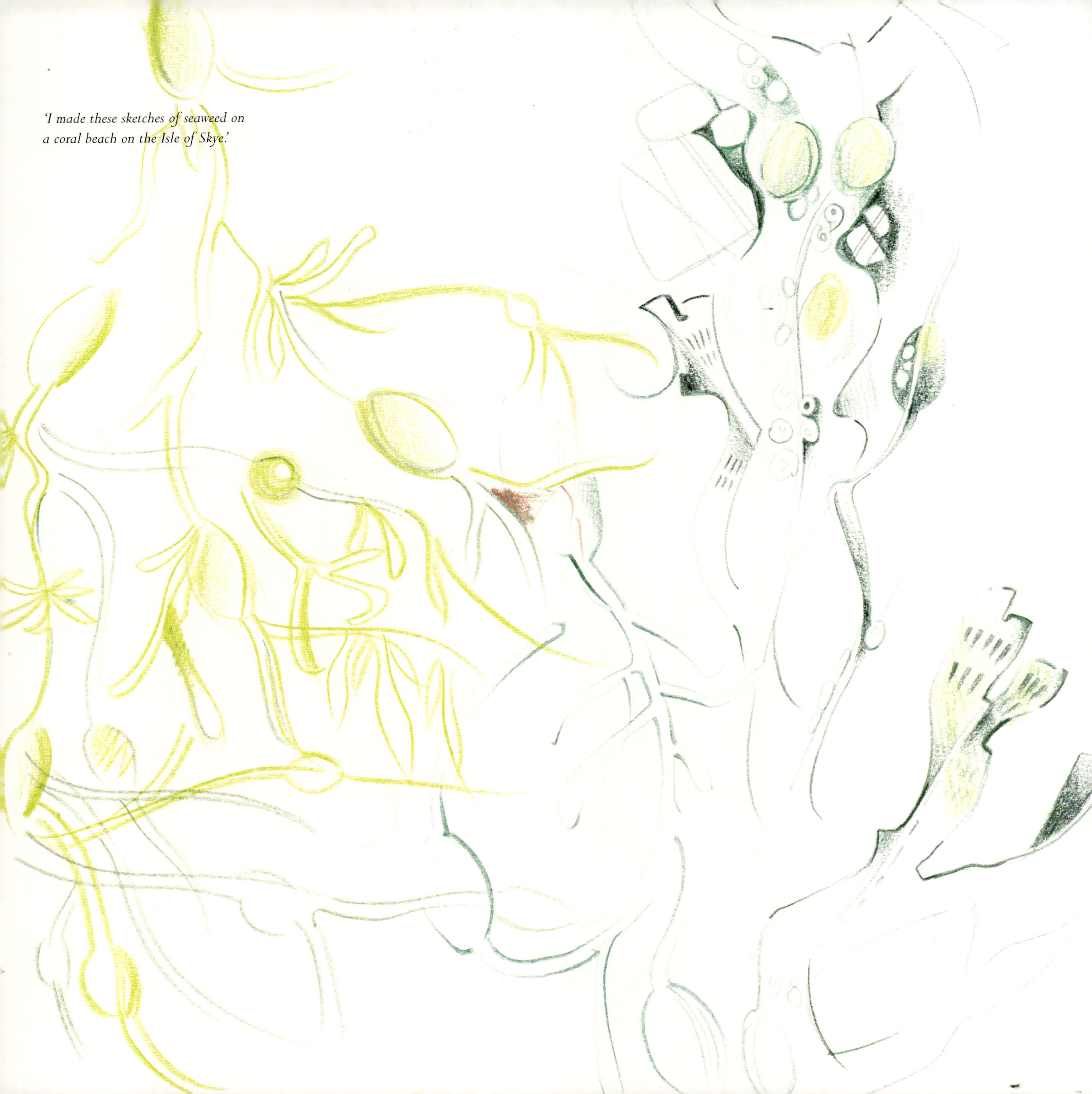

'I made these sketches of seaweed on
a coral beach on the Isle of Skye.'

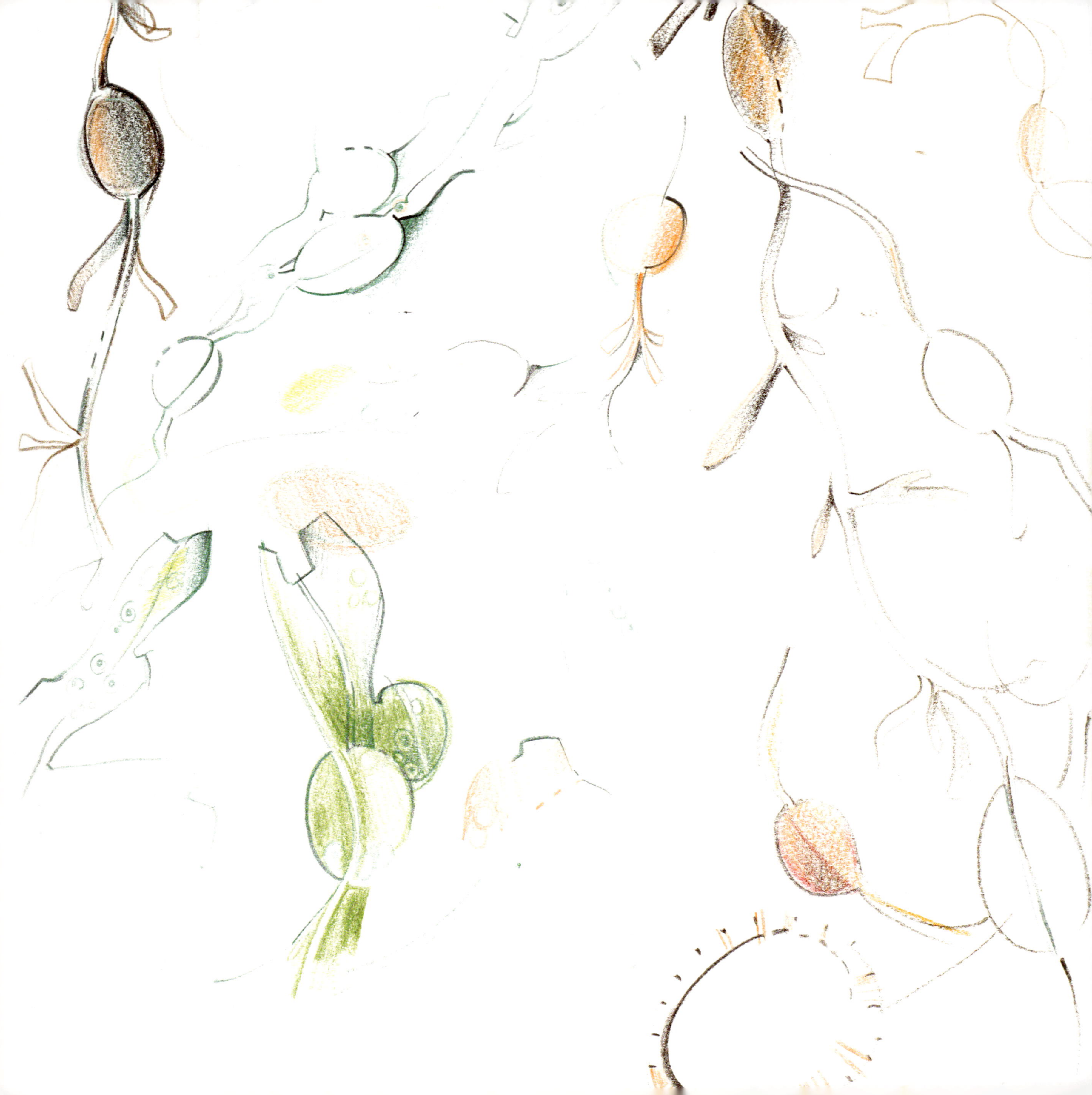

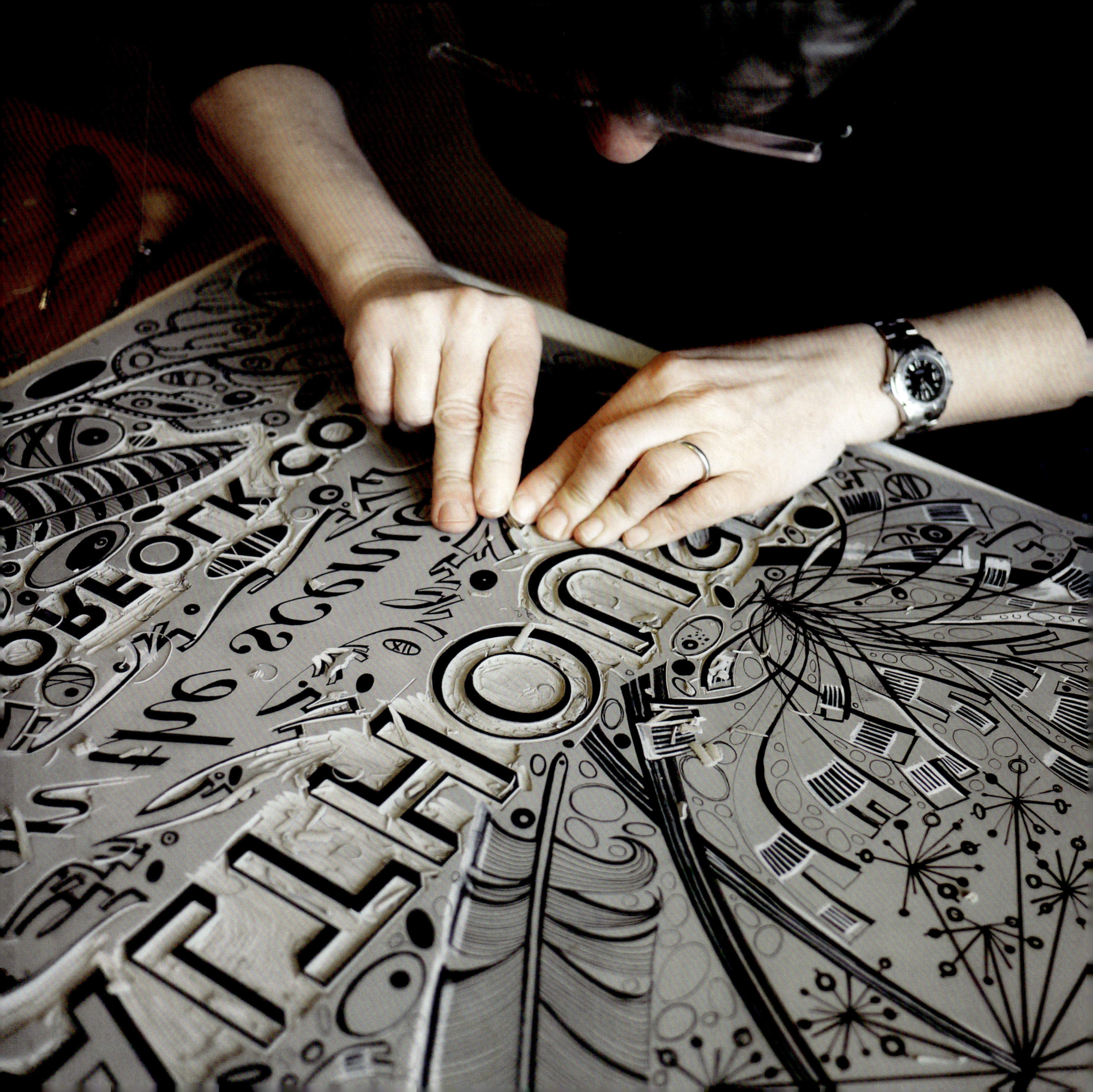

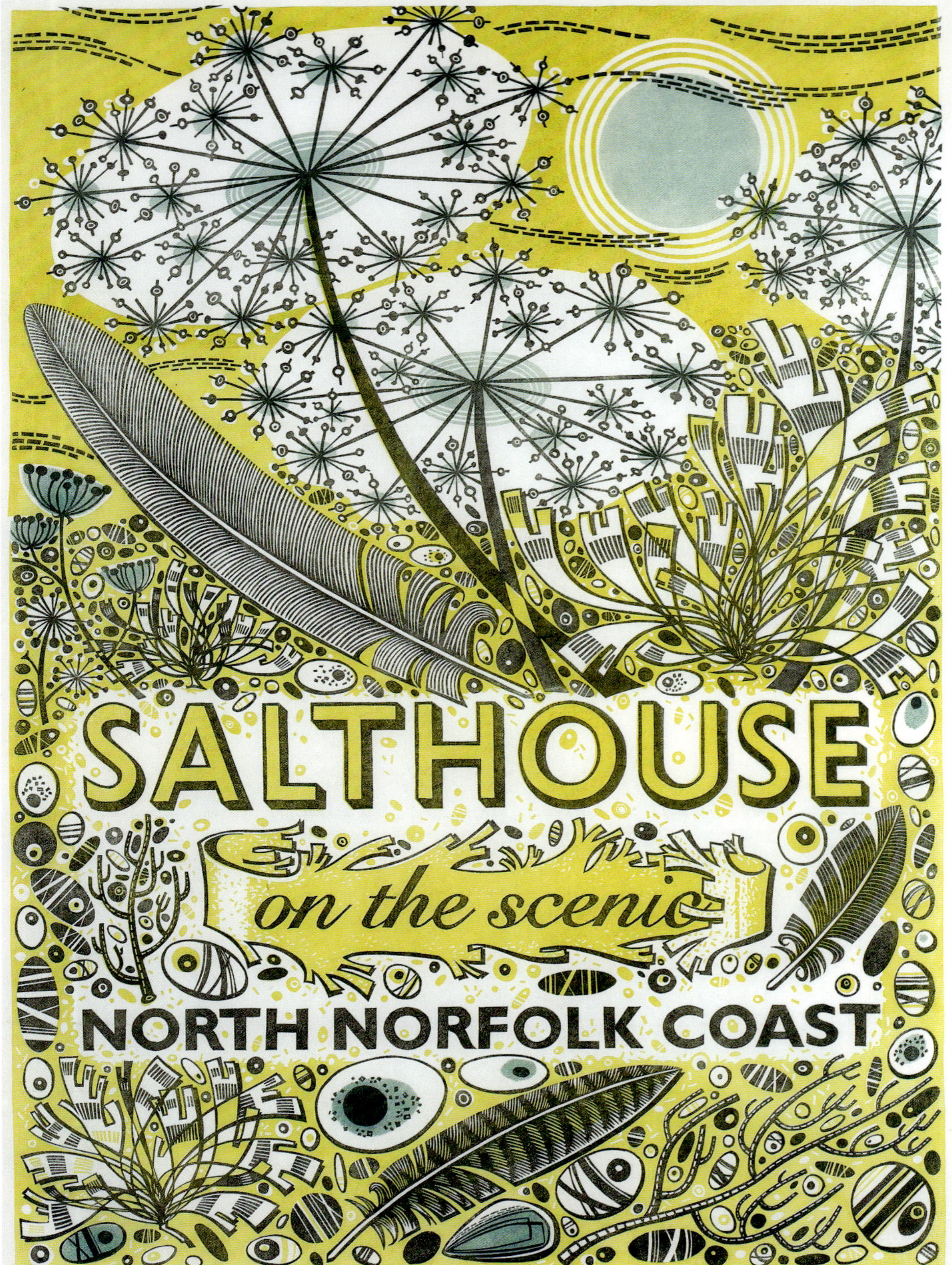

'When I was working on the grey block for the Salthouse poster, I cut the text in mirror image so that it would read correctly when printed (right).'

Poster: Salthouse on the Scenic North Norfolk Coast

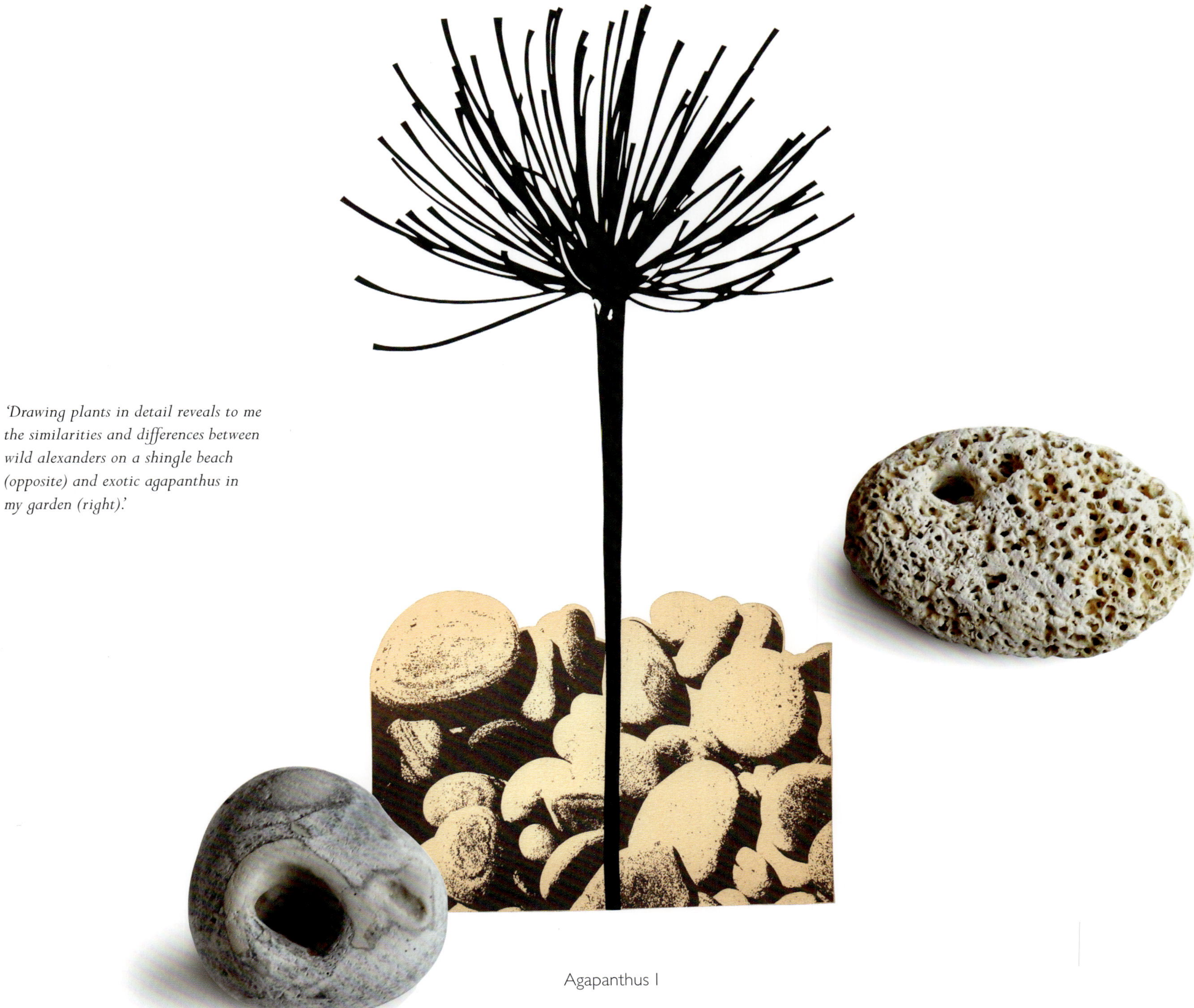

Agapanthus I

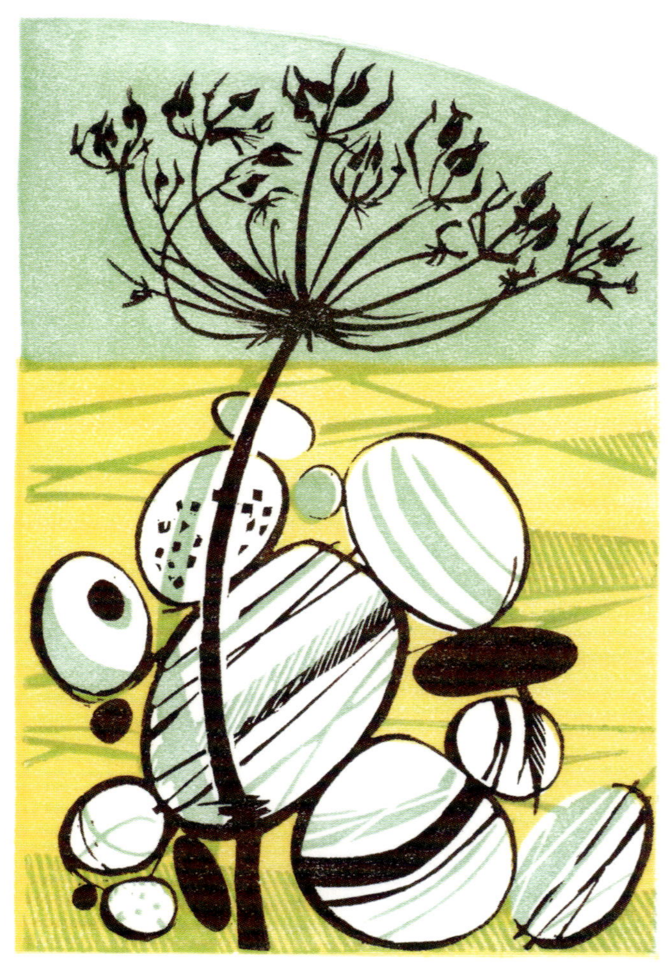

Alexanders

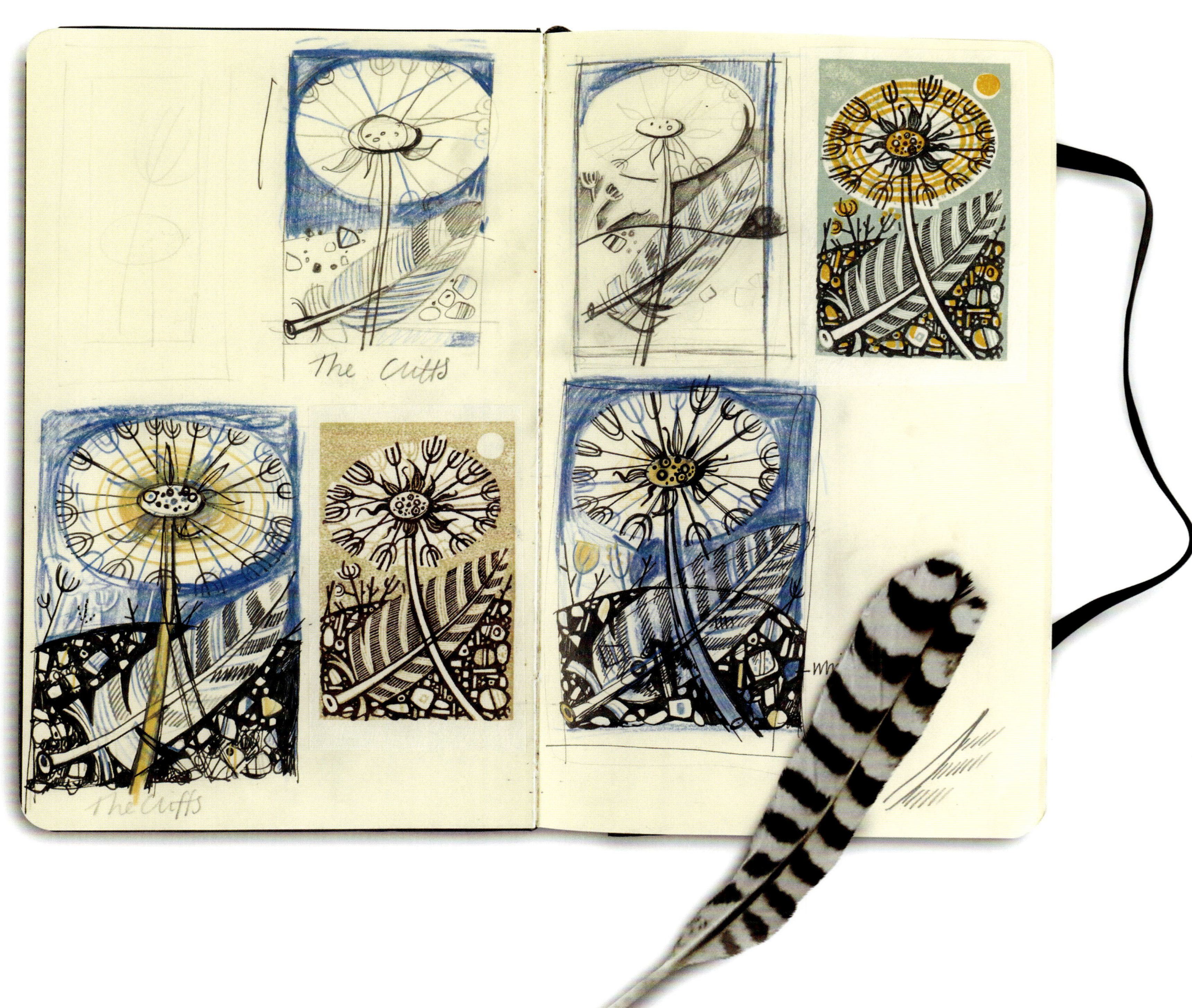
The Cliffs
The Cliffs

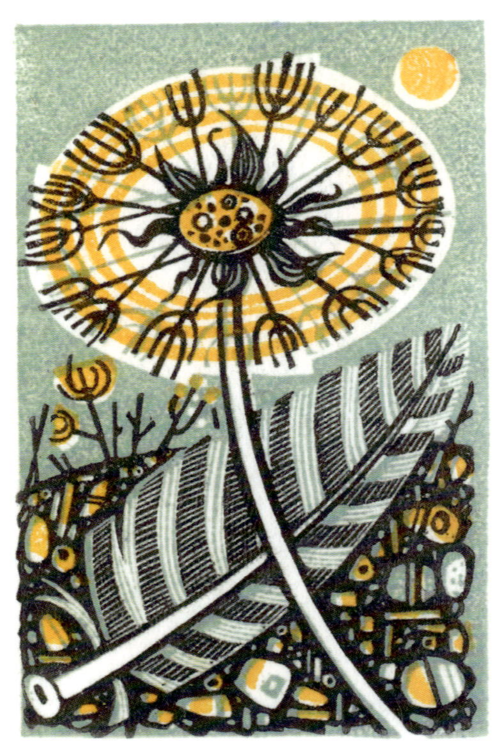

Dandelion III

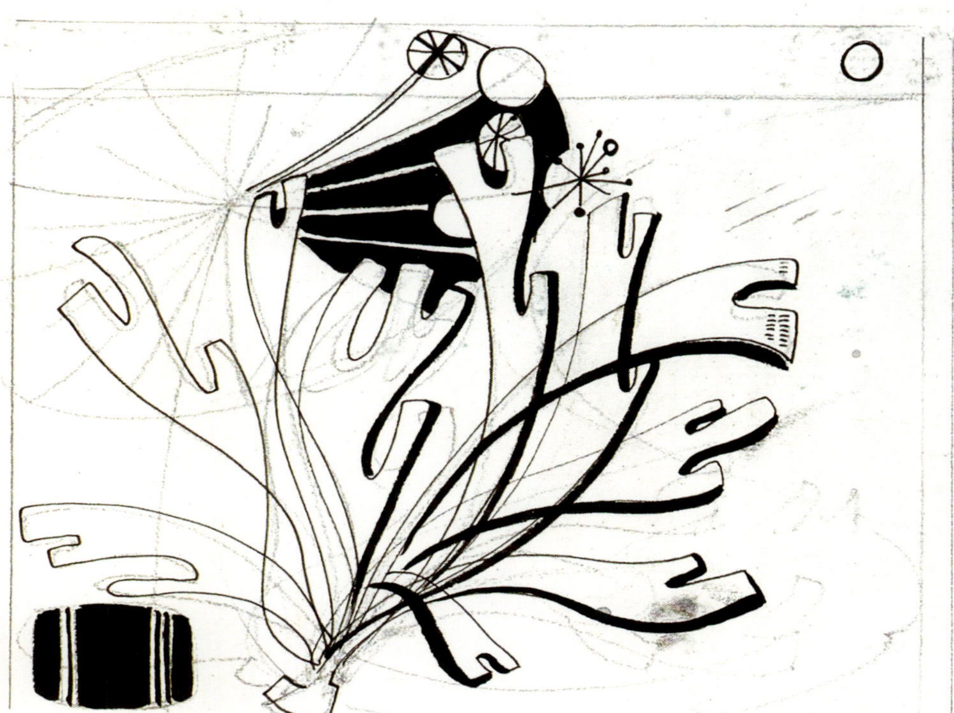
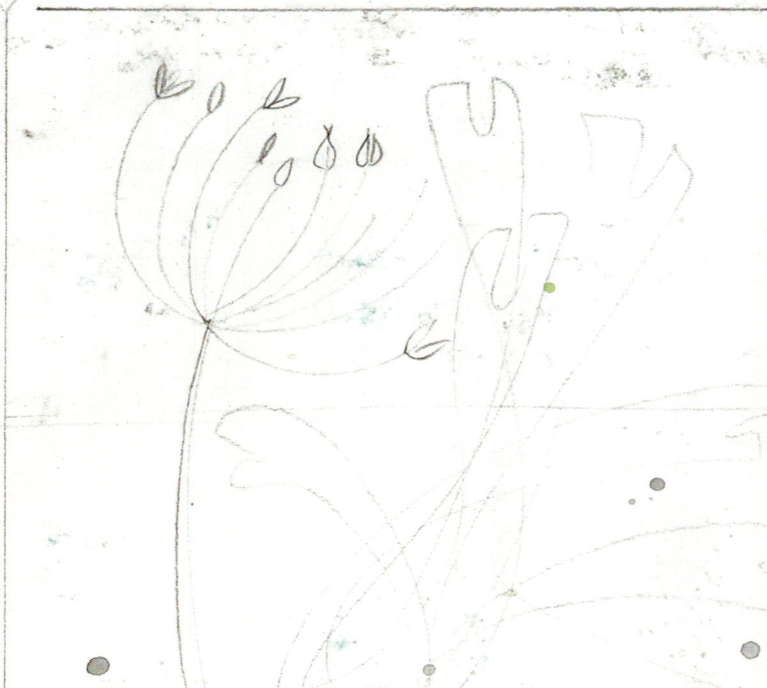
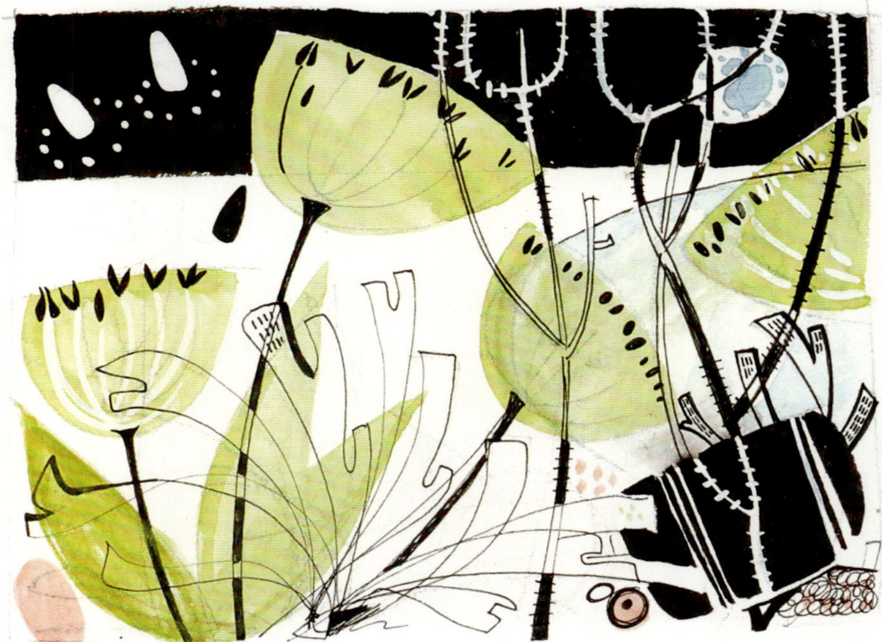
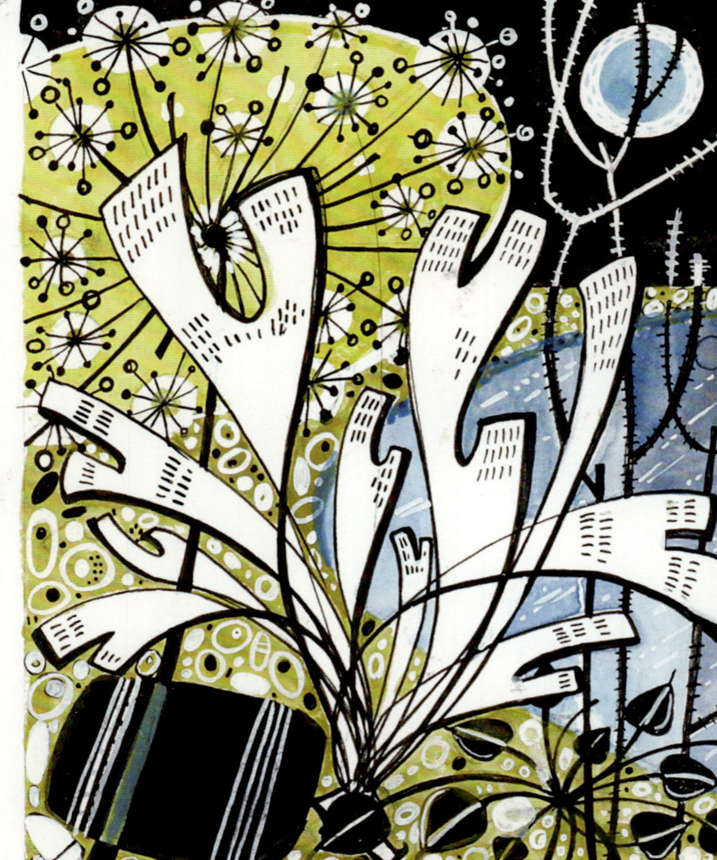

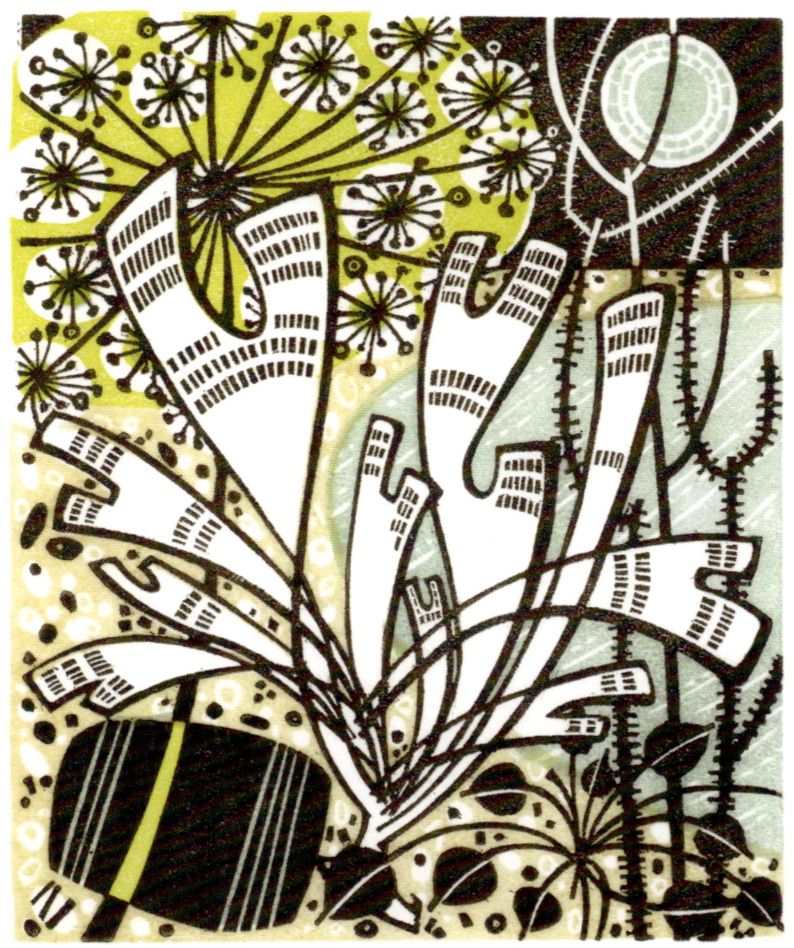

Beach with Alexanders

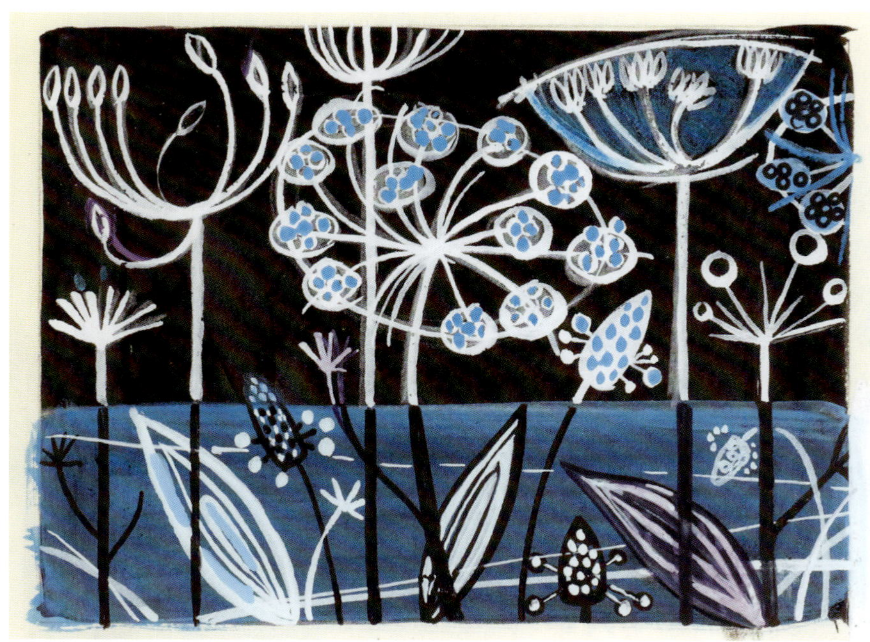

'The way structural seed heads break
the line between sea and sky along the
north Norfolk coast inspired my series
of "Clifftop" prints.'

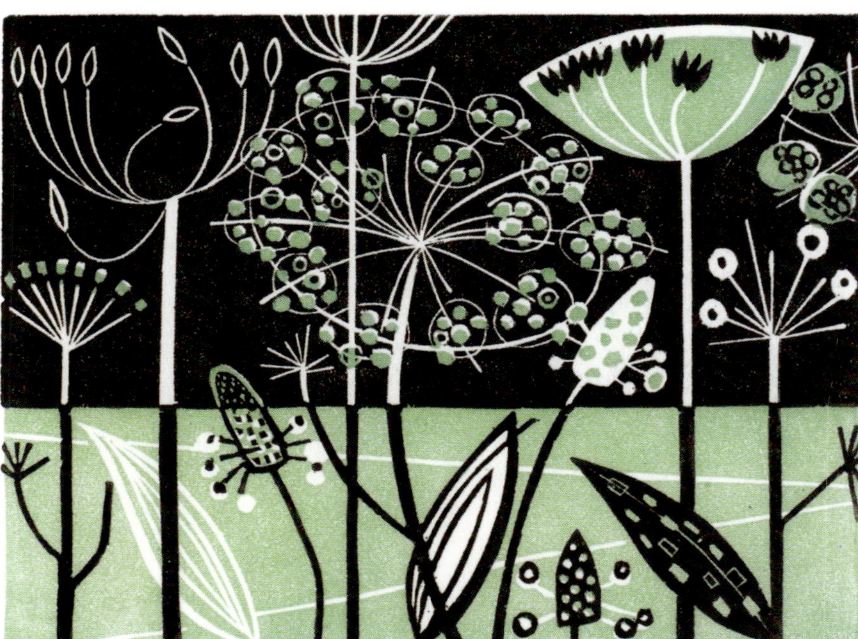

Clifftop

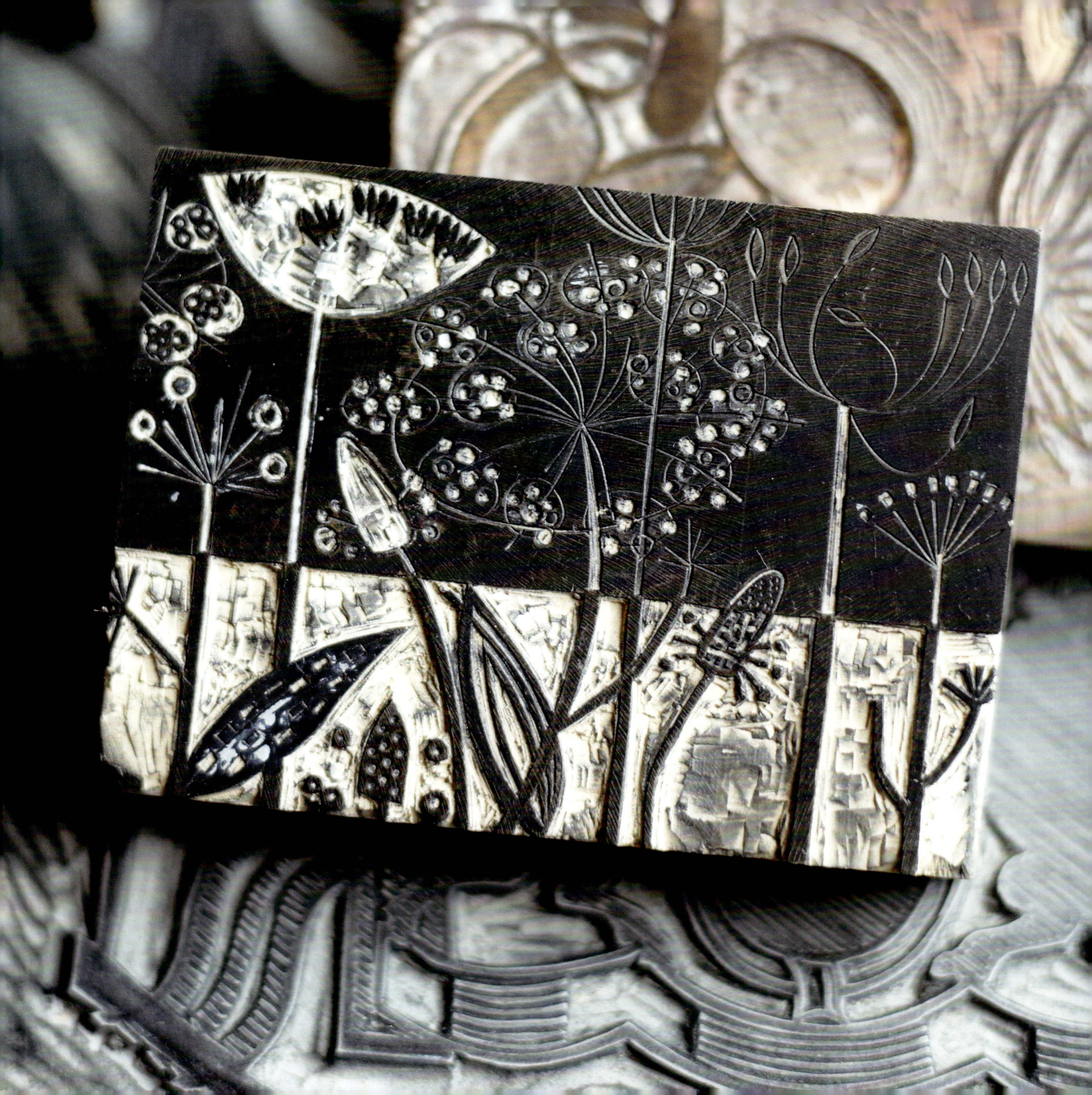

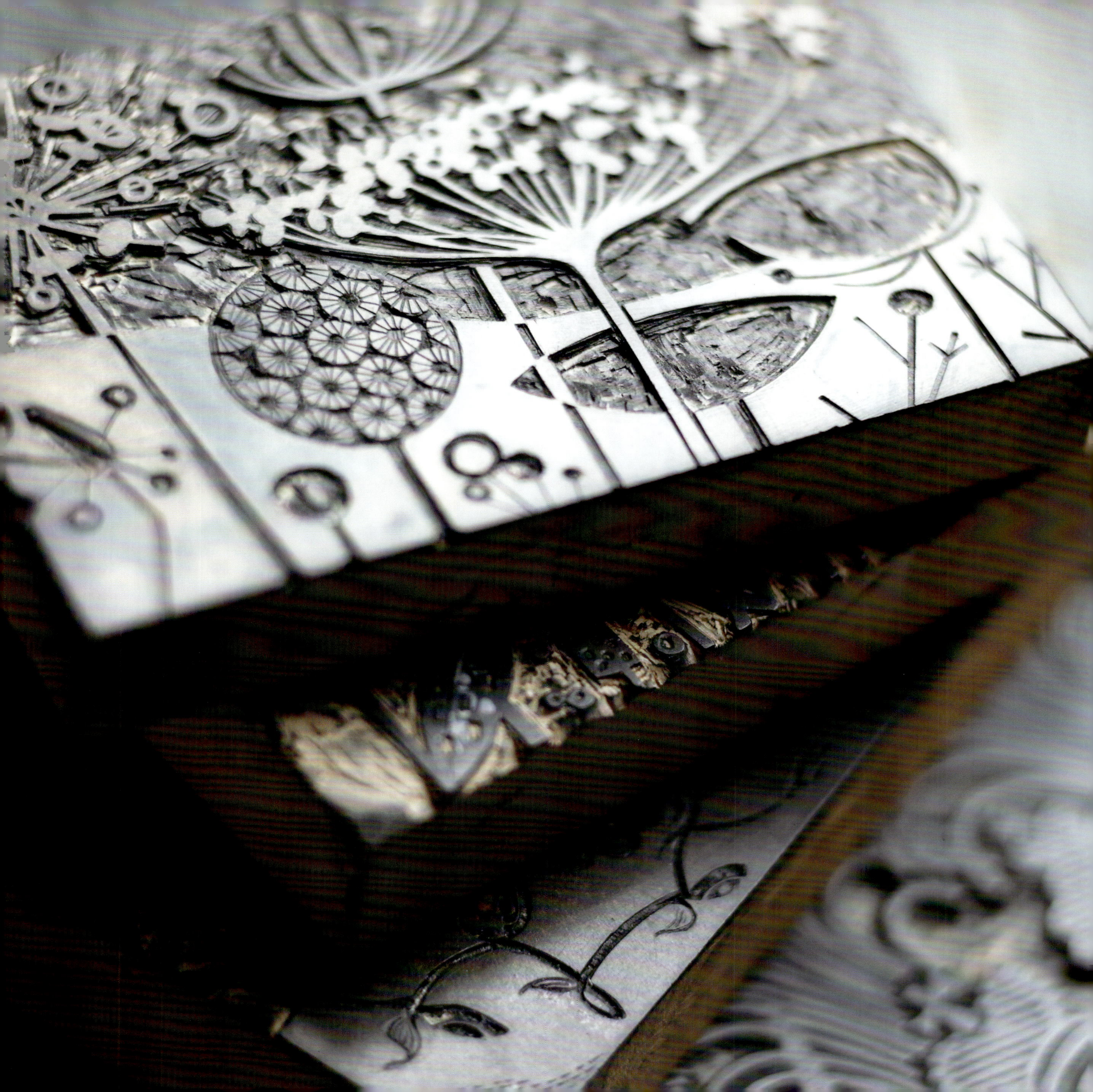

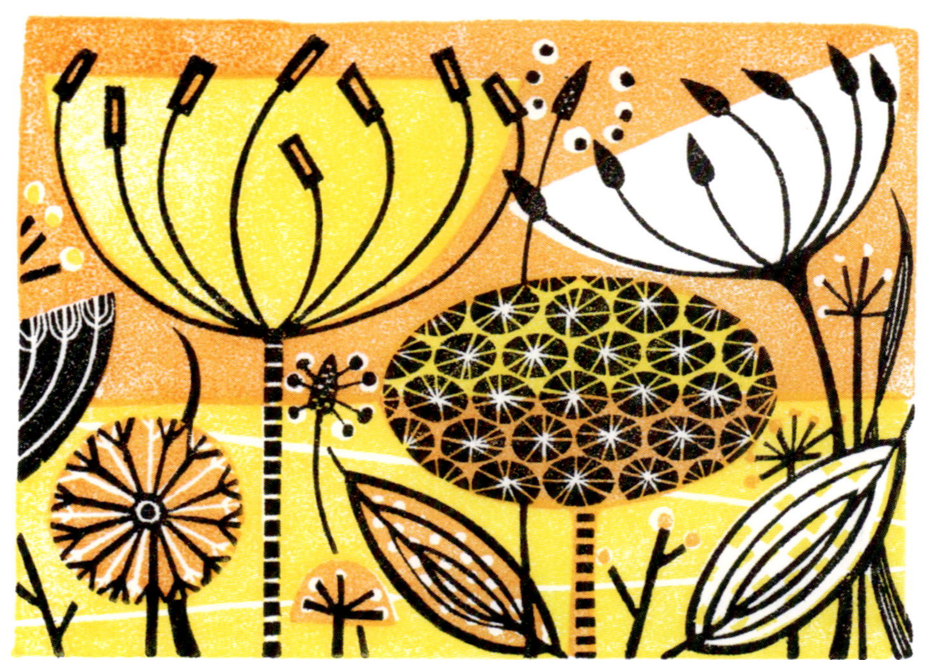

Clifftop III

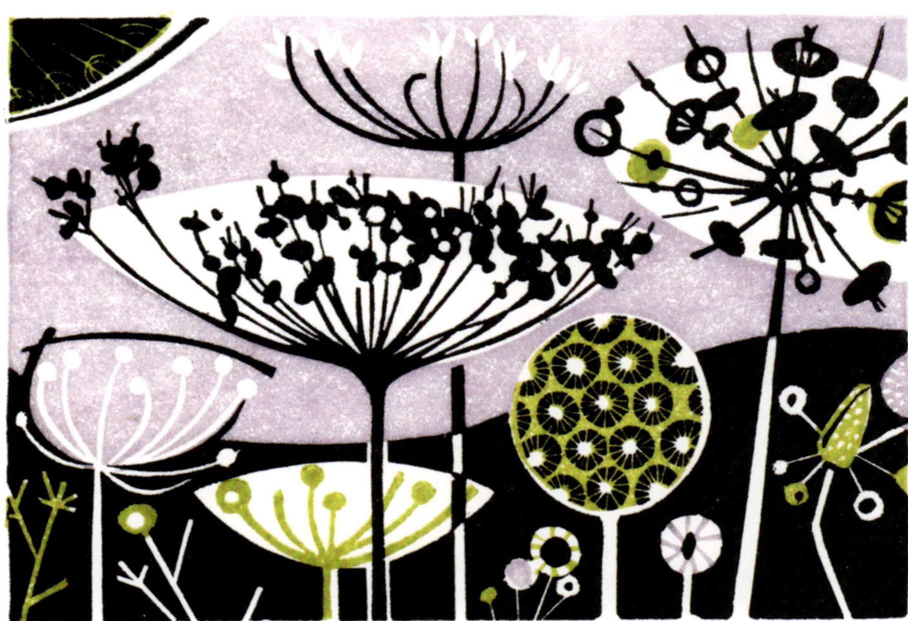

Clifftop II

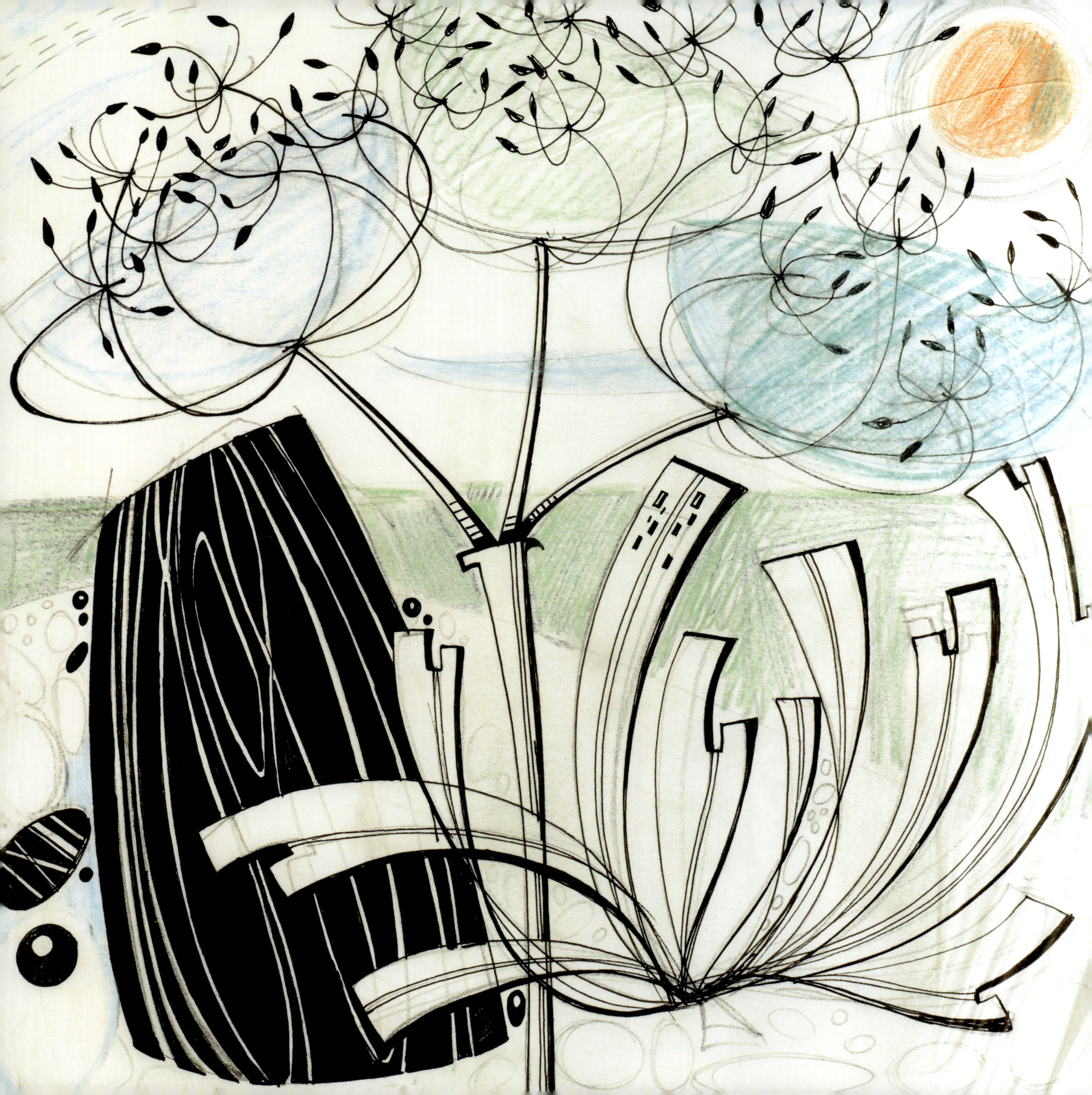

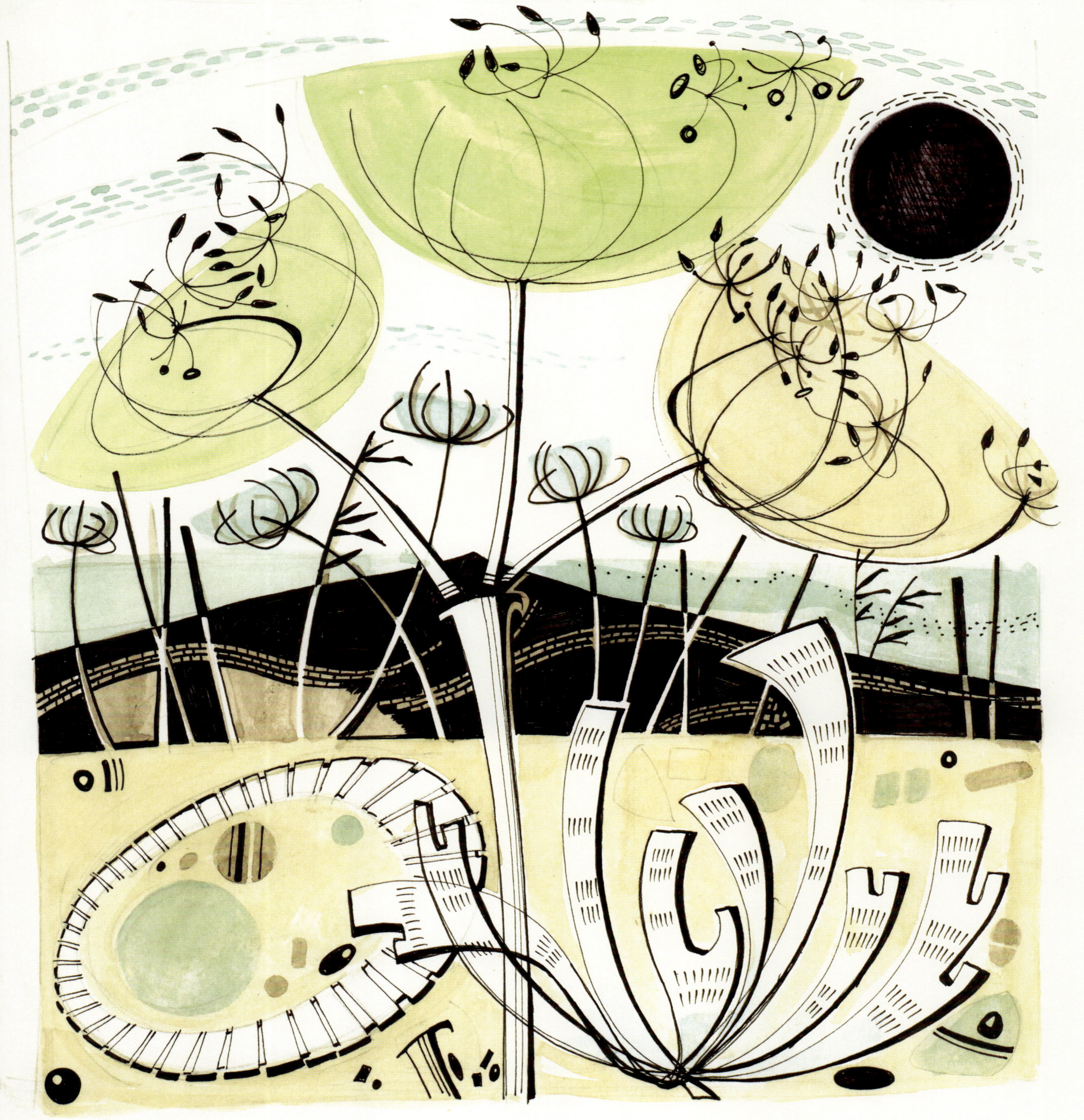

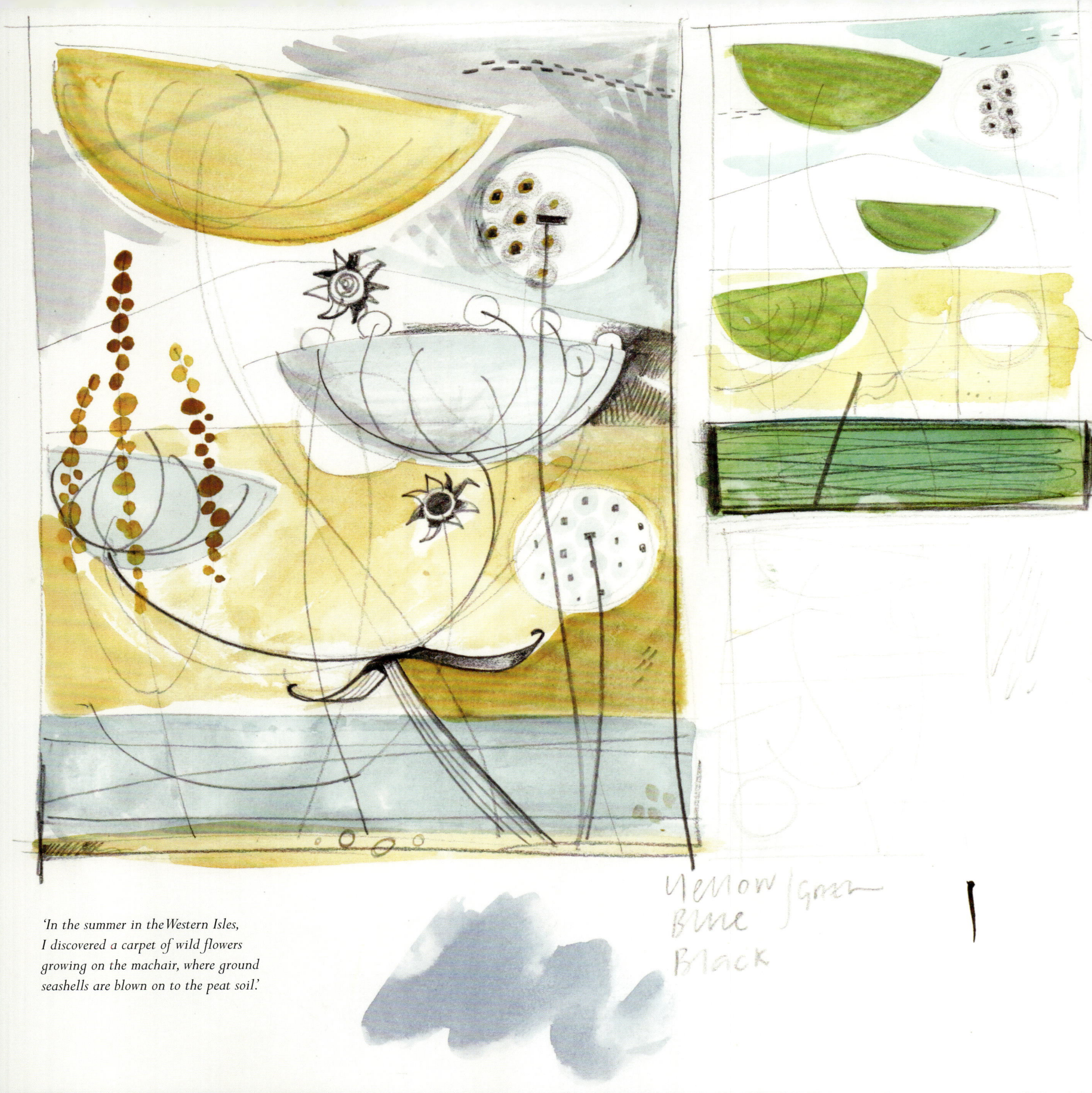

'In the summer in the Western Isles,
I discovered a carpet of wild flowers
growing on the machair, where ground
seashells are blown on to the peat soil.'

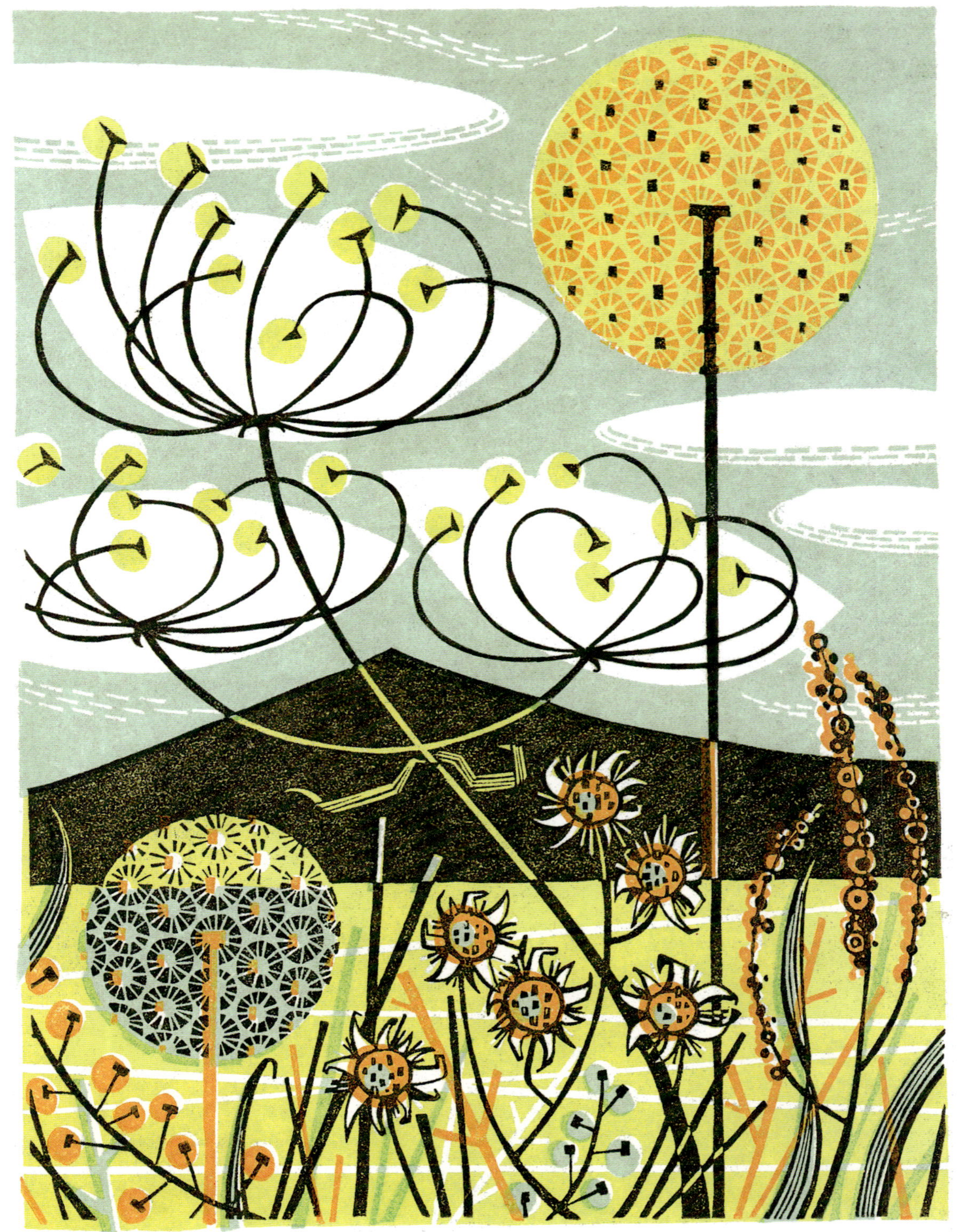

Scarista

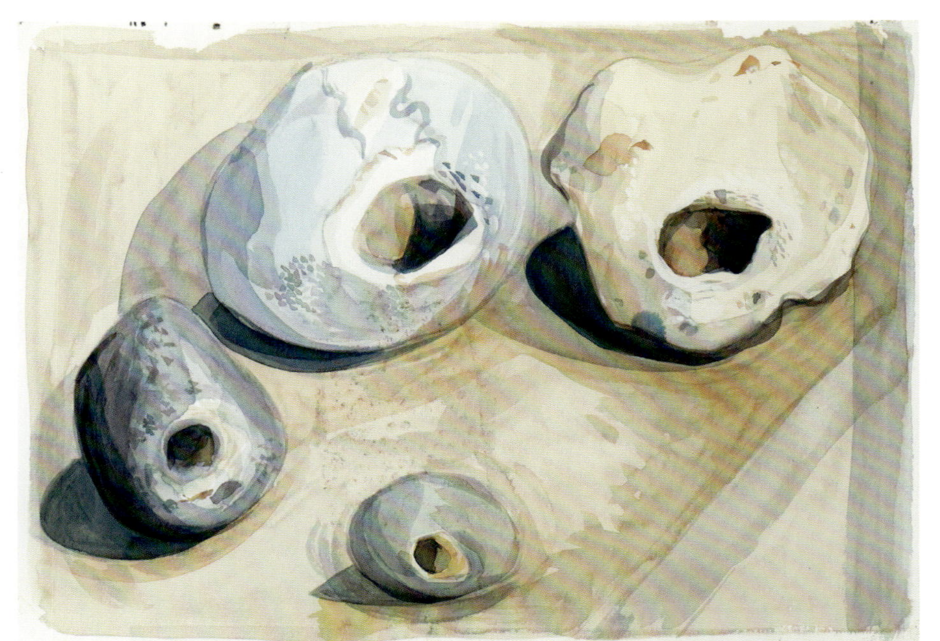

'the pebbles and
flints, striated
and pockmarked,
ground the plants
and the prints'

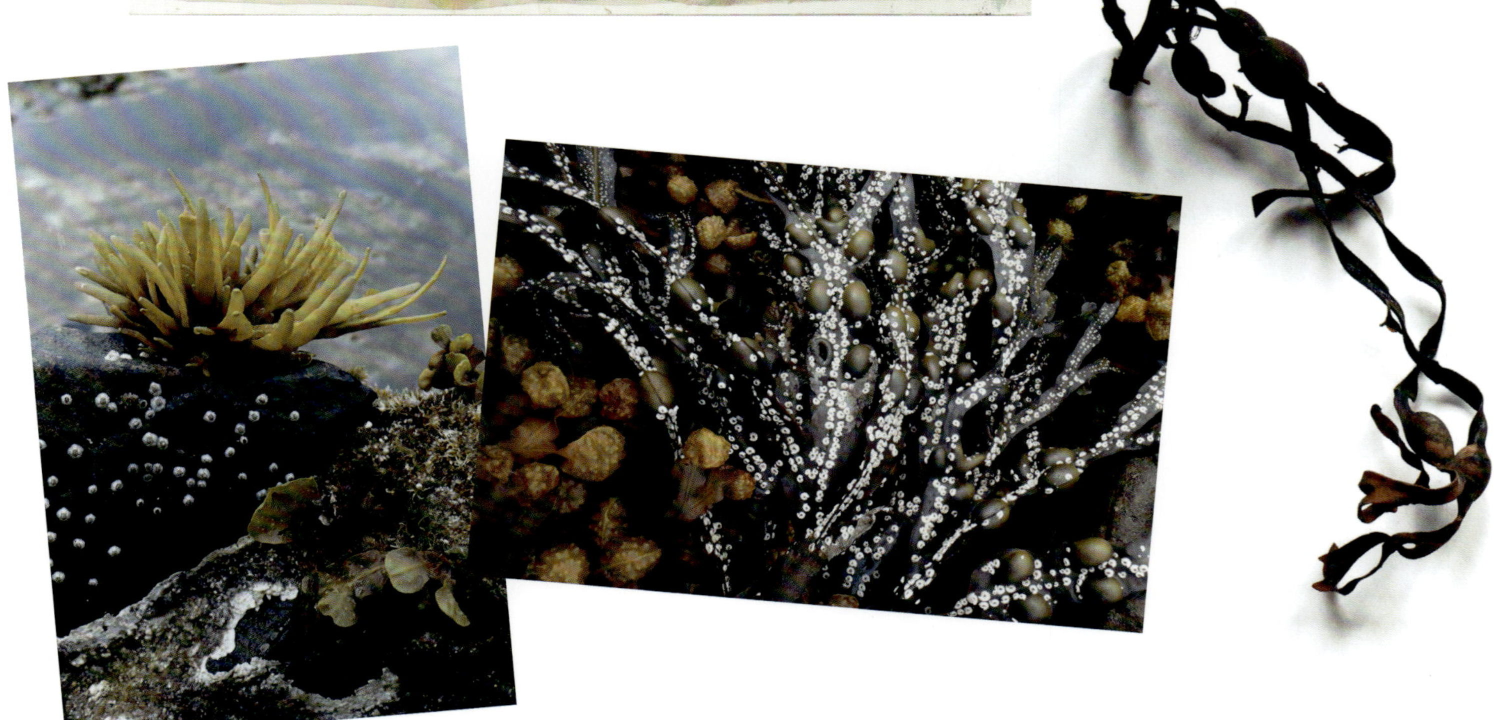

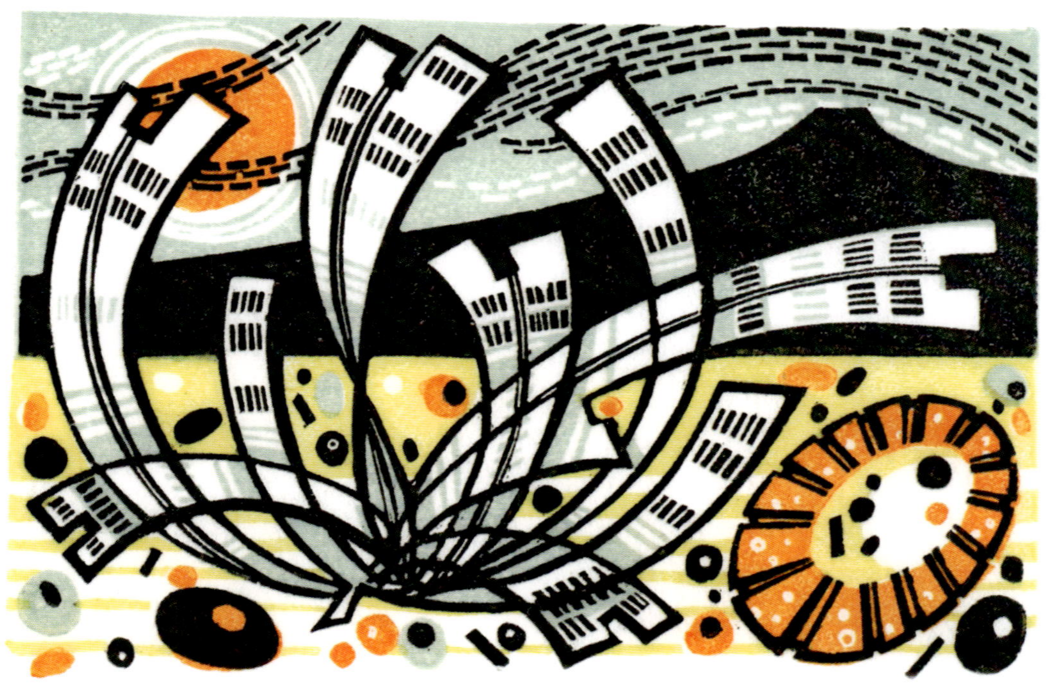

Seaweed, Buried Shell

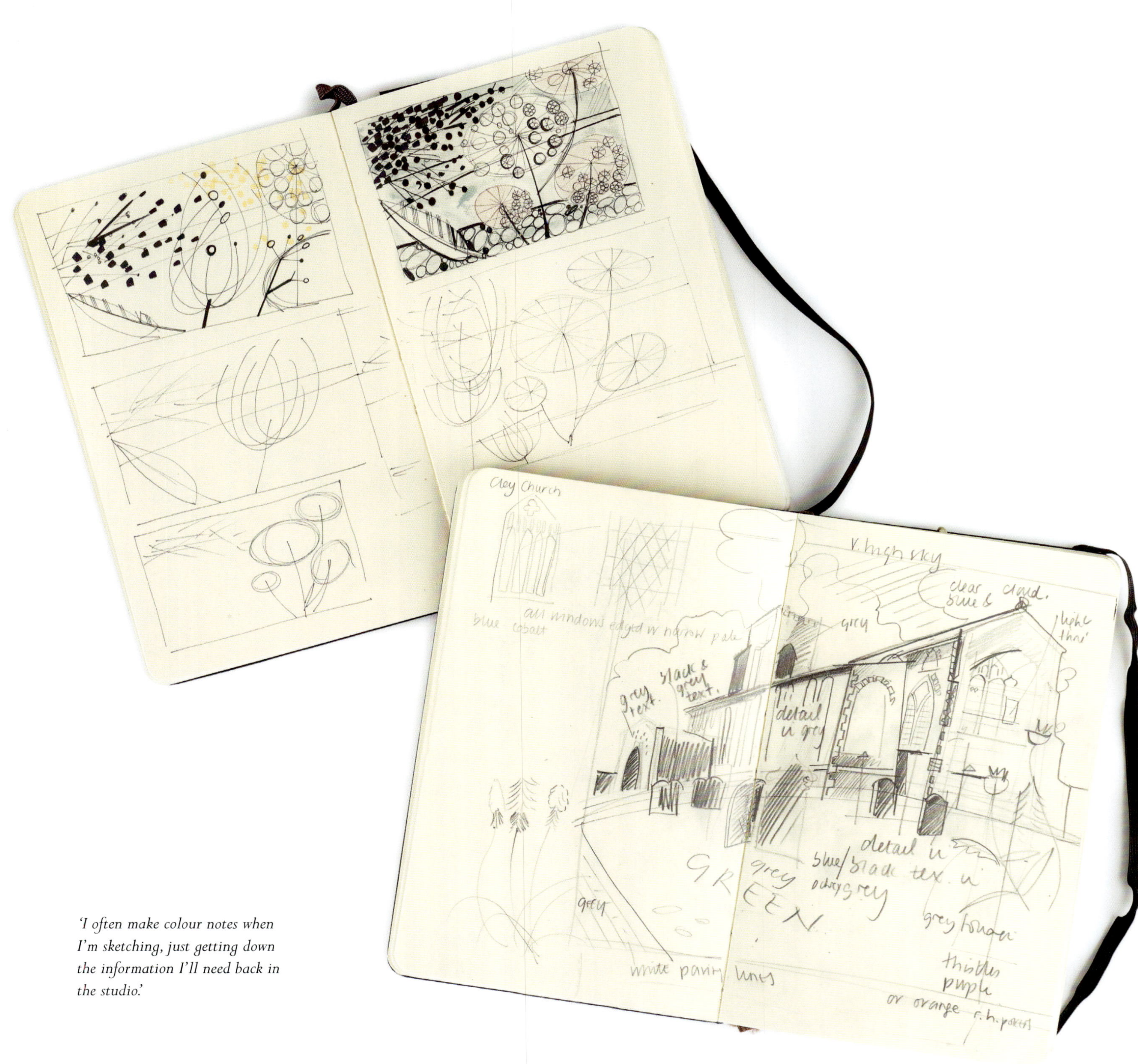

'I often make colour notes when I'm sketching, just getting down the information I'll need back in the studio.'

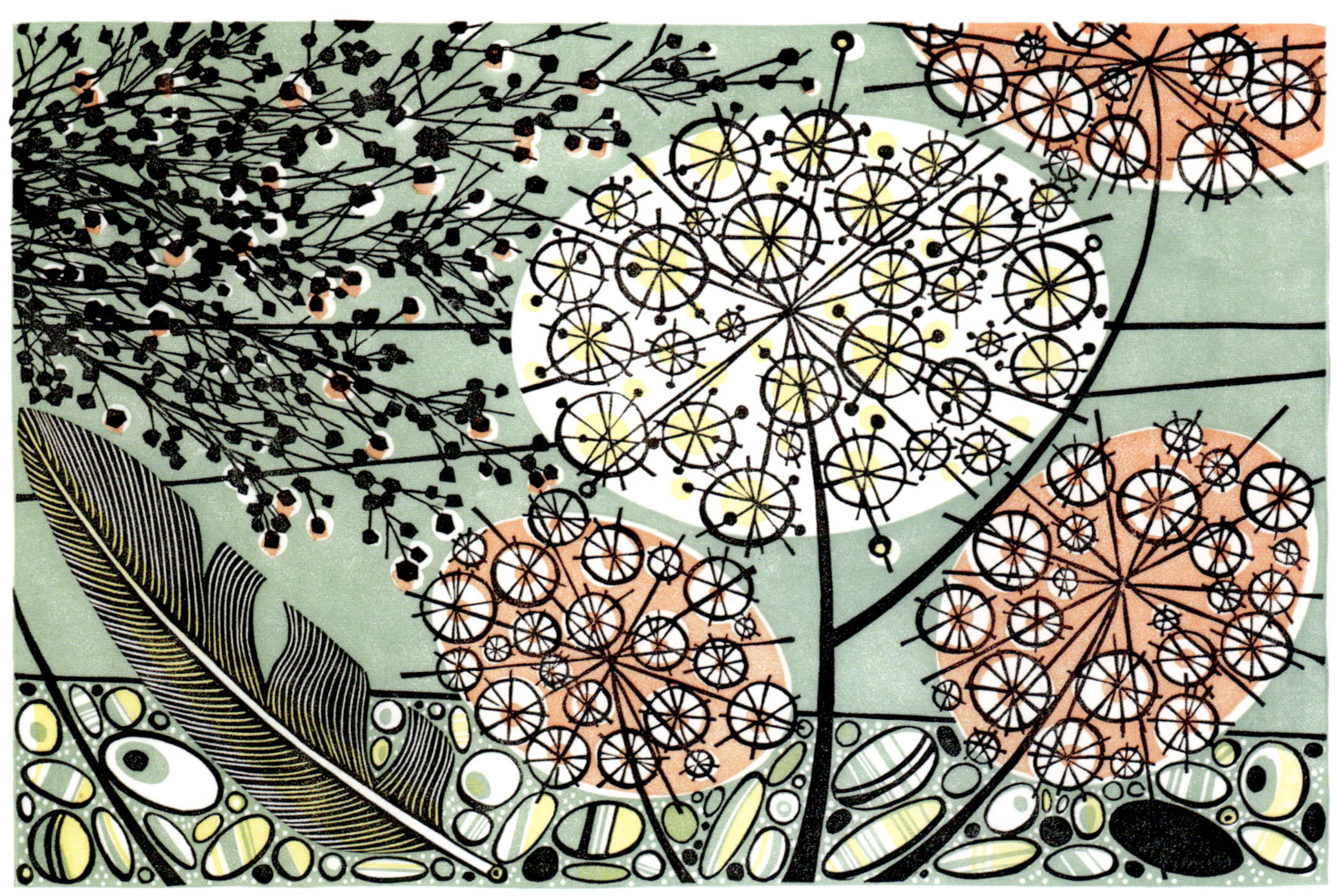

Salthouse

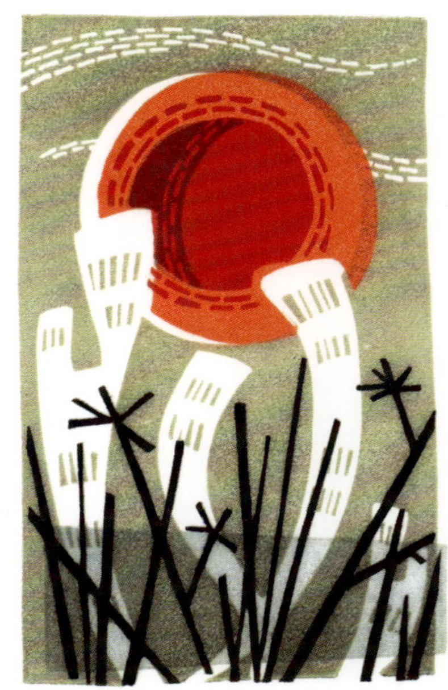

Skye

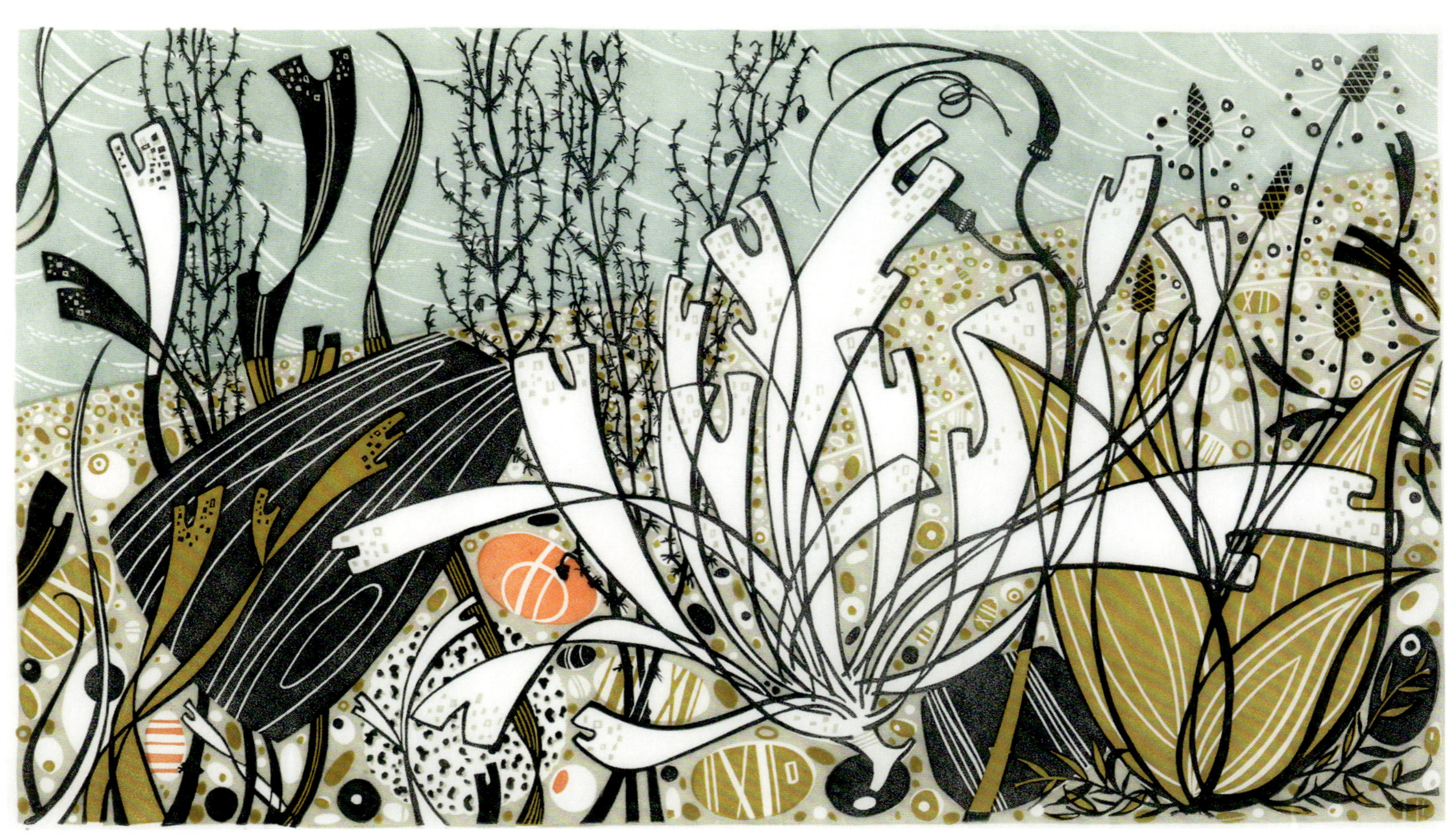

The Beach, Aldeburgh

'I made the print opposite, and the
one entitled The Church, Salthouse
(see page 61), for an annual group
exhibition that is held in Salthouse
village's flint church.'

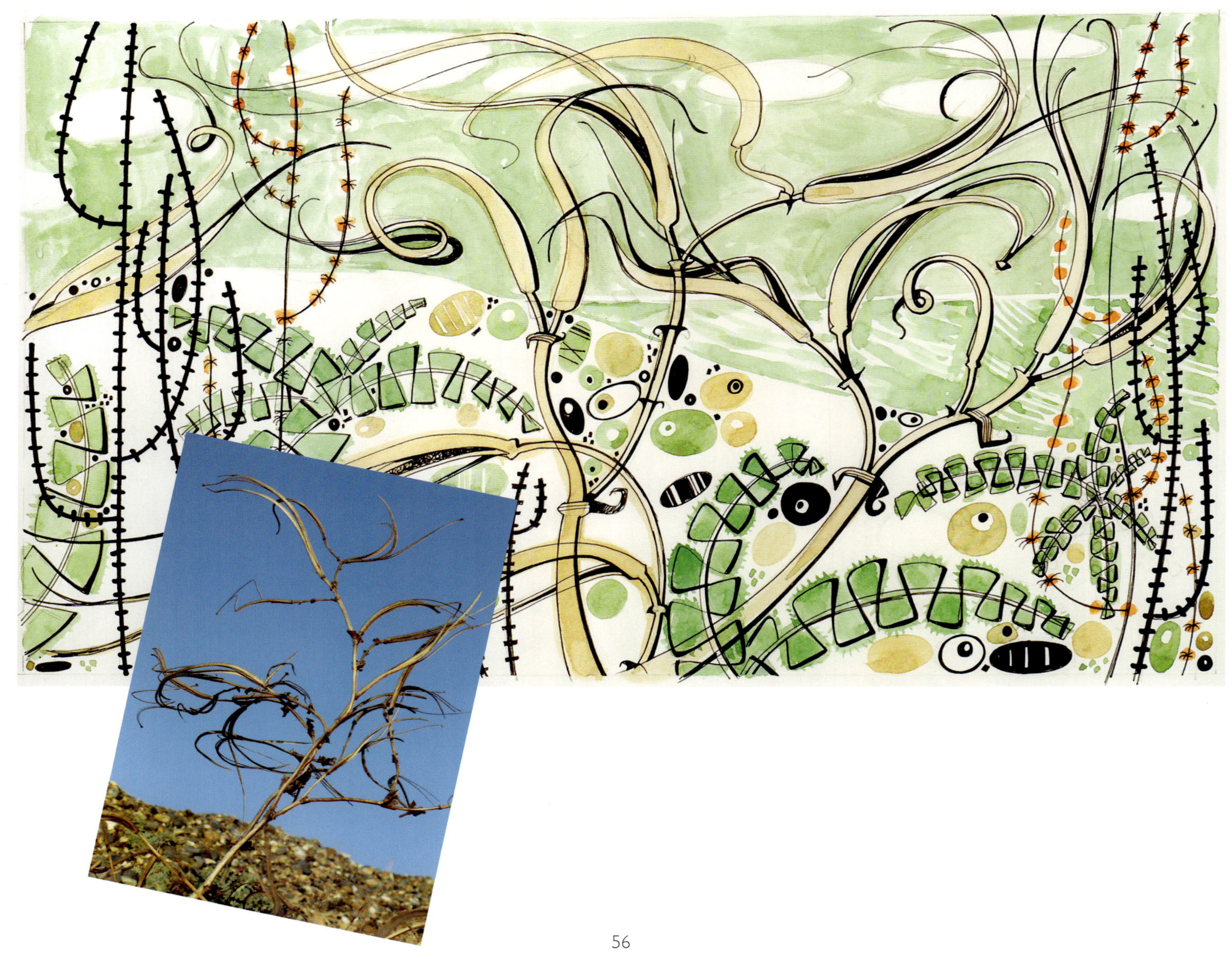

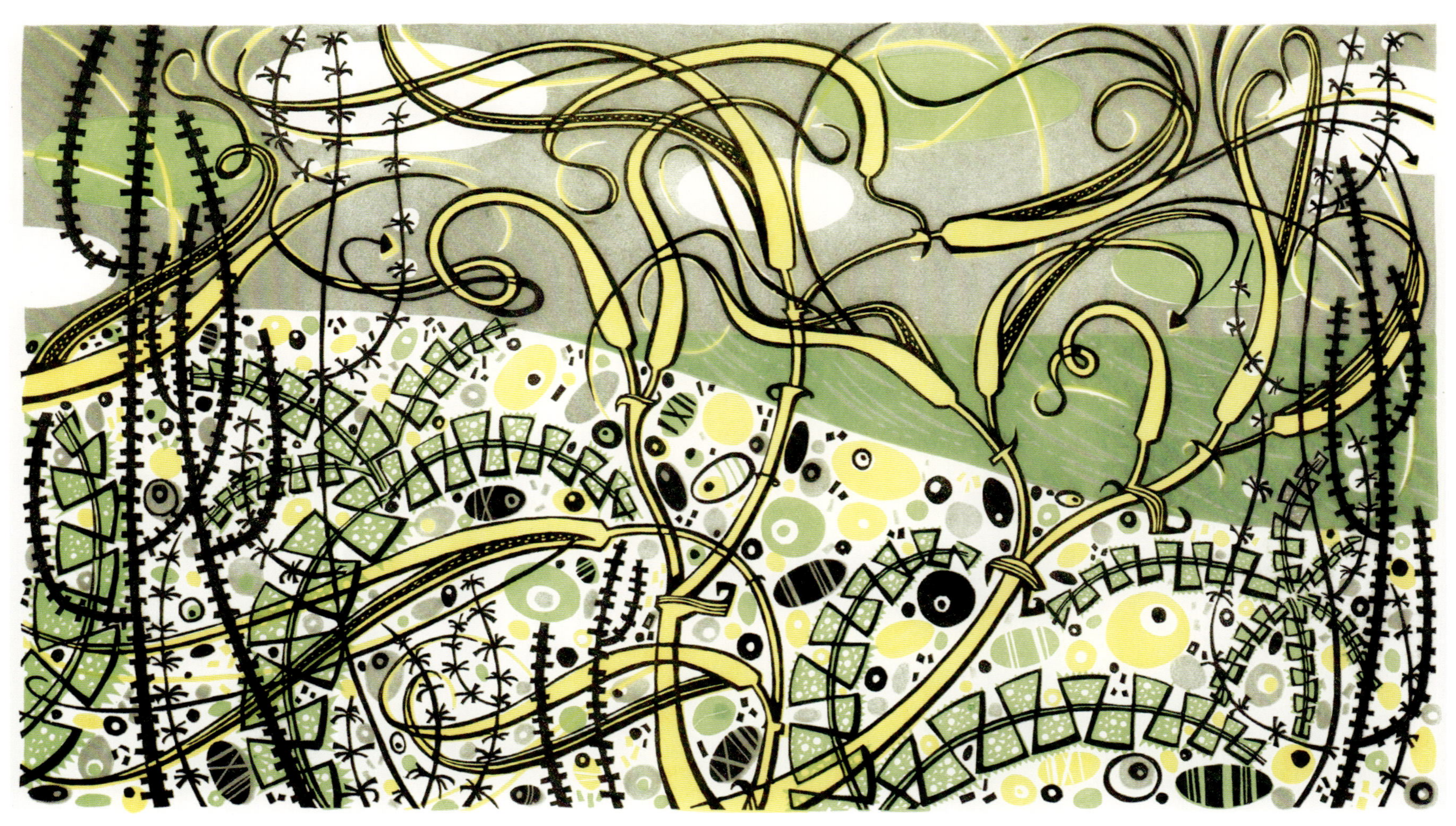

The Beach, Salthouse

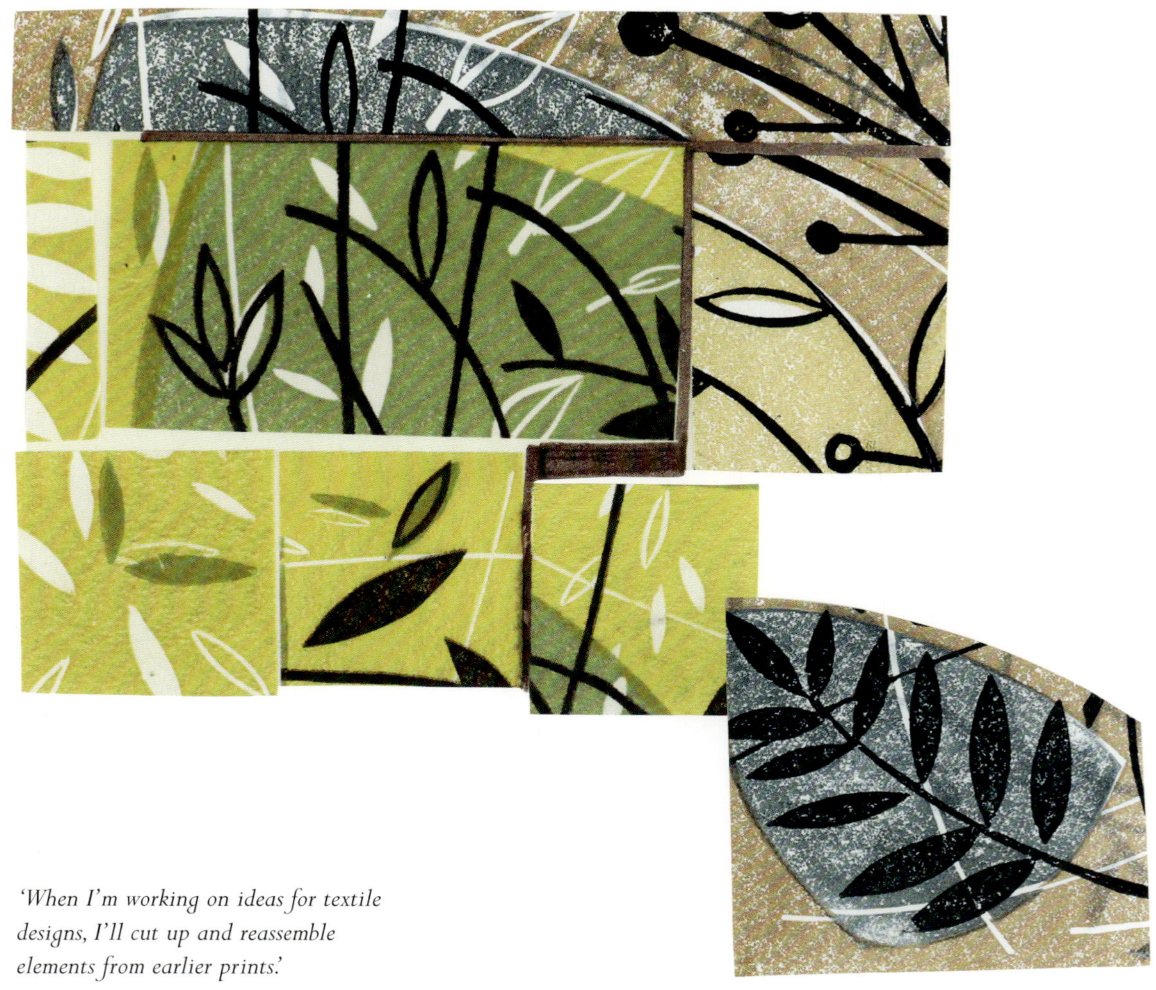

'When I'm working on ideas for textile
designs, I'll cut up and reassemble
elements from earlier prints.'

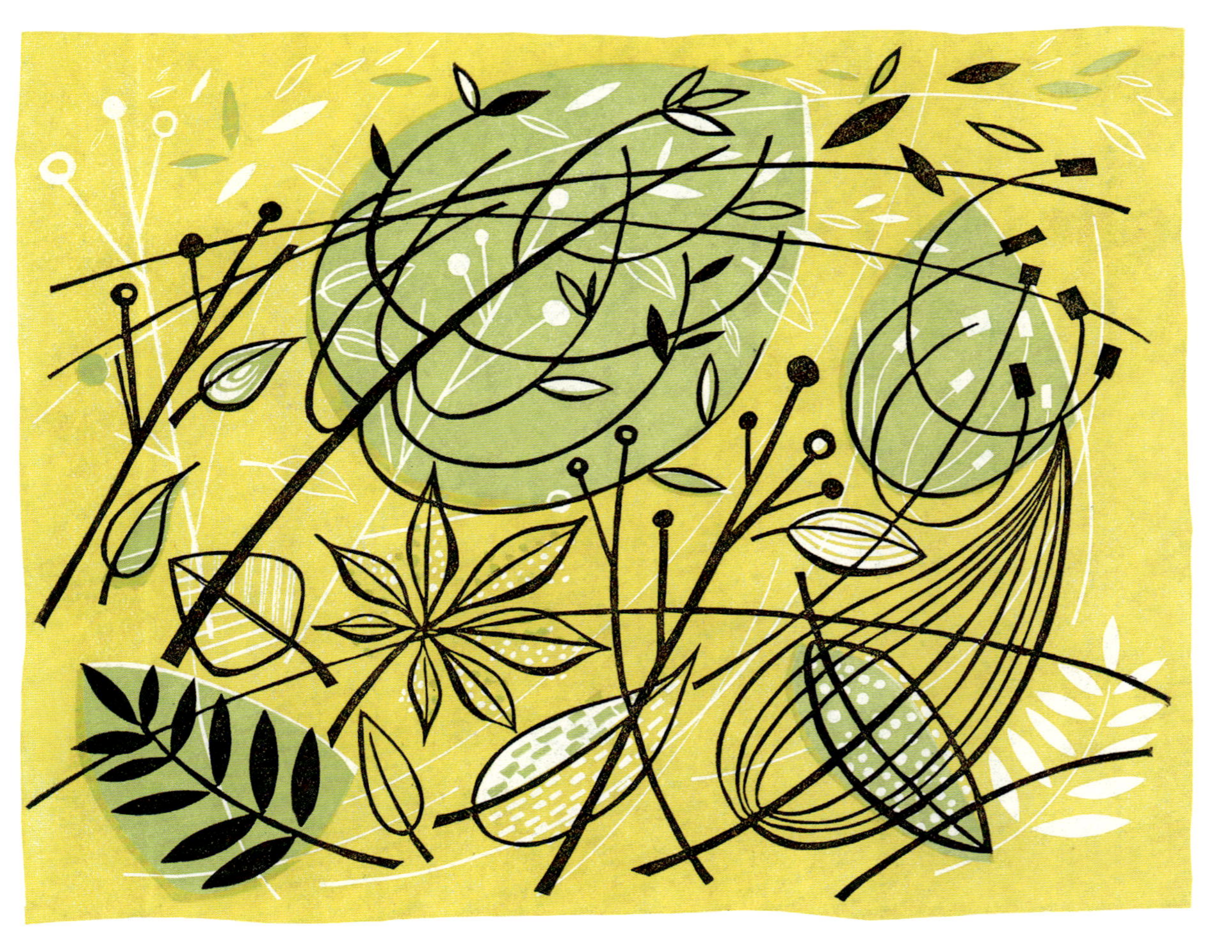

Weybourne to Sheringham

'In the churchyard above the beach,
I sketch ivy flowers poking over the
flint walls and alexanders outlined
against the pale sky.'

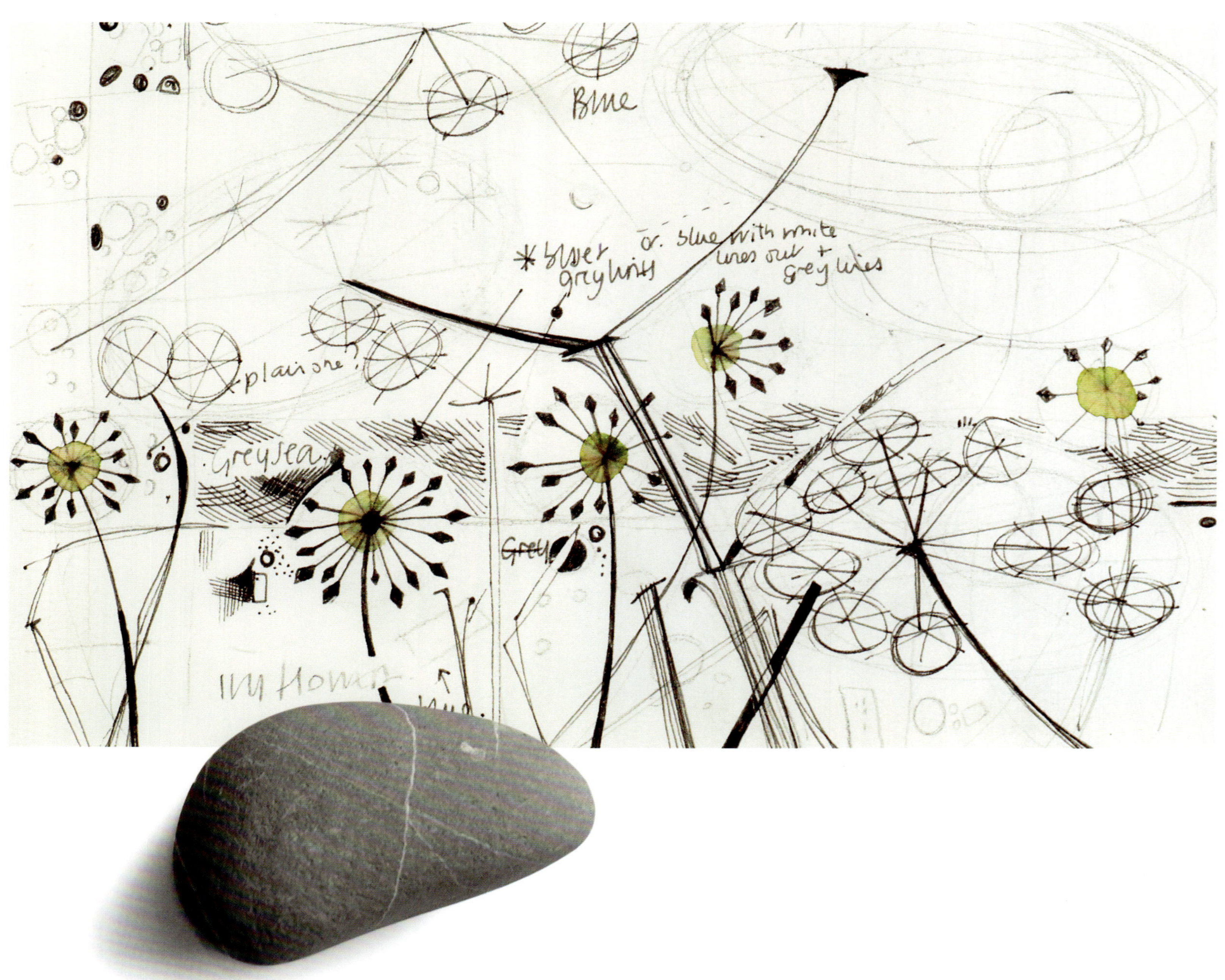

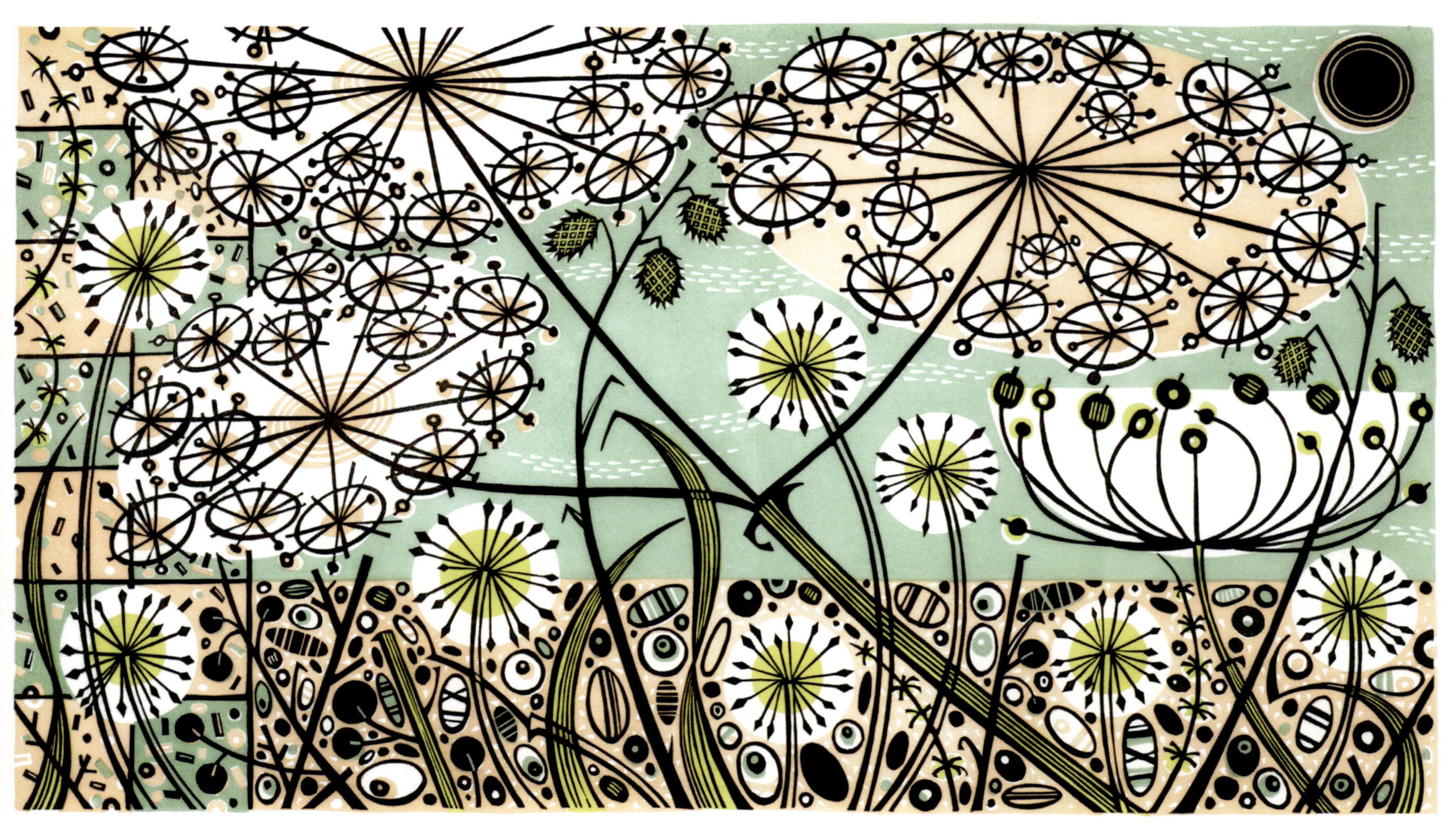

The Church, Salthouse

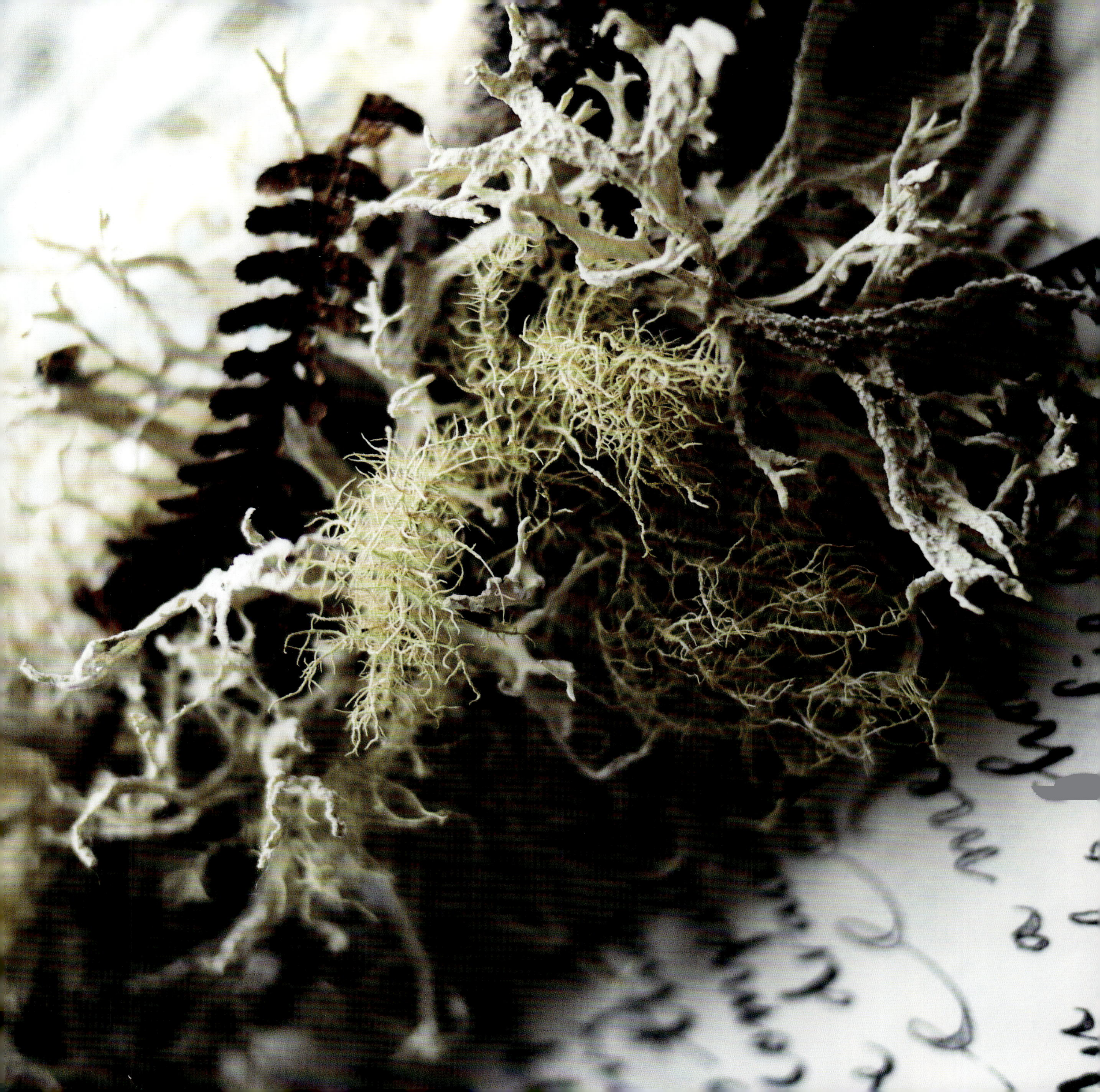

Woodland and Hedgerow

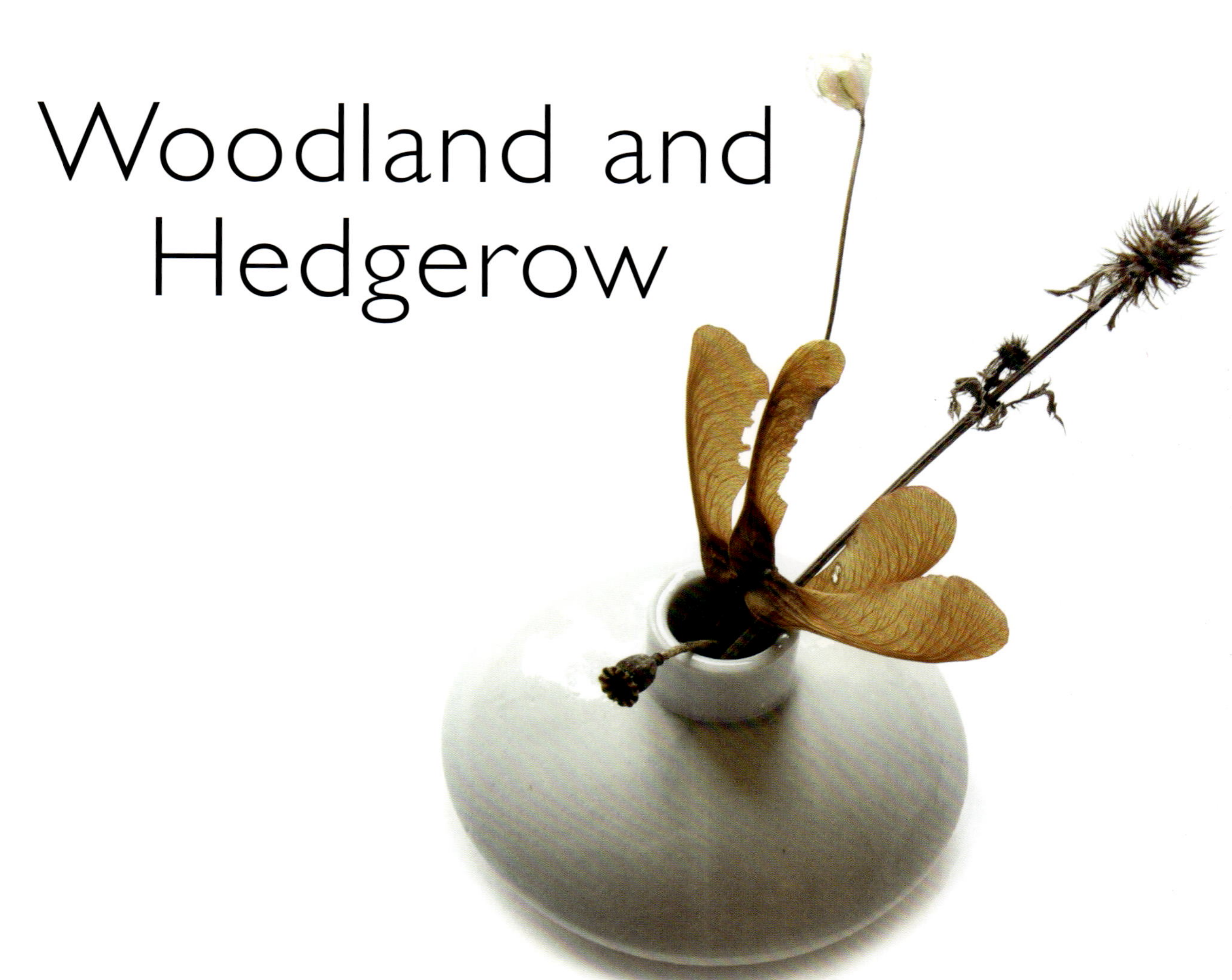

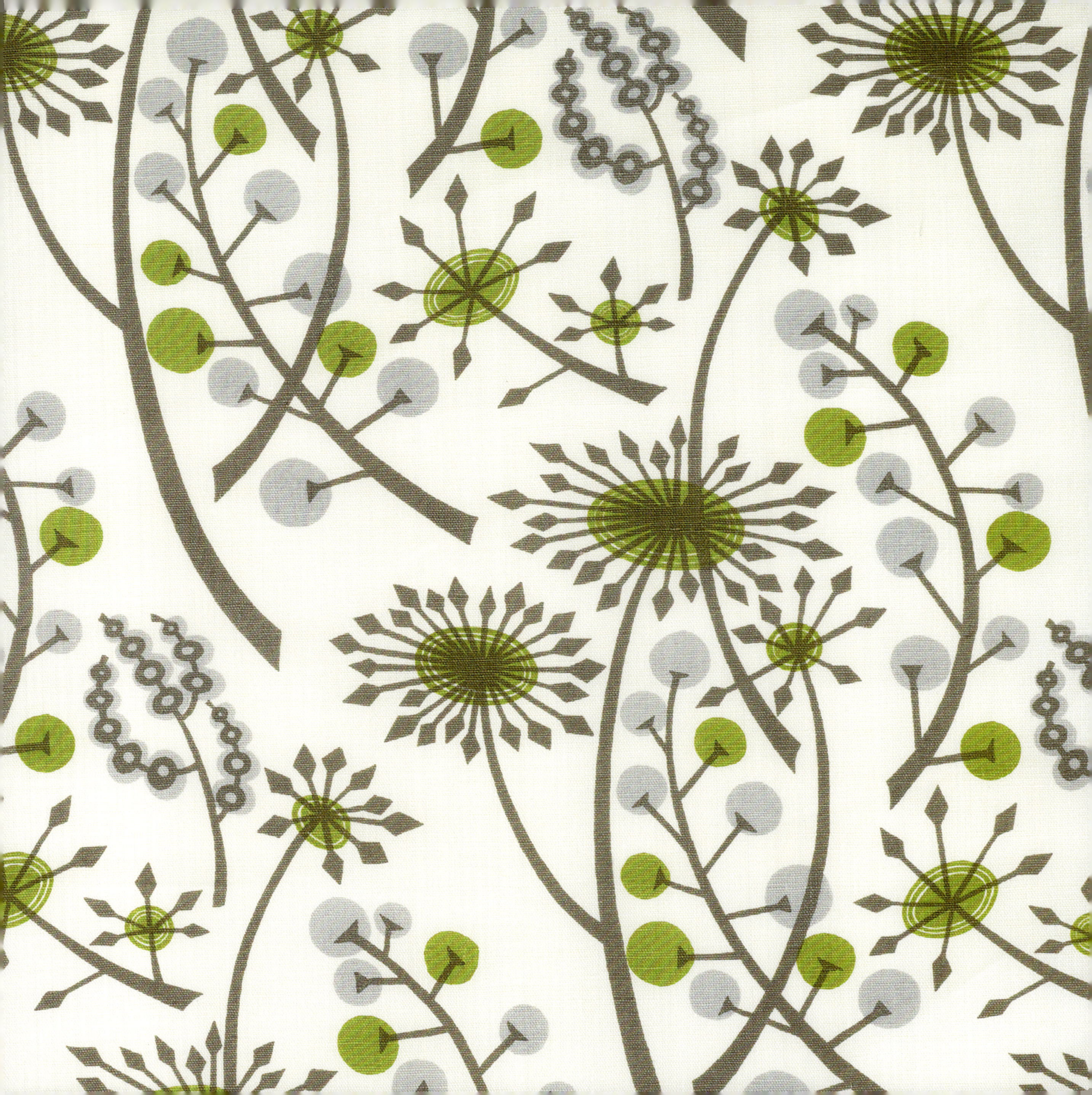

The small scale of many of Angie Lewin's prints
means that, to examine them properly, you
need to get up close to her work in order to
gain a sense of where the inspiration comes from.
So have a look at the wood engraving entitled *5 Trees*
(see page 69), which shows five almost unbranched
but striated trunks silhouetted against a brilliant
sun. When you understand that they are birch
trees, the stripy bark makes sense.

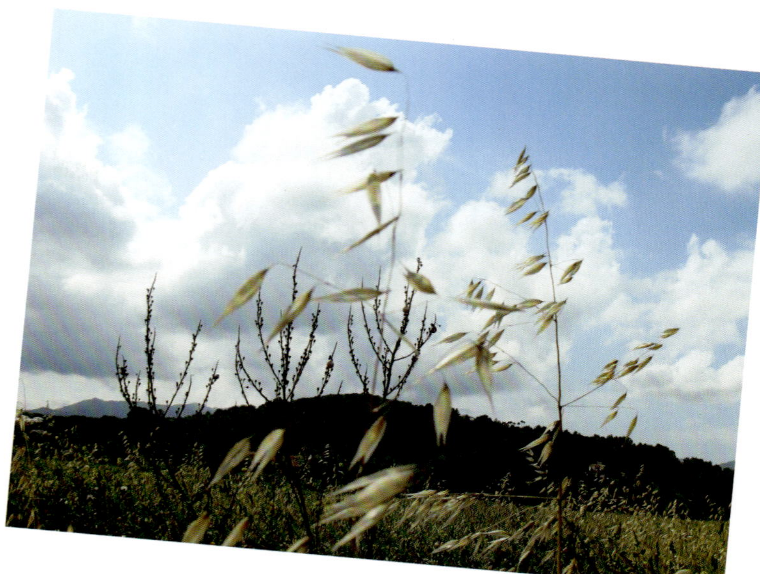
Northern Mallorca.

Contrast this with the screenprint *Winter Birches* (see page 85), which
Lewin made as a sequel to *5 Trees*. 'I felt that the [engraving's] image would scale up
successfully, and *Winter Birches* is inspired by heavy snow and freezing winter weather on
Speyside', she recalls. From the engraving's five trunks, there are now eight, similarly flexible
and striped; in the foreground are grasses and seed heads. The sun from *5 Trees* has changed
from a brilliant yellow to a dull, greenish one, and the background is pale blue with swirls
of snow. In *Ballindalloch* (see page 67), the background birch trunks are white.

Lewin is attracted to the less obvious elements of trees and woodland plants: 'the chalky
grey-green lichens on trees, and golden-green ones,
too; bright-red rowan berries, frost-blackened wild
roses, valerian, comfrey and rosebay willowherb'.

In *Ramsons* (see page 83), the print is filled with
the broad leaves and white umbels of the herb. As
you would expect in woodland, the prints show
a green and busy underworld. Another plant that
Lewin often draws is goat's beard, which grows in
both woodland and meadows; *Goat's Beard II* (see
page 133) shows green seed heads inside strong
black lines.

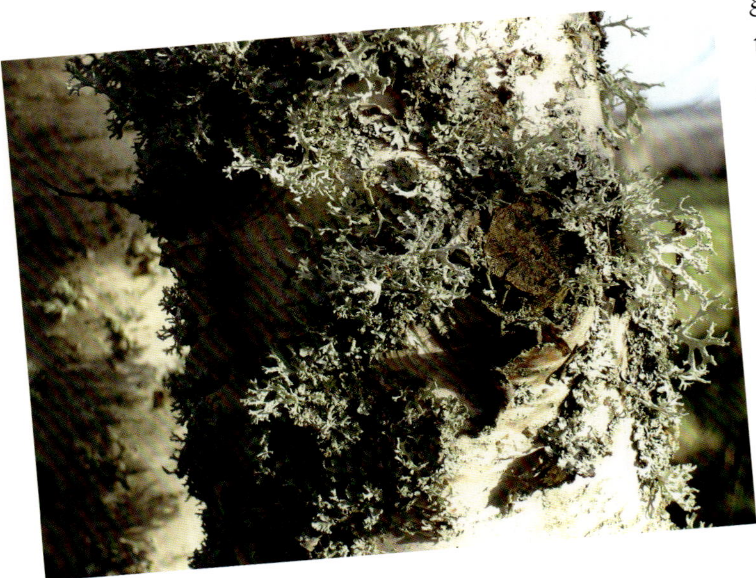
Lichen on a birch tree.

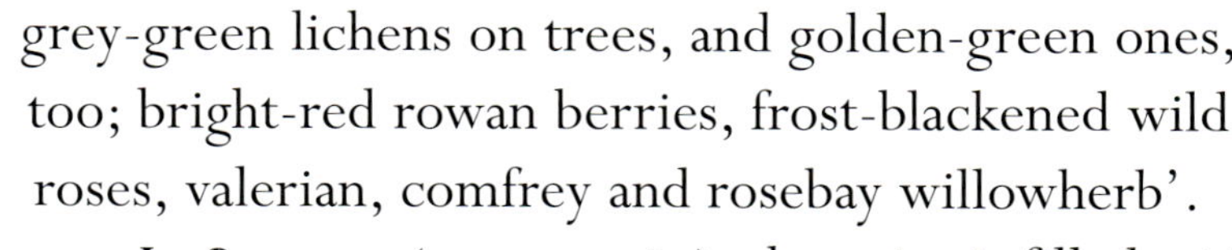

*Opposite: Lewin's 'Hedgerow' textile design, 2009, printed on to
heavyweight linen union.*

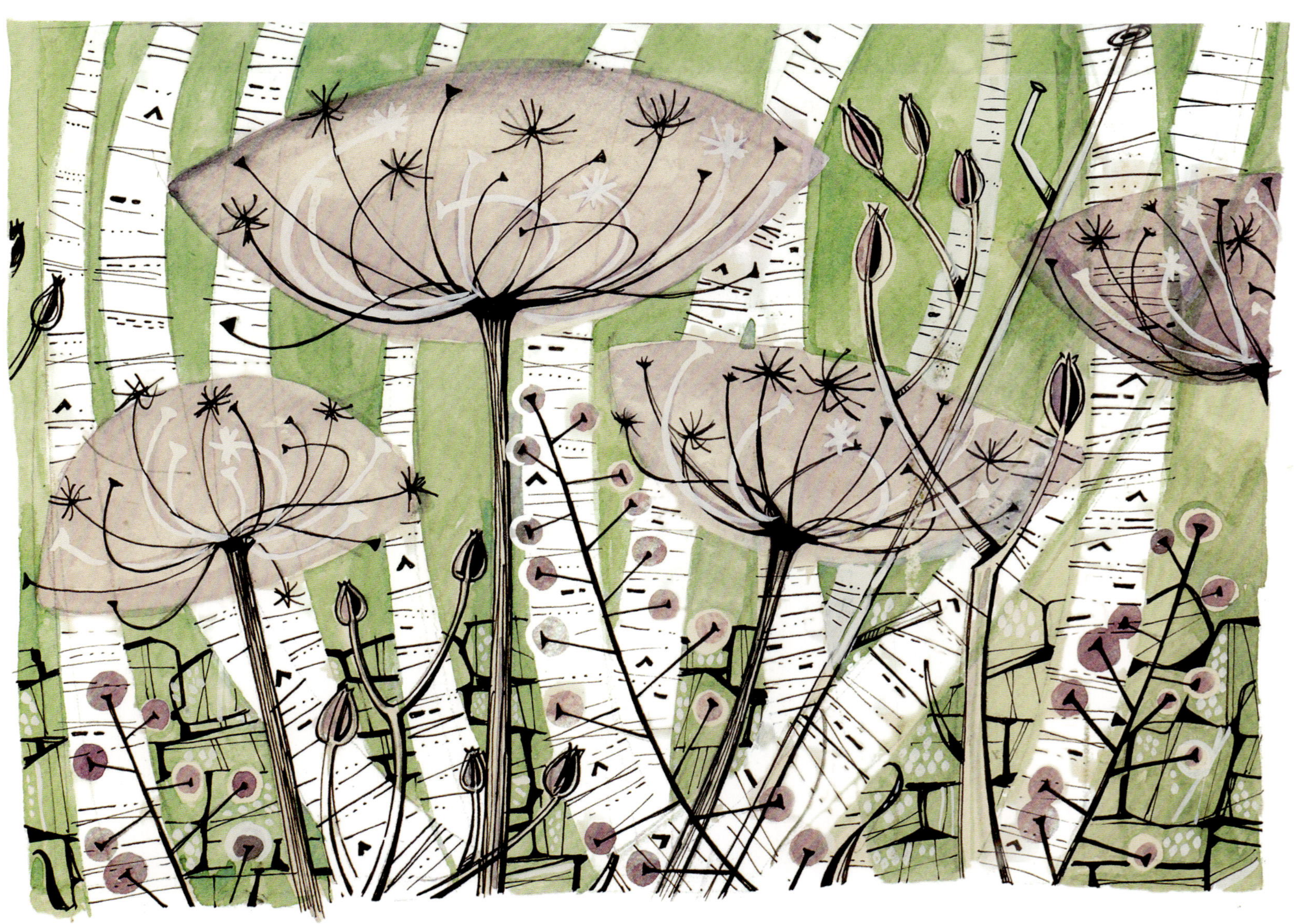

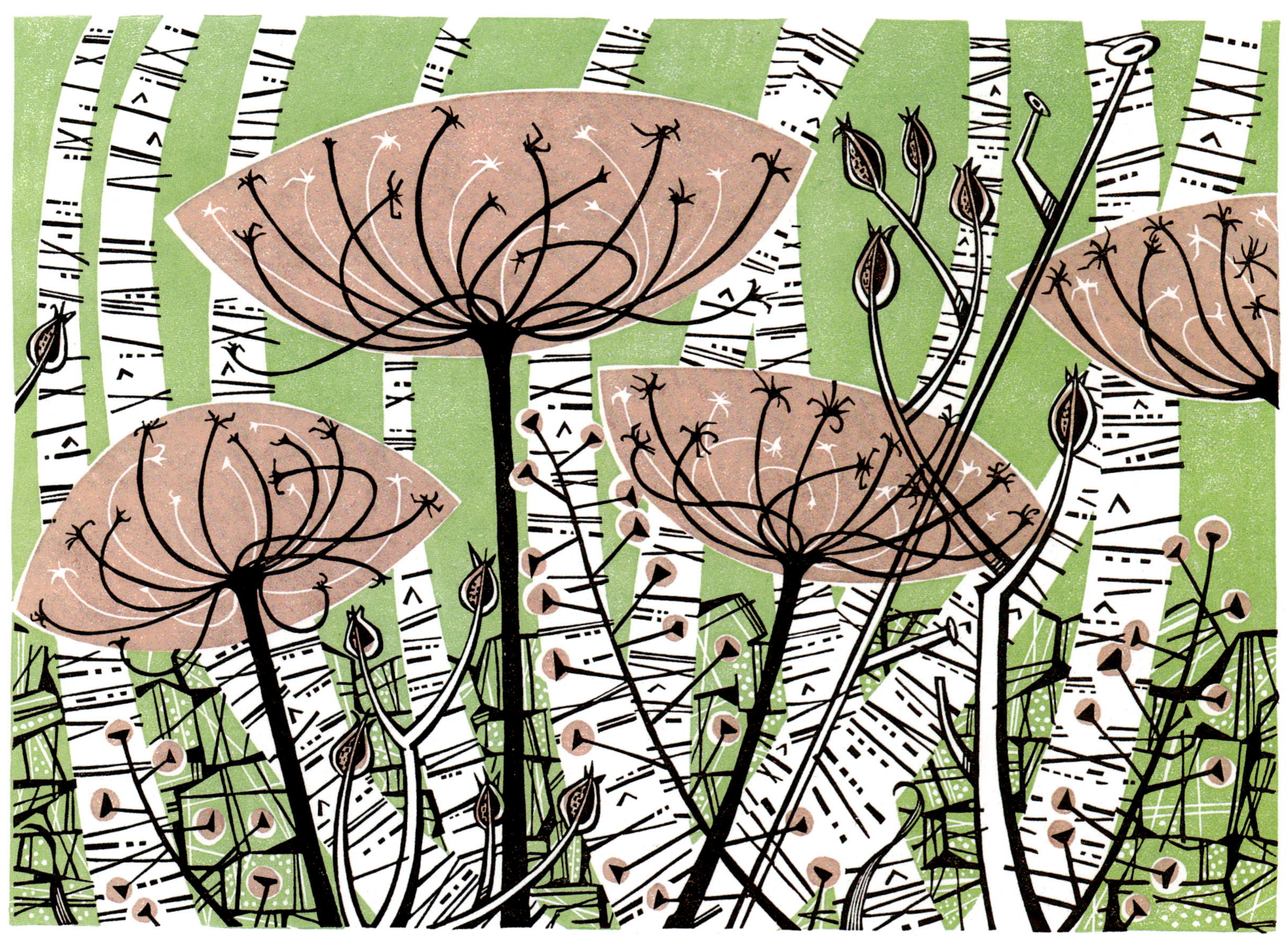

Ballindalloch

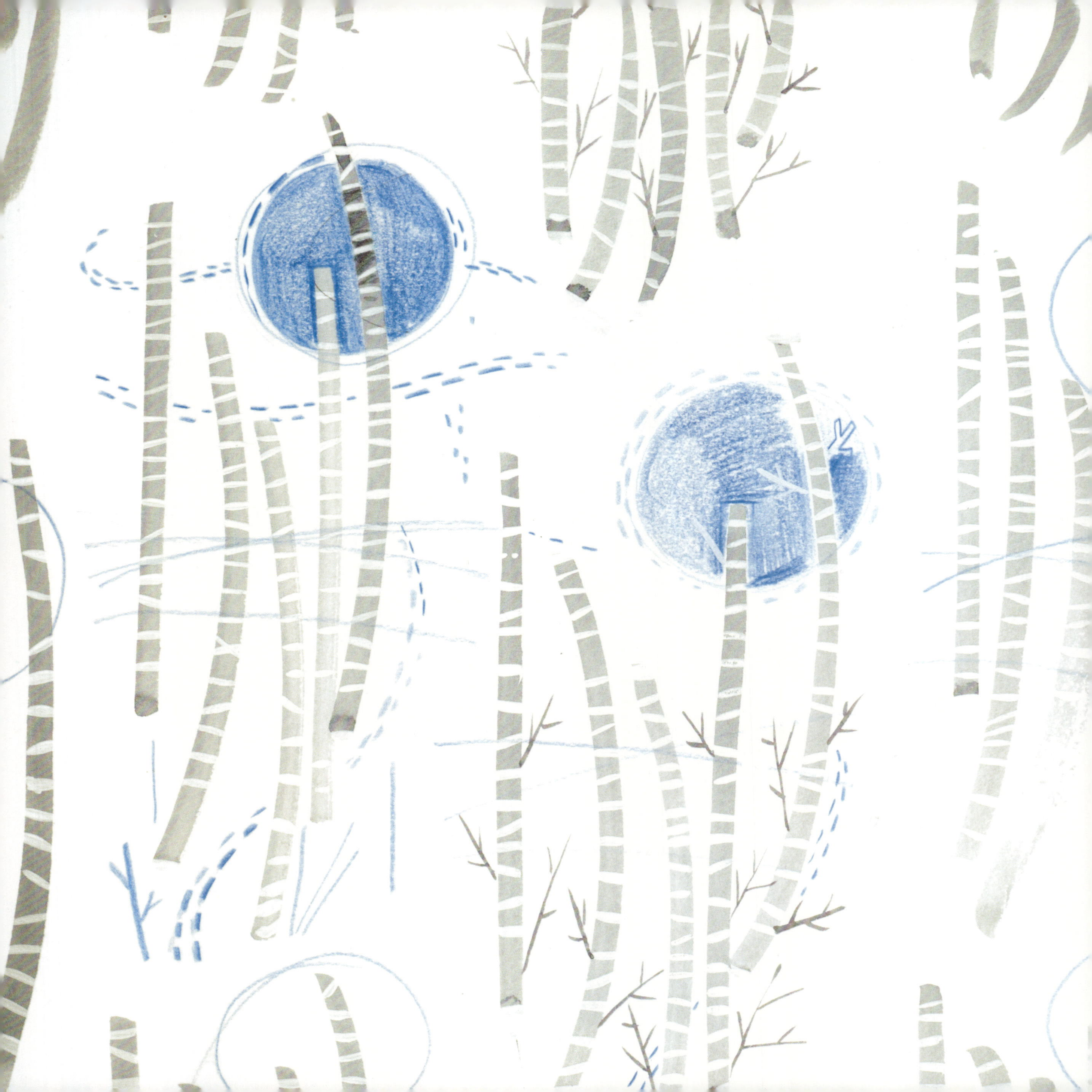

*‘My sketchbook pages may be
the starting point for a print
or a textile design.’*

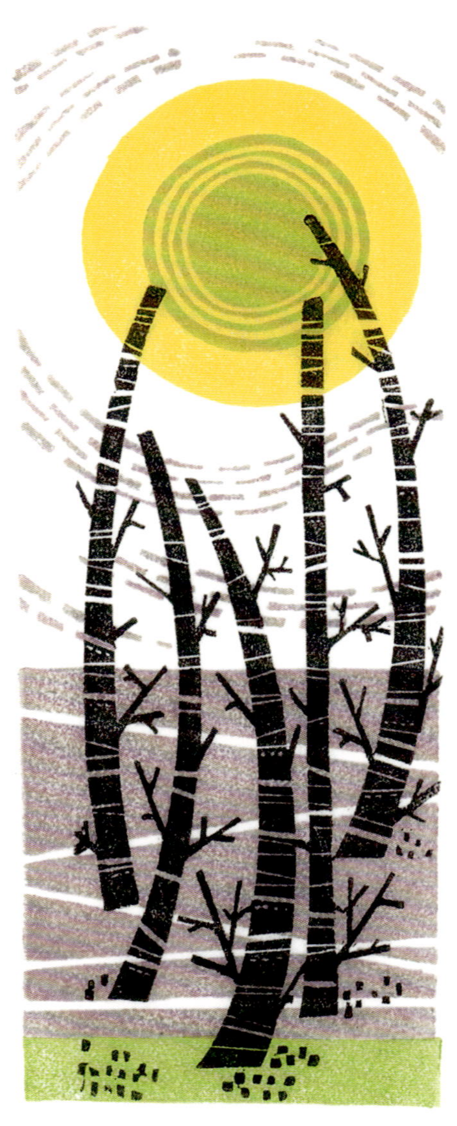

*‘striated trunks
silhouetted against
a brilliant sun’*

5 Trees

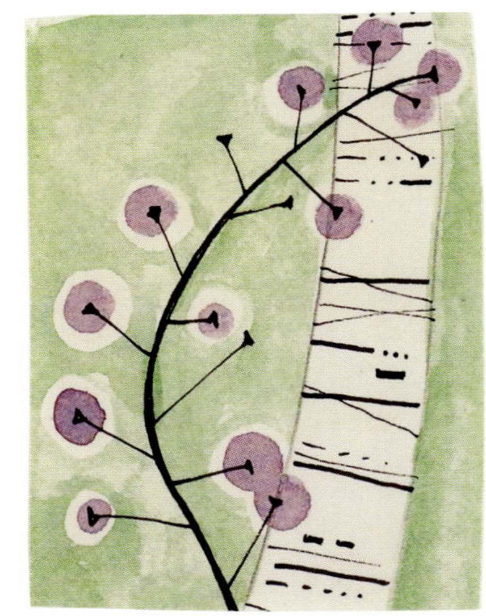

'When I'm out walking in woods, I'm struck by the black patterning on the gleaming white trunks of birch trees, and how this contrasts with fresh green foliage and bright berries.'

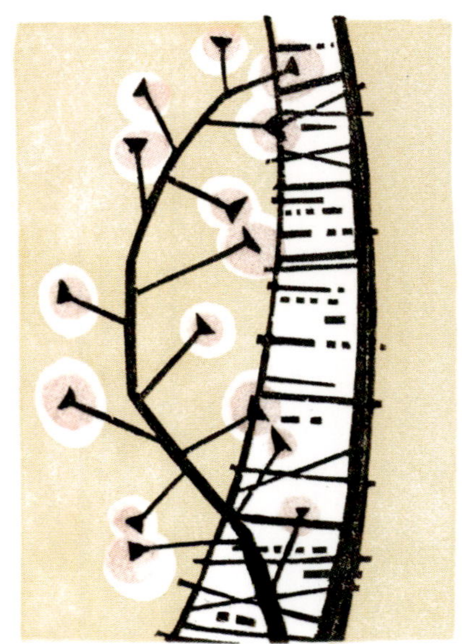

Birch

'*I've drawn a pencil grid over this
small sketch to help when making
a larger drawing for the screenprint*
Birches, Ballindalloch *(overleaf)*.'

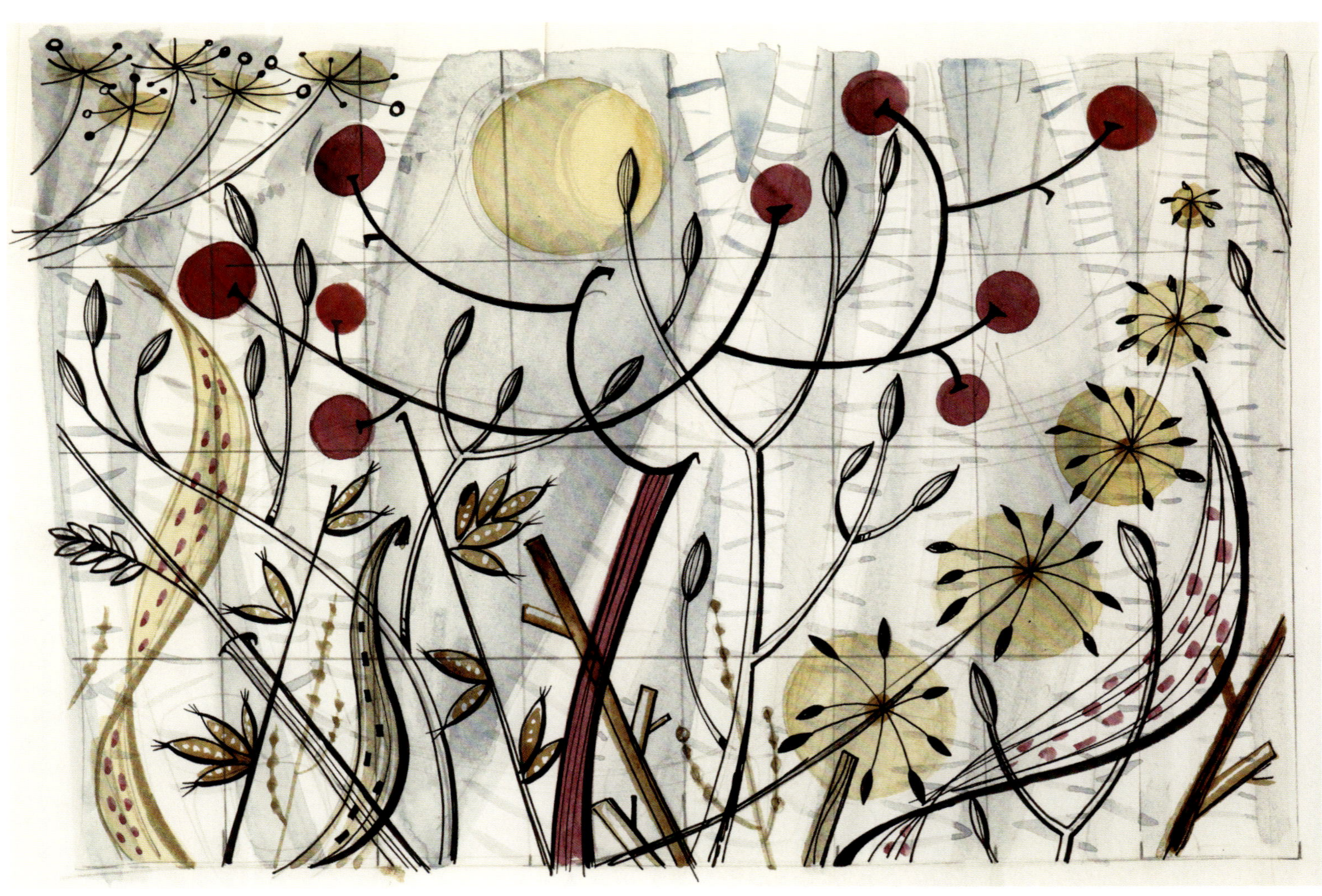

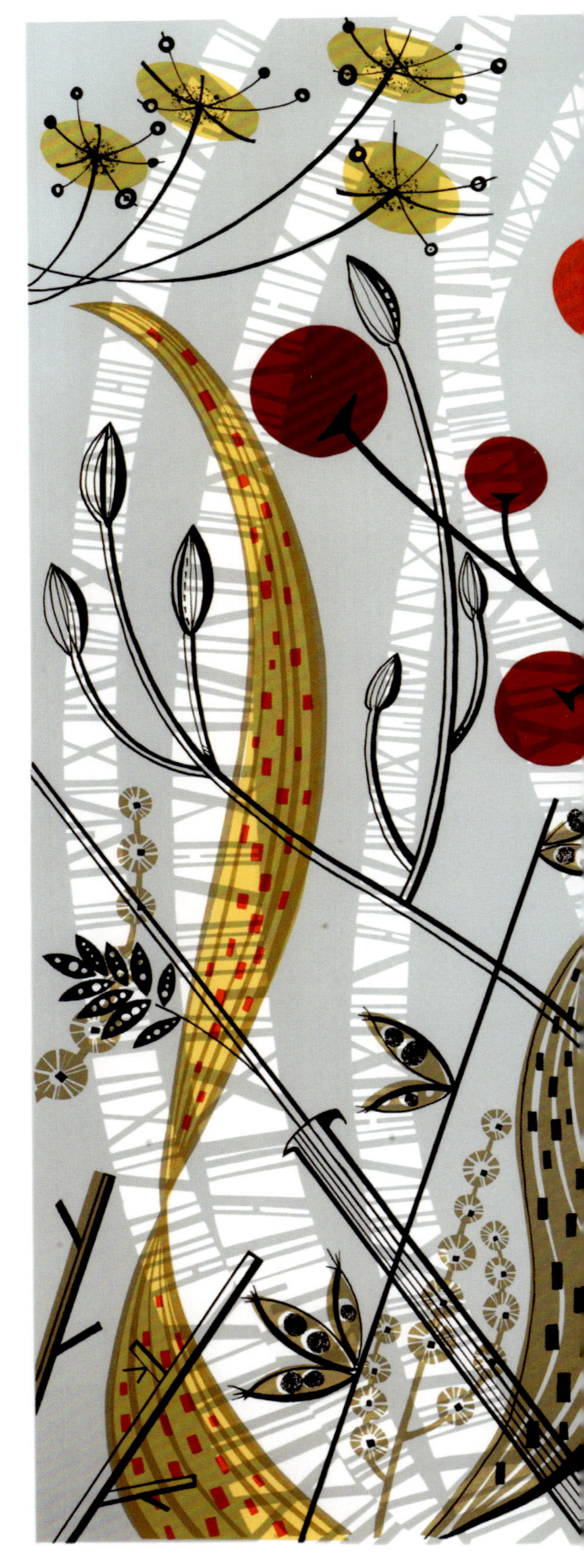

Birches, Ballindalloch

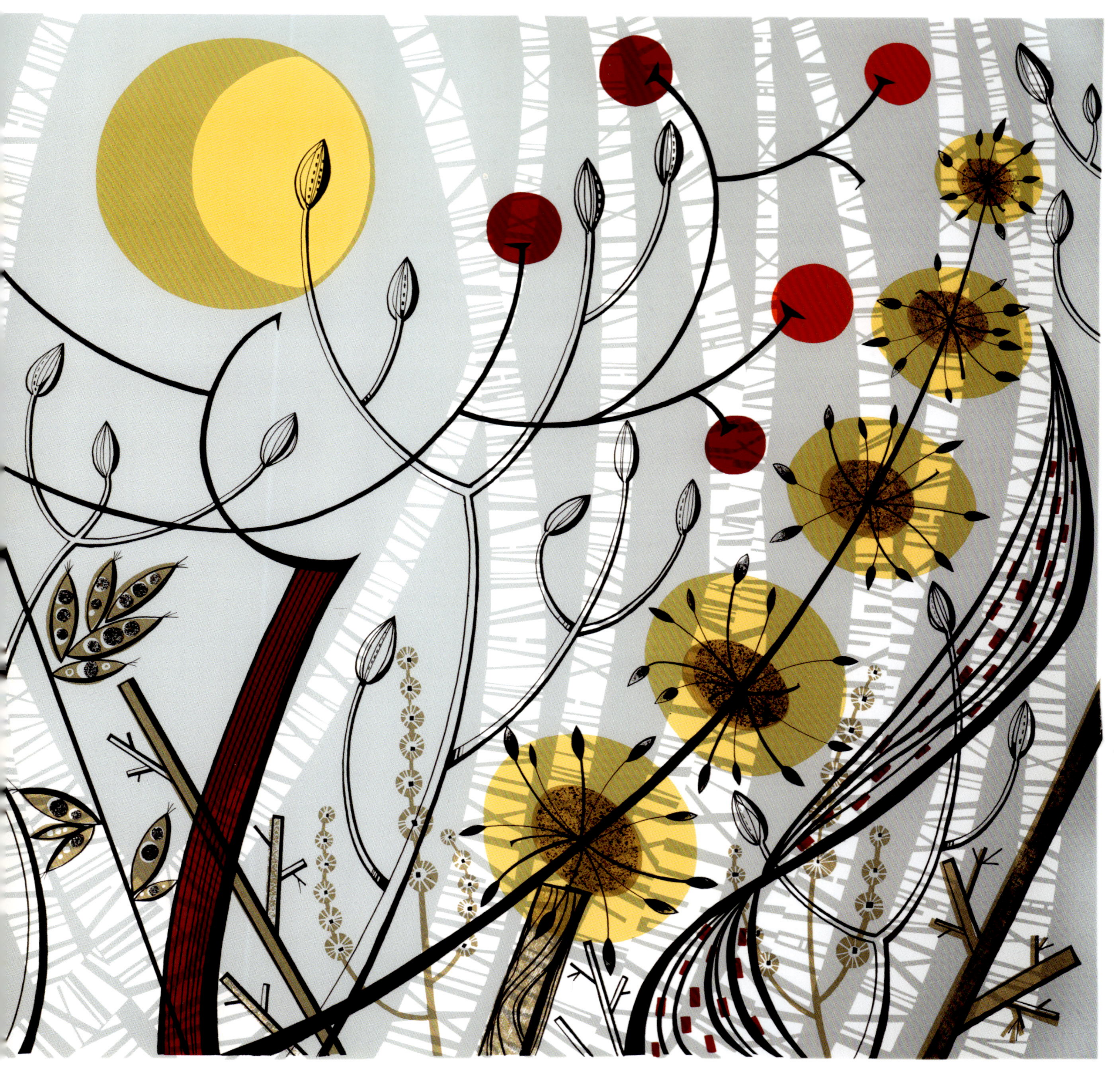

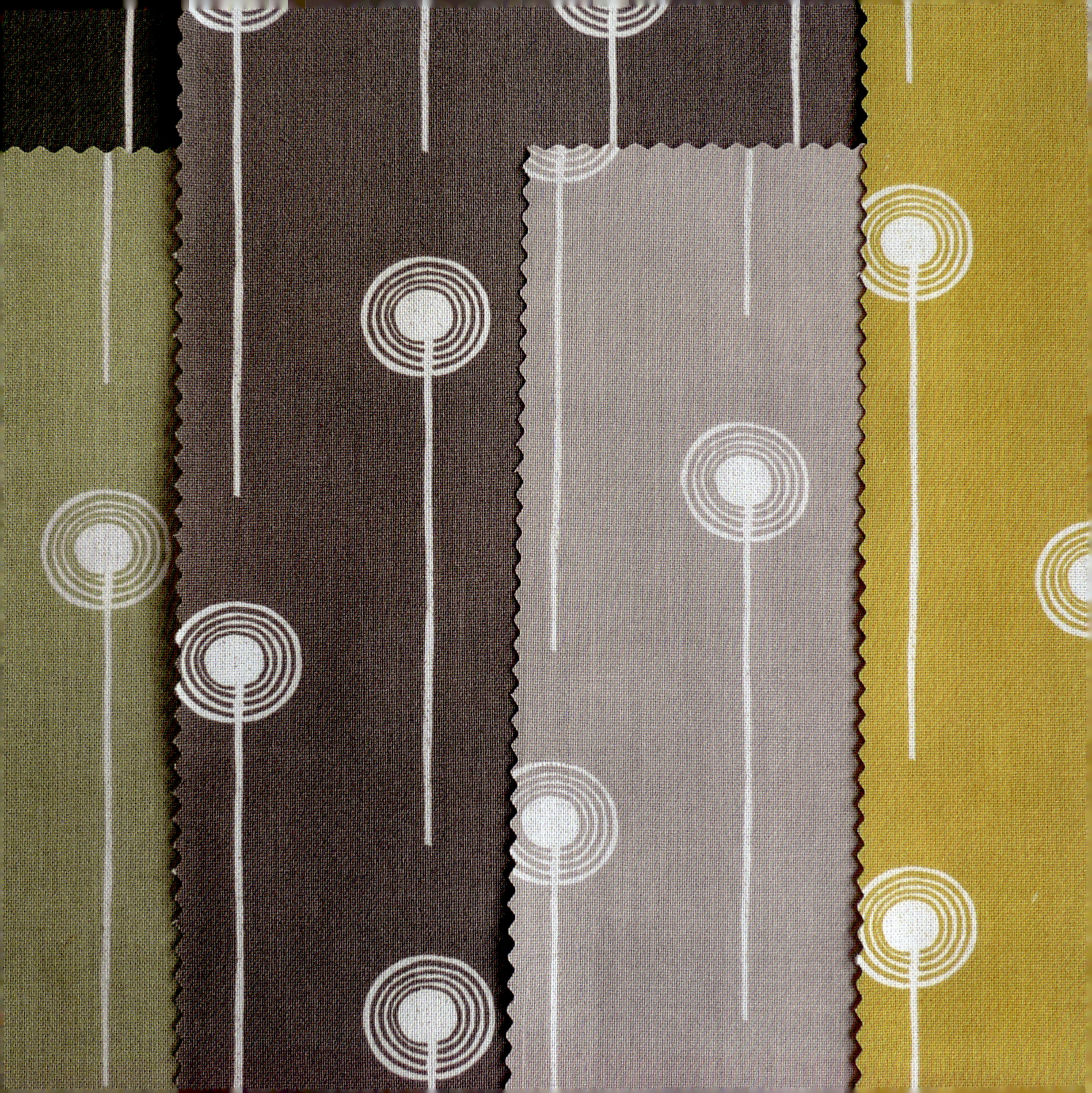

'Before colour samples of my
textiles are printed commercially
I'll try out possibilities by printing
the linocut on to Japanese paper.
Opposite are swatches of my
"Dandelion 2" design.'

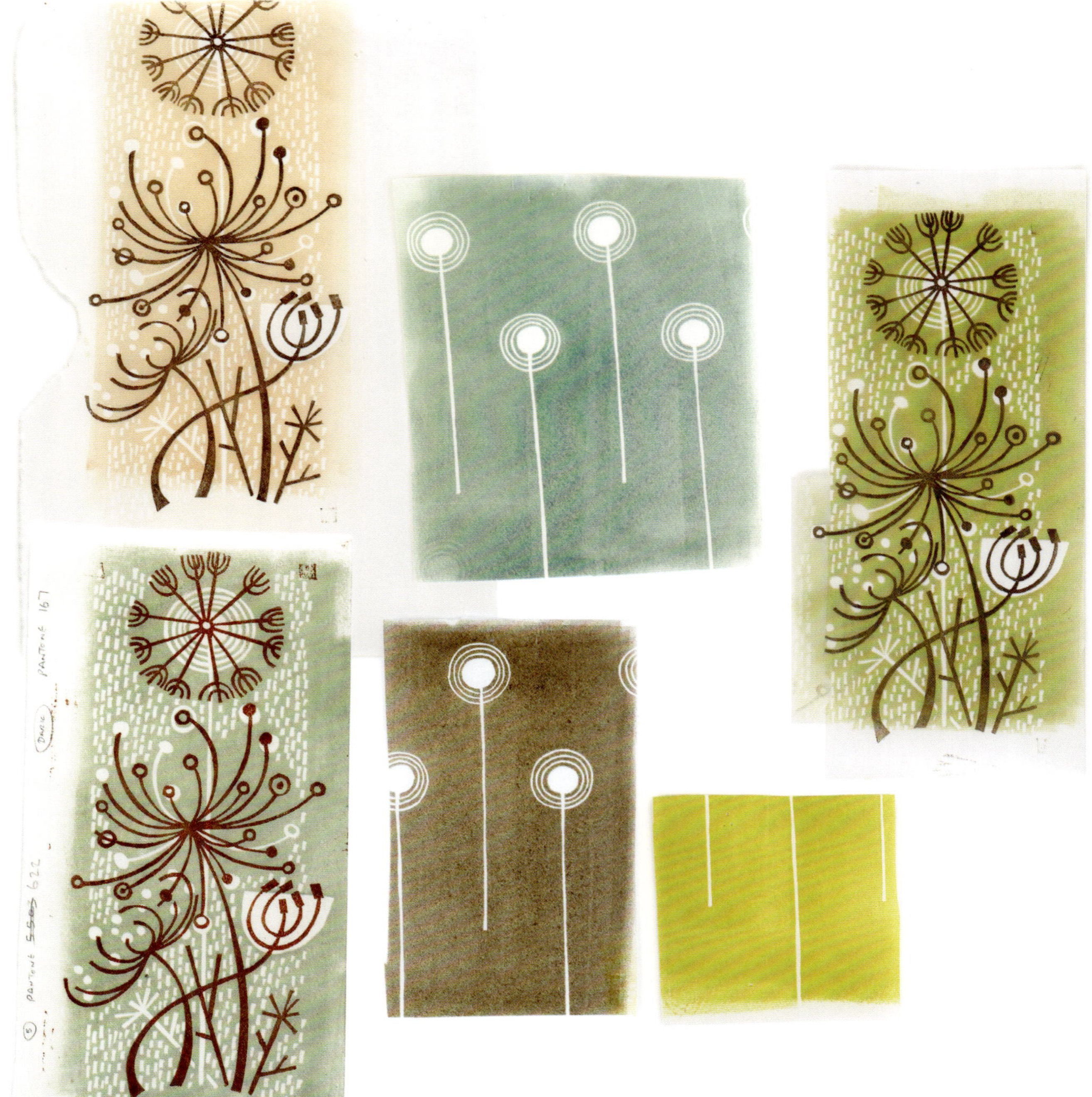

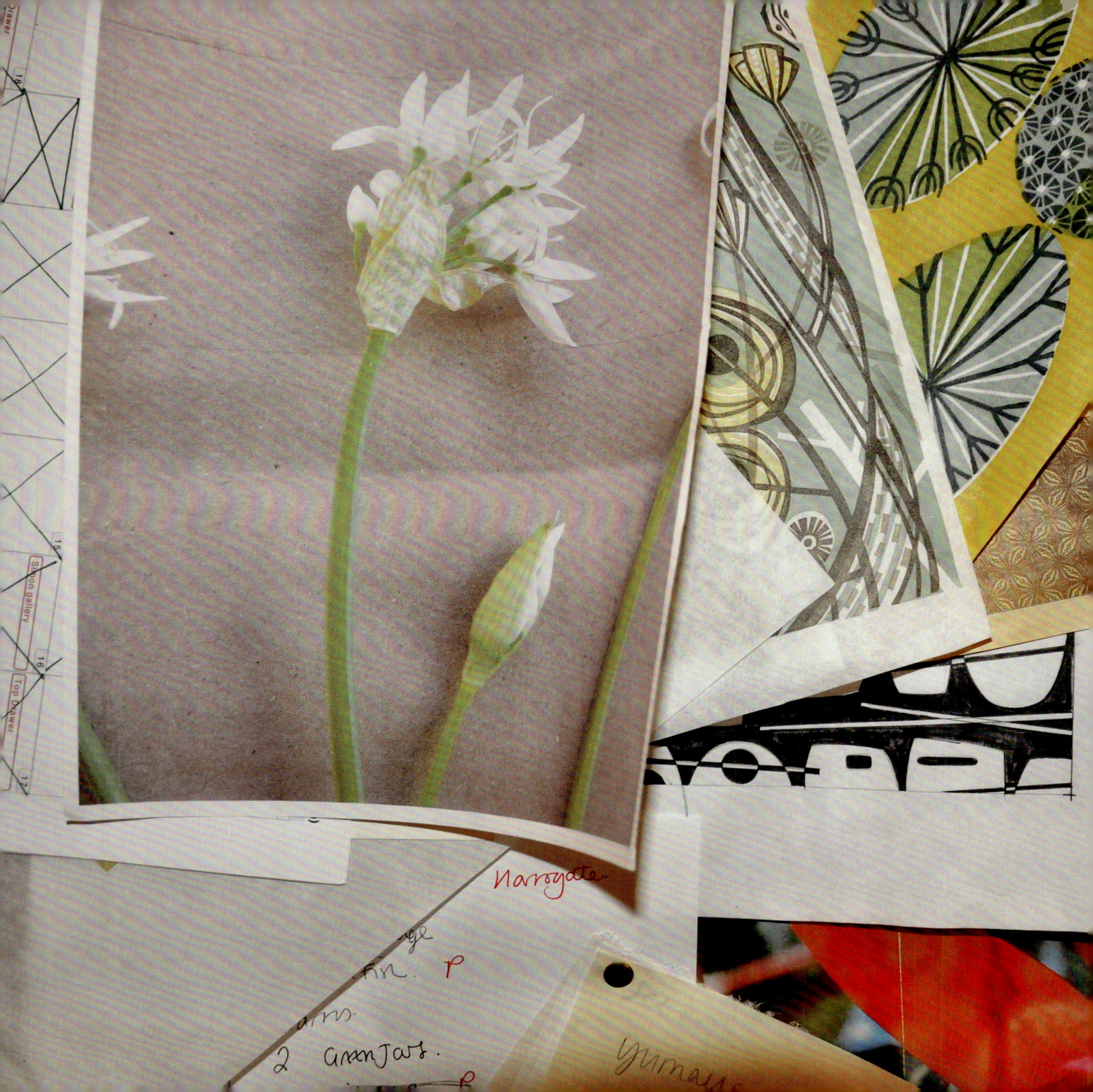

Shoon gallery
Top Drawer
Harrogate.
2 Granjars.
yumays

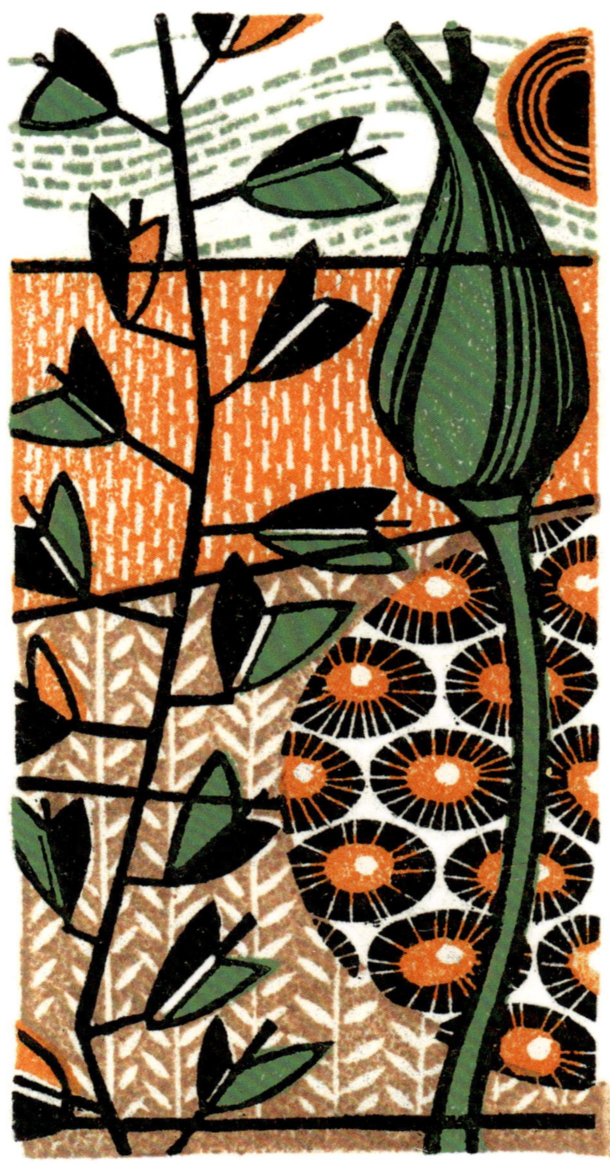

Dandelion II

*'I created this repeat pattern
with the block for Ivy (opposite),
by turning the woodblock through
90 degrees at a time.'*

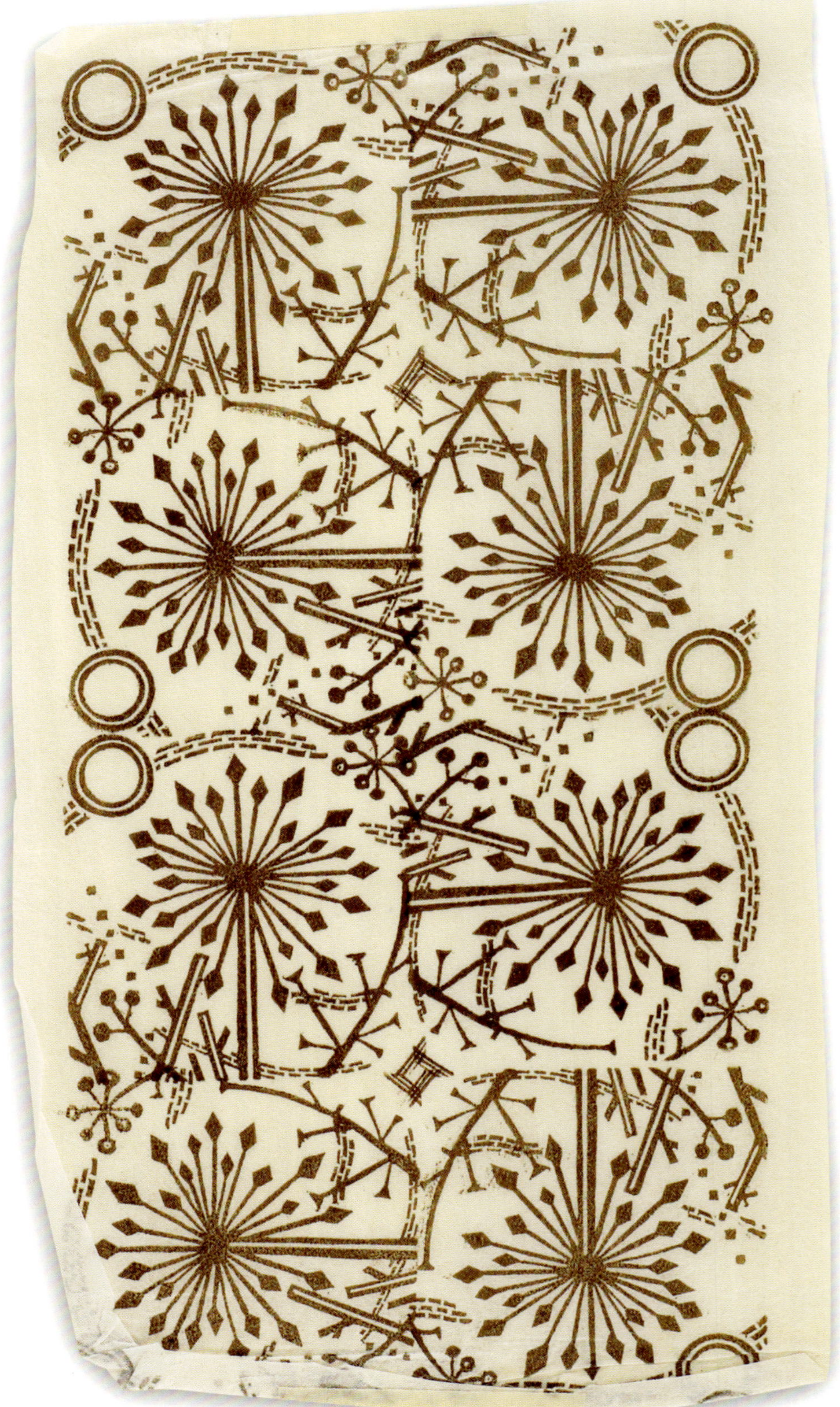

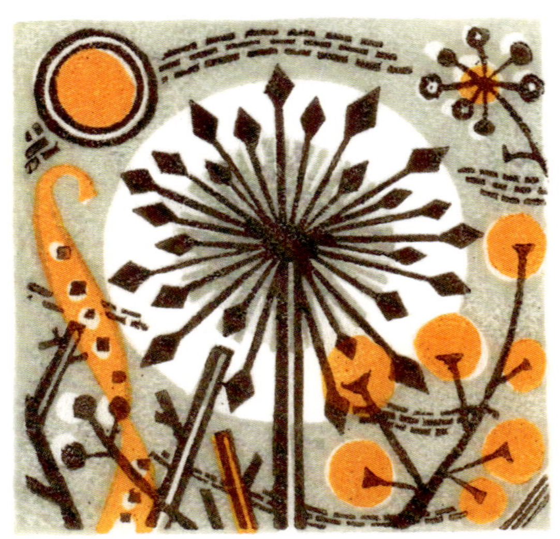

Ivy

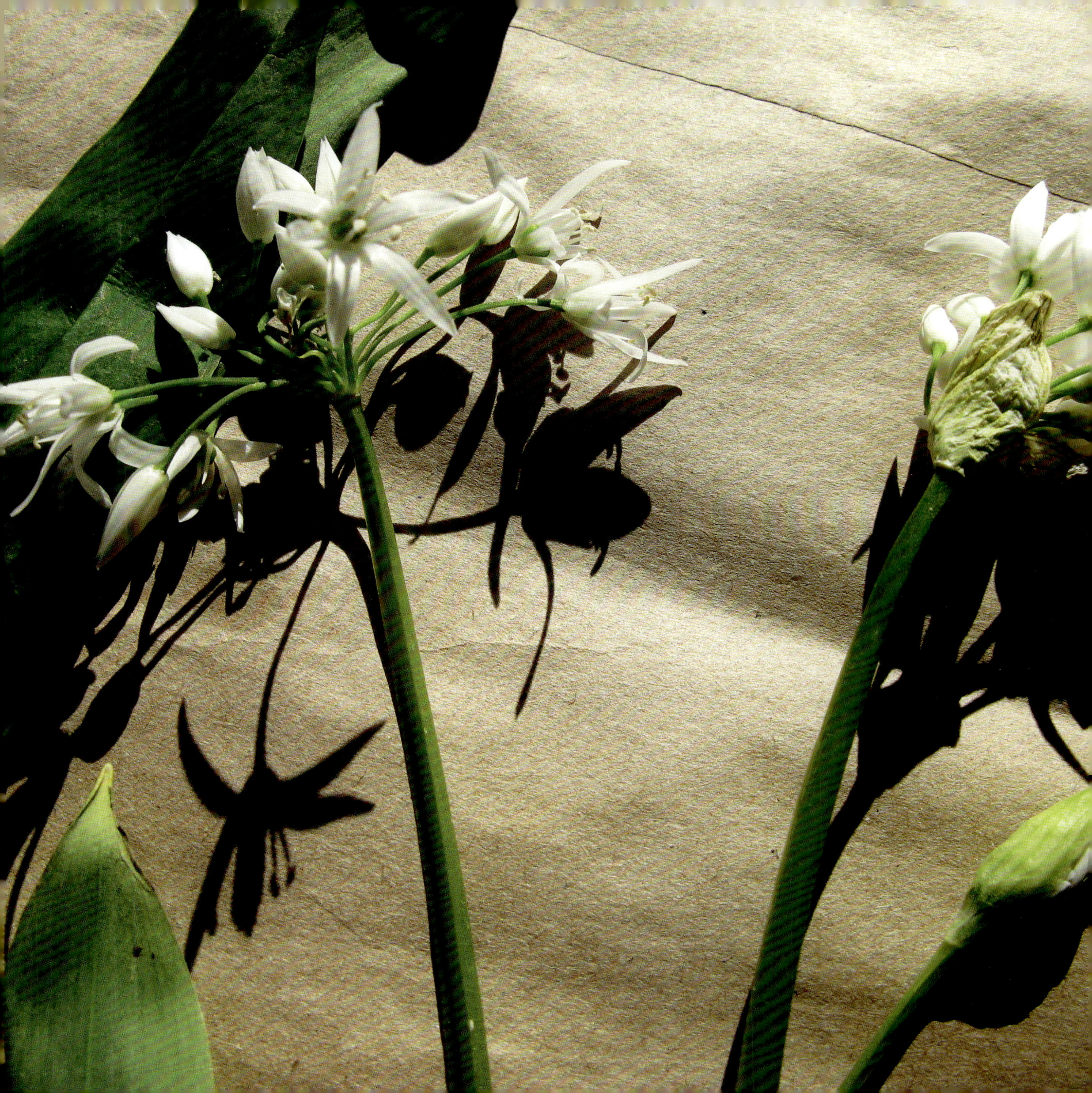

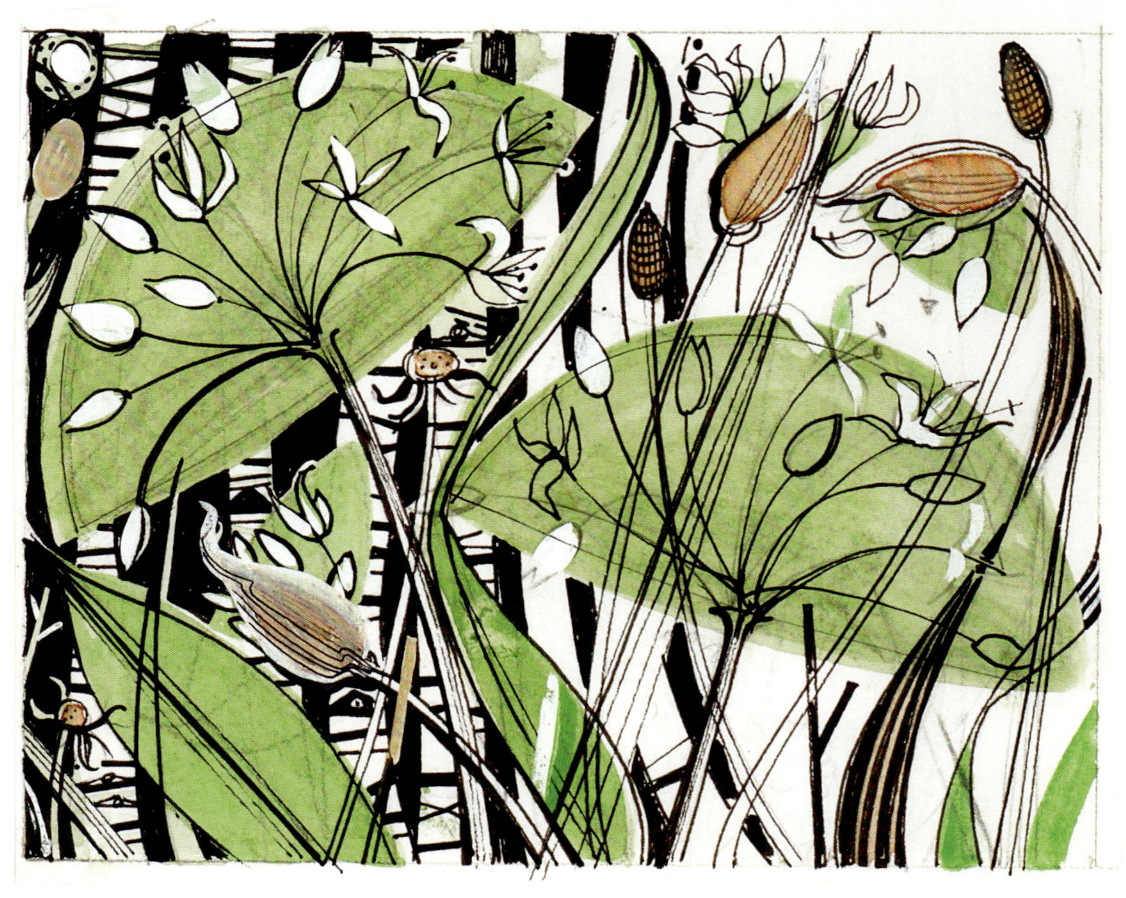

'a green and busy
underworld'

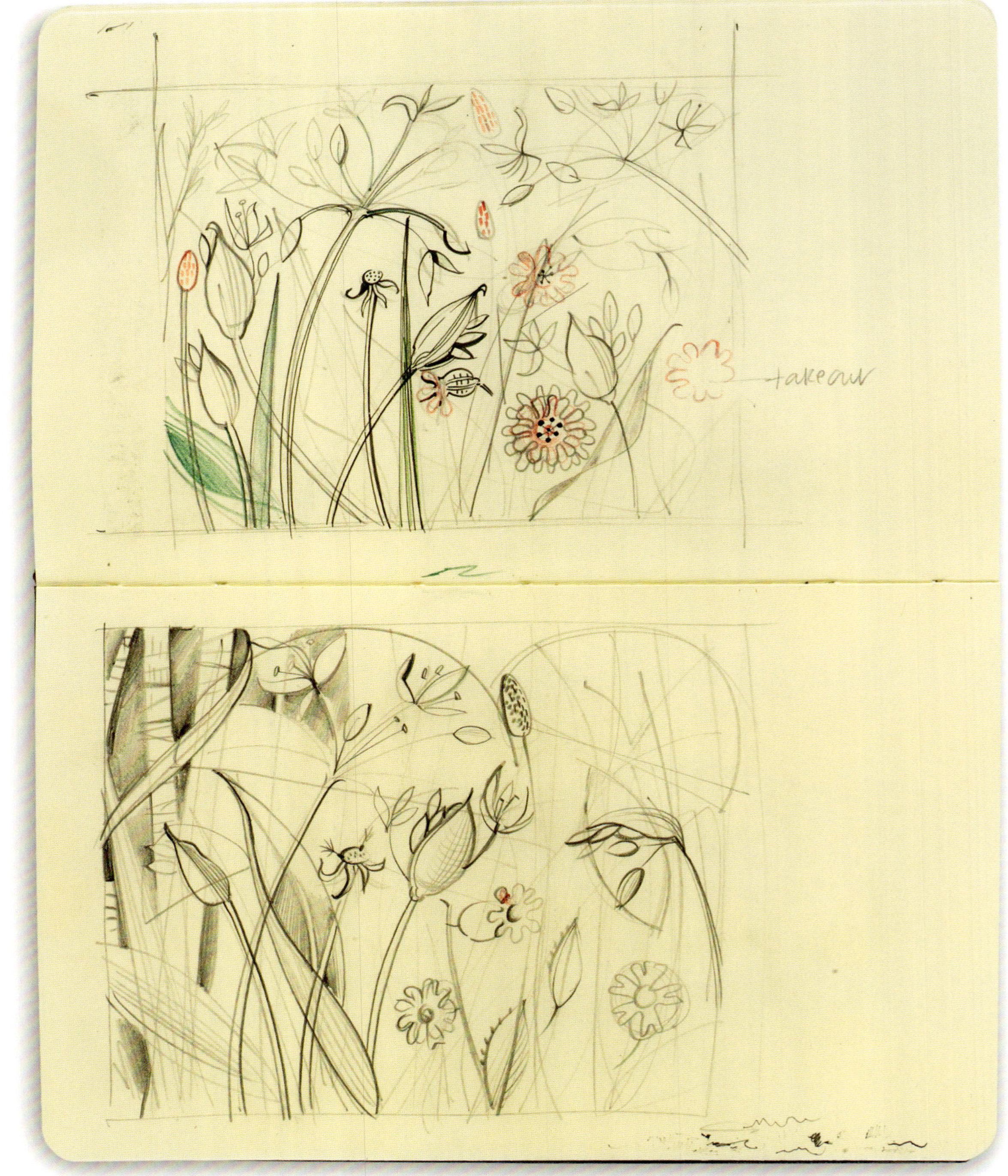

'Ramsons (wild garlic) often grows in the shade beneath trees in deciduous woodland. I collect the leaves to use them in cooking.'

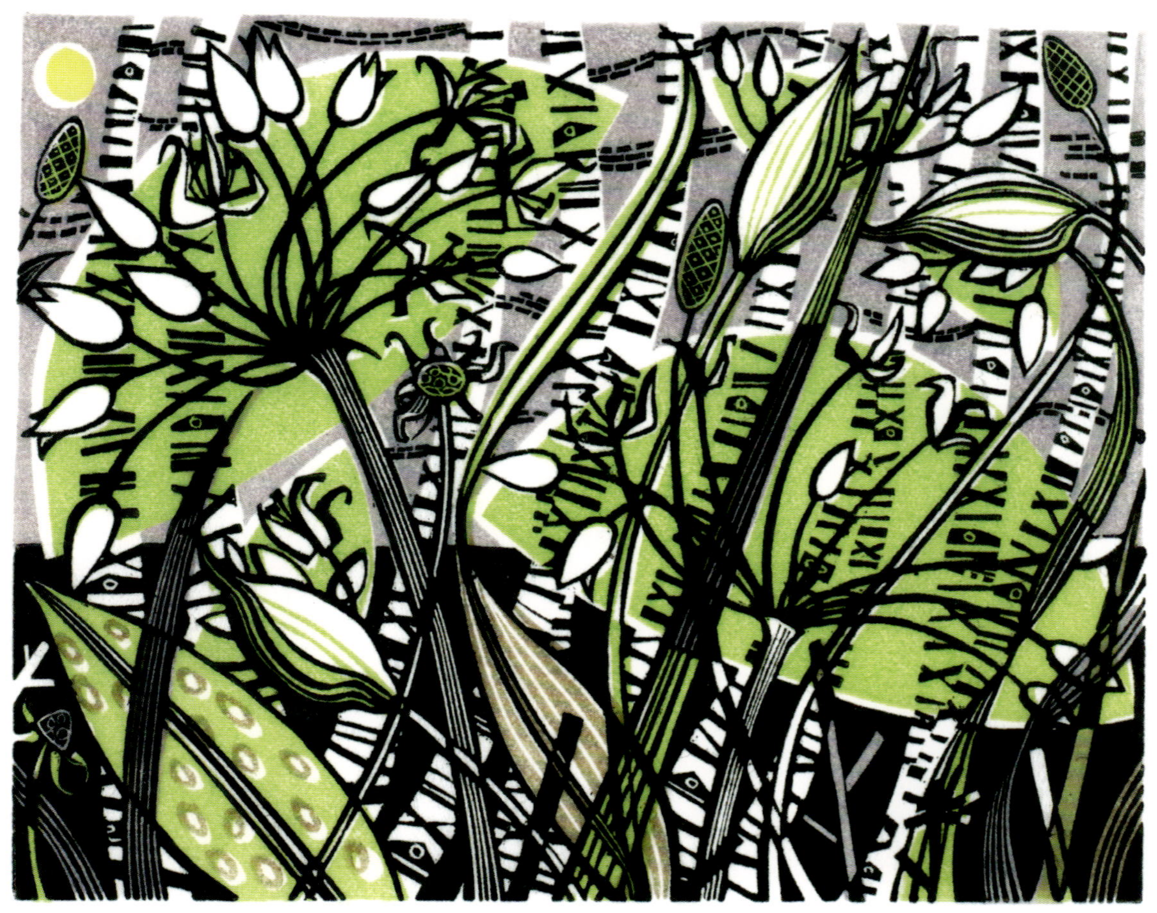

Ramsons

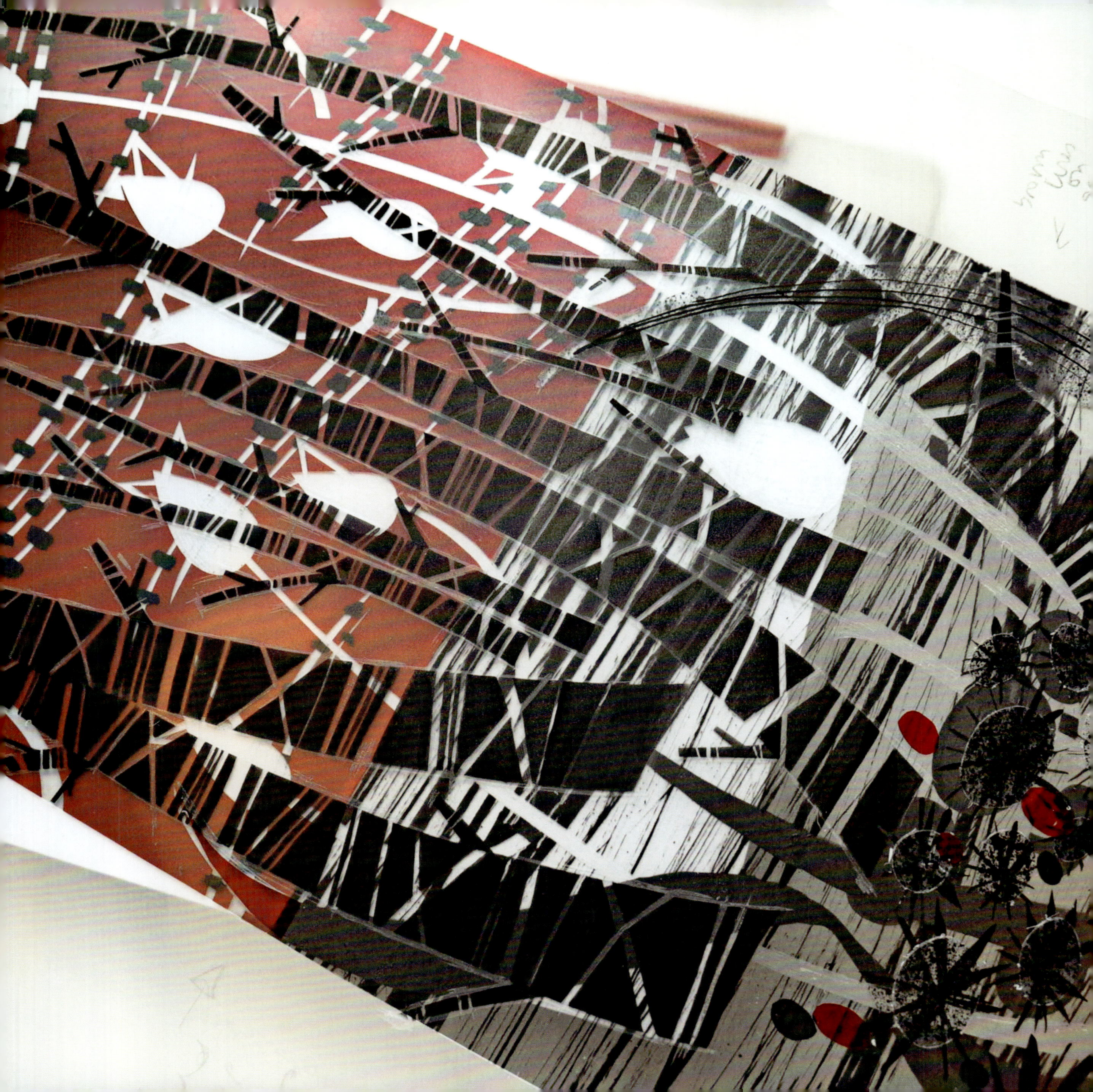

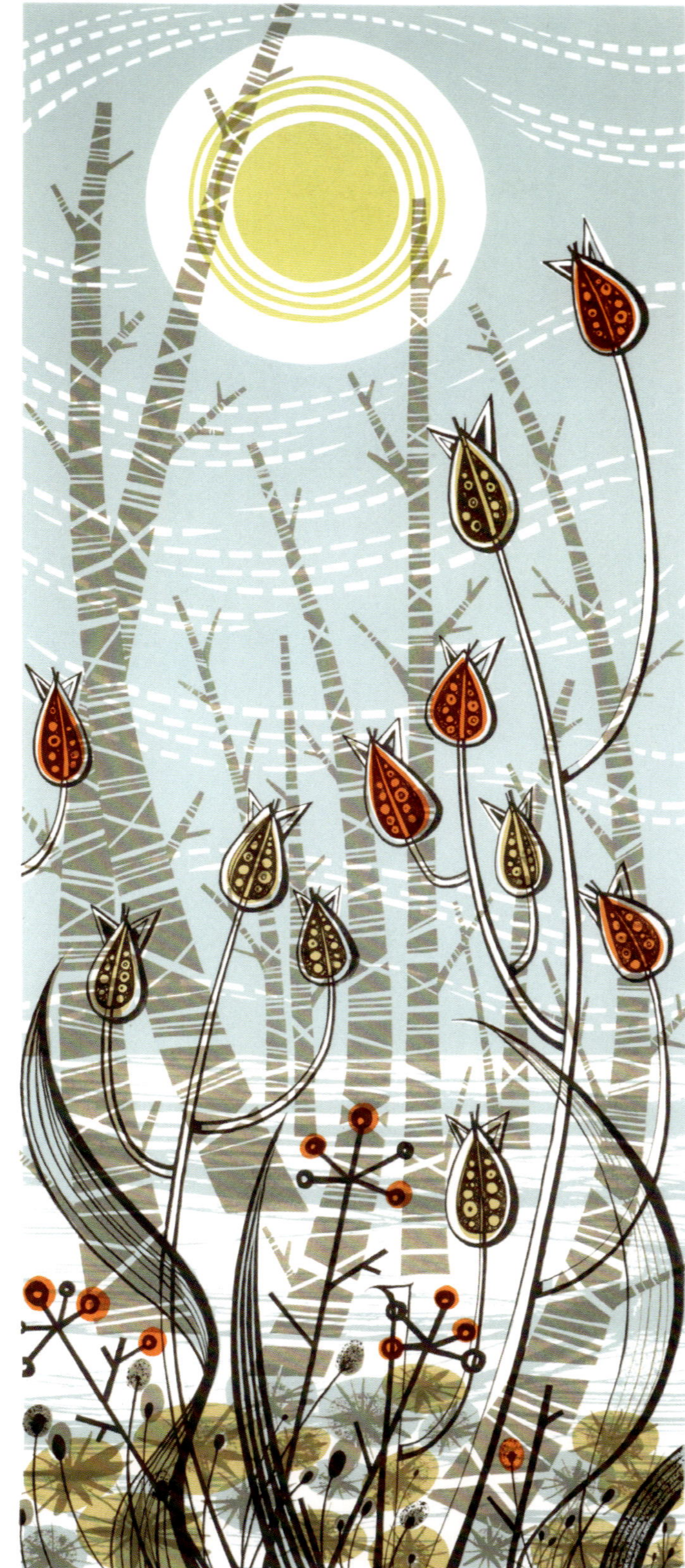

Winter Birches

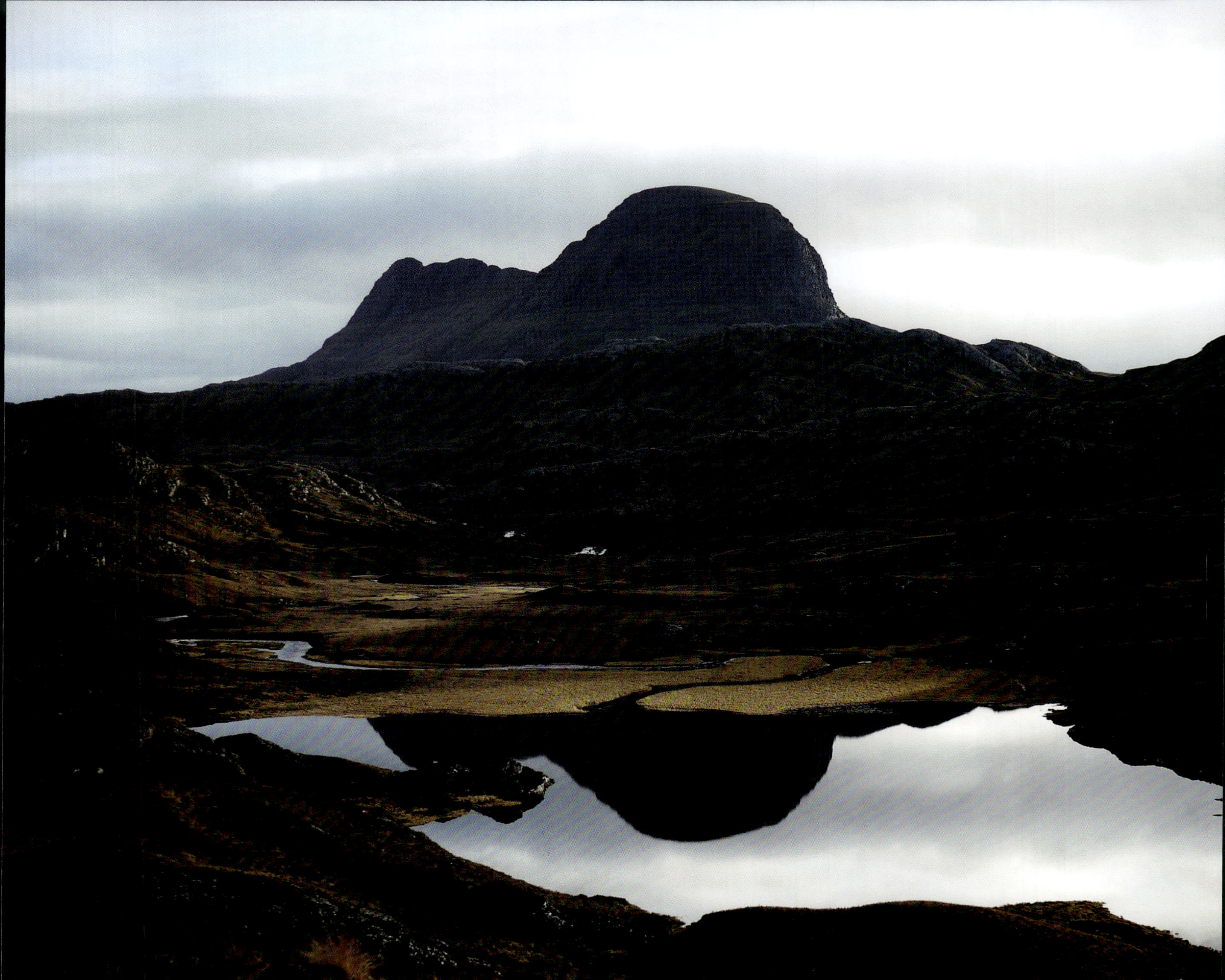

River and Loch

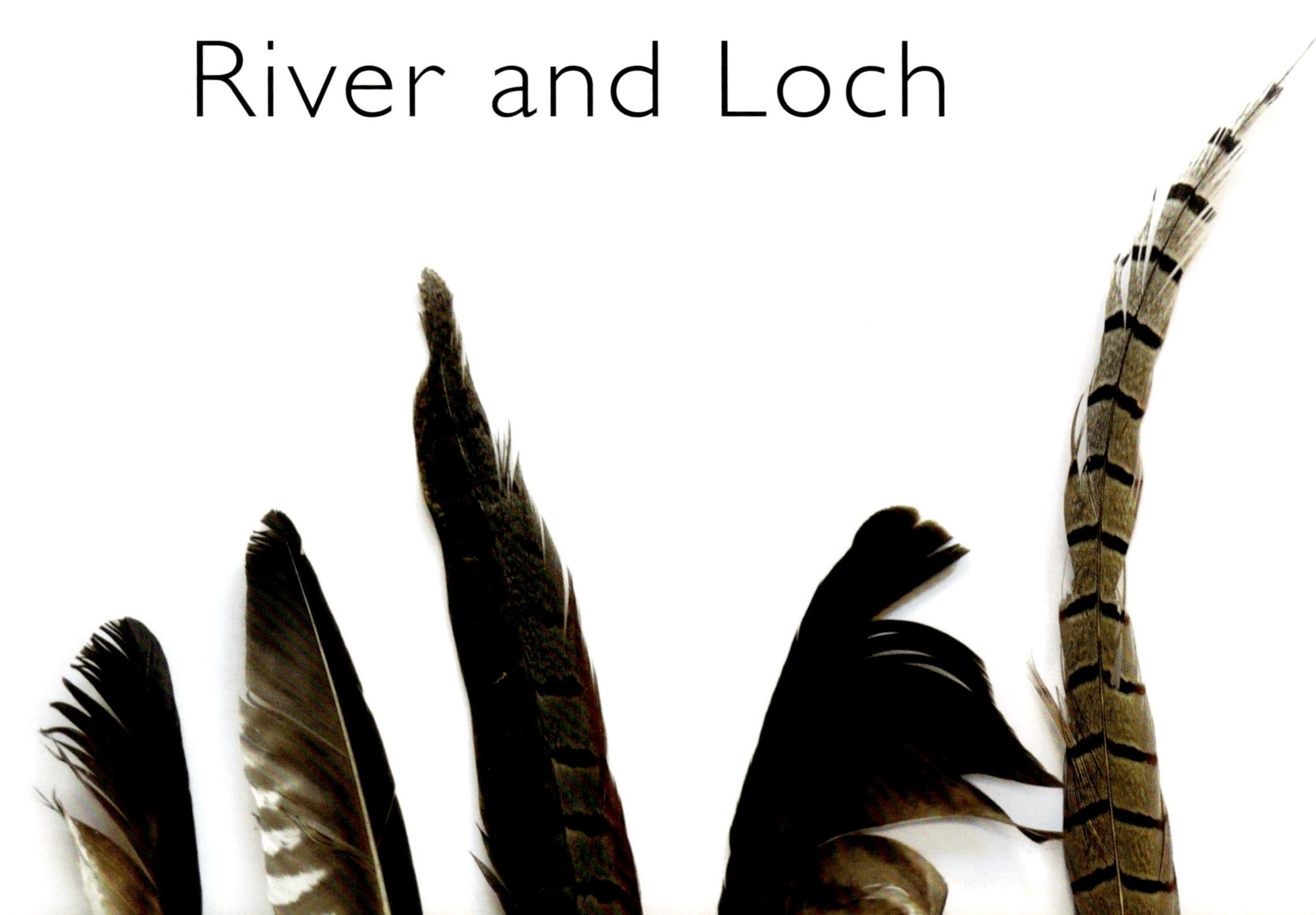

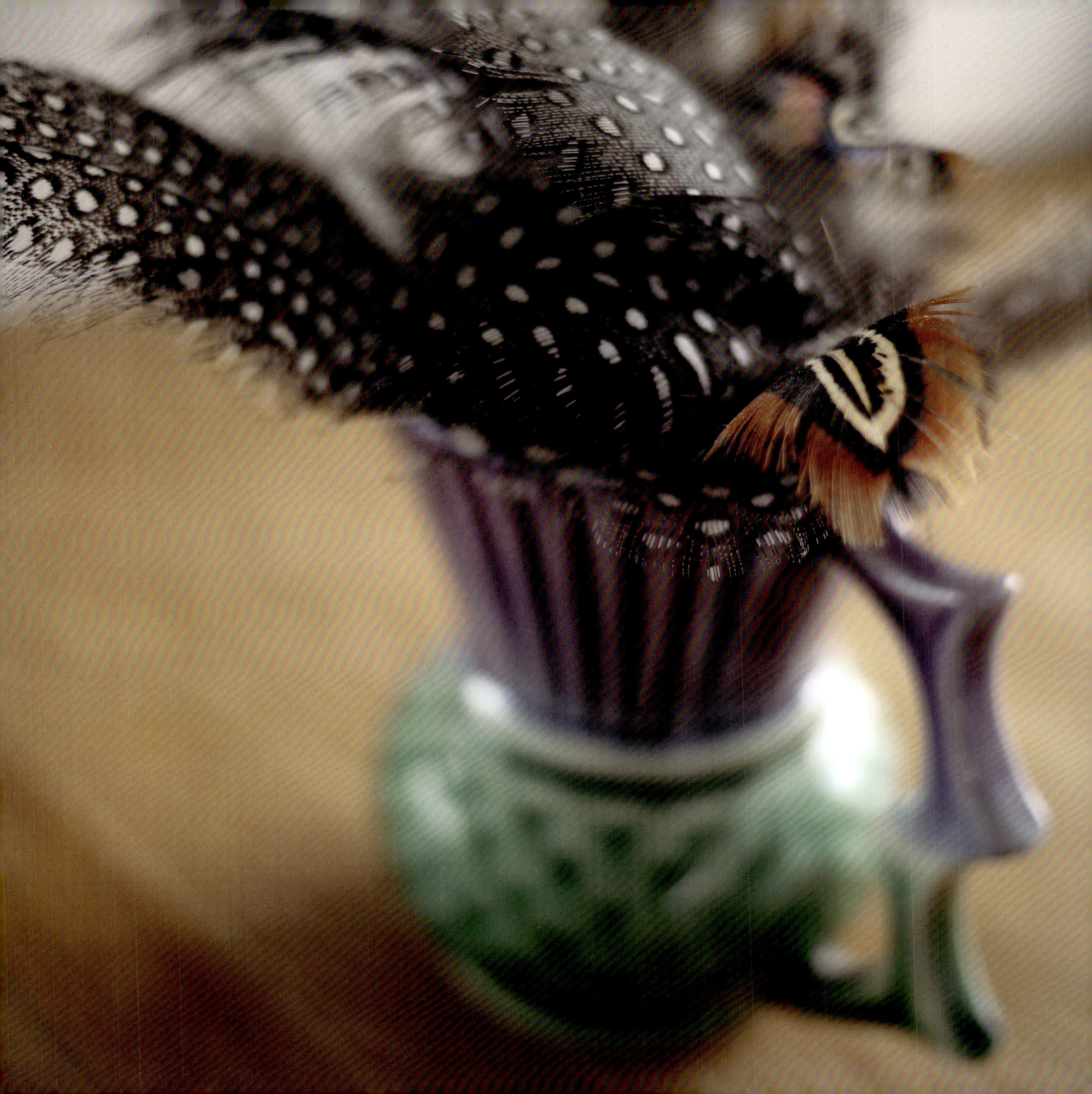

A ngie and Simon Lewin spend part of the year in Scotland, attracted, among other things, by the walking and the fishing on the River Spey. Speyside and the coast of the Moray Firth provide a different habitat from East Anglia for the prints. Angie says: 'We accidentally "found" a derelict croft on the side of a hill looking out on to Ben Rinnes, and later bought it. We're close to the Spey itself and have mountains all around us, and I take great inspiration from all this. The views are truly wonderful and ever-changing. The house itself is a traditional stone crofter's cottage, which had been uninhabited since probably the 1960s. On our first visit I tore some layers of wallpaper from the bedroom wall, which I've since used in collages – I needed a memento.'

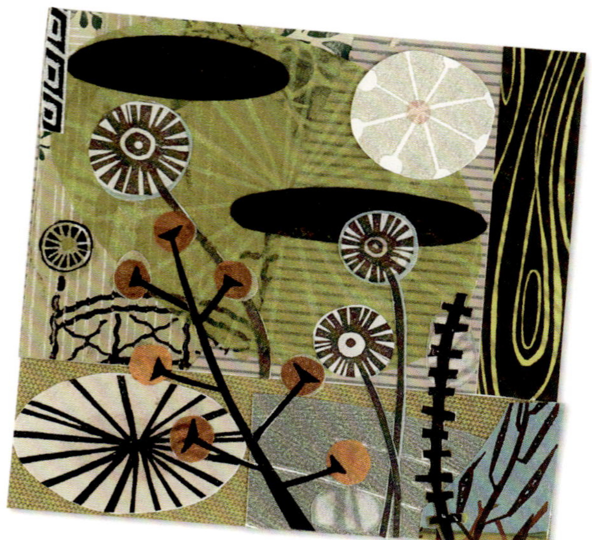

Lewin's prints often feature lochs and mountains. In *Loch with Dandelions* (see page 96), in which the dandelion clocks tower in the foreground, the background hill is rendered by a single dark shape, the water by a pale, elongated semi-circle. In the linocut *Moonlit Loch* (see page 101), the water is as green as the sky above, and the ebony-black hills are streaked with white moonlight.

The screenprint *By Green Bank* (see pages 92–93) shows the Spey flowing behind local plants, such as scabious, yellow rattle and plantain, its sense of movement created, Lewin explains, 'by painting Indian ink with broad brushstrokes on to a clear film, exposing this on to the silkscreen and then printing in soft green over a heather-purple background'. The lithograph *Autumn Spey* (see page 91) is inspired by the surroundings of the old Knockando wool mill, which is powered by a tributary of the Spey.

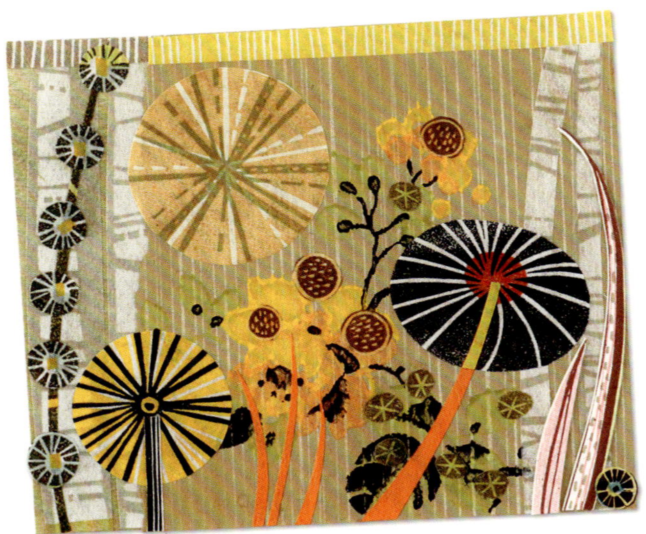

Opposite: Guineafowl and pheasant feathers in a 'thistle' pot at Lewin's Scottish studio.

The collages Derelict Croft III *(above) and* Derelict Croft IV *(left) incorporate salvaged wallpaper.*

'When sitting on a riverbank, I am at
the same level as the plants and can
focus on intricate details and patterns.'

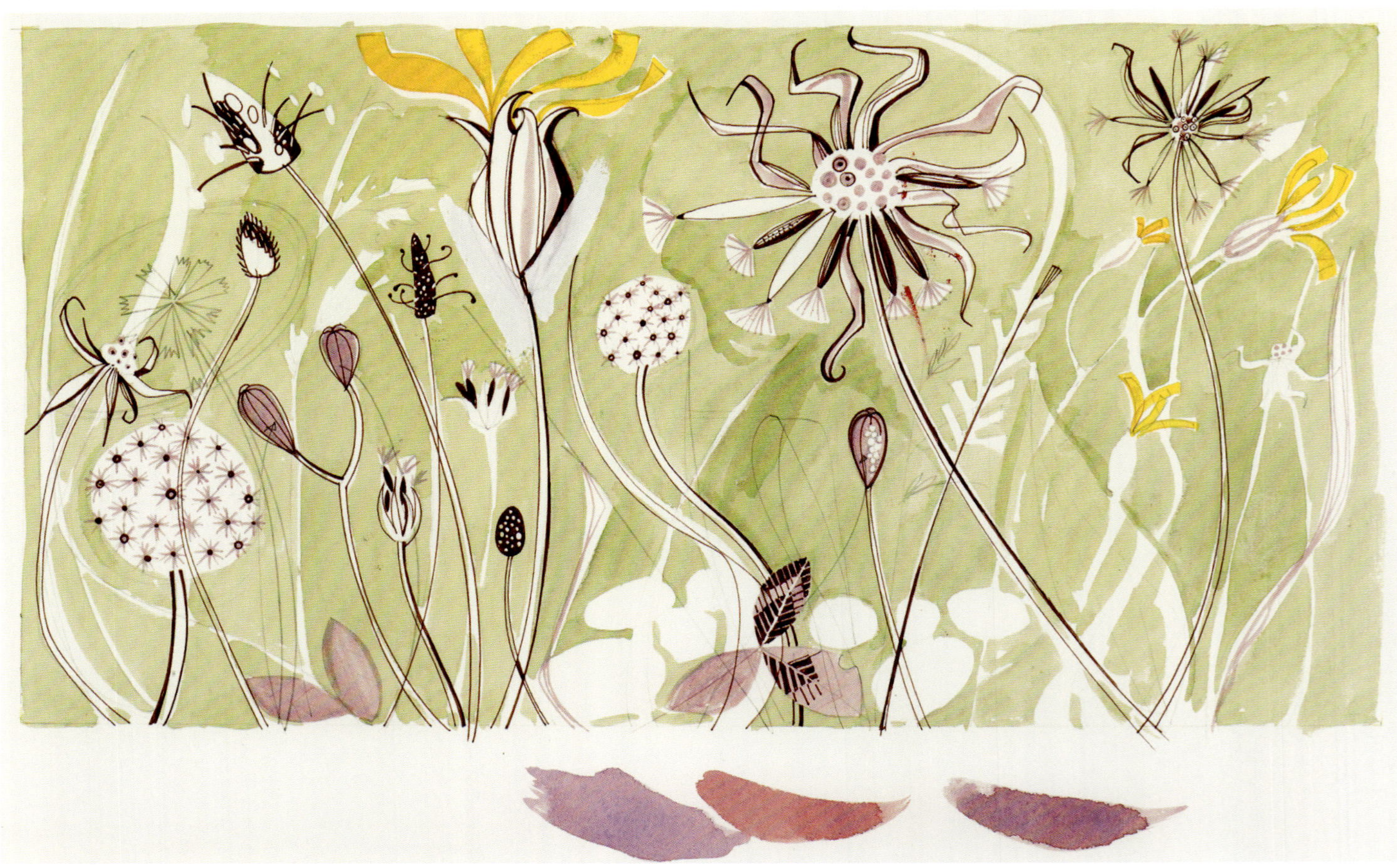

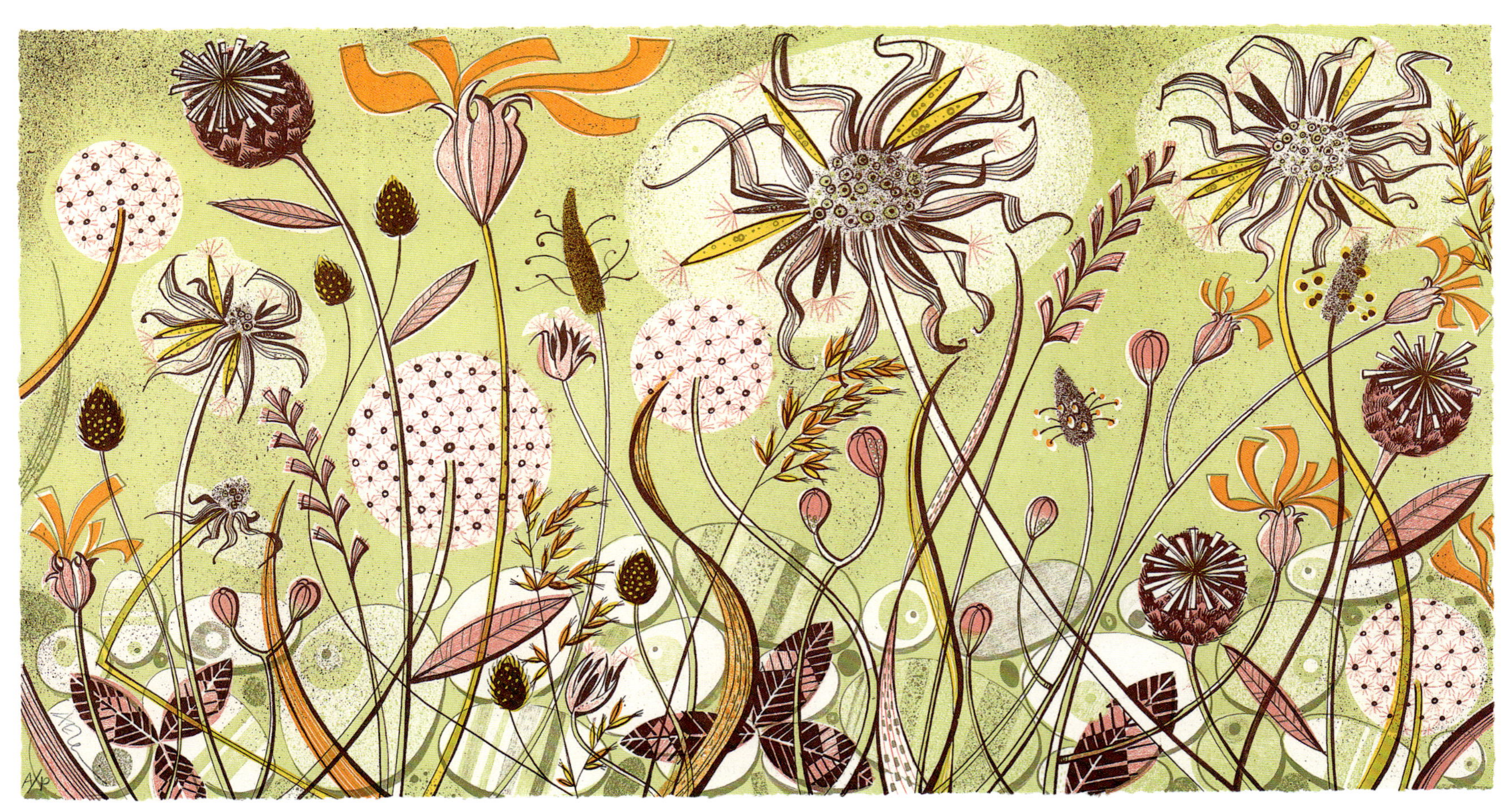

Autumn Spey

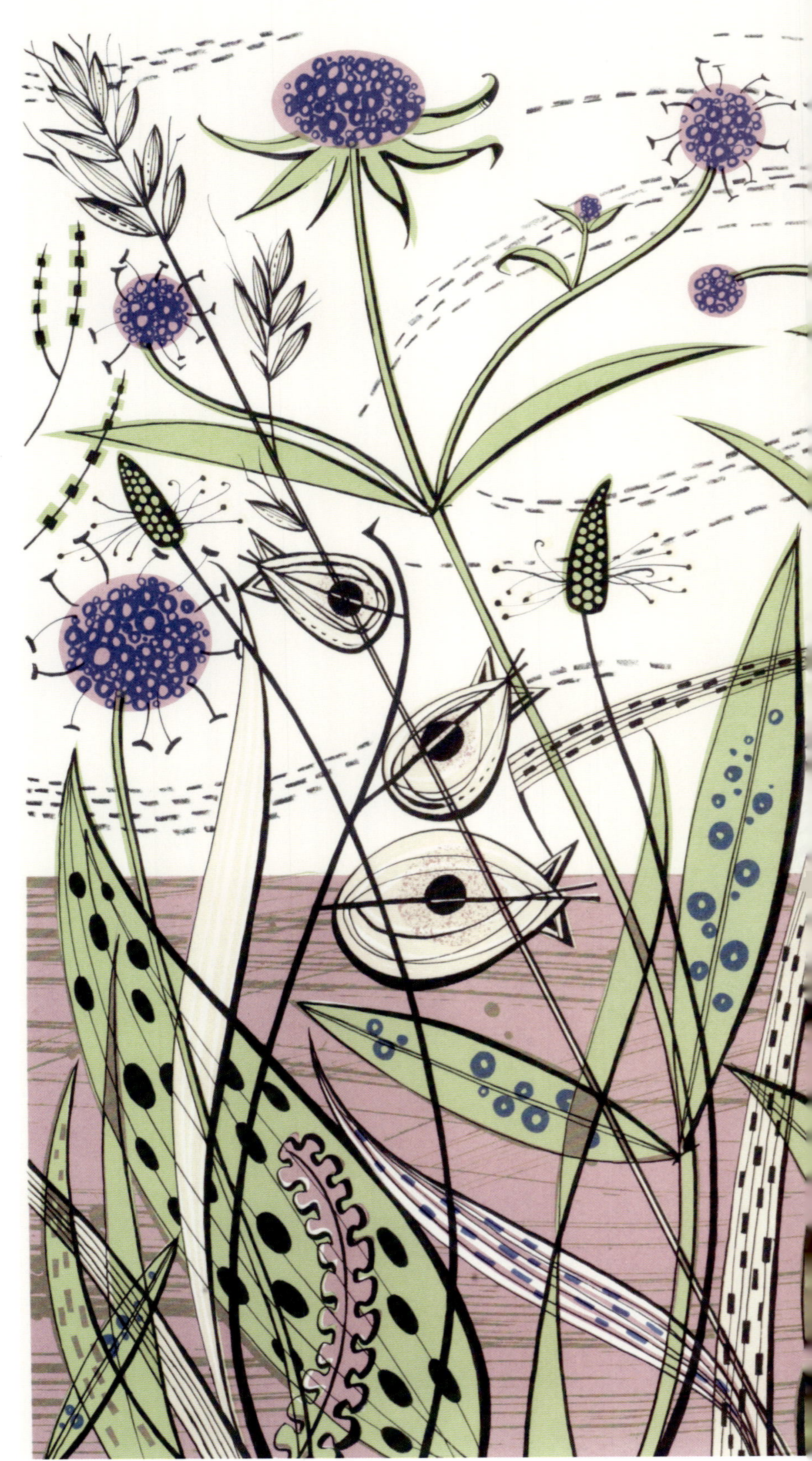

'*the Spey flowing behind local plants, such as scabious, yellow rattle and plantain*'

By Green Bank

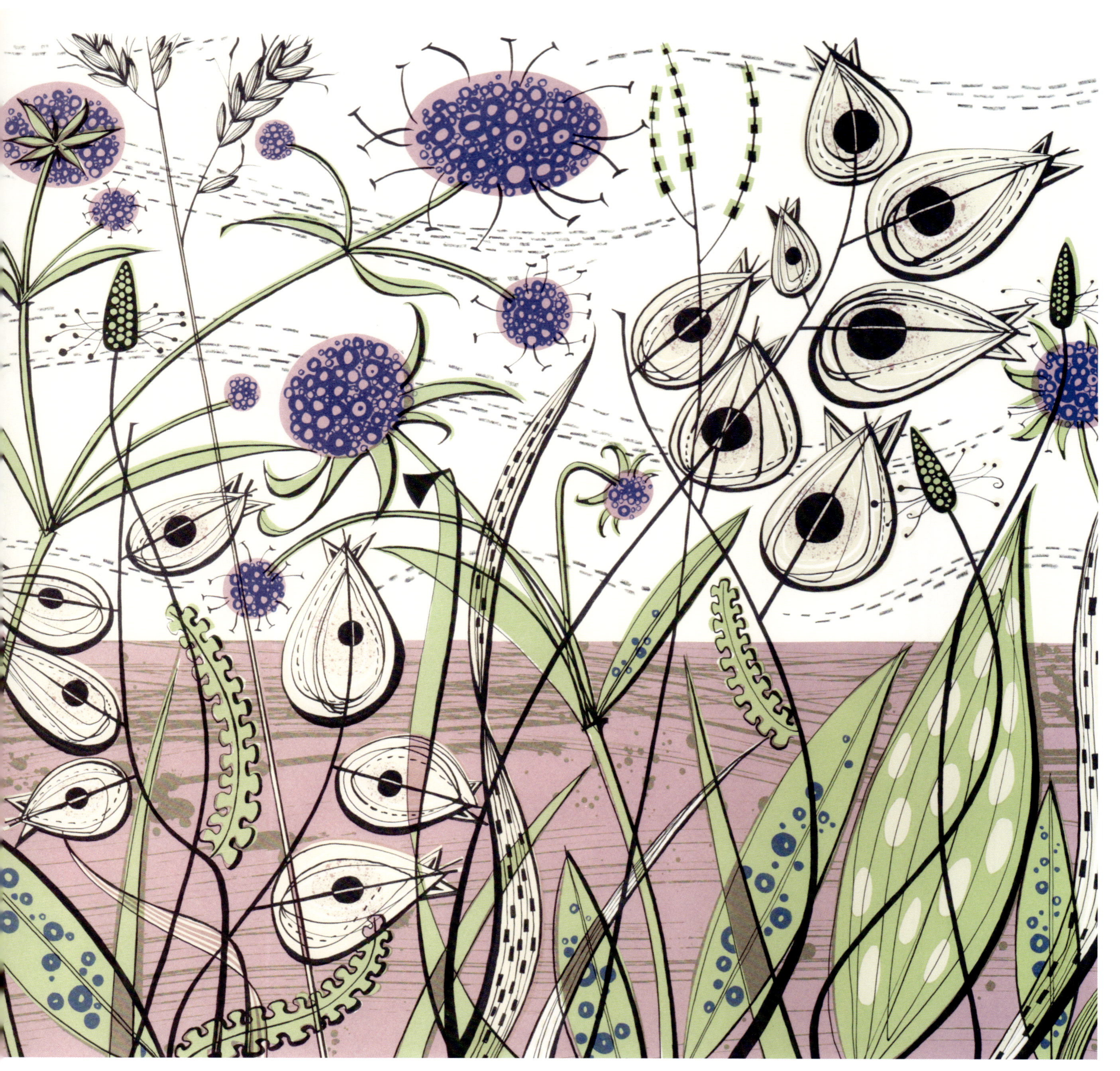

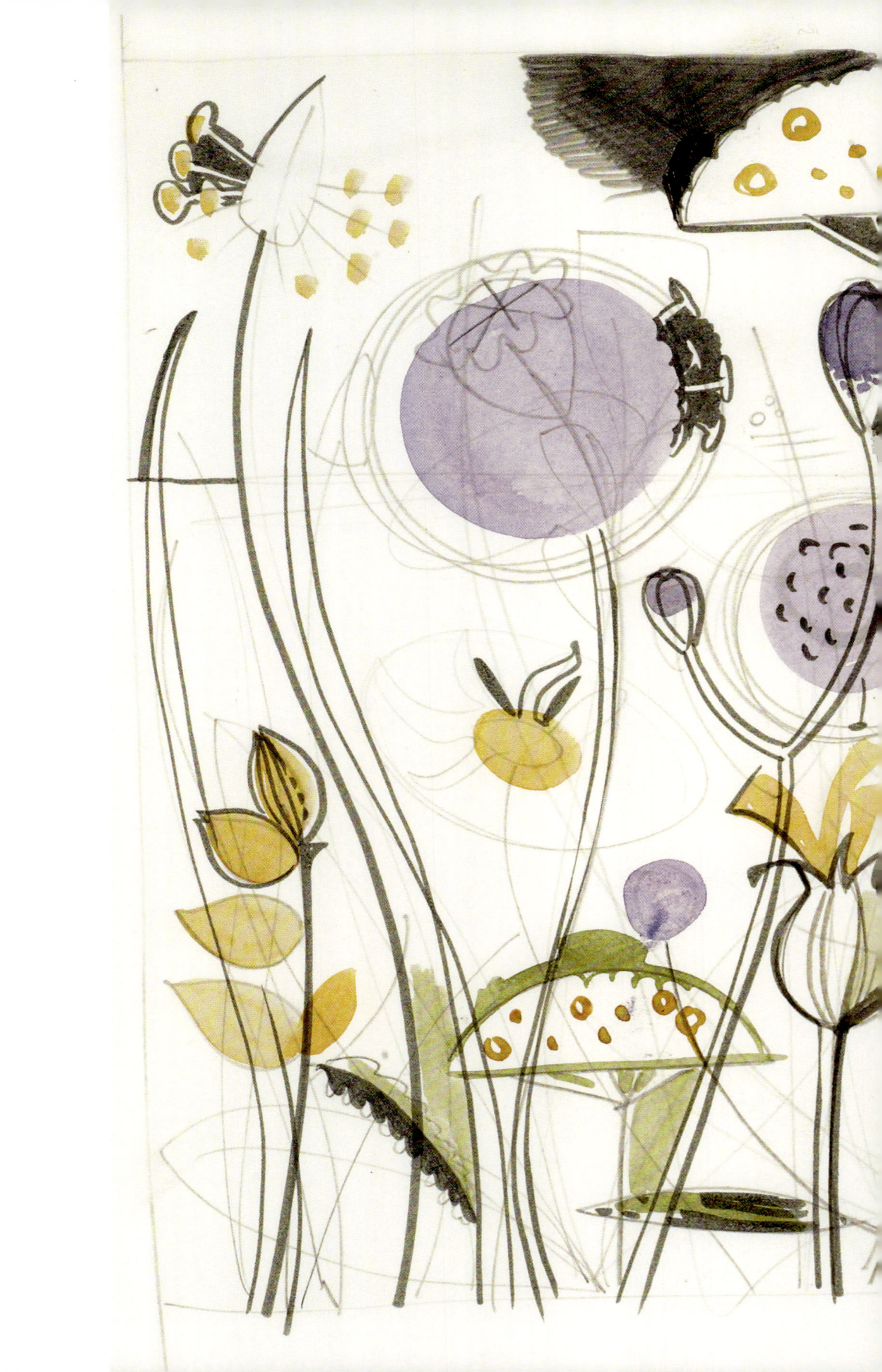

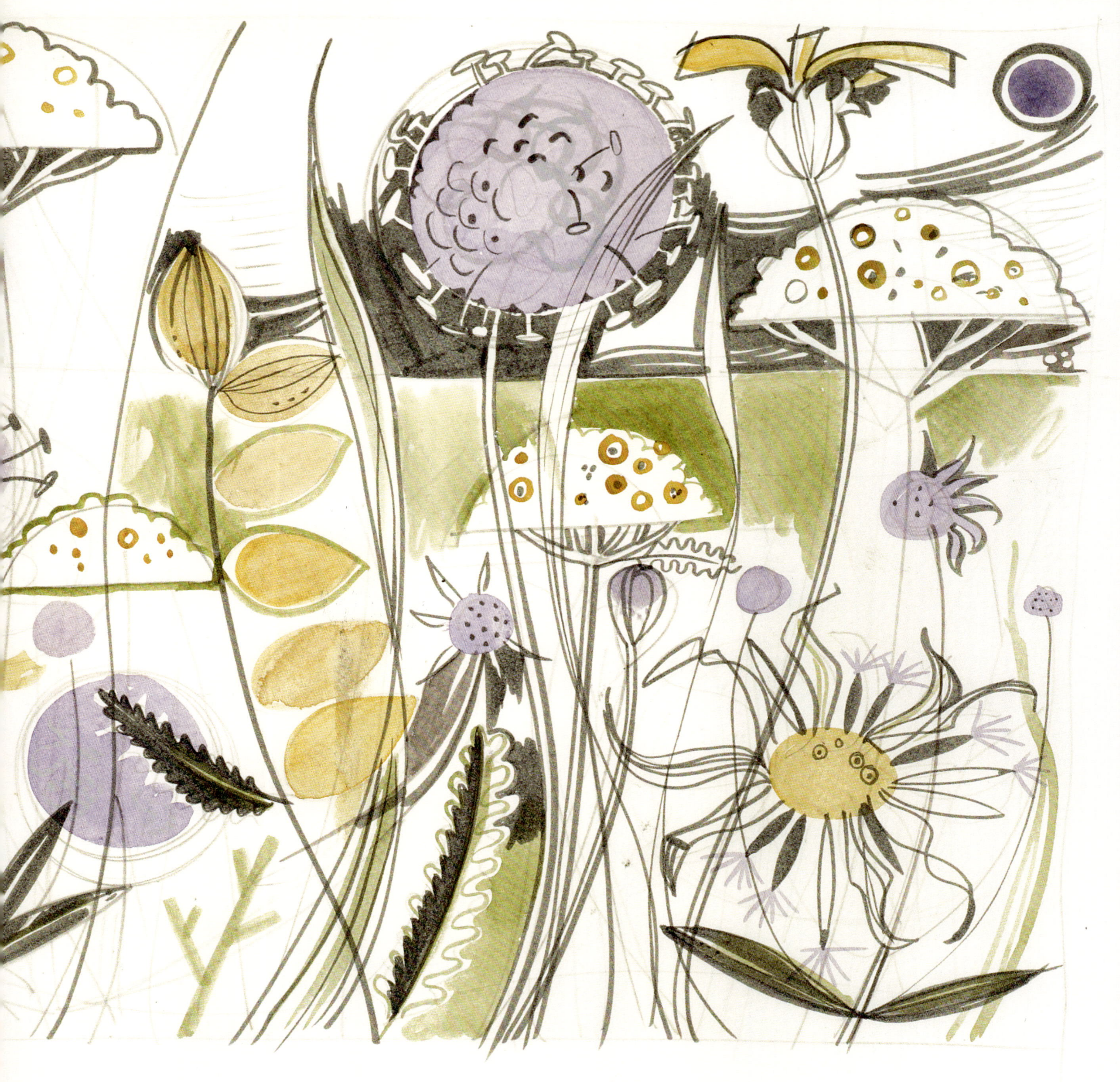

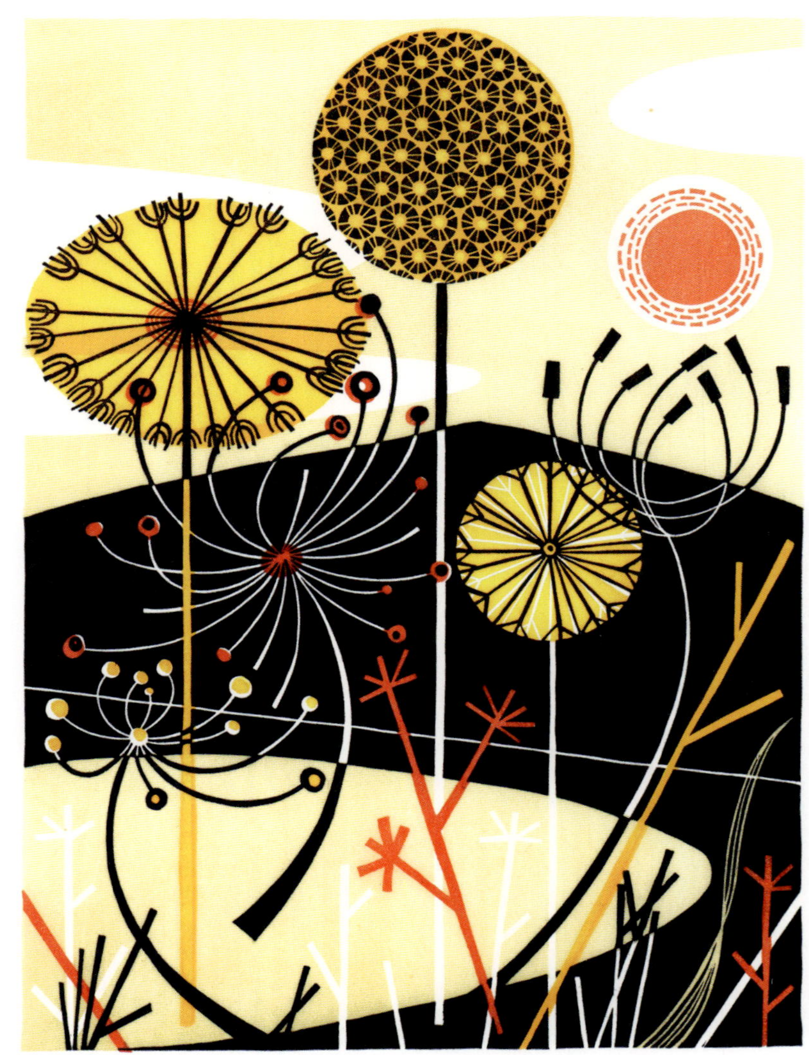

Loch with Dandelions

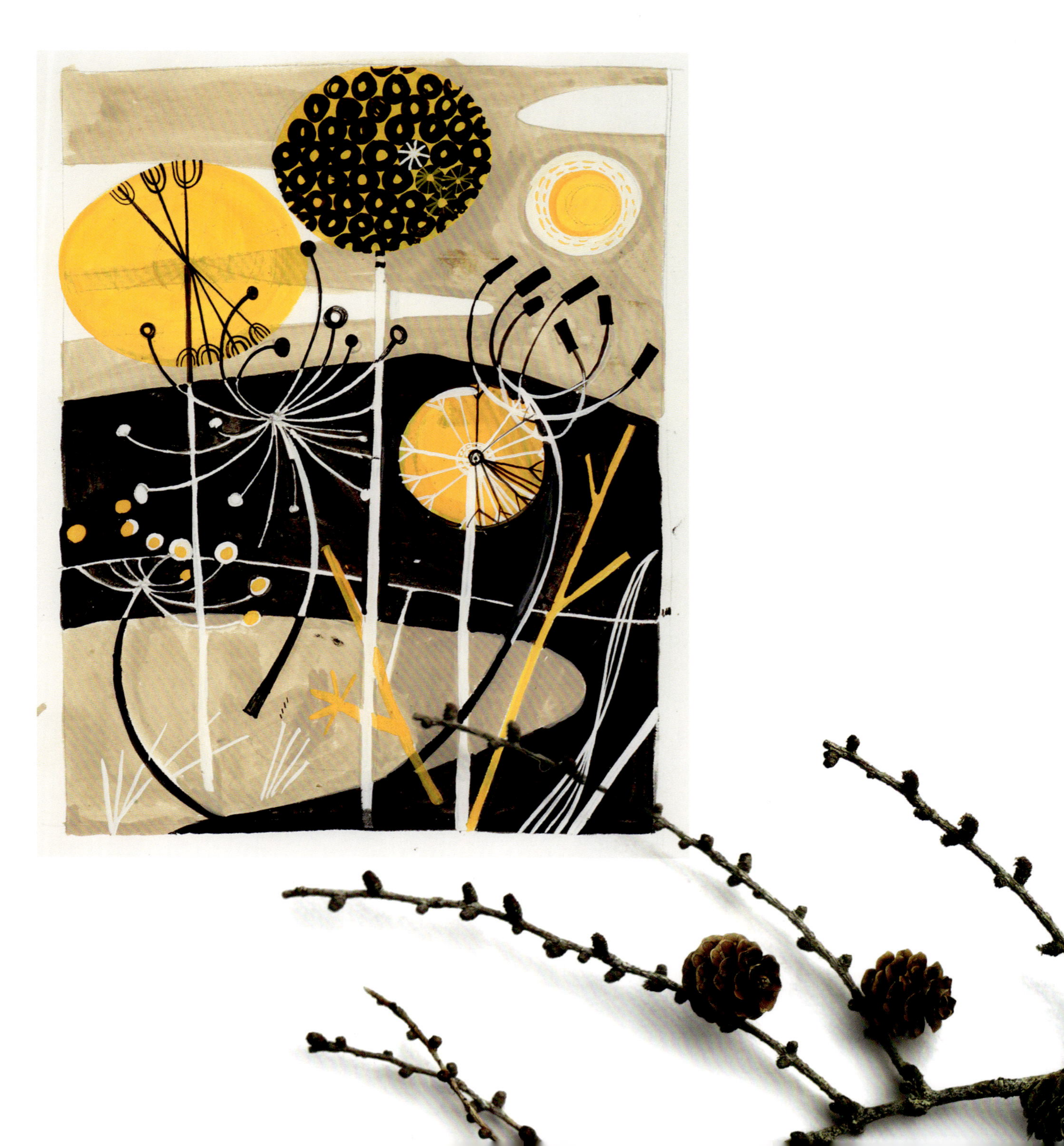

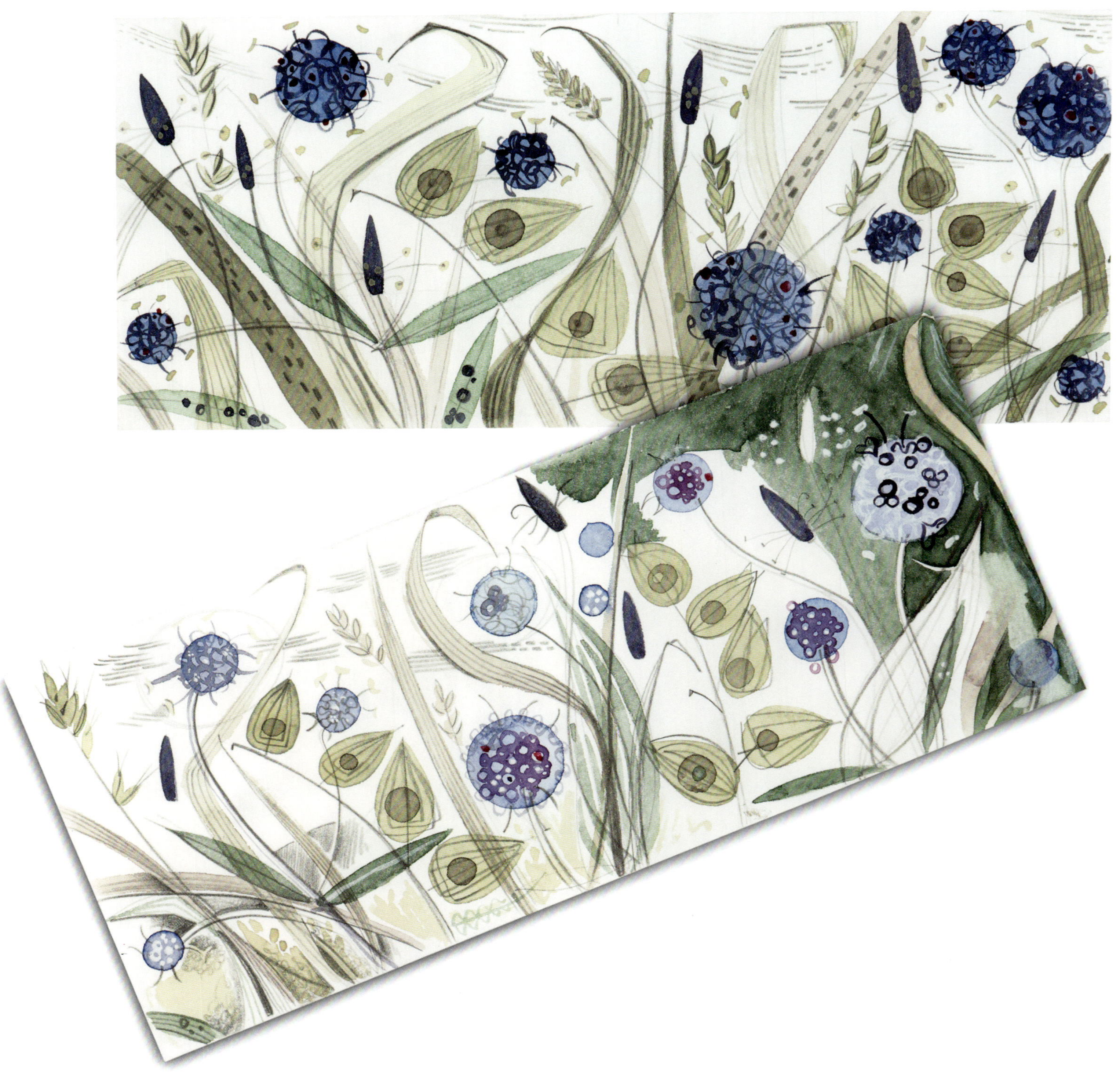

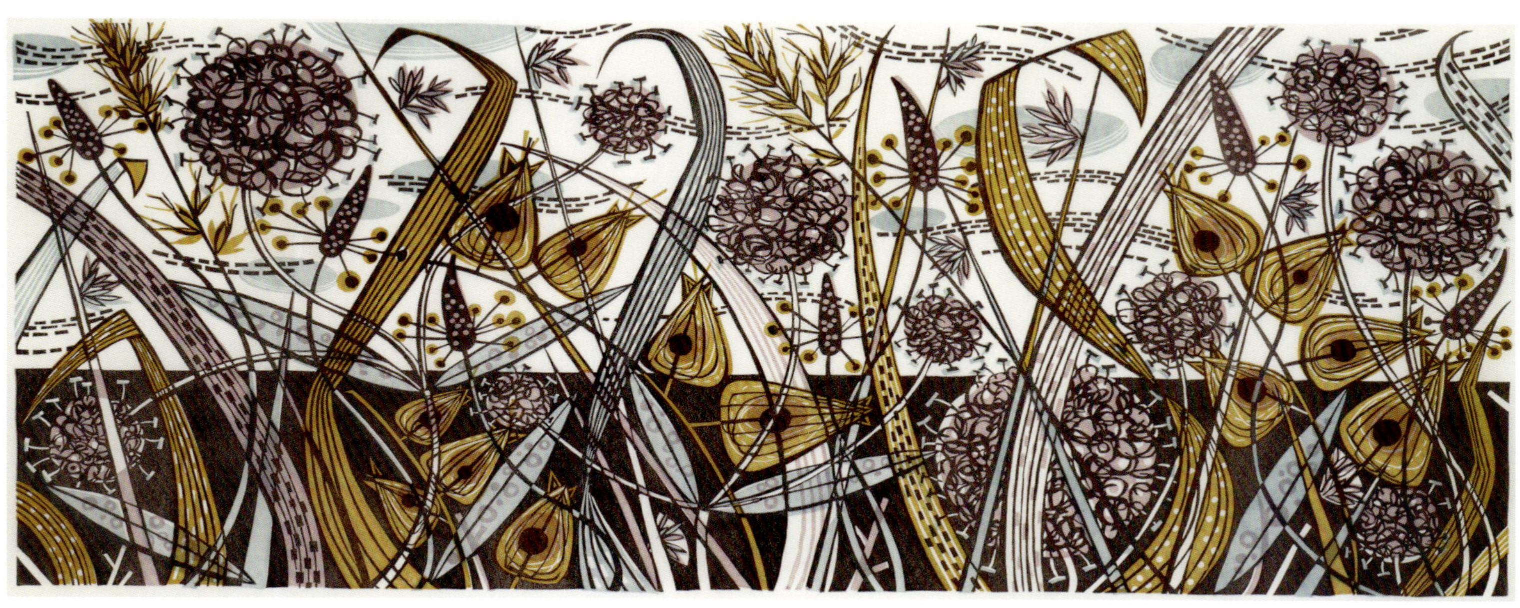

Late Summer Spey

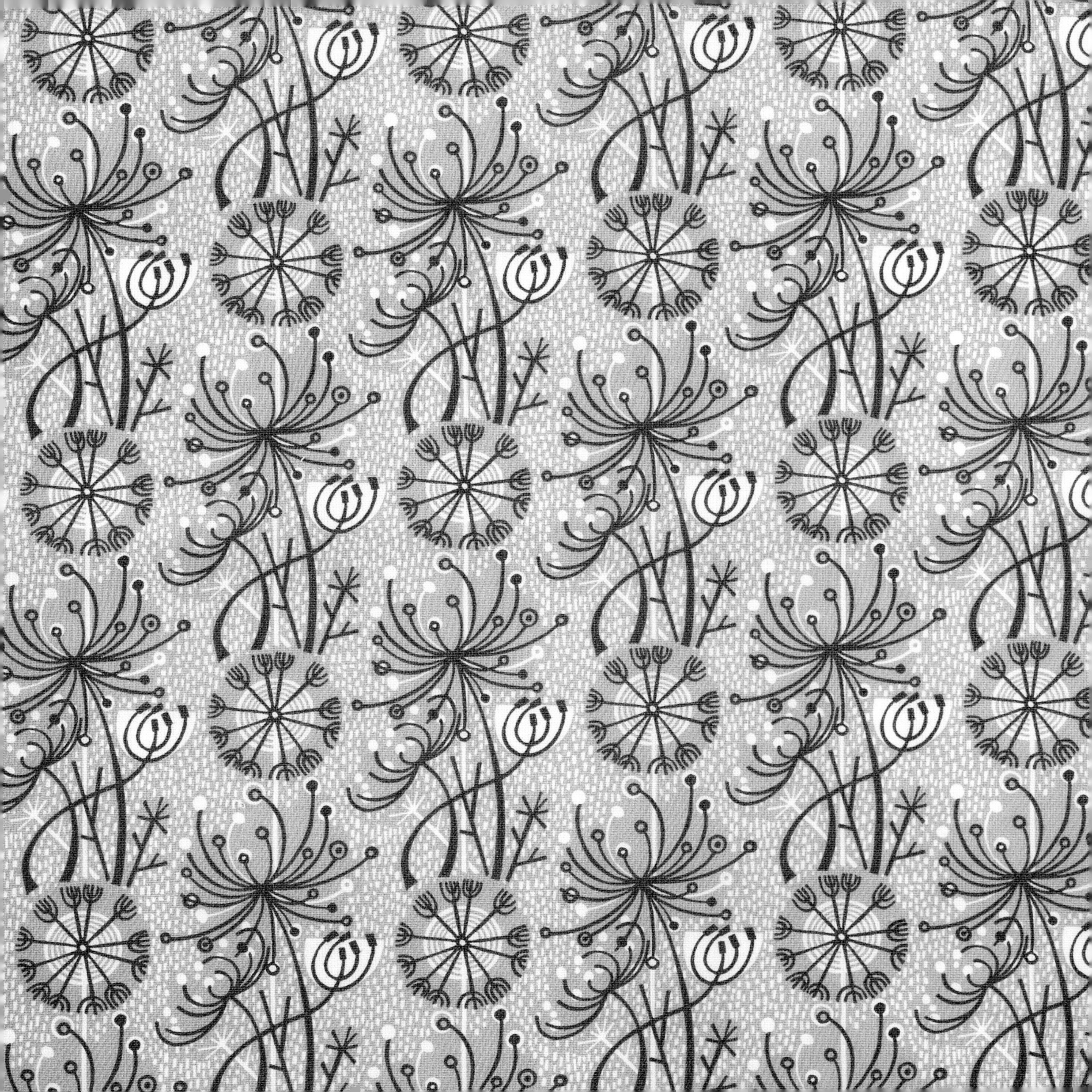

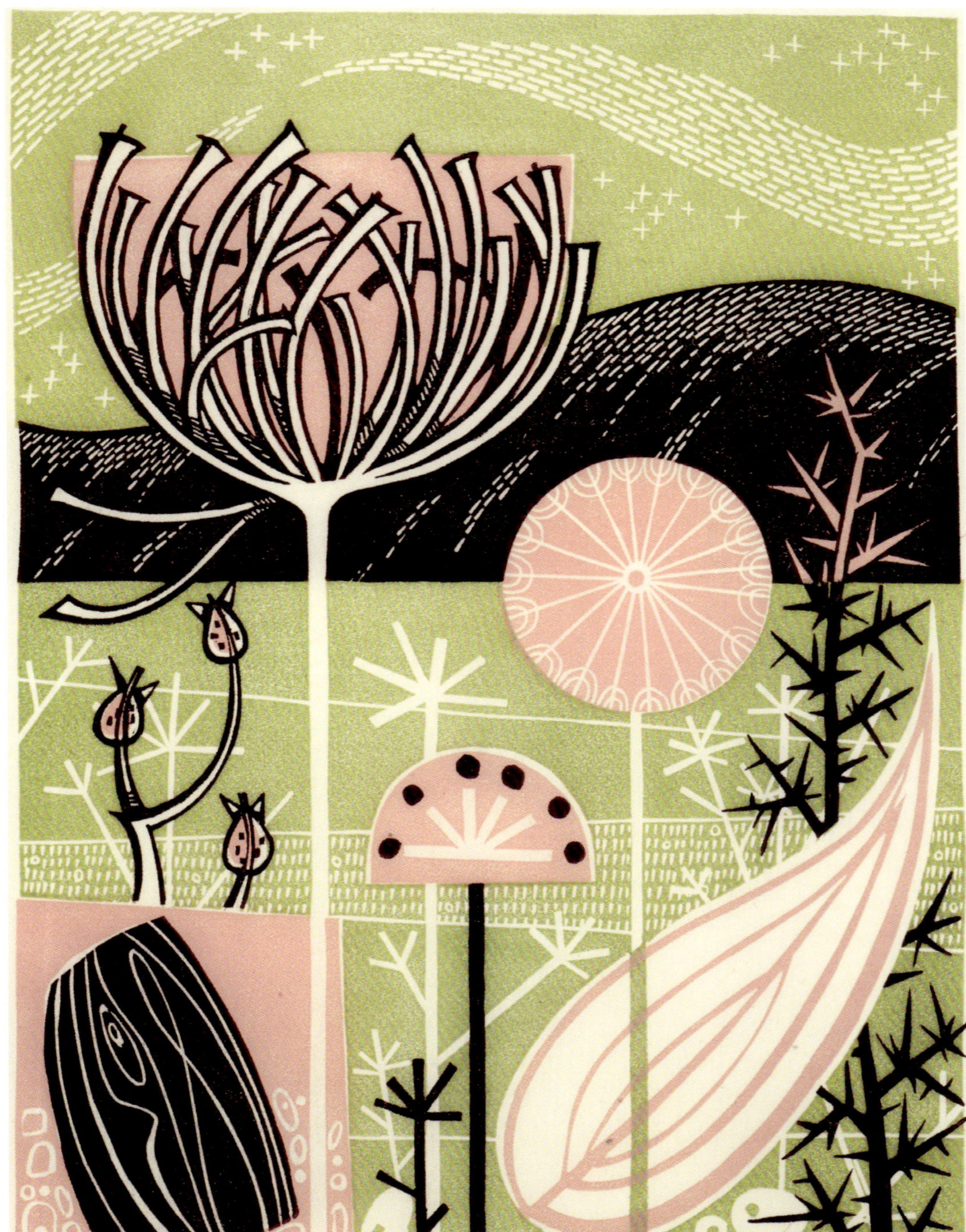

Moonlit Loch

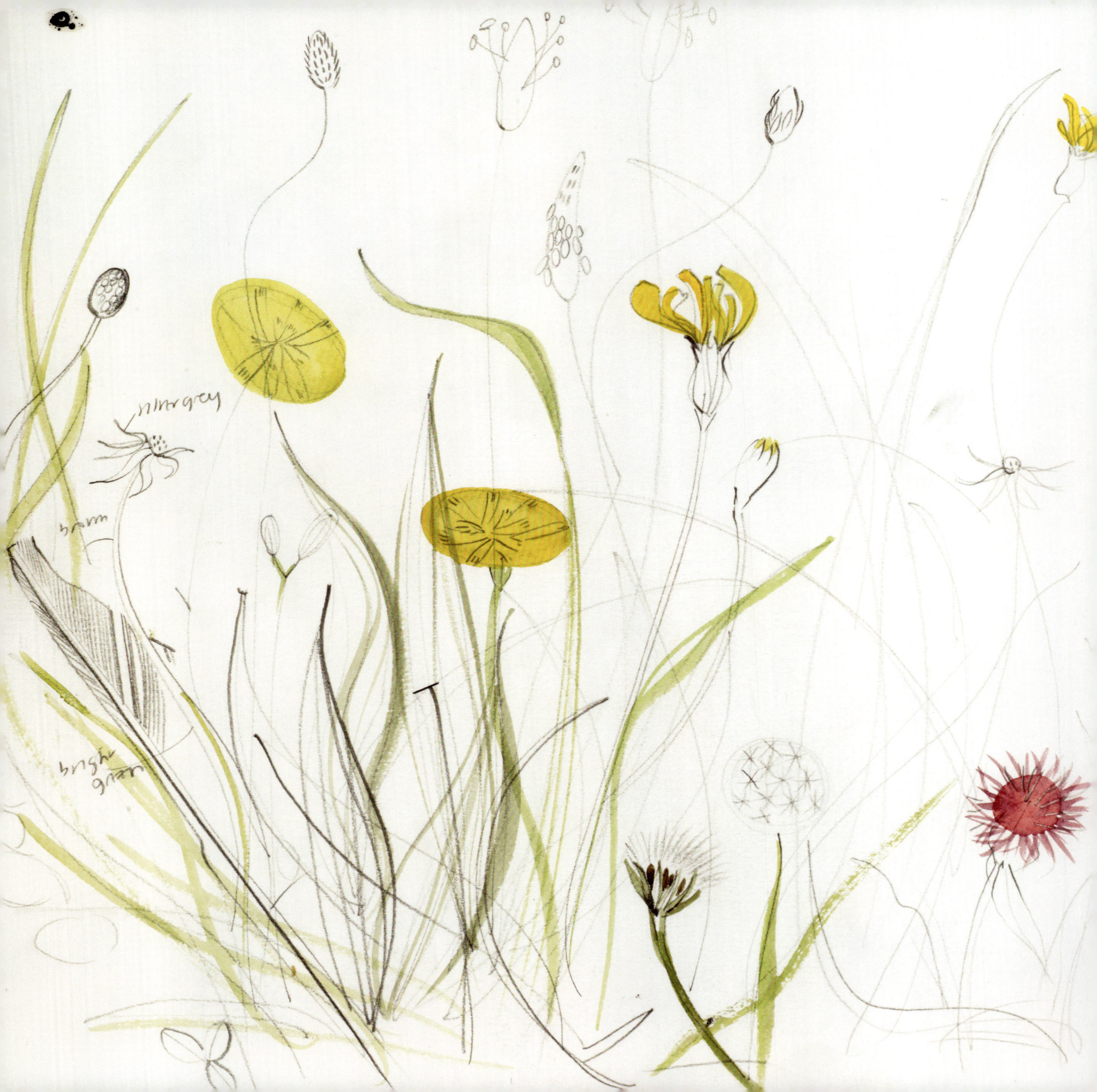
nlnrgrey
brown
bright
green

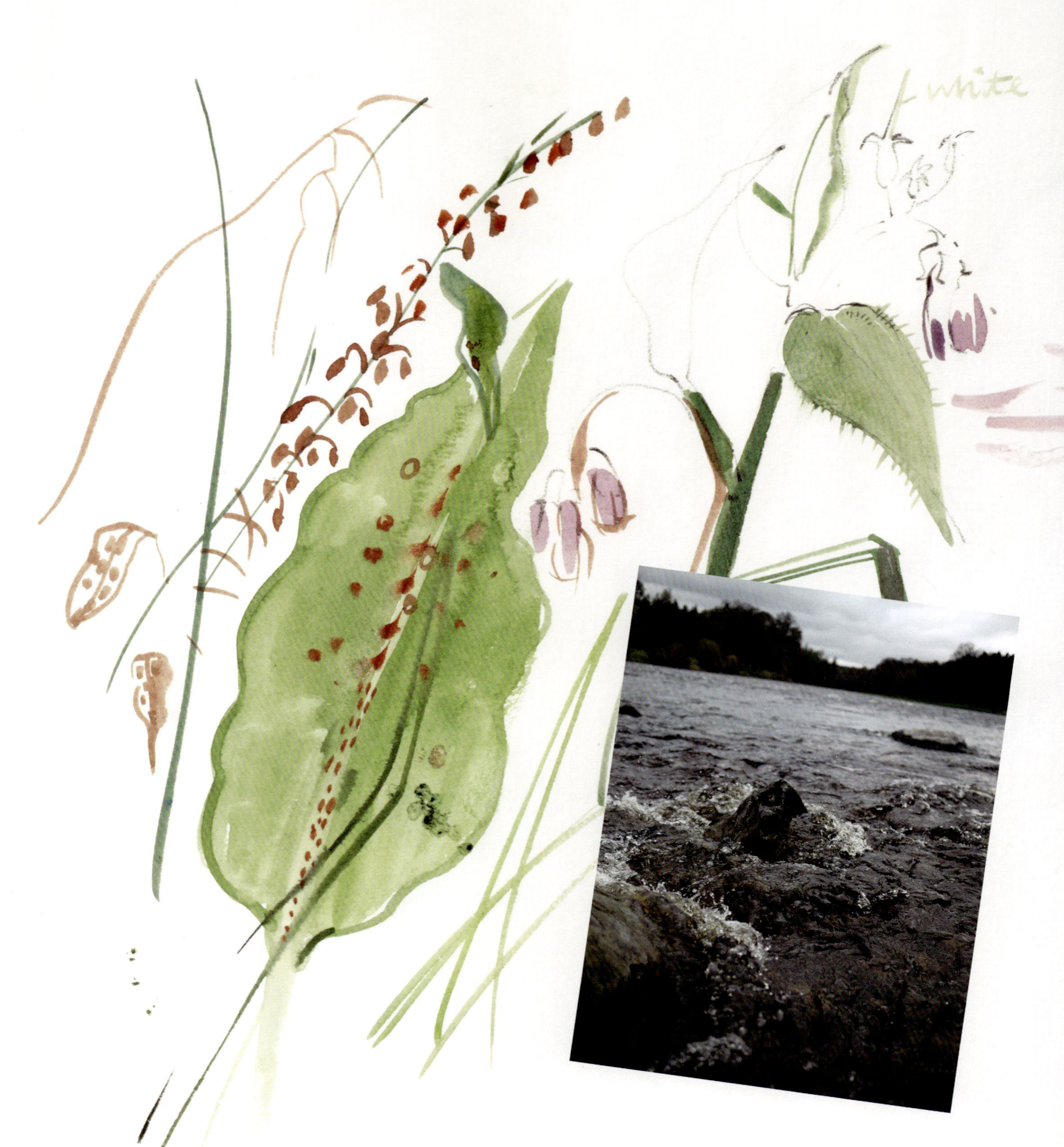
white

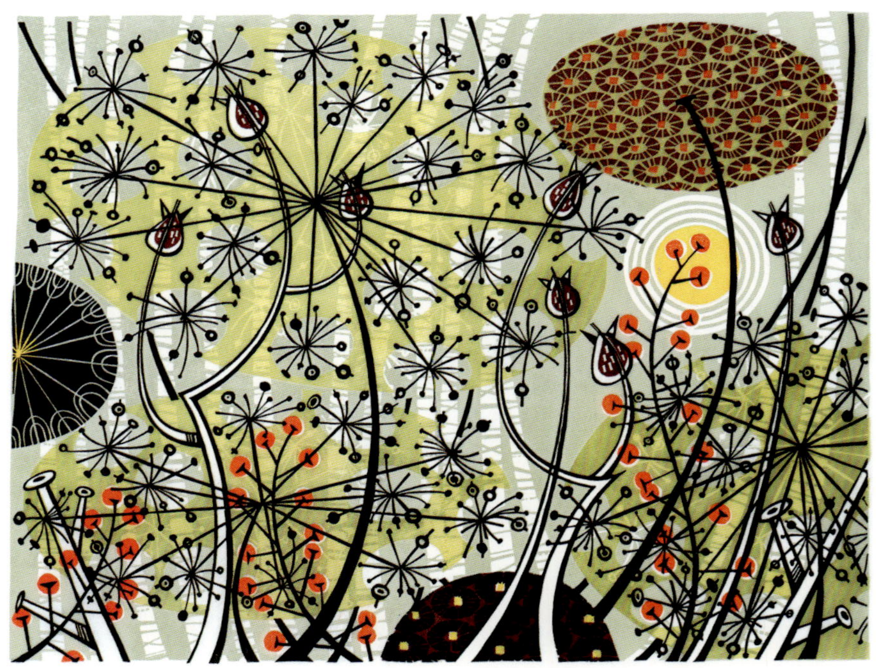

Spey Path II

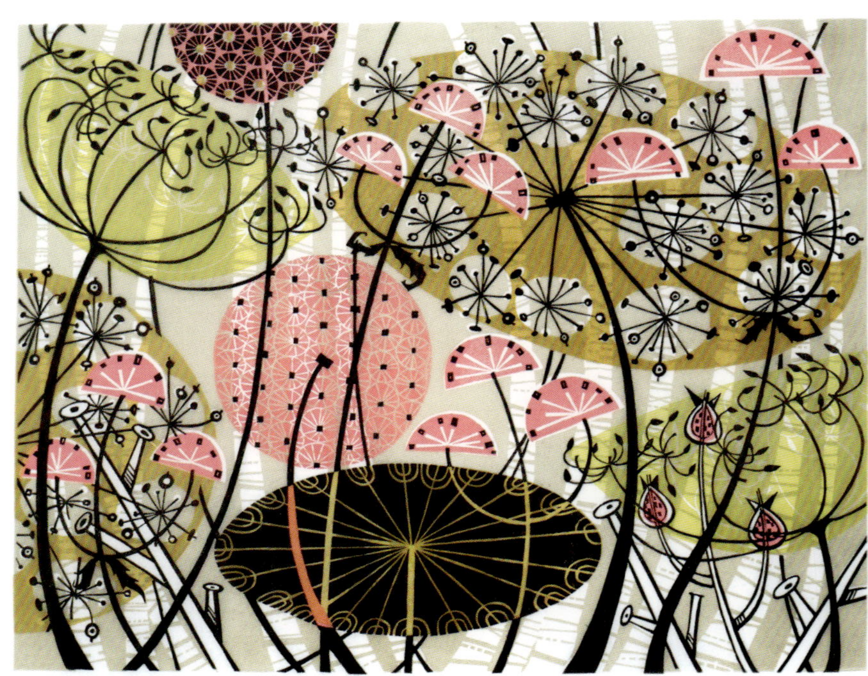

Spey Path III

'I use white-barked birch trees as
a backdrop for plants through the
seasons: cow parsley, valerian, rosebay
willowherb and rowans.'

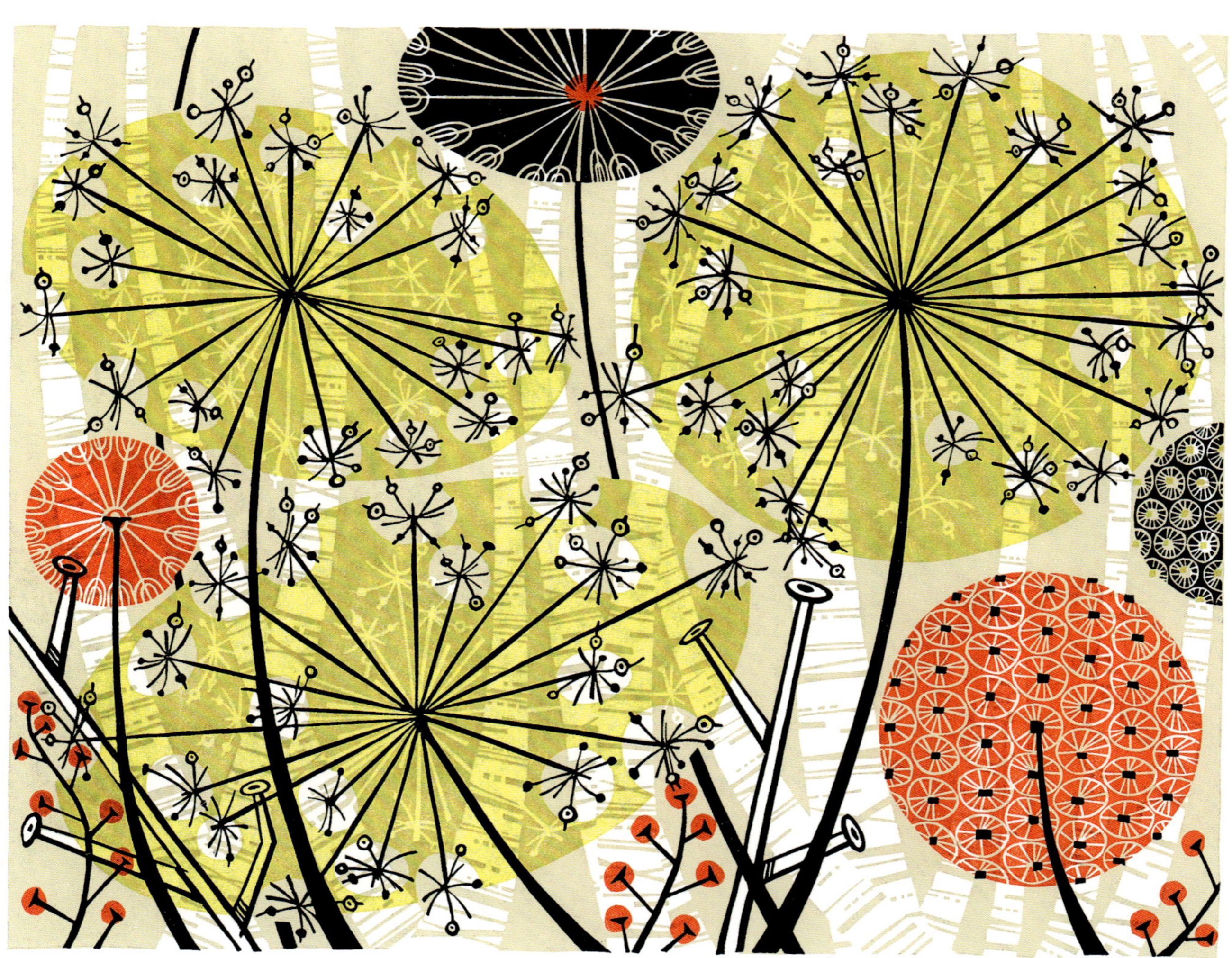

Spey Path I

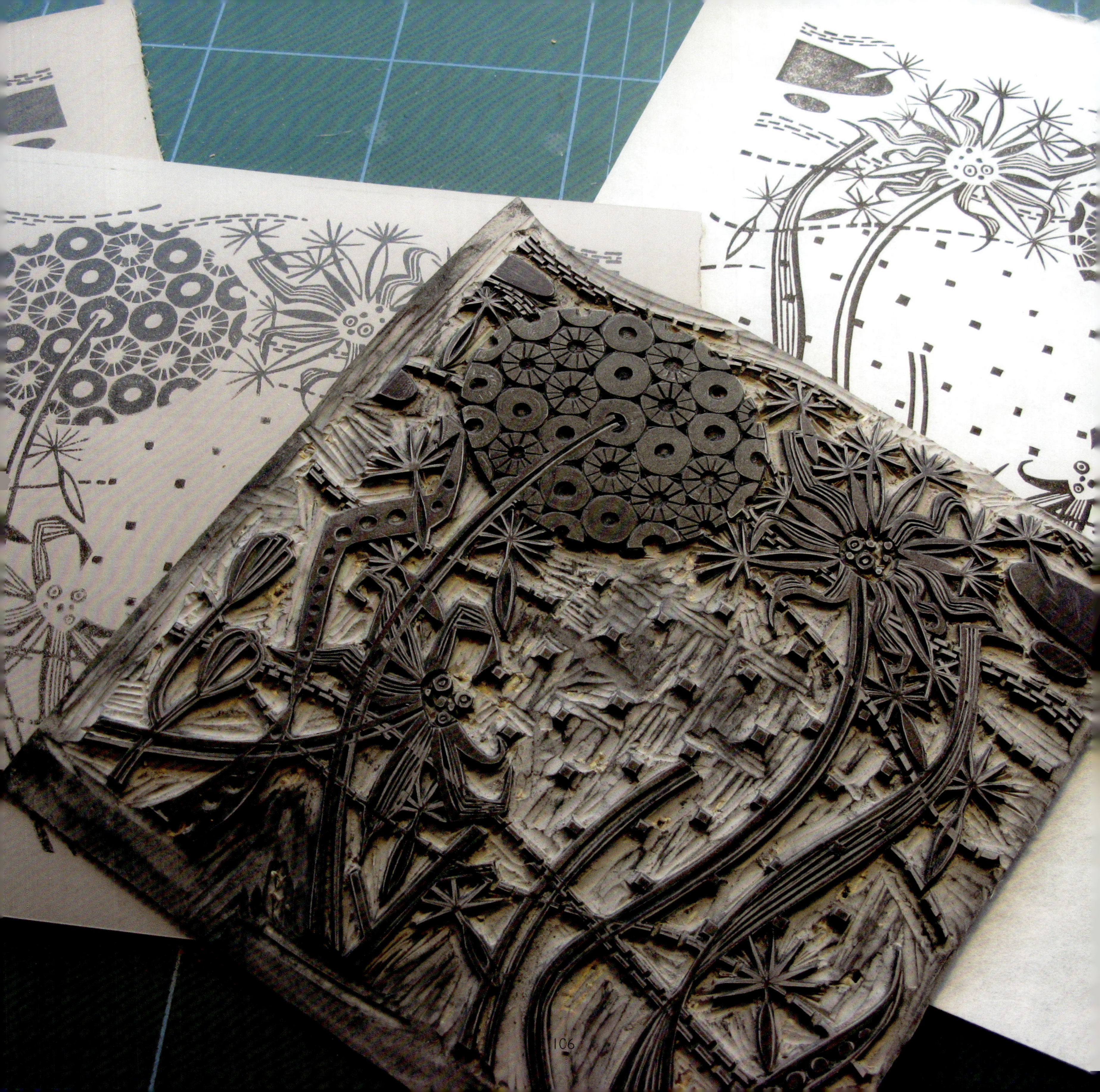

106

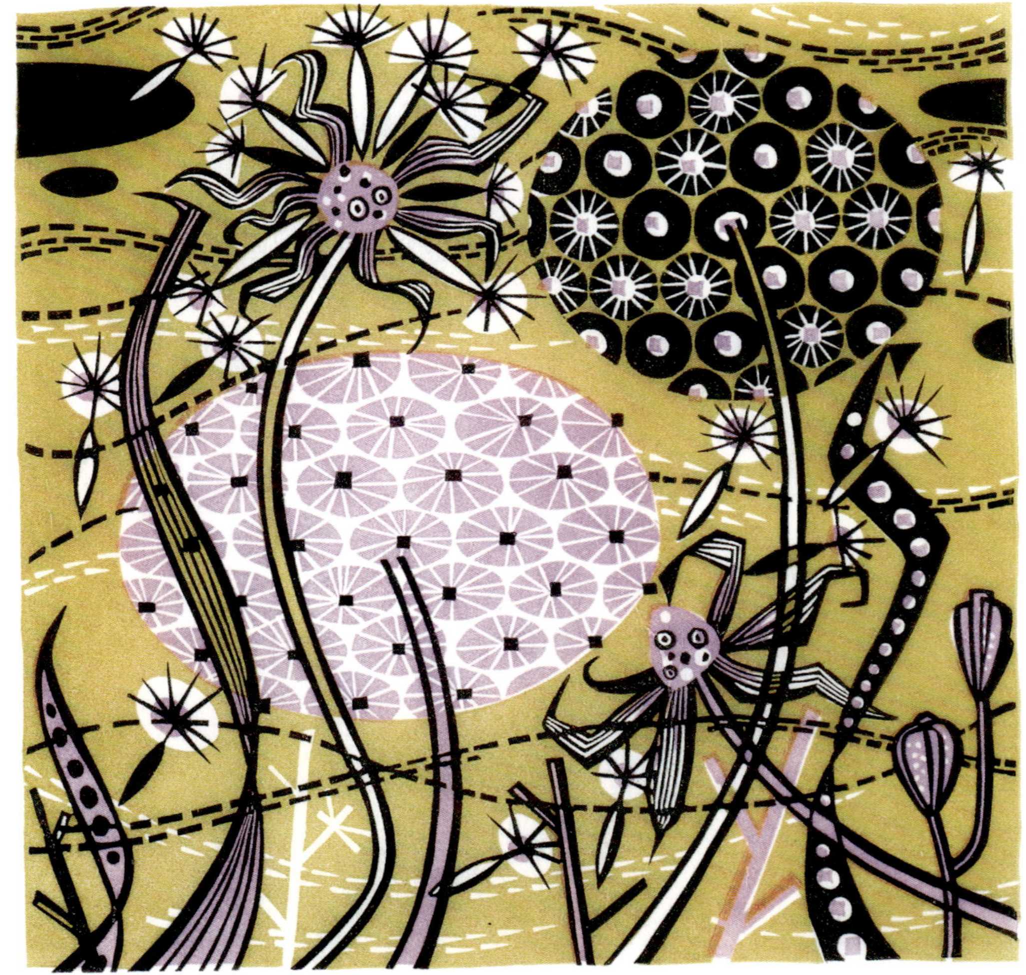

Spey Seedheads

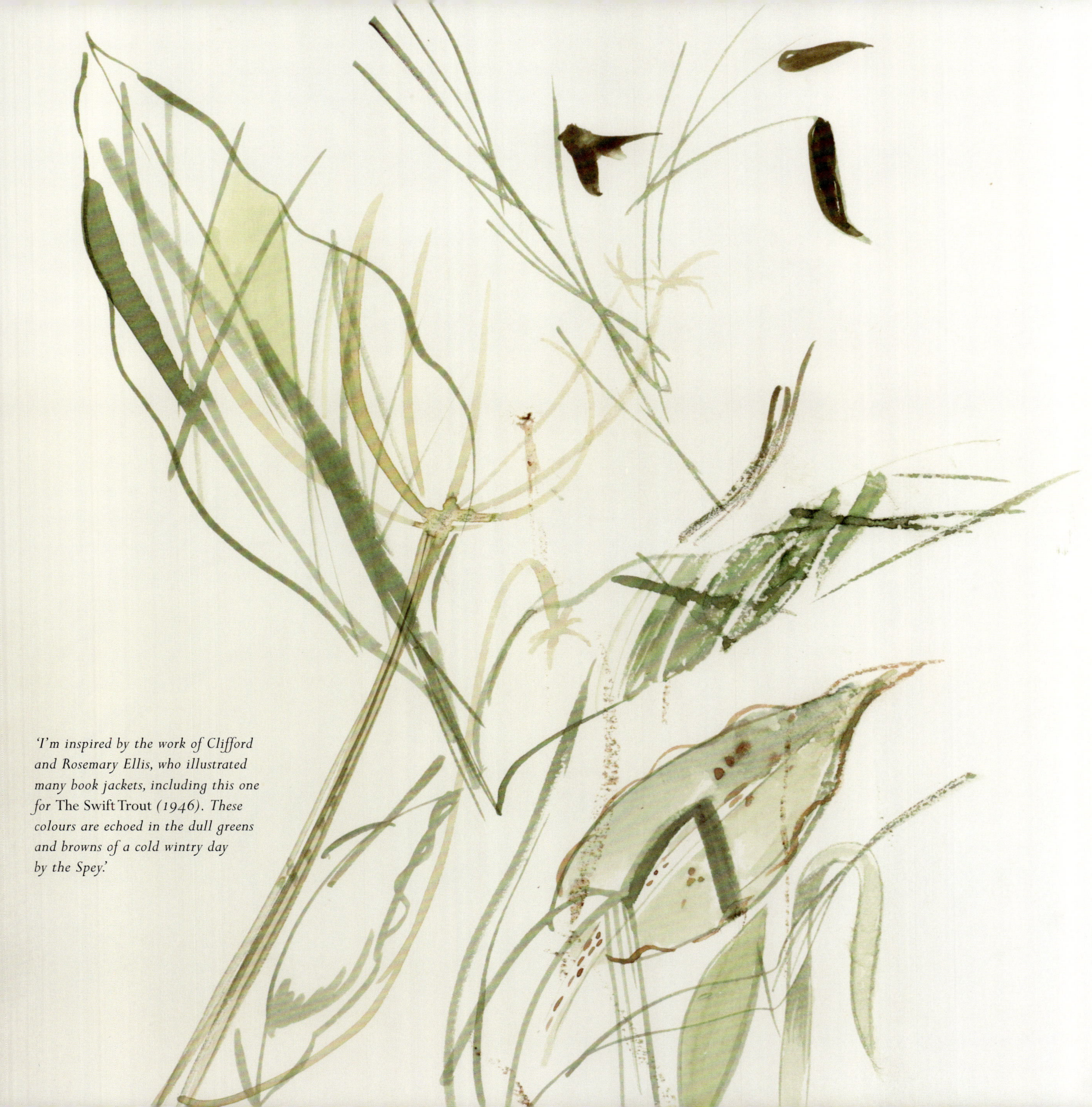

'I'm inspired by the work of Clifford and Rosemary Ellis, who illustrated many book jackets, including this one for The Swift Trout (1946). These colours are echoed in the dull greens and browns of a cold wintry day by the Spey.'

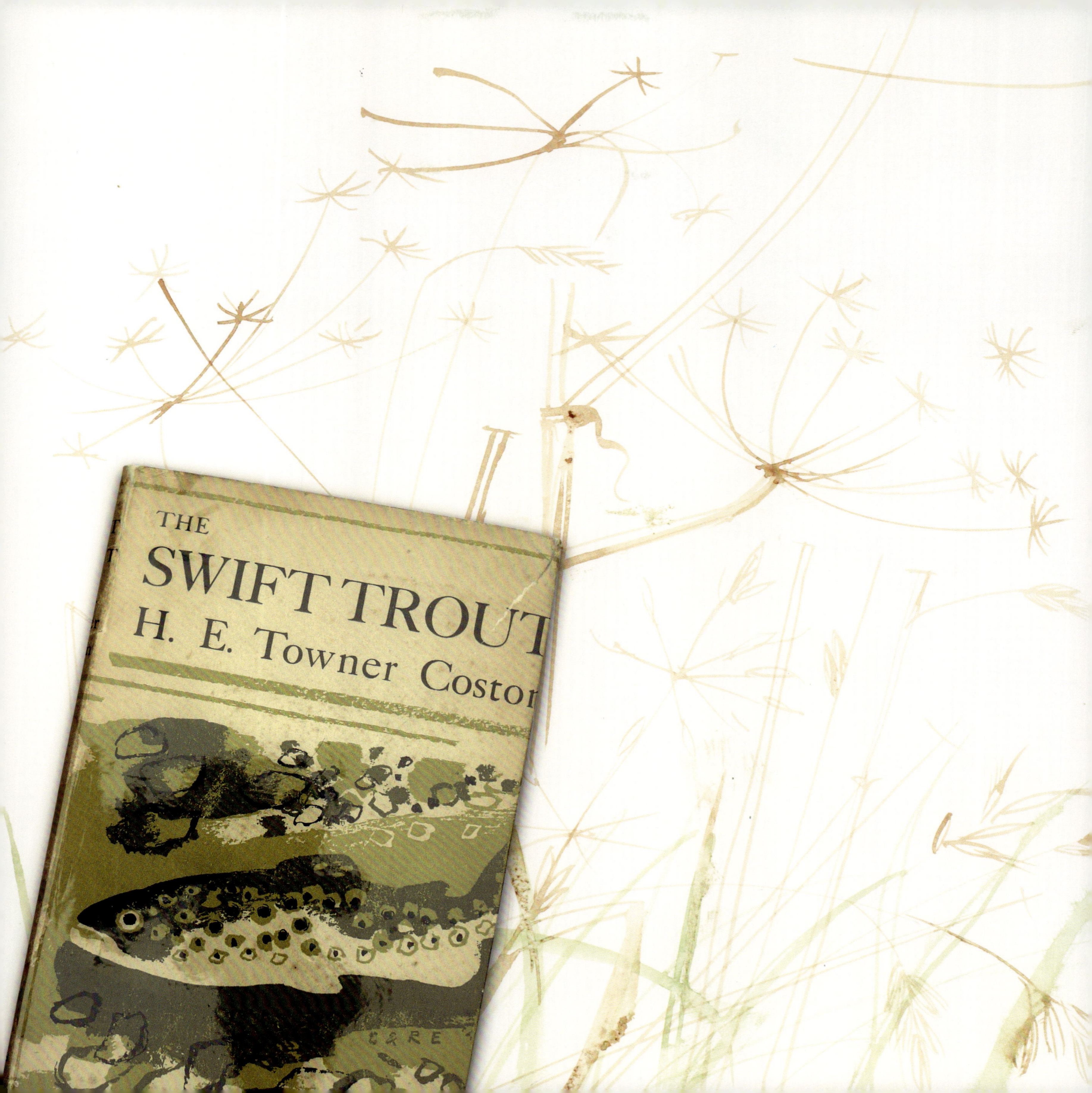
THE
SWIFT TROUT
H. E. Towner Coston

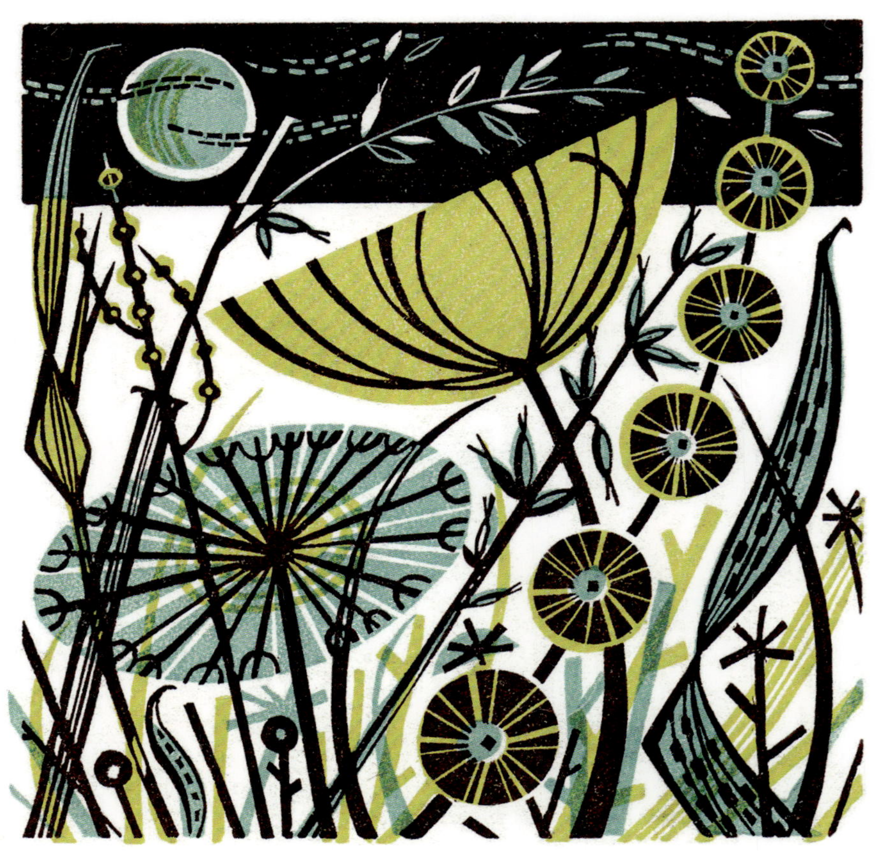

Winter Spey II

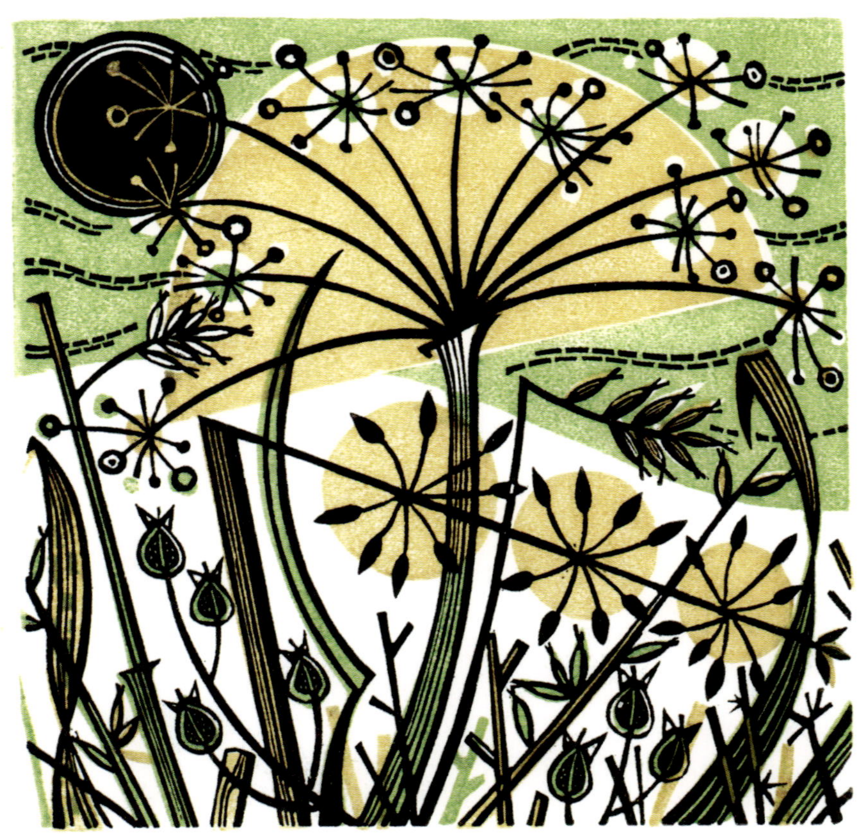

Winter Spey III

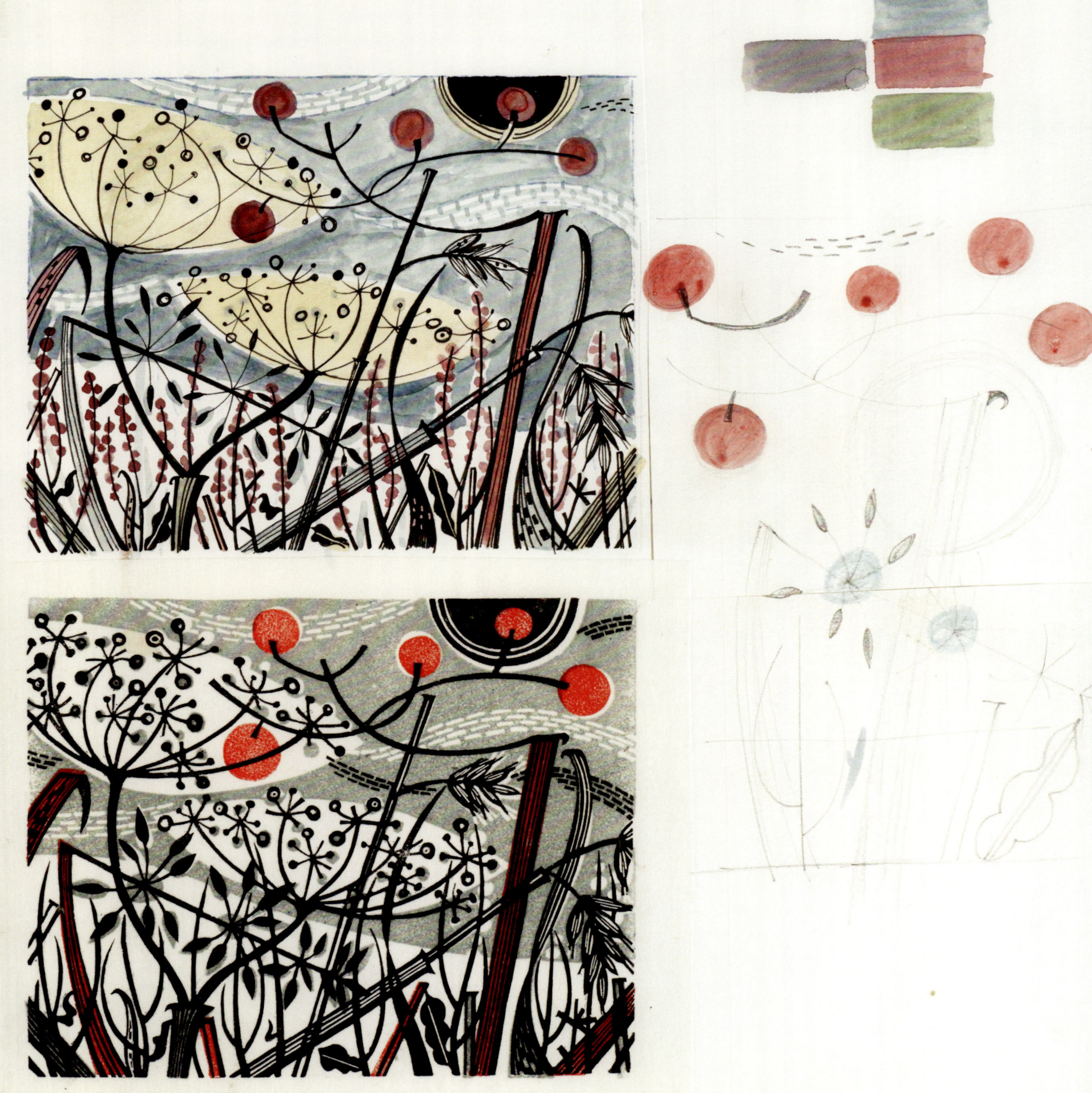

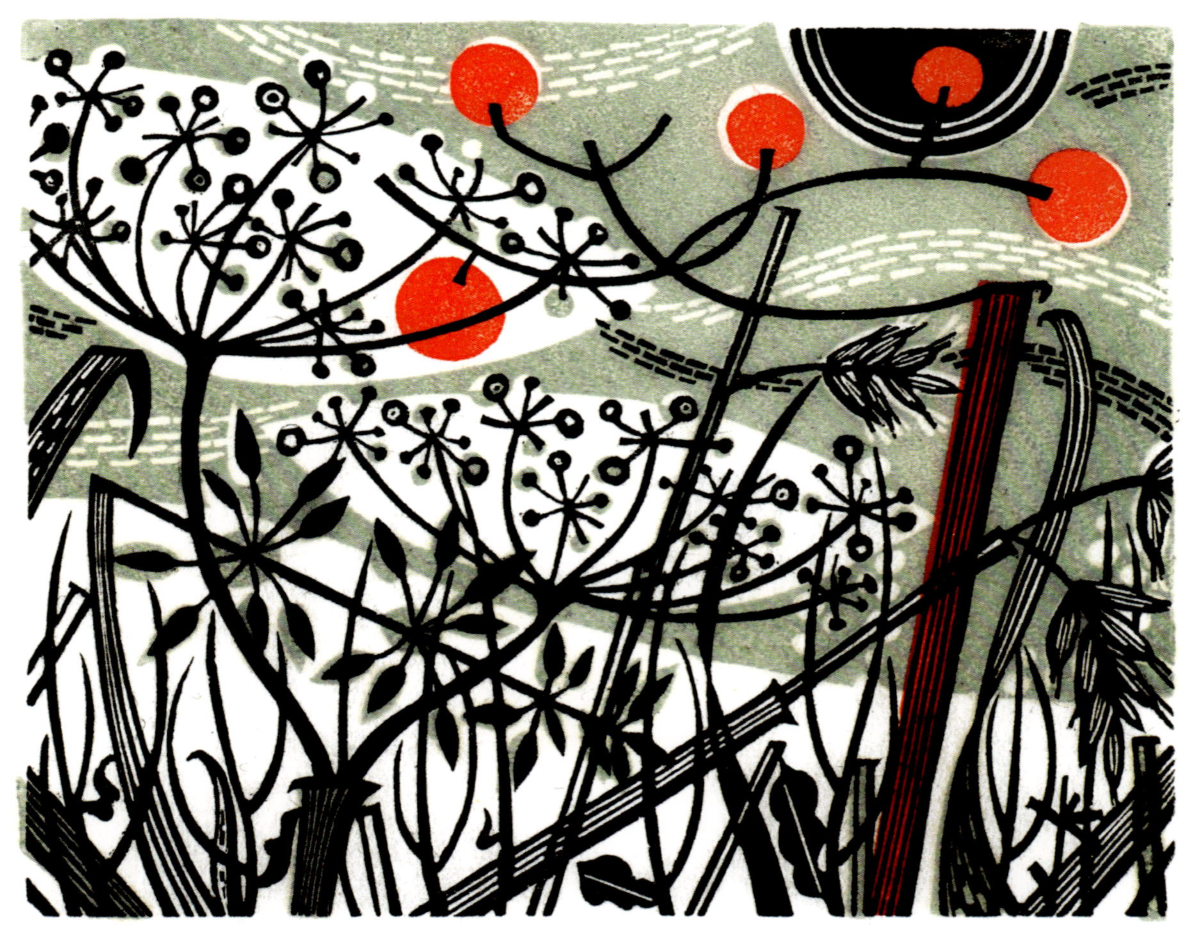

Winter Spey

'Before starting to cut blocks I sketch
out compositions and consider the
number of colours that might be used
in the print (see overleaf).'

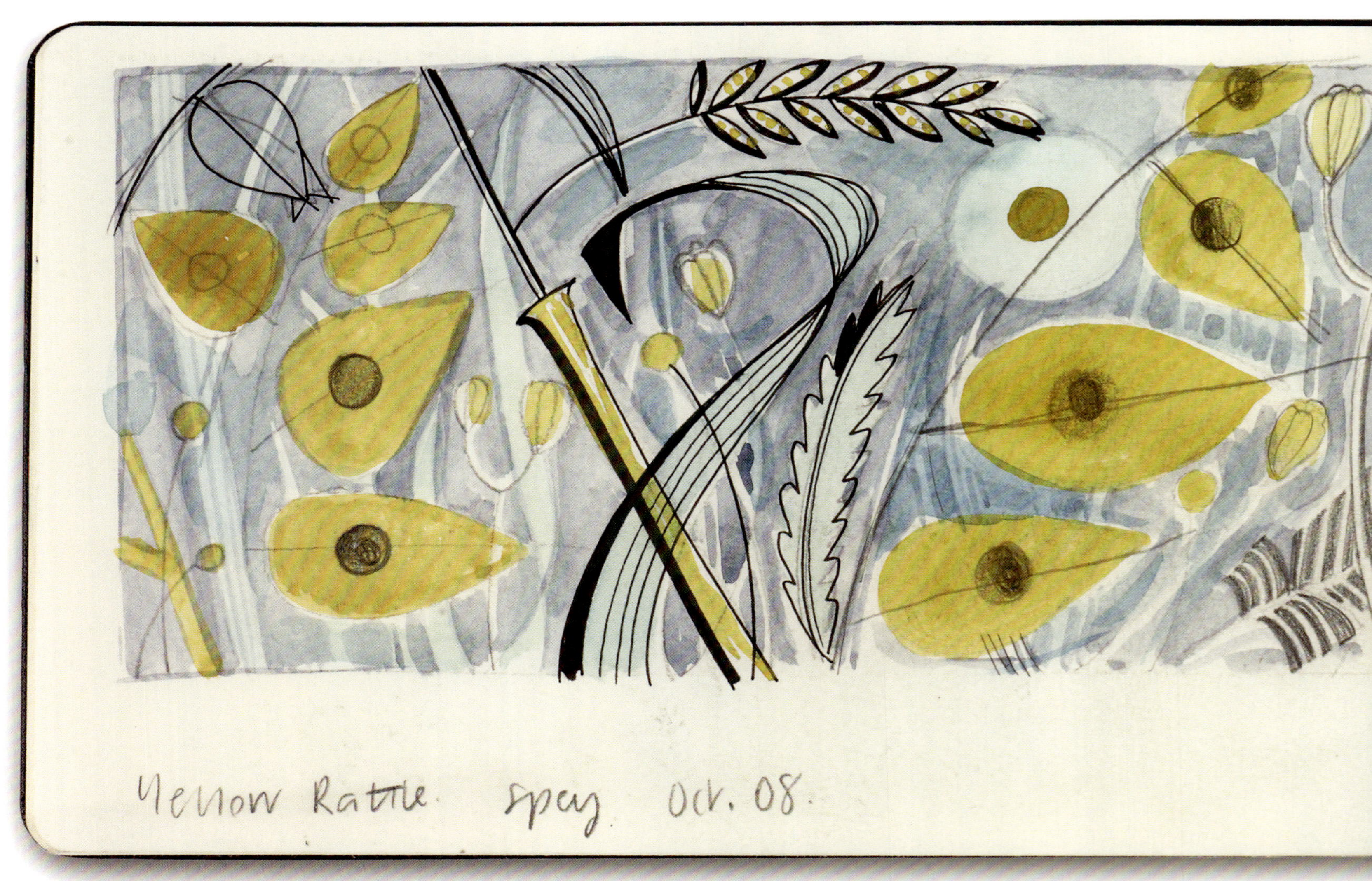

Yellow Rattle. spey. Oct. 08.

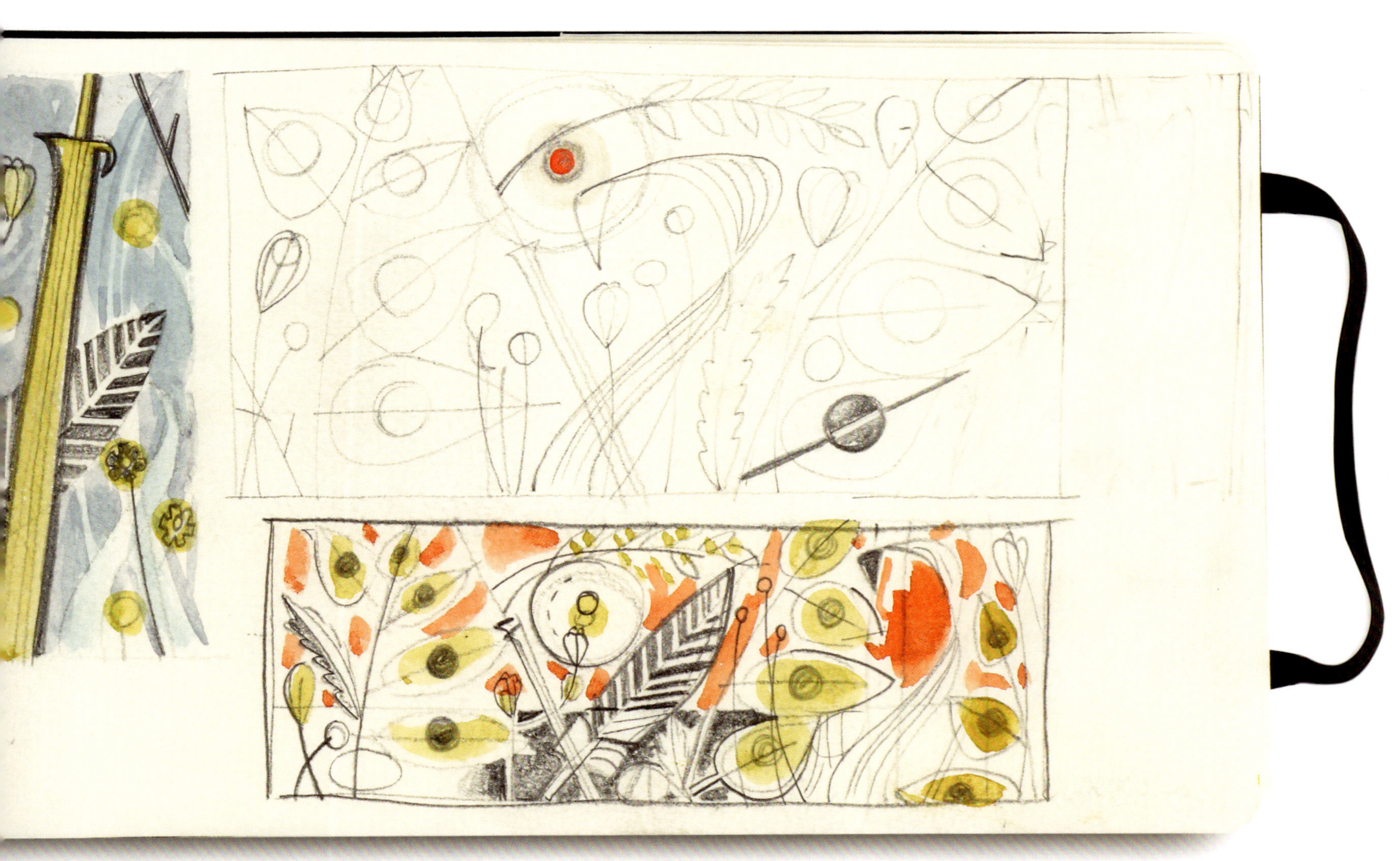

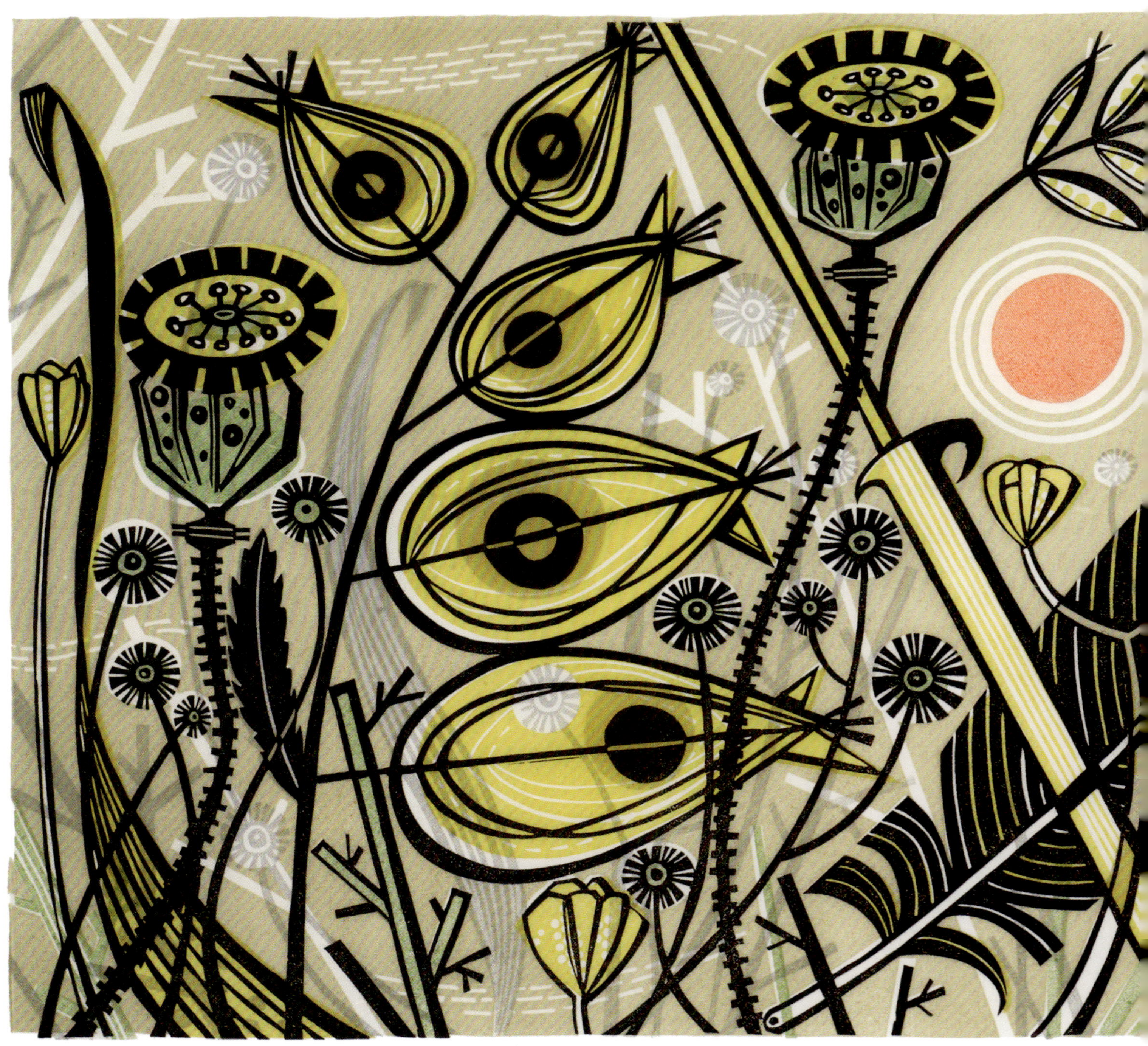

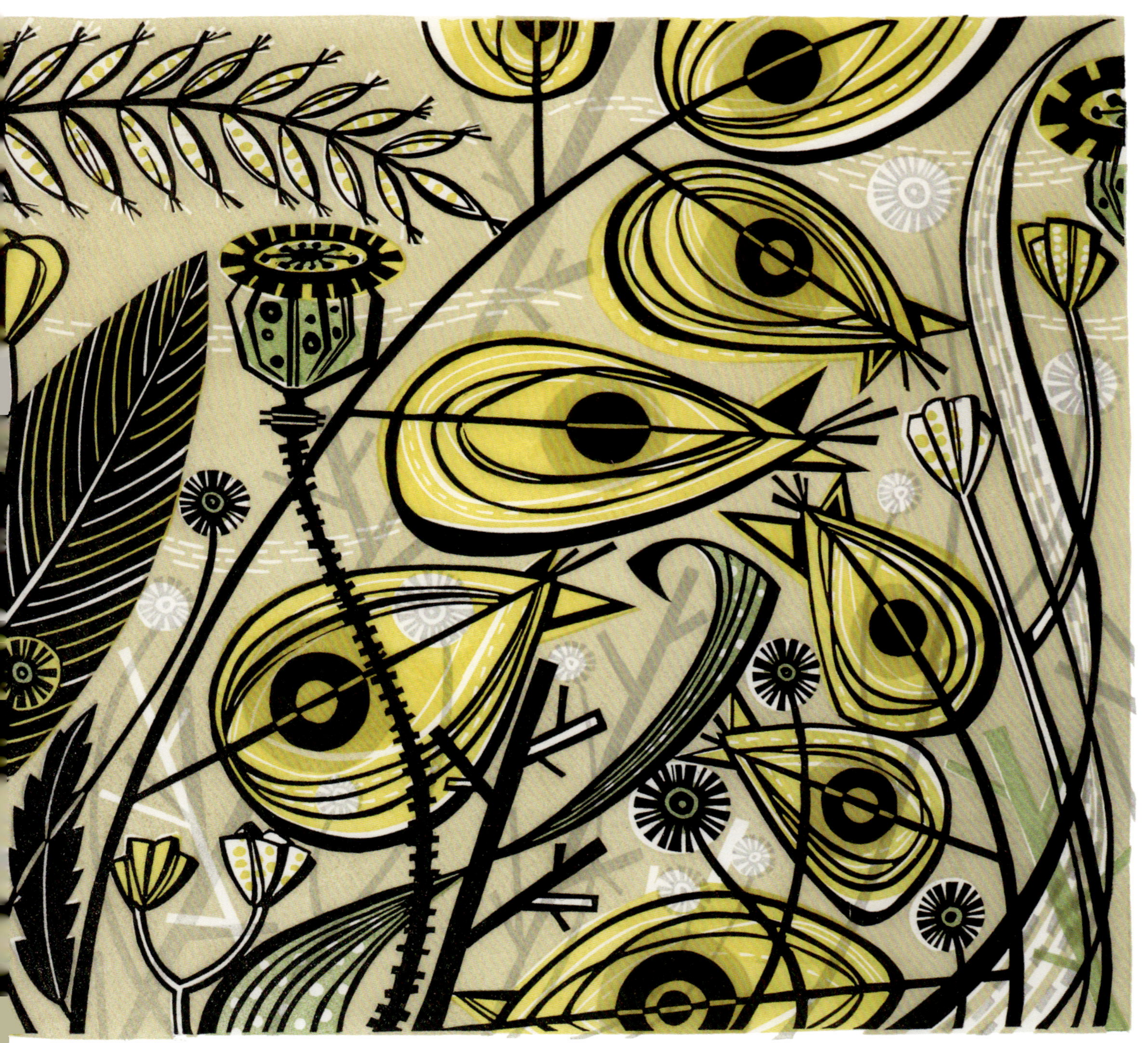

Yellow Rattle

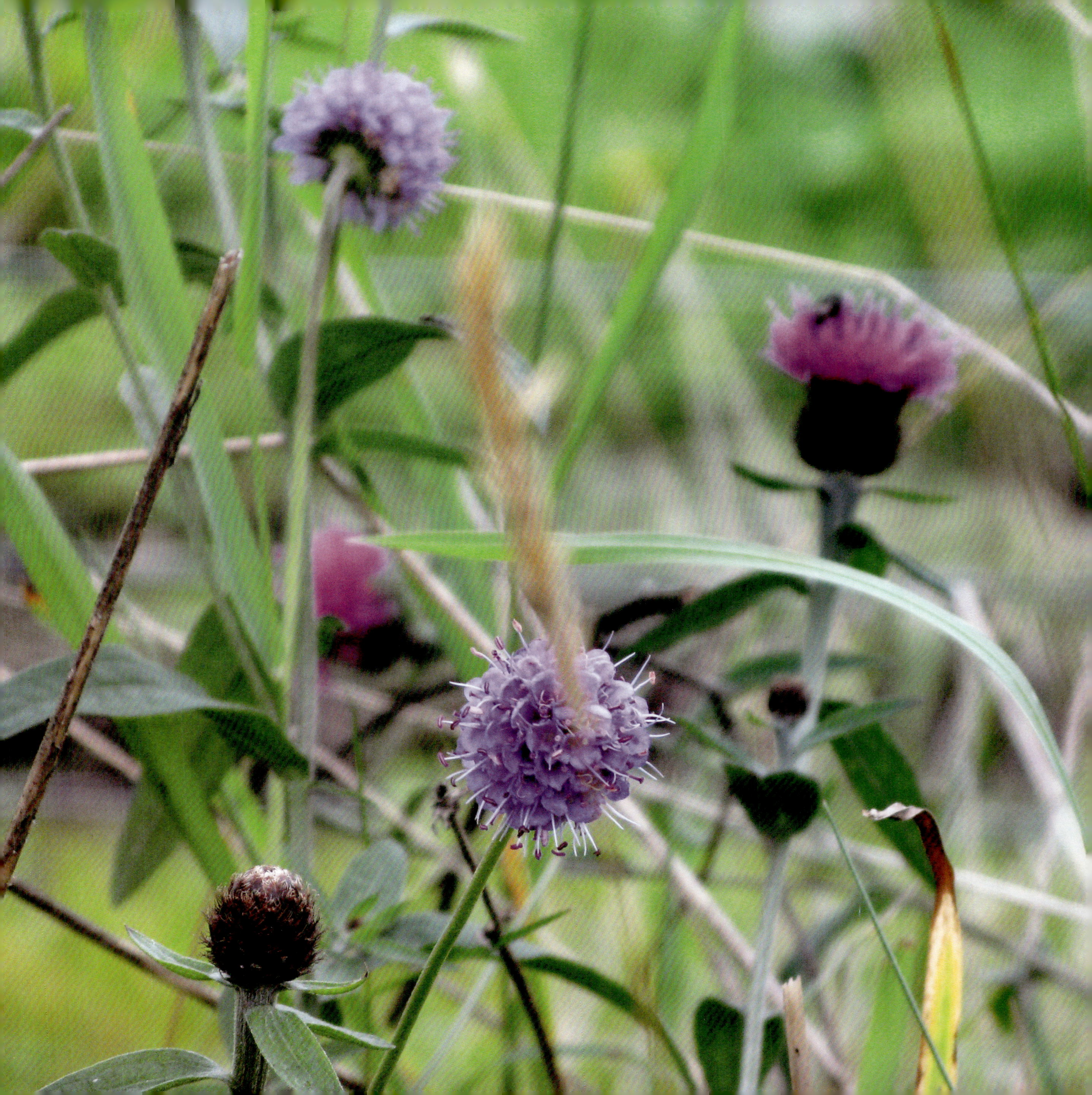

Meadow and Garden

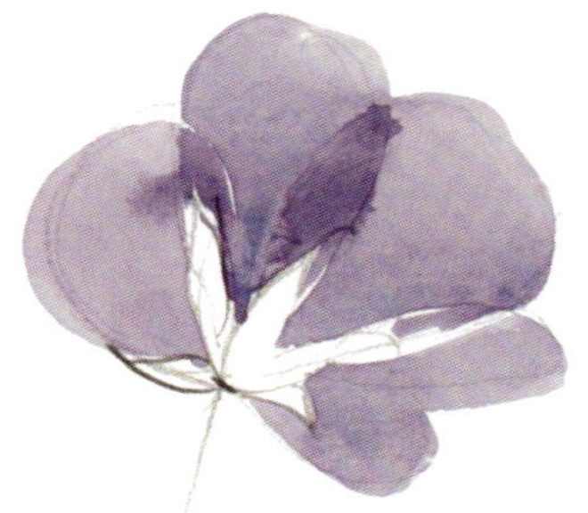

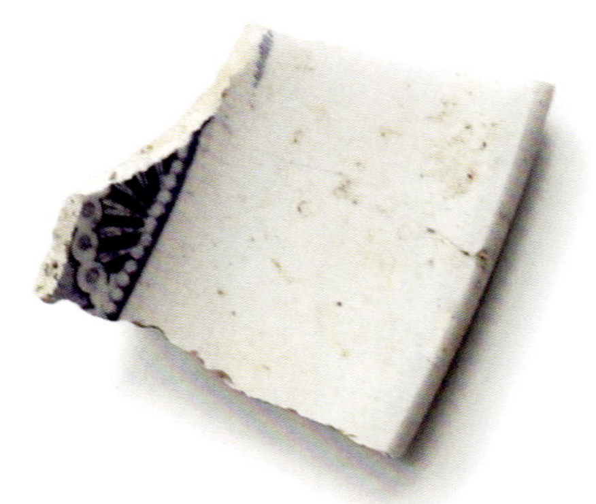

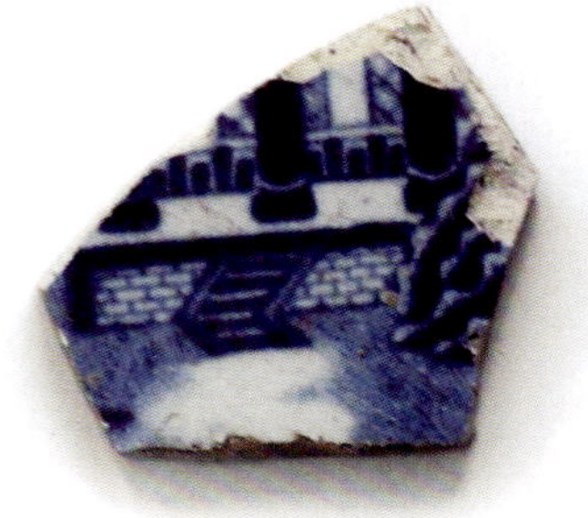

The prints representing plants that grow in meadows and those that show plants Angie Lewin grows in her garden are, she says, closely related, and if Lewin's Scottish coastal prints are the harsh side of her work, these are its gentle side. Some people consider many native British plants that grow in the wild to be weeds, but for Lewin their spiky looks and strong contours make them valuable: 'I love the huge variety of wild grasses, left uncut. When I get down to ground level, there are clovers, plantains, chickweed and dandelions, in close-up.'

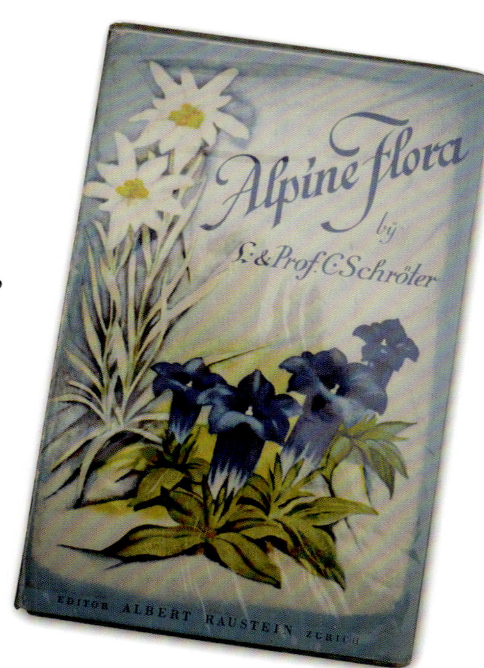

Among Lewin's early work is a group of prints based on dandelions. These are interesting because they show how images of a single plant can be developed by a skilled printmaker. The dandelion prints vary from a close-up look at the seed head (*Dandelion IV*, measuring less than 5 × 5 cm/2 × 2 in.; see page 132) and a larger image that includes both the buds and seed heads (*Clocks II*; see page 135), to an image in which the clock is accompanied by a small plantain (*Dandelion I*; see page 132). *Dandelion III* (see page 39) teams the clock with a striped feather.

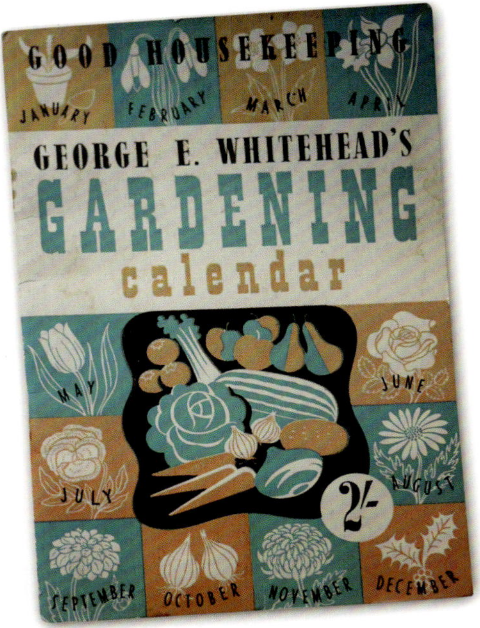

Lewin's botanically derived prints are rarely highly colourful – many are subdued, soft or downright monochrome – but among those that show her at her most decorative are the ones taken from her garden, where she grows geraniums, lupins, daisies, poppies and evening primrose. 'I grow plants that I am inspired to sketch and develop into prints', she says. 'How a plant appears when it has gone to seed is important. Structure is important, as are plants with open frameworks that create a sense of depth and make the layering of plants visible.'

The screenprint *Wild Garden II* (see page 161) relies on native plants to produce one of Lewin's most decorative works, showing the seed heads of columbines, the flat heads of achillea (yarrow) and the herb *Sanguisorba* (burnet). The daisy-like shapes that spring against a pale-yellow sky turn out to be seed heads. This print was, she says, inspired by illustrated natural history books of the 1950s.

A tiny wood engraving, *Anemone* (see page 129), represents Japanese anemones' round, white seed heads and their tiny black seeds. The print shows Lewin working at her most abstract, although still with plant forms.

Most of Lewin's prints are quite small, some of them smaller than 5 × 5 cm / 2 × 2 in., but one of the largest is *Agapanthus* (see page 123), a lithograph measuring 45 × 71 cm (17⅝ × 28 in.). A row of these tender garden plants, which have the same cup-shaped heads as, say, alexanders or fennel, reaches proudly up into a green sky; beneath them a mix of plants includes *Phlomis* (Jerusalem sage), scabious, the seed pods of *Lychnis coronaria* (rose campion) and the heads of *Coreopsis* (tickseed, or calliopsis) after the petals have fallen. The whole writhes with energy.

The plants Lewin represents are not exclusively native to Britain. *Blue Meadow* (see page 131) was sketched in northern Mallorca: wild carrot, its purple umbels here portrayed in a brilliant scarlet-orange, make the foreground, almost obscuring a blue-grey stone wall and background mountain; the umbels' brilliant orange is reprised in the sun shining in the sky. Watermelon-pink is used for the poppy heads and umbels in *Red Meadow* (see page 149) – another foreign field, judging by the full tangerine sun in the sky.

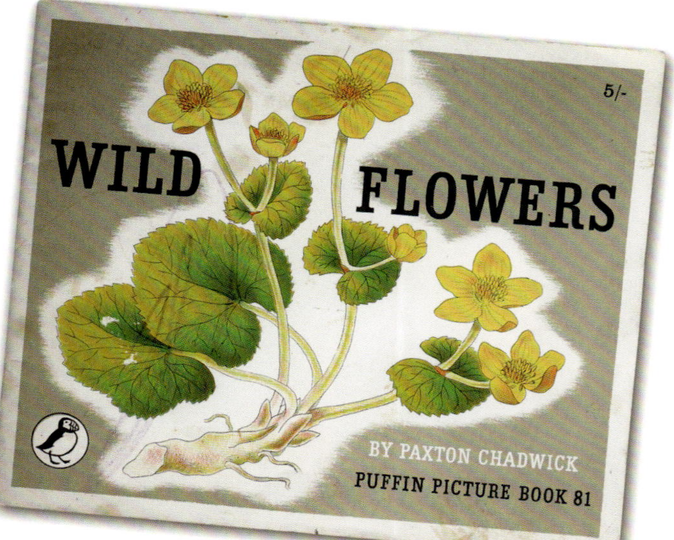

Opposite and left: Some of Lewin's collection of old gardening books and wild-flower guides. Above: Sketch for Hidden Fish *(see page 139).*

'A row of these tender garden plants
reaches proudly up into a green sky'

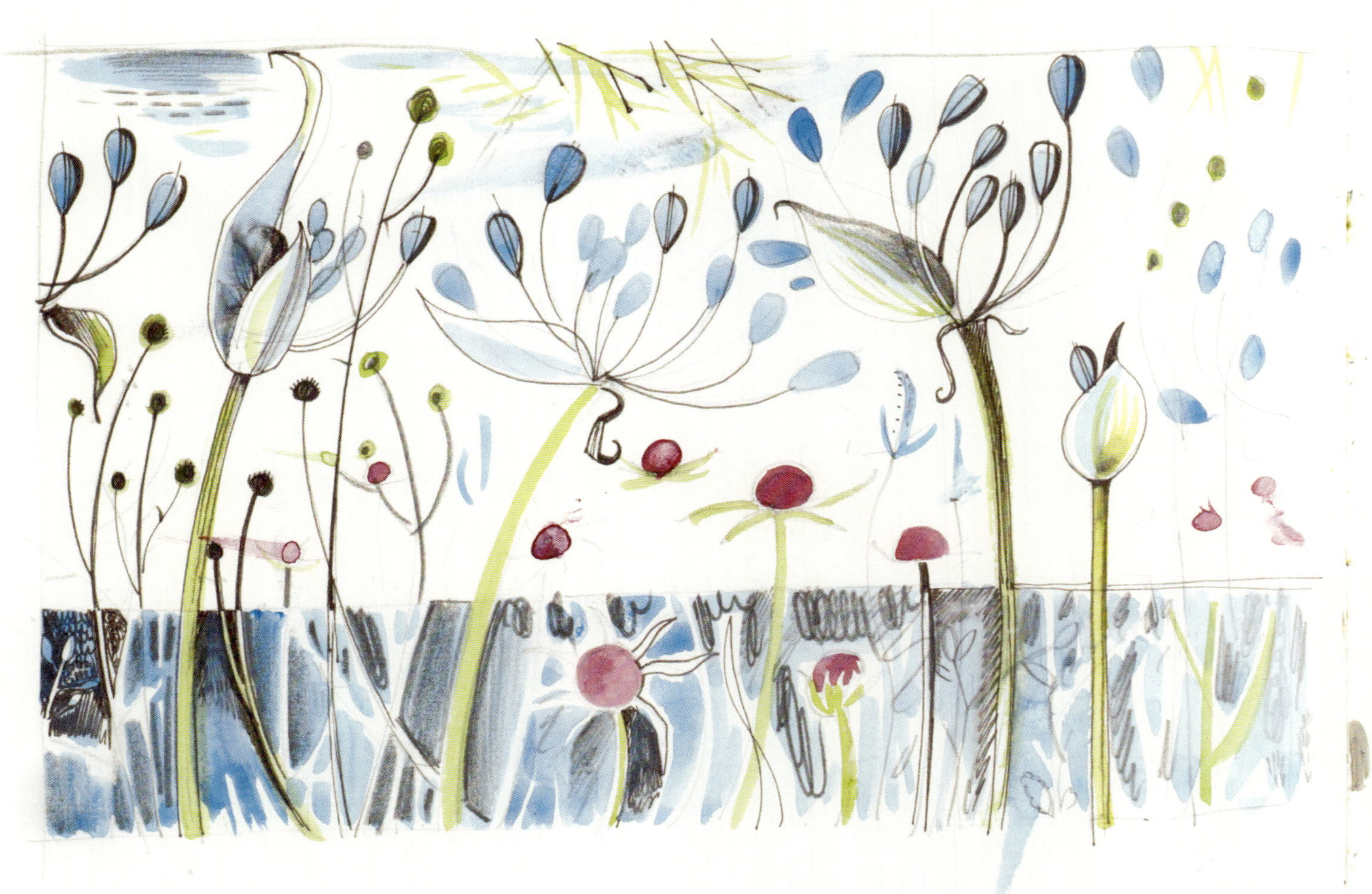

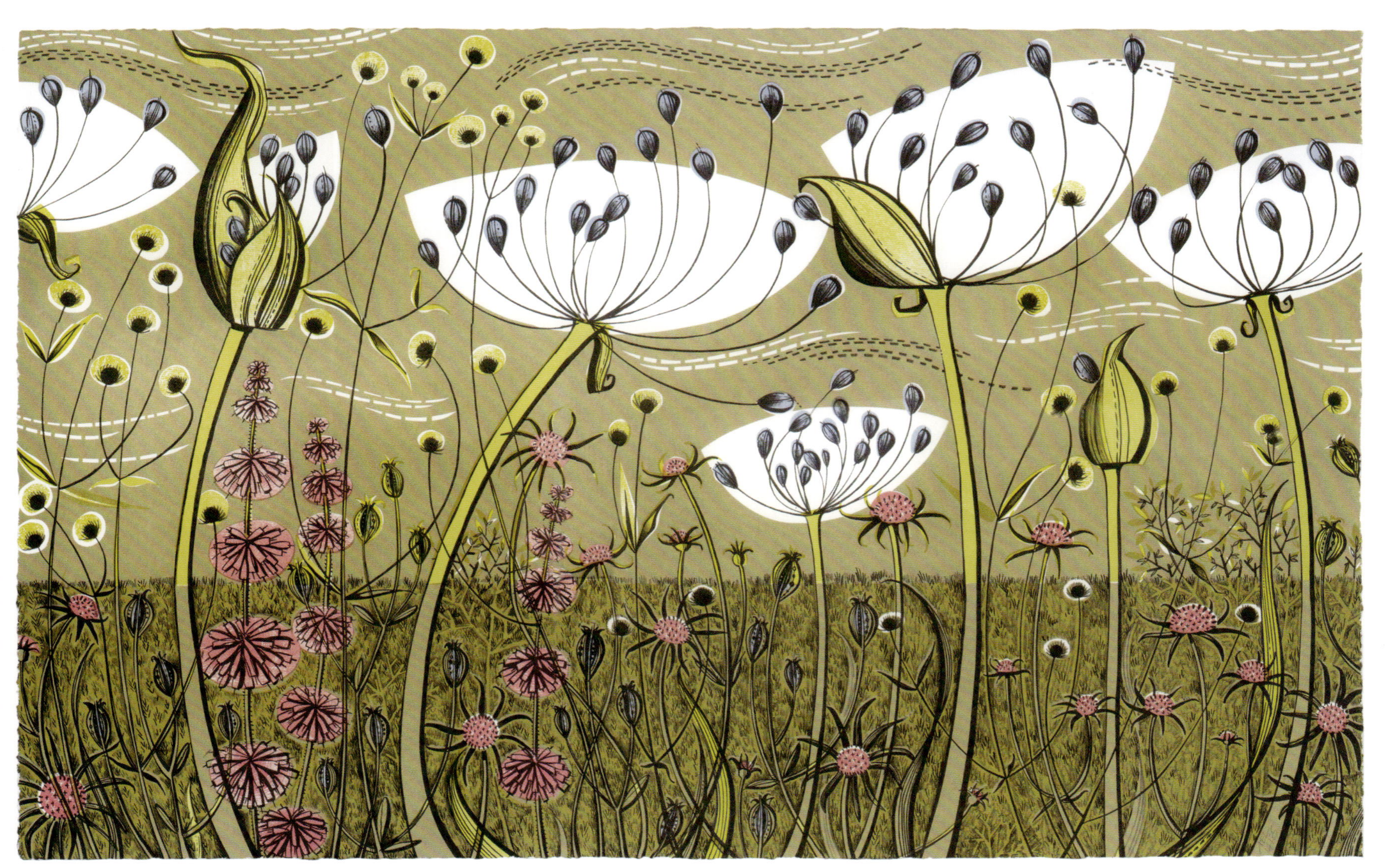

Agapanthus

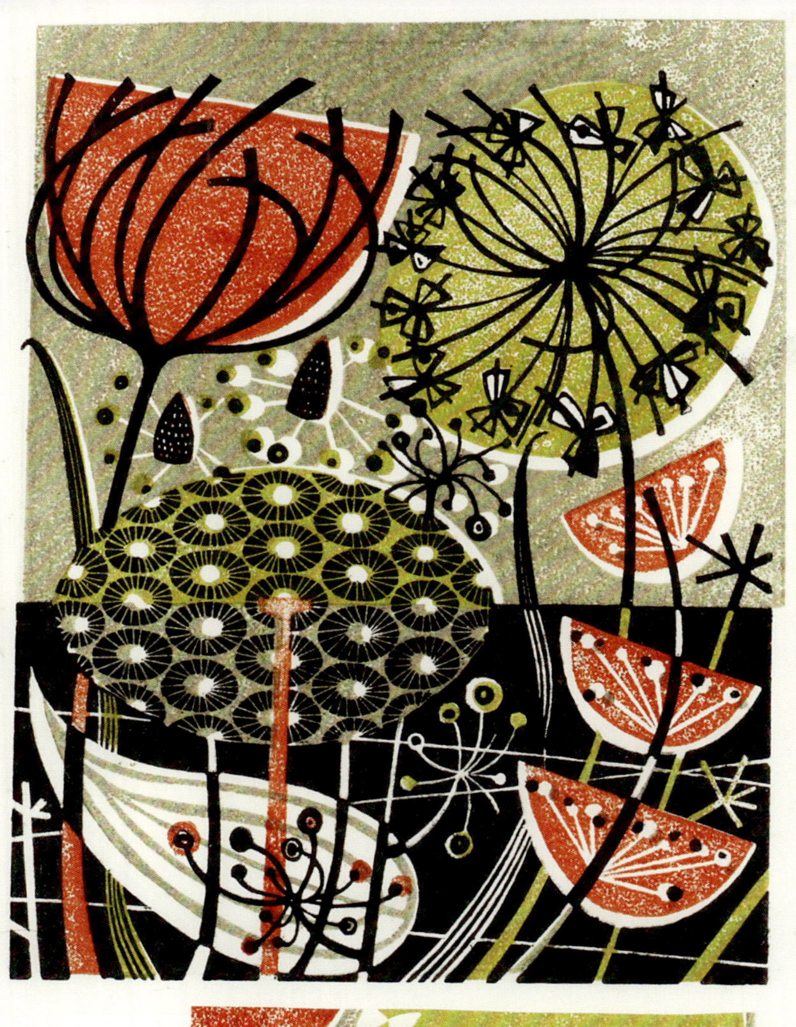

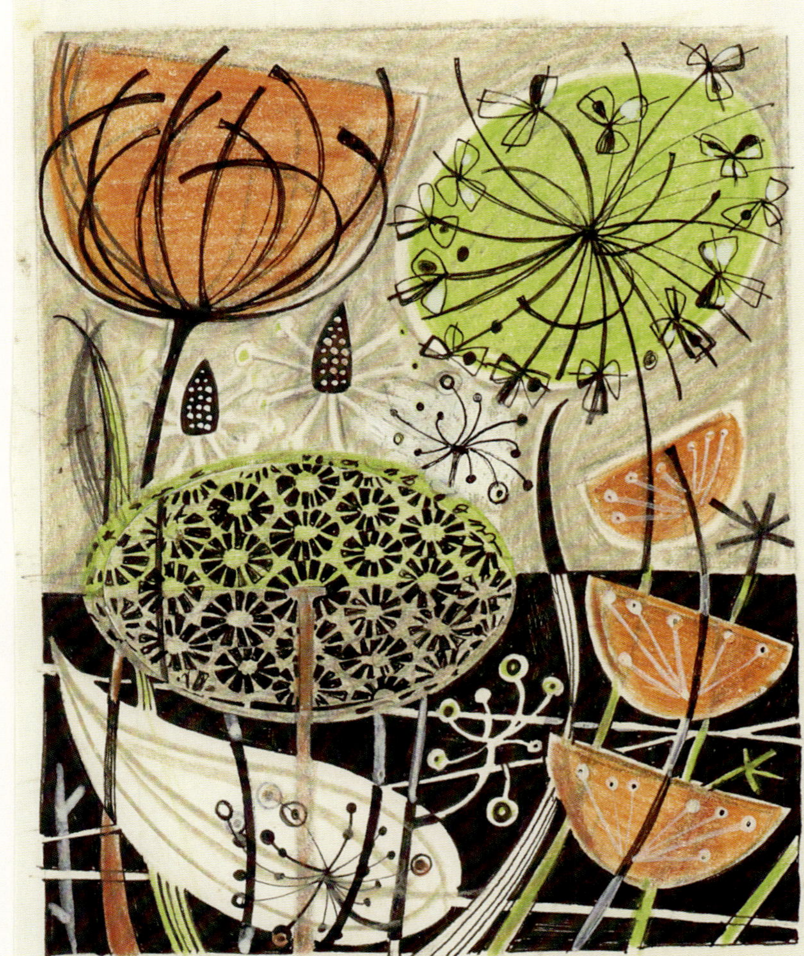
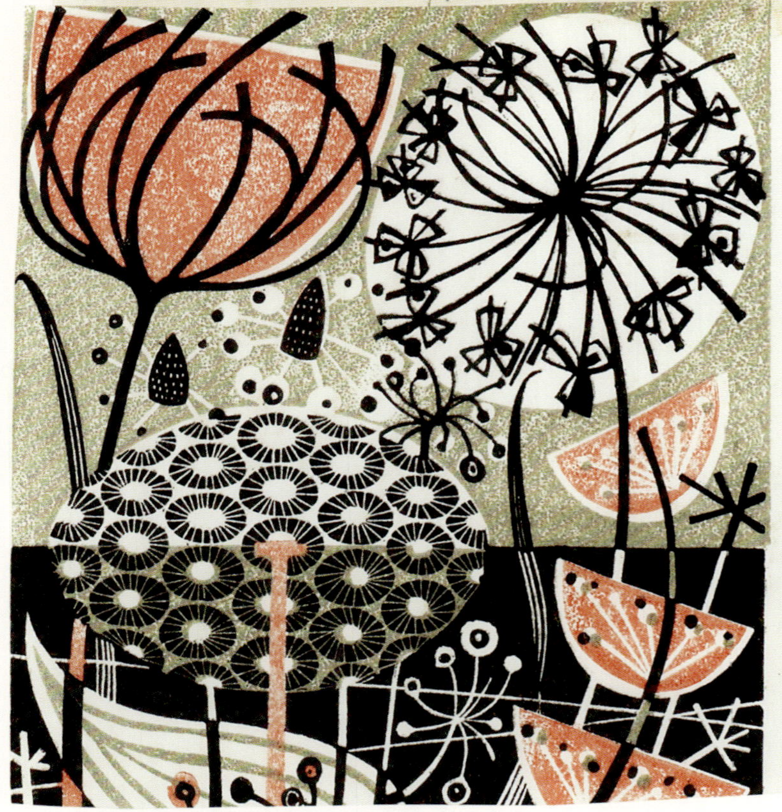

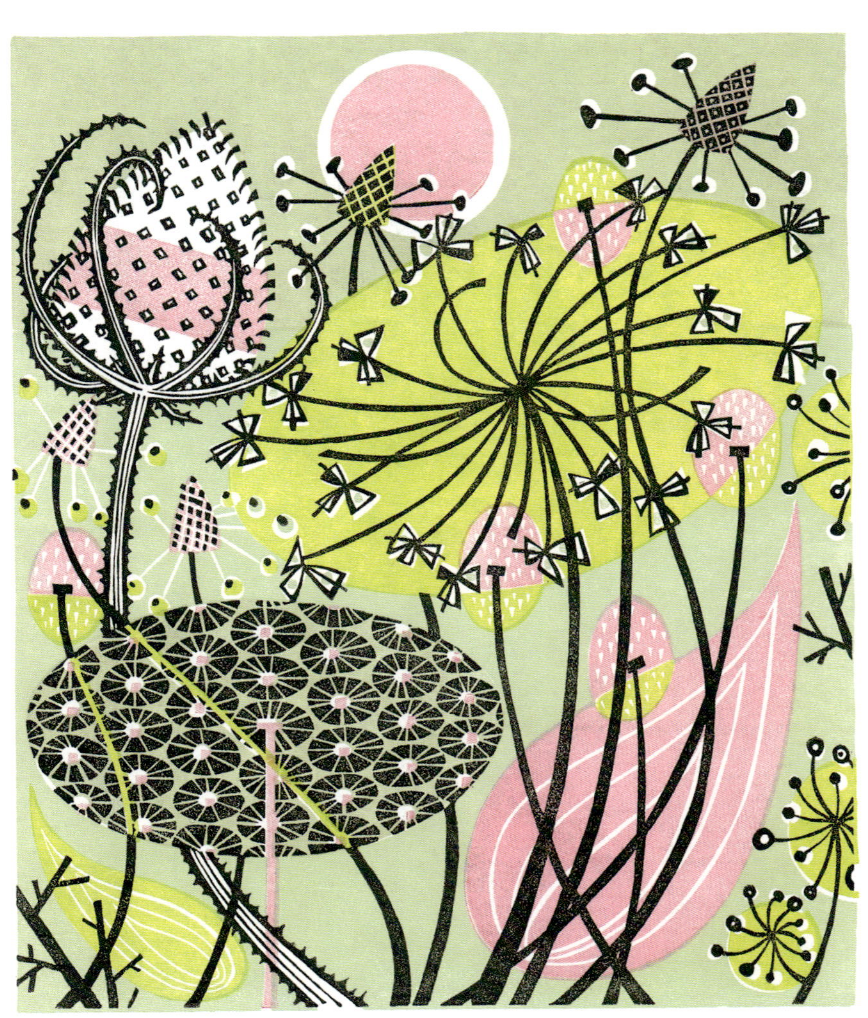

Alliums

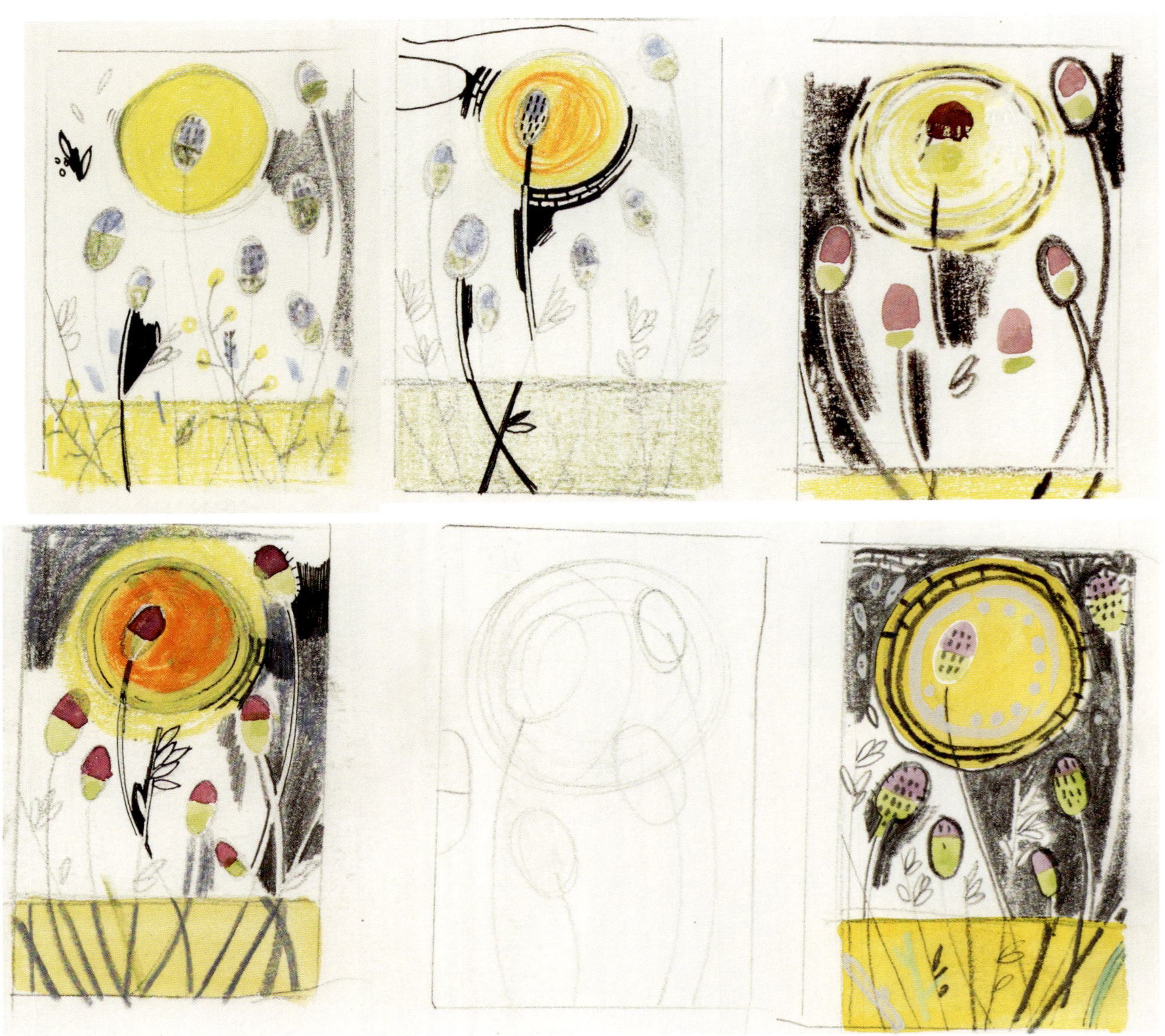

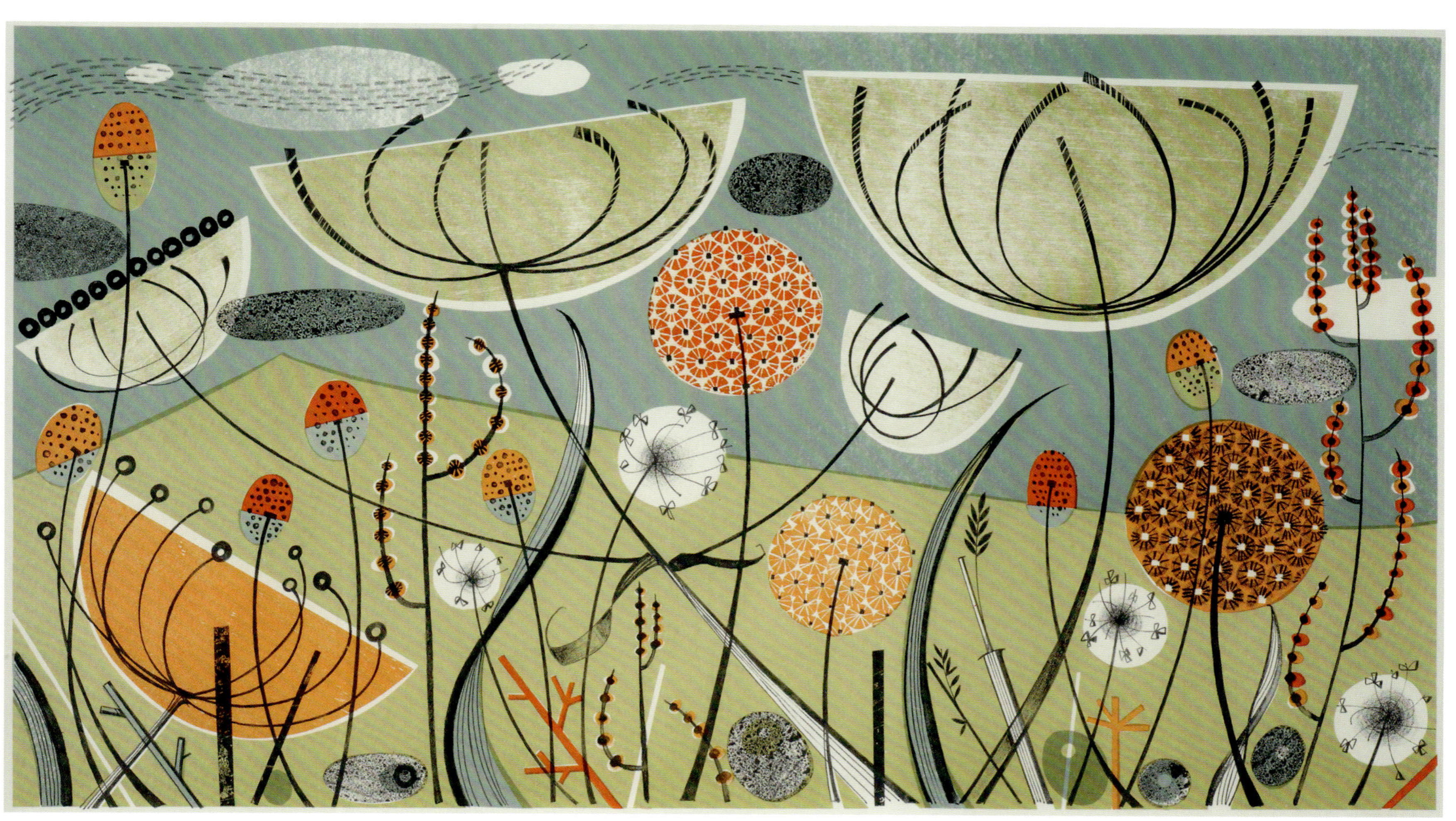

Alliums and Fennel

'The silhouettes of Japanese anemone
seed heads on their twisting stems
recur in my drawings and prints.'

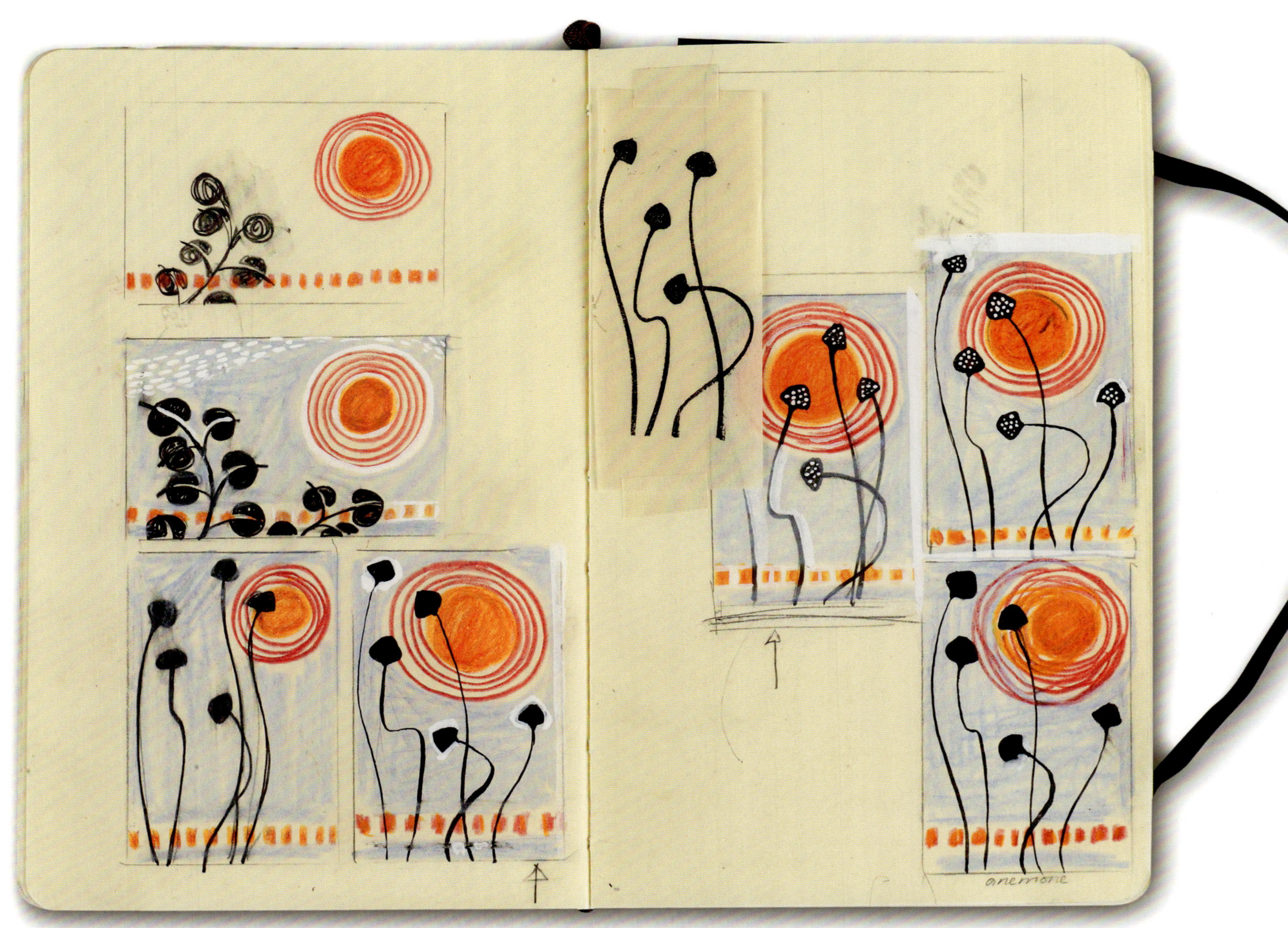

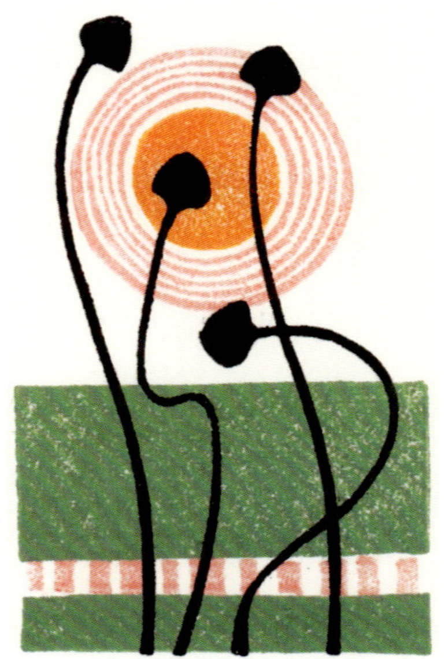

Anemone

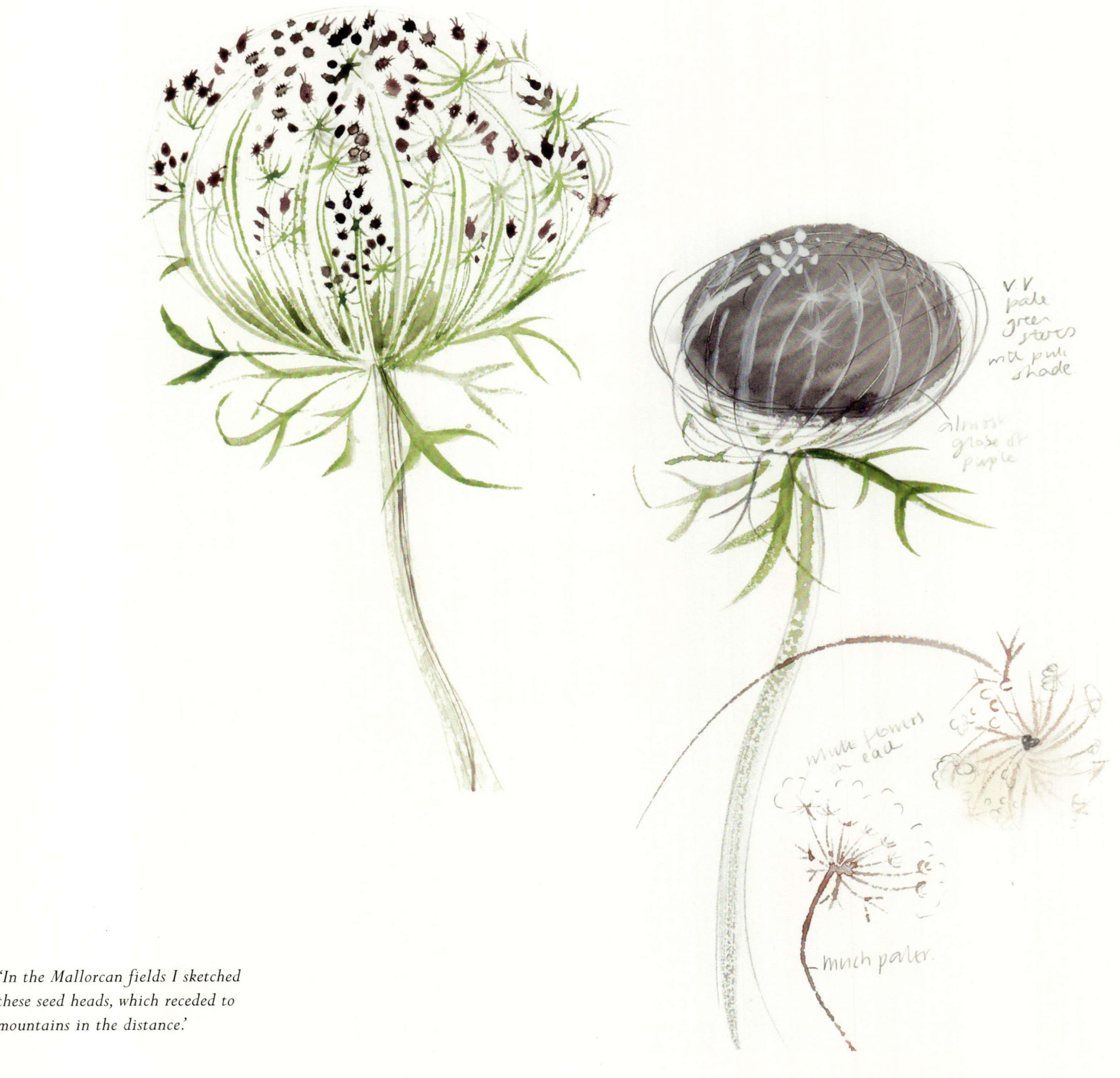

'In the Mallorcan fields I sketched
these seed heads, which receded to
mountains in the distance.'

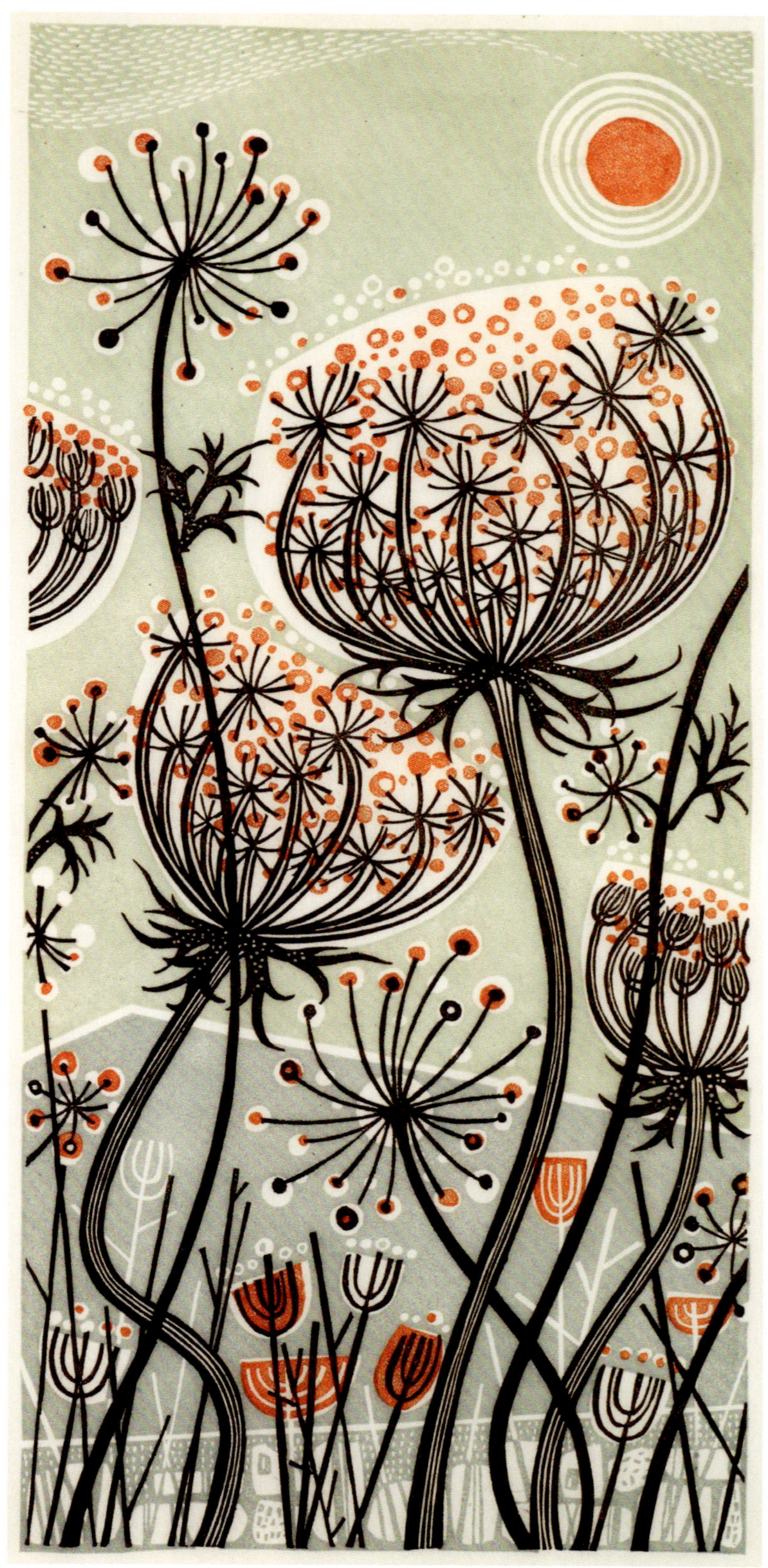

Blue Meadow

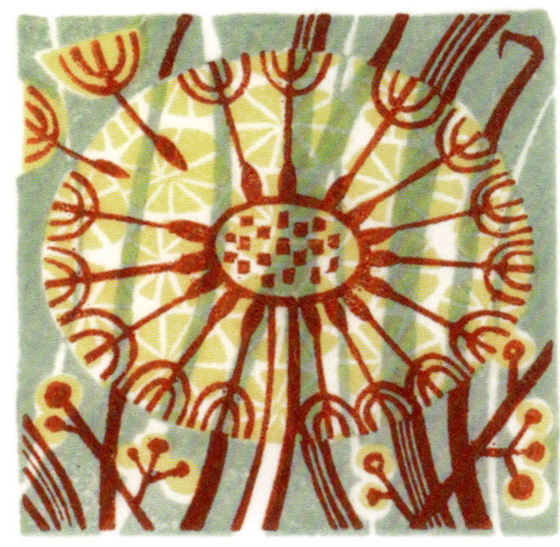

Dandelion IV

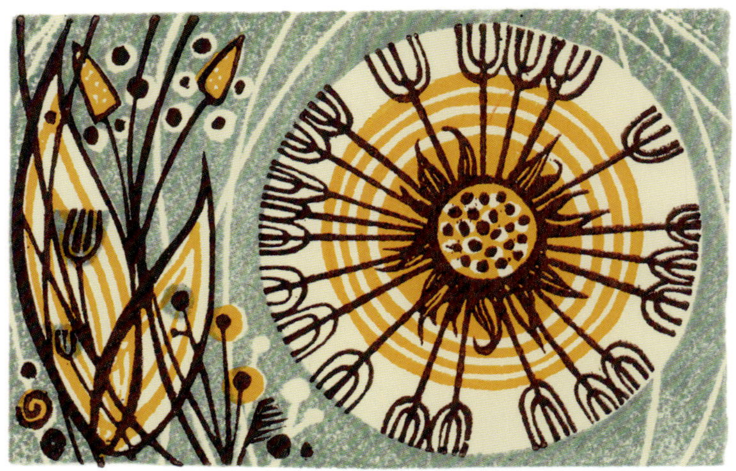

Dandelion I

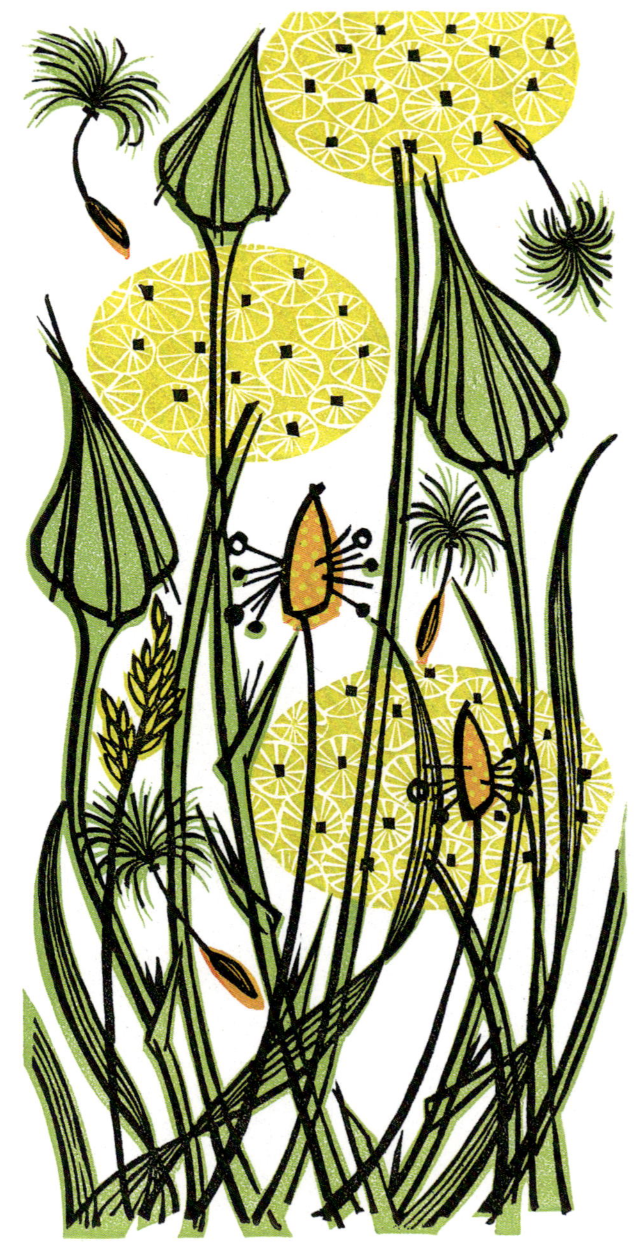

Goat's Beard II

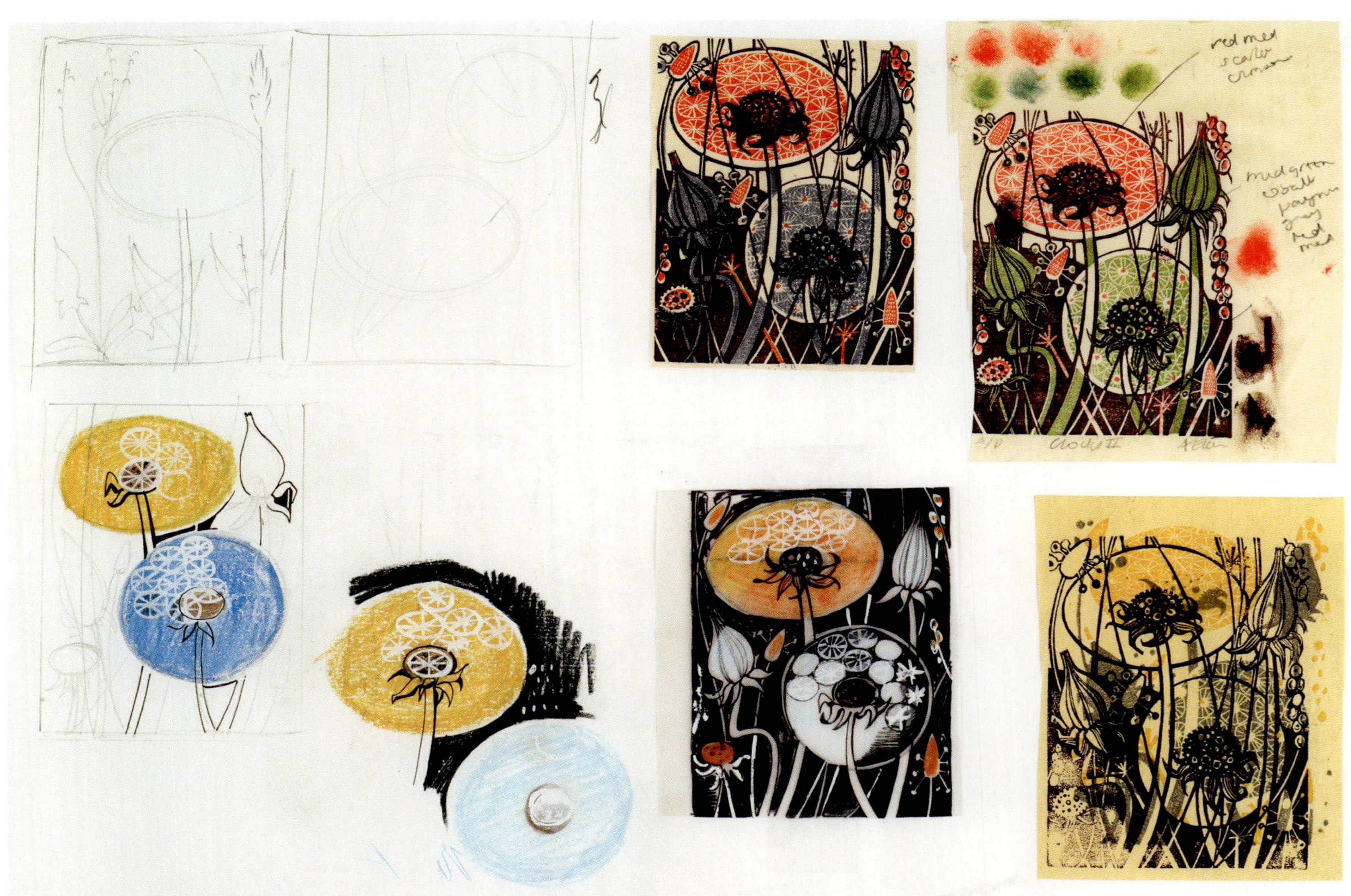
red med
scarlet
crimson
mid green
cobalt
payne
grey
red
med

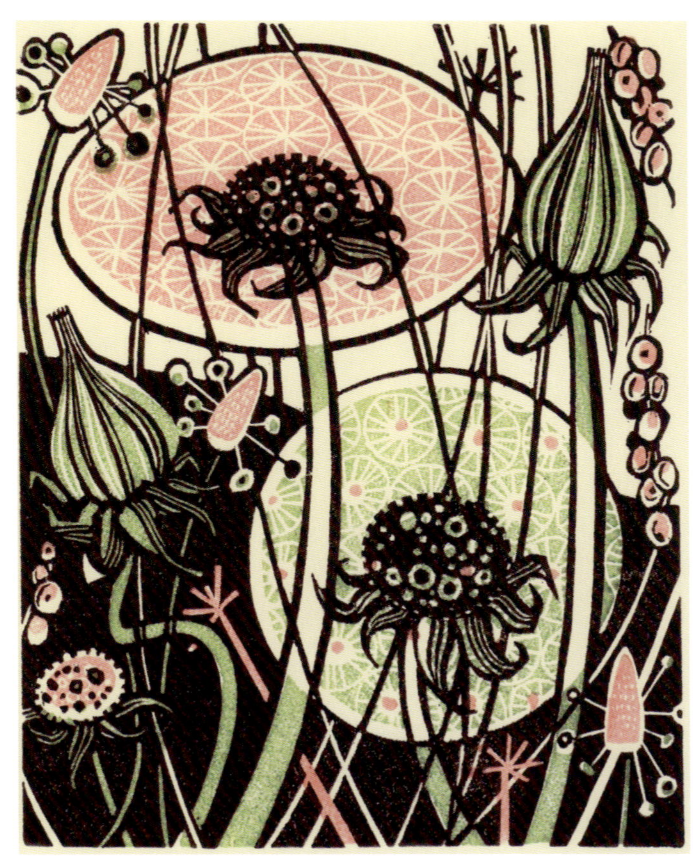

Clocks II

'open frameworks that create
a sense of depth'

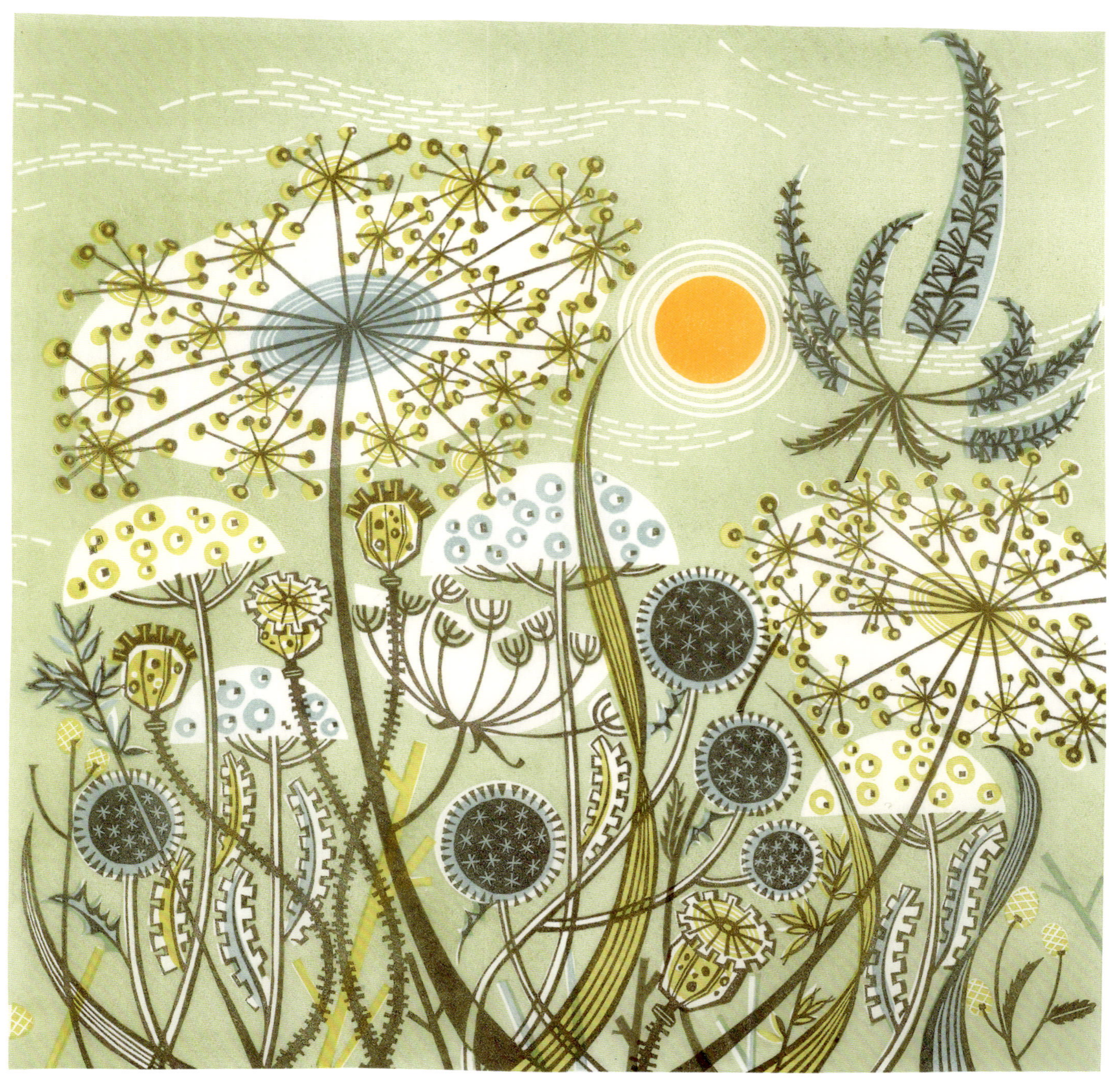

Green Meadow

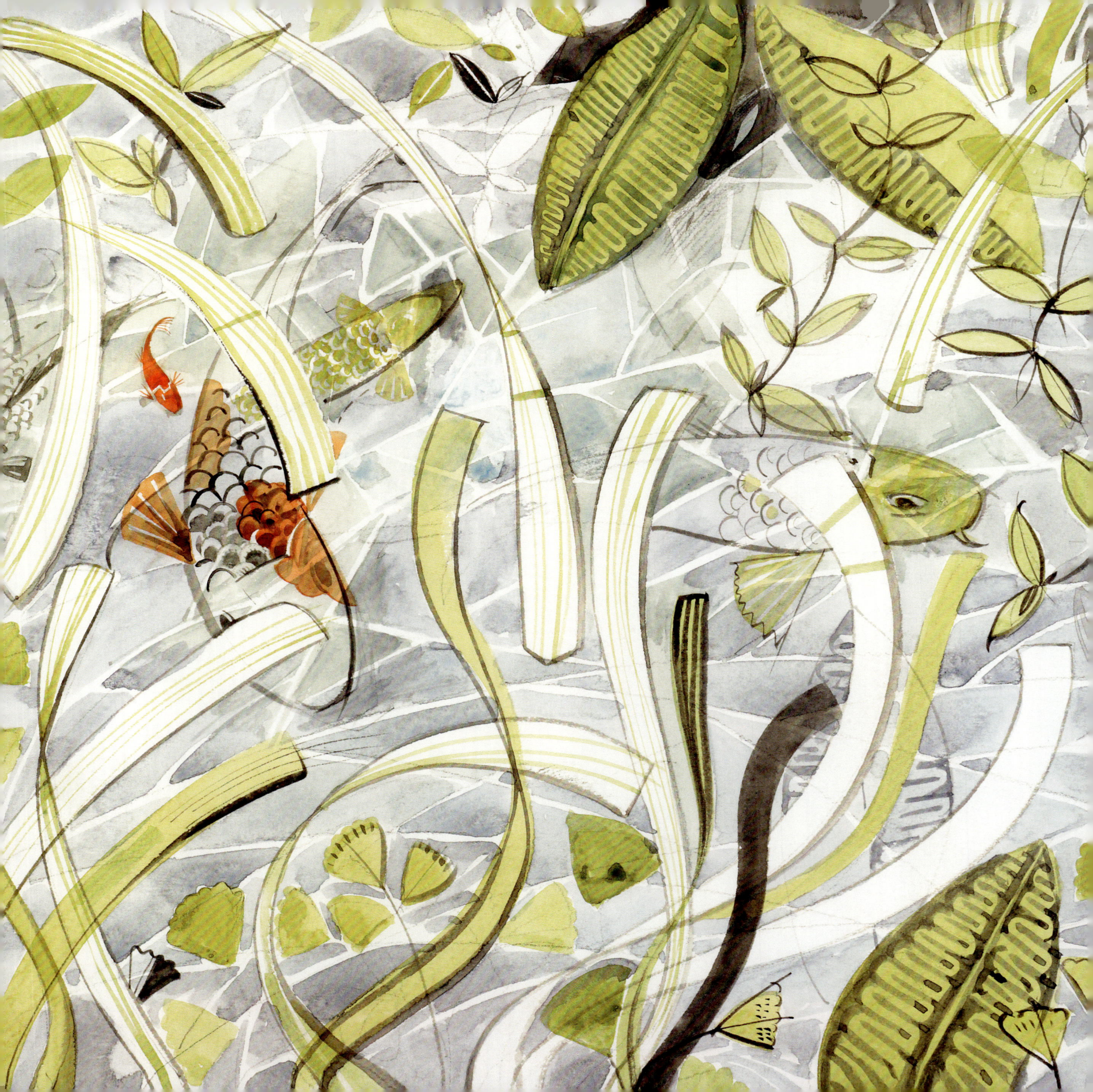

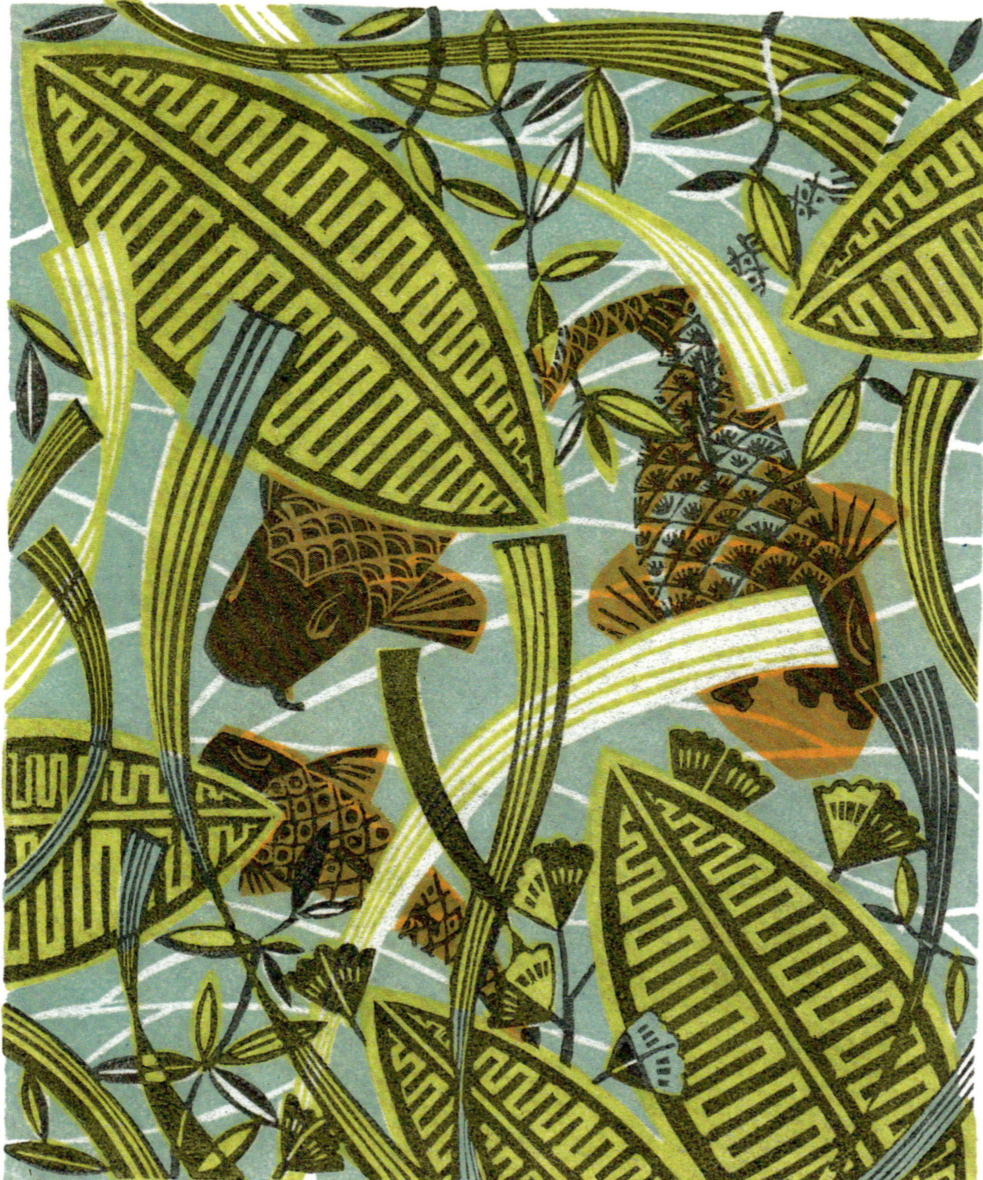

'I usually draw less exotic plants than these. Here koi carp swim beneath lush overhanging foliage in the conservatory at the Barbican, in London.'

Hidden Fish

'In my garden the boundaries between
wild and cultivated plants are blurred.'

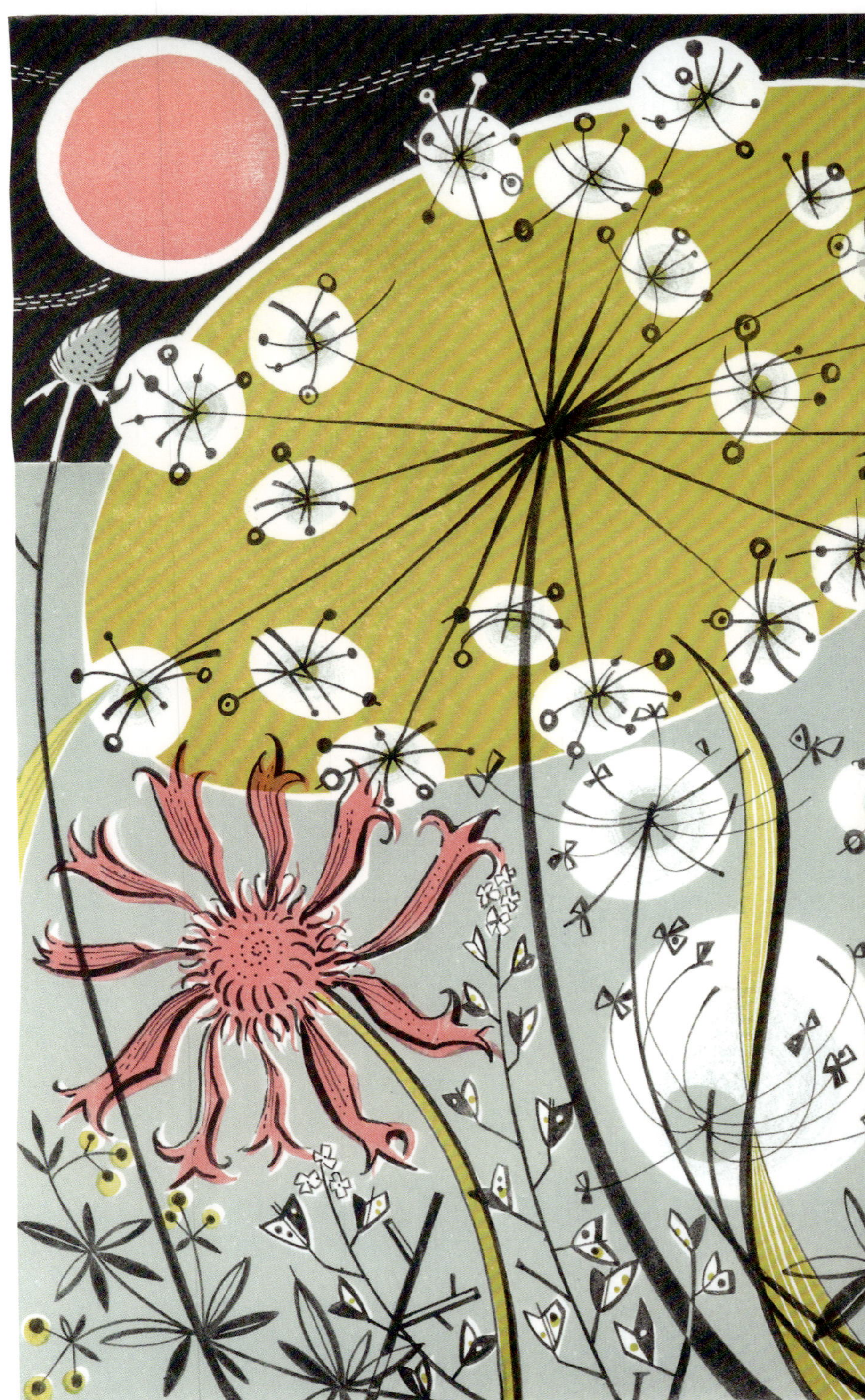

Meadow II

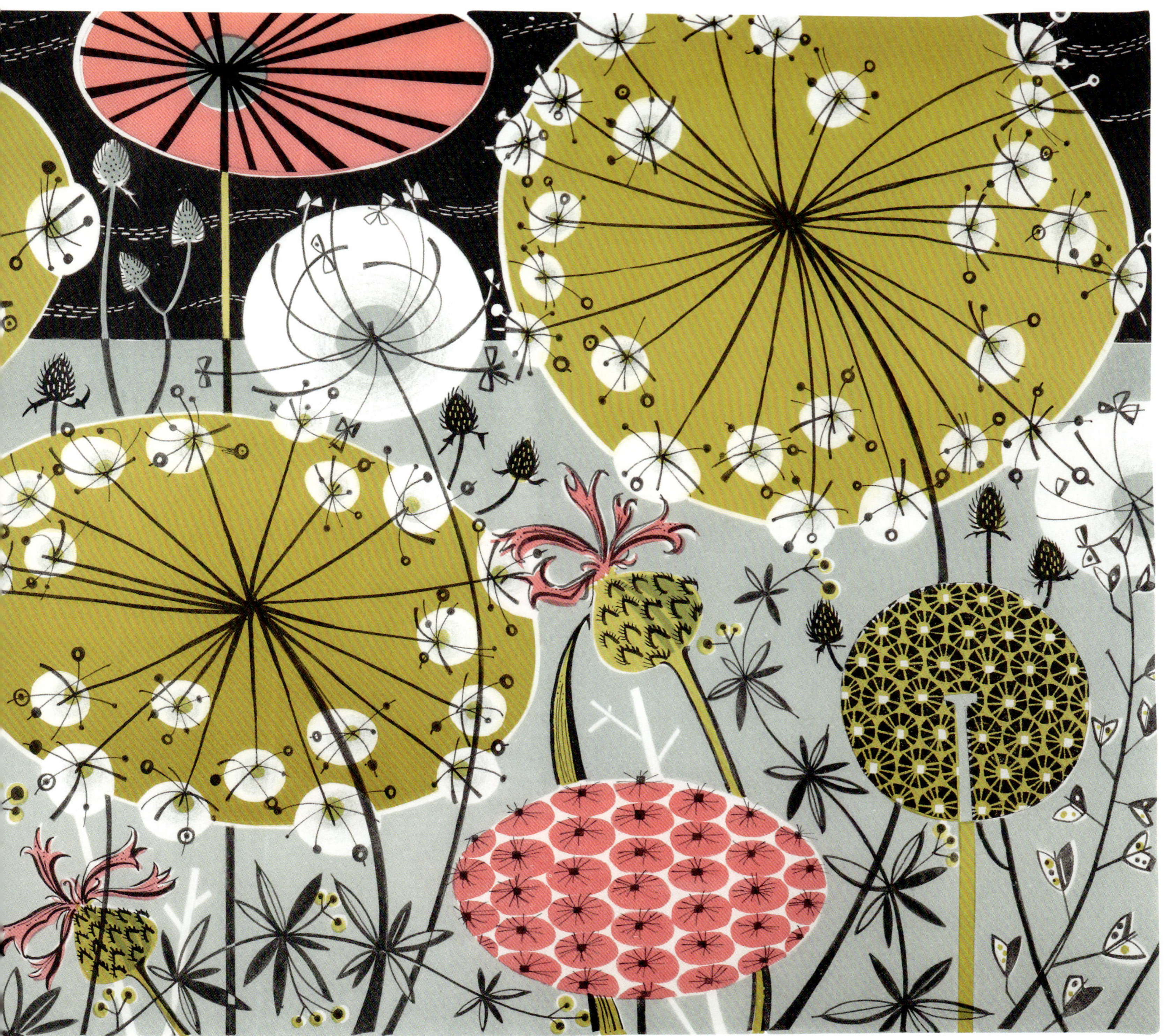

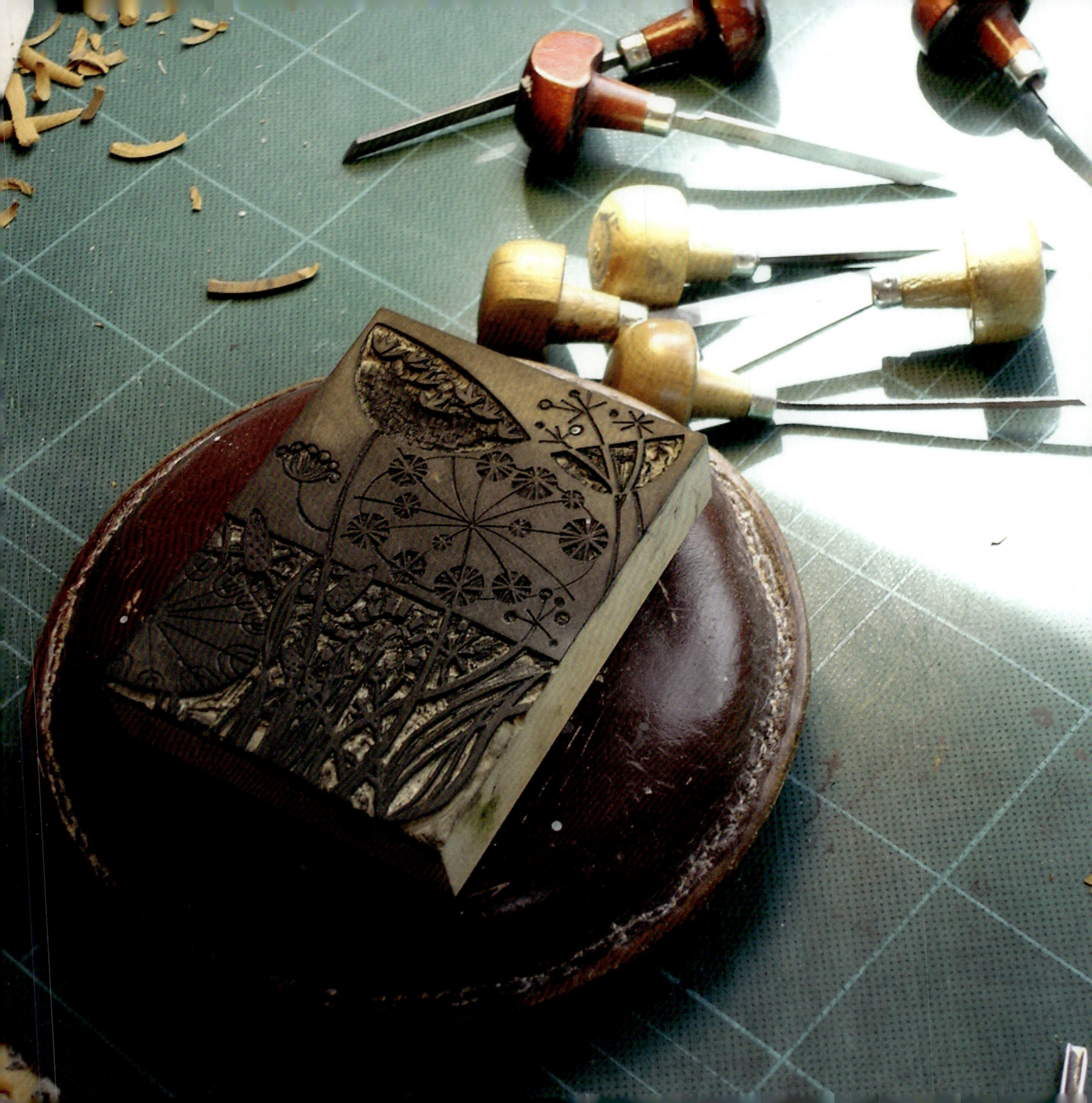

'Resting the woodblock on a leather
sandbag allows me to turn it smoothly
as I engrave.'

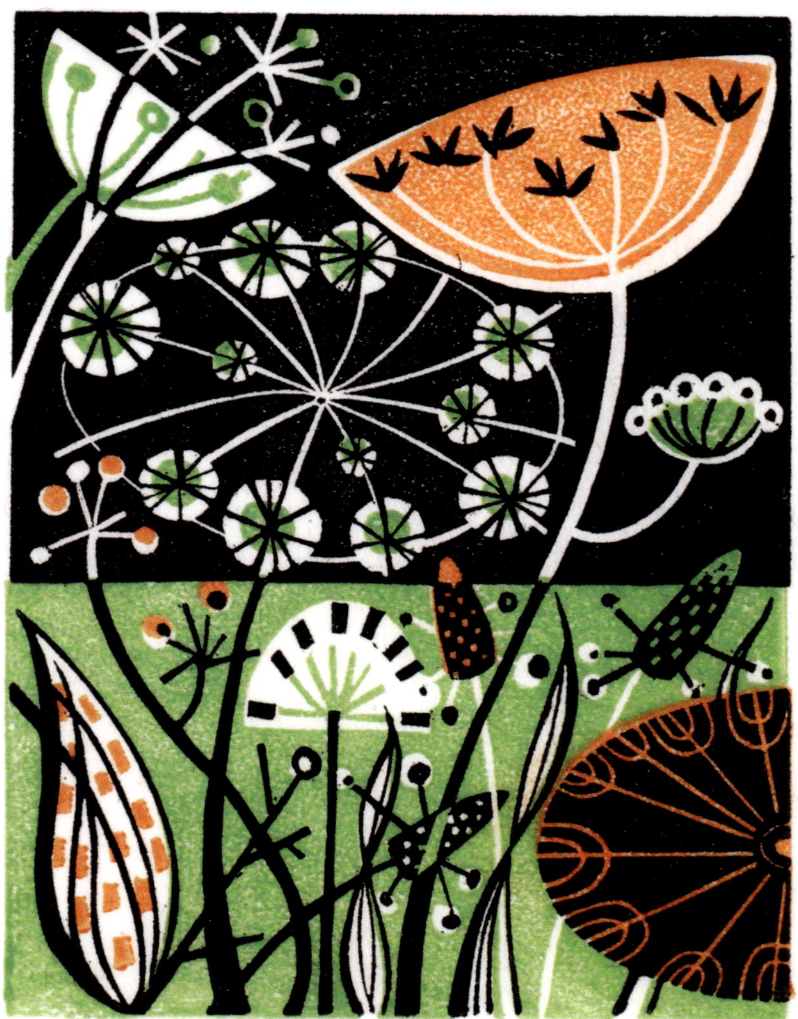

Meadow

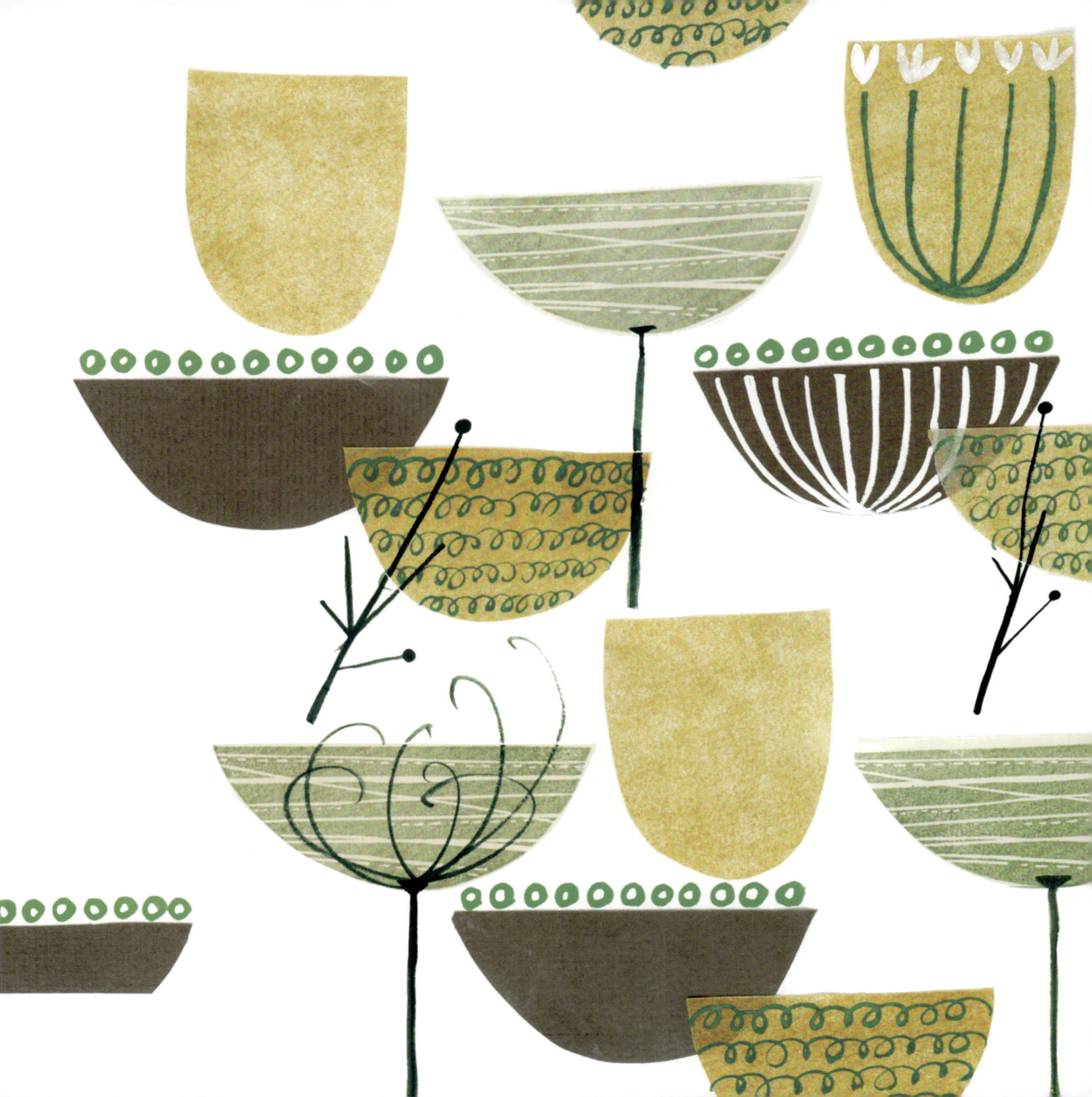

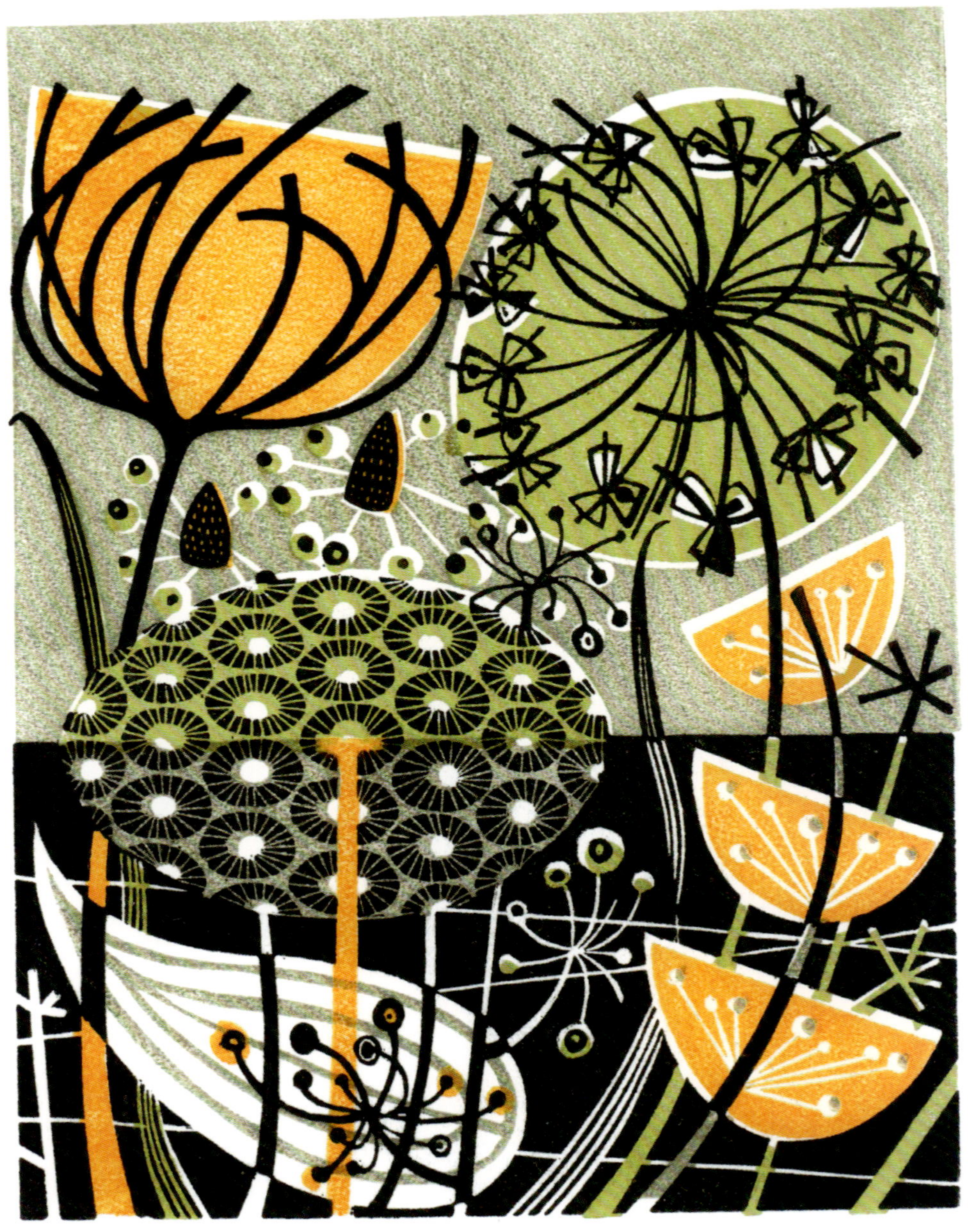

Meadow's Edge

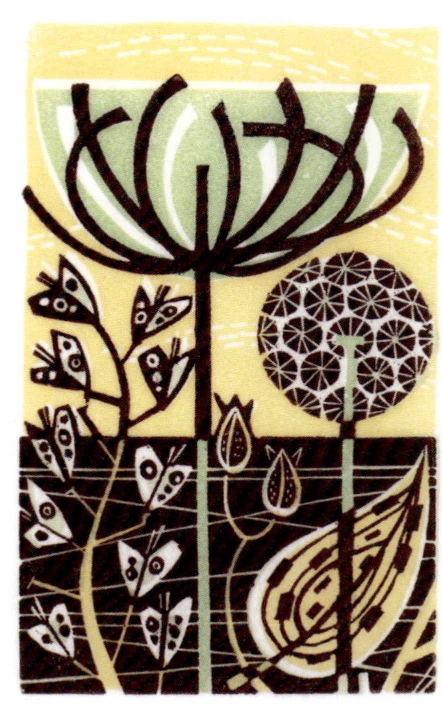

Pale Day

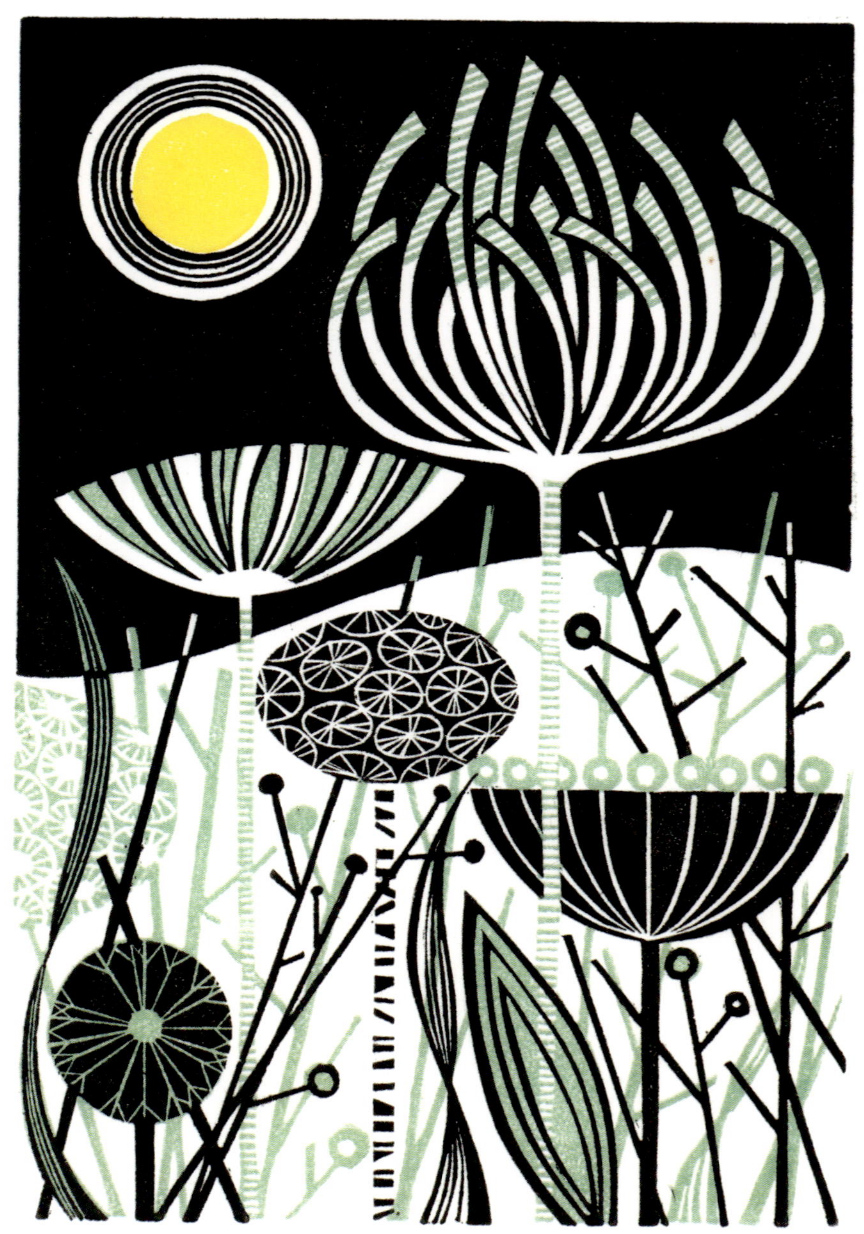

Moonlit

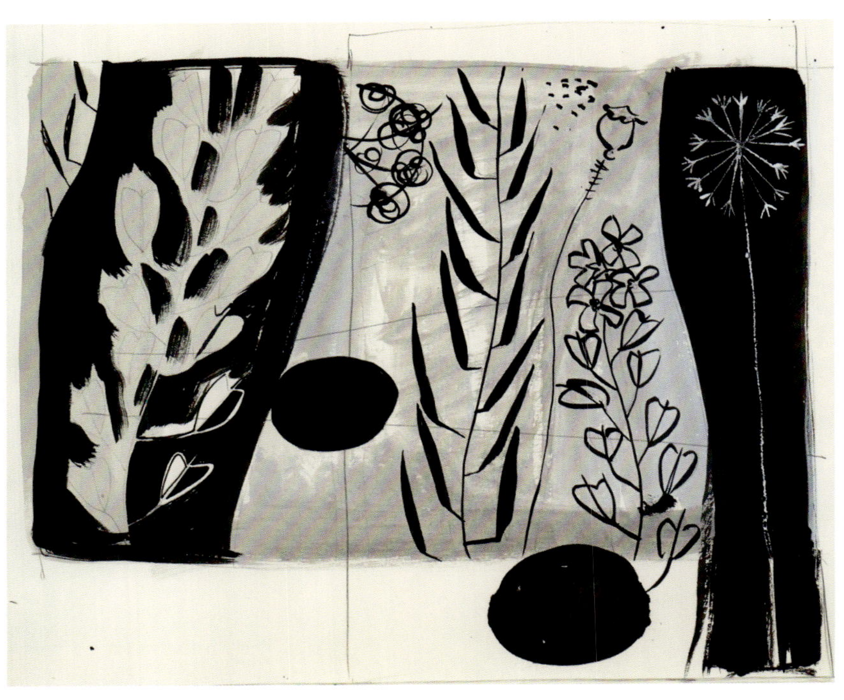

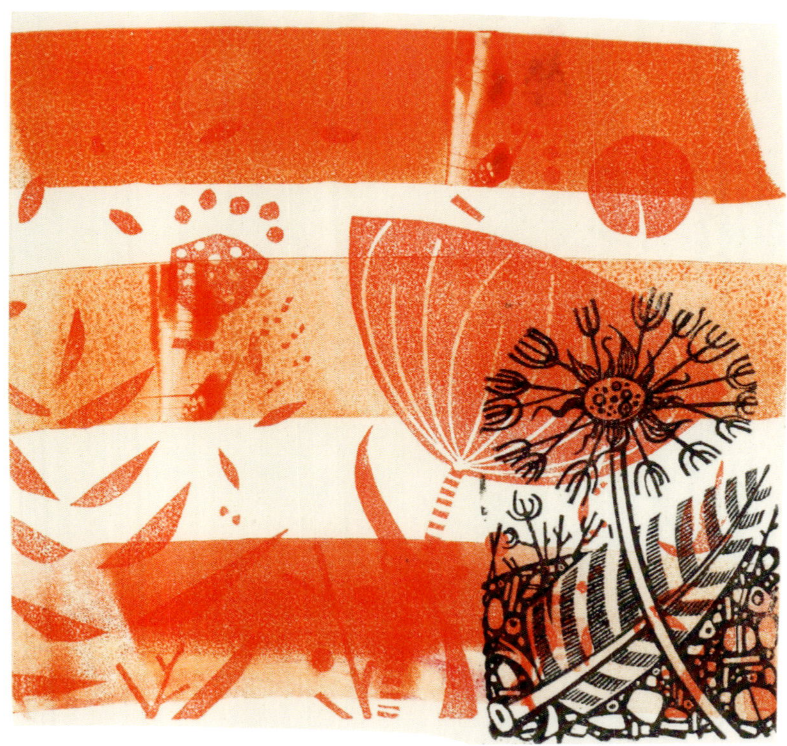

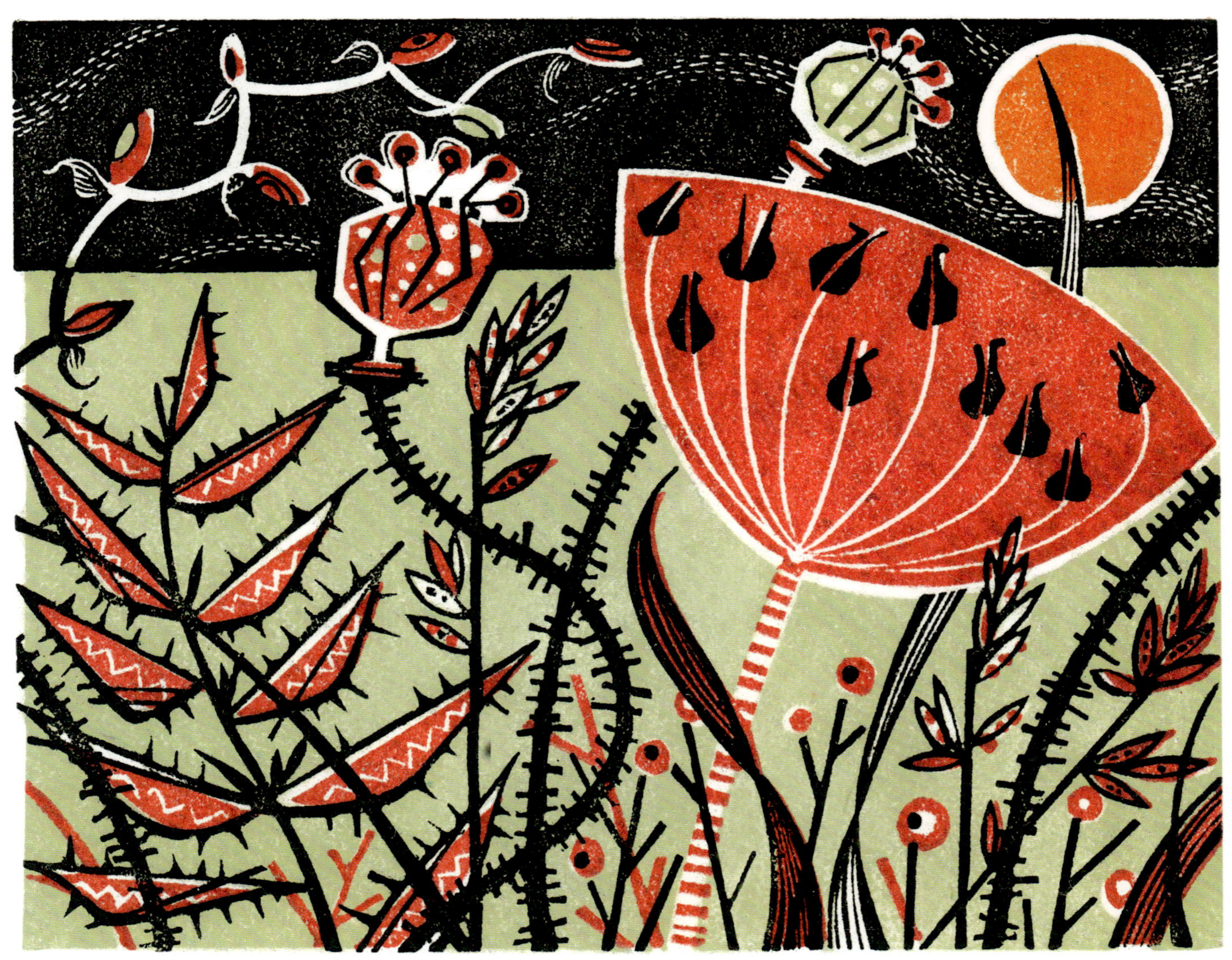

Red Meadow

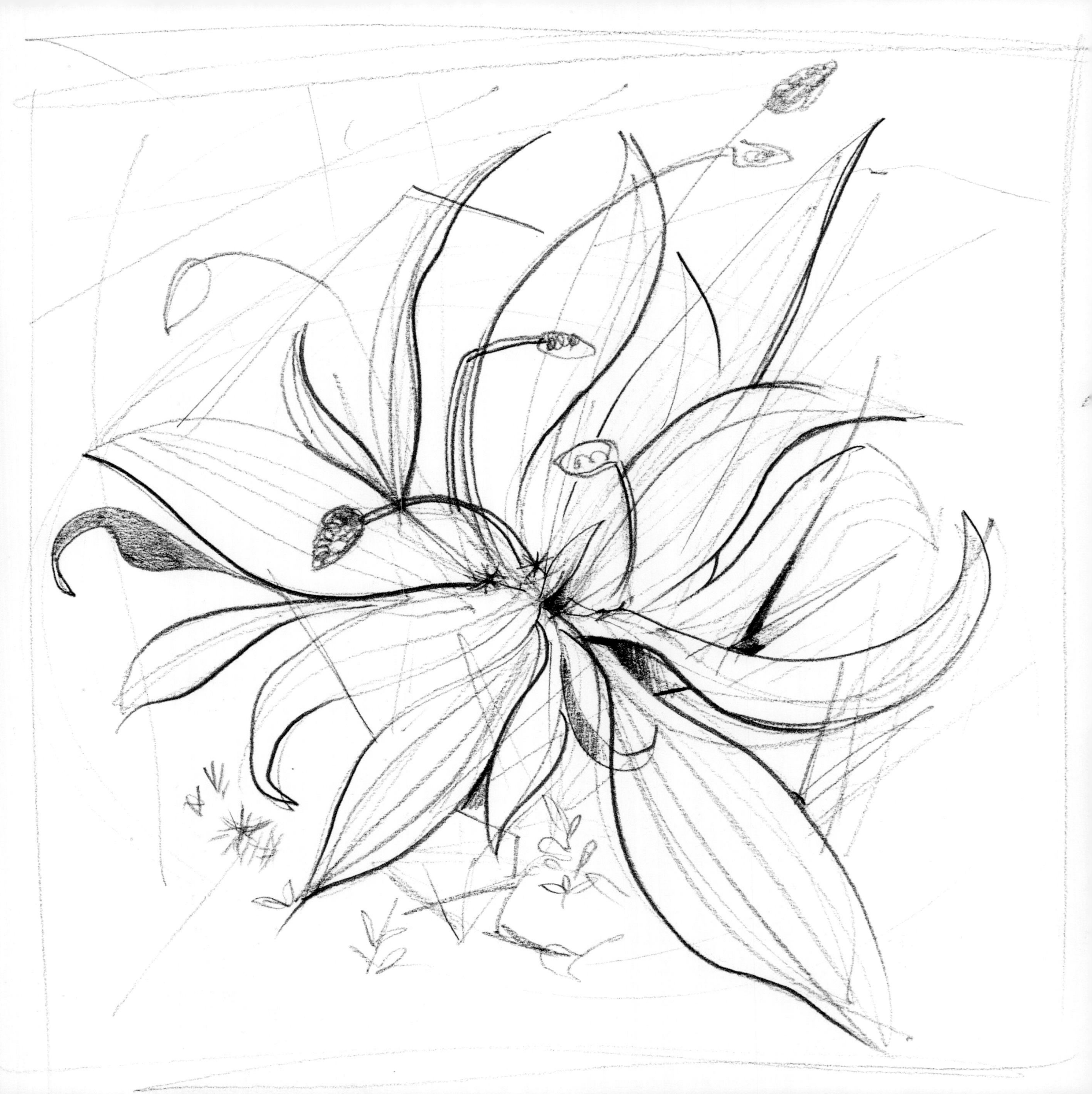

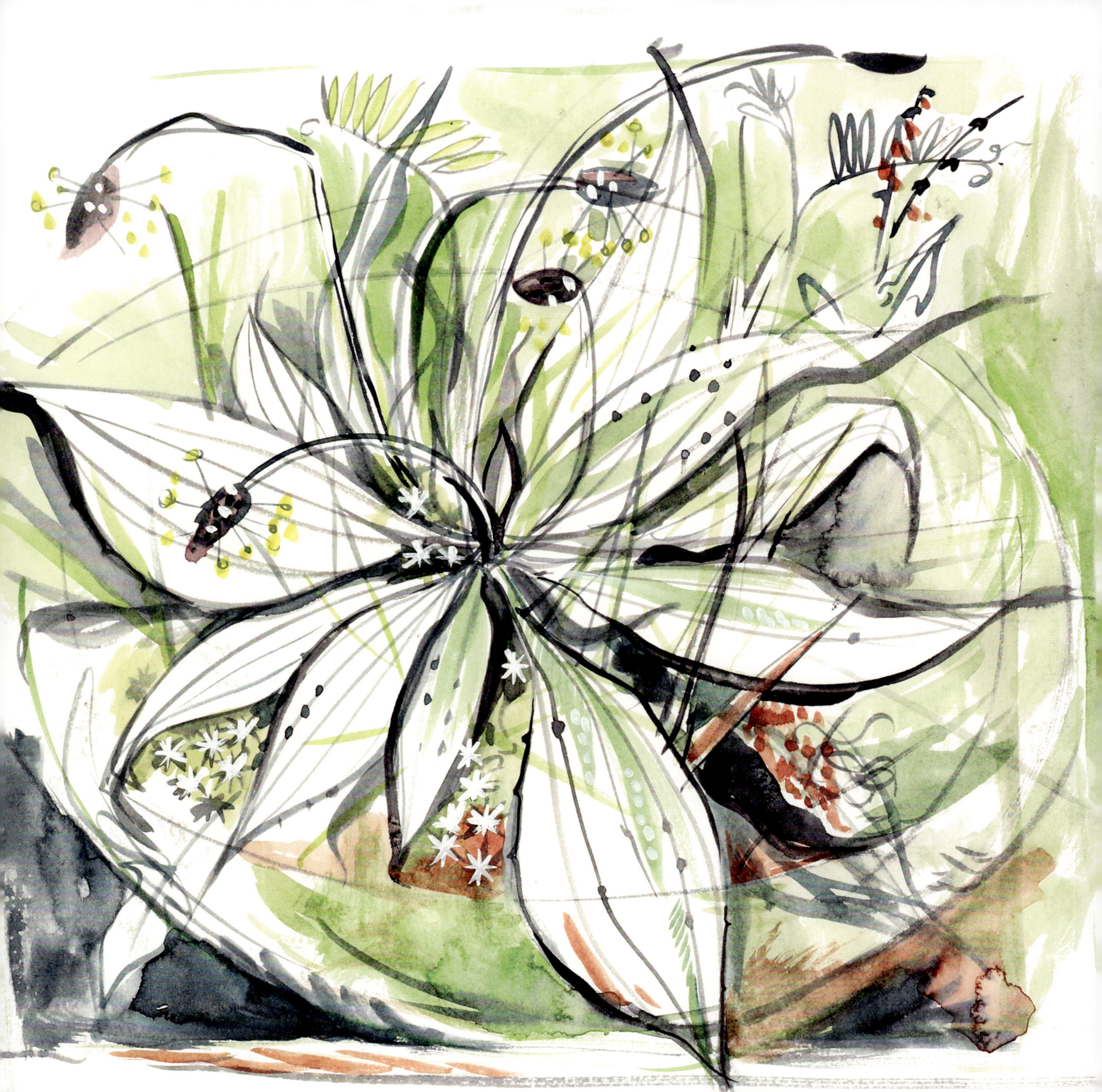

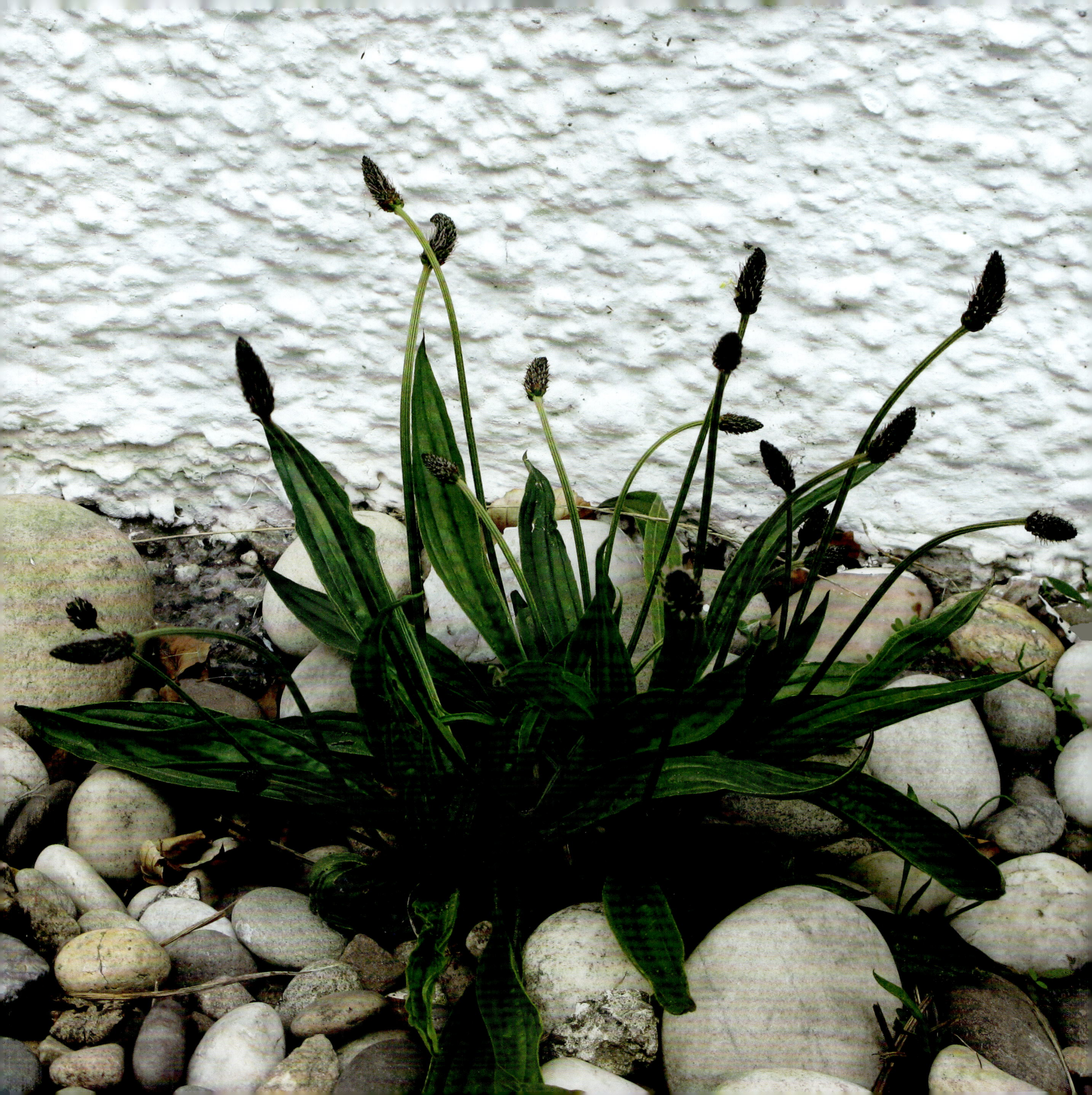

Ribwort Plantain

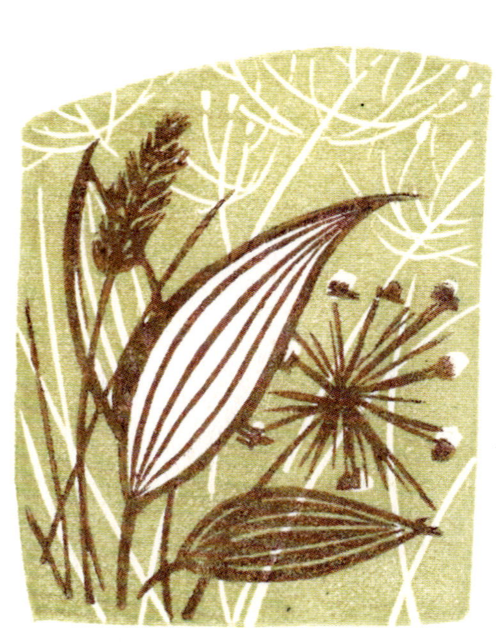

Plantain

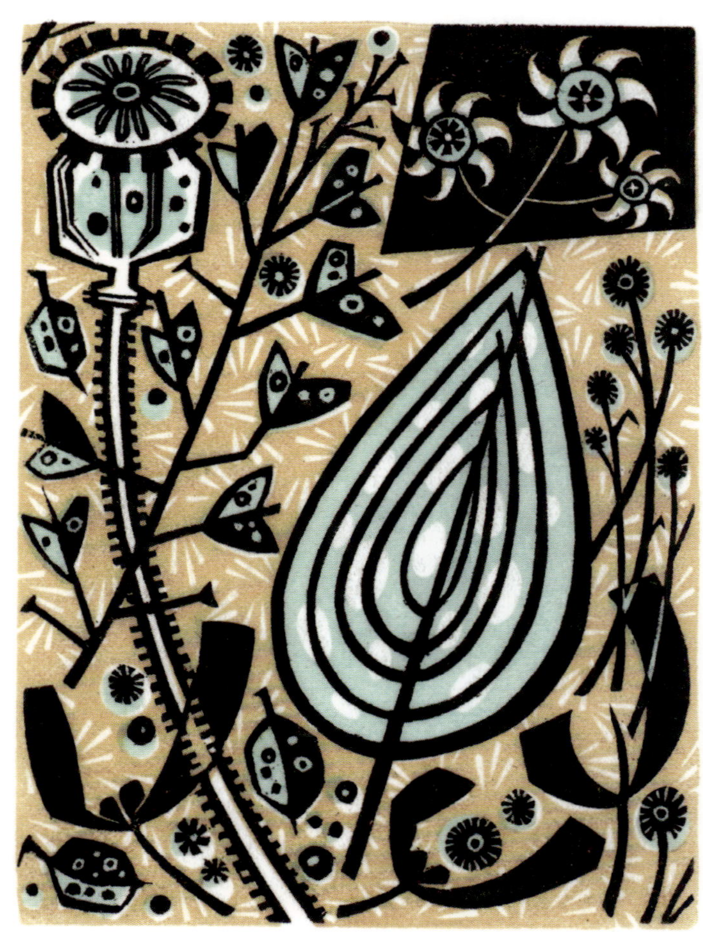

Spotted Leaf

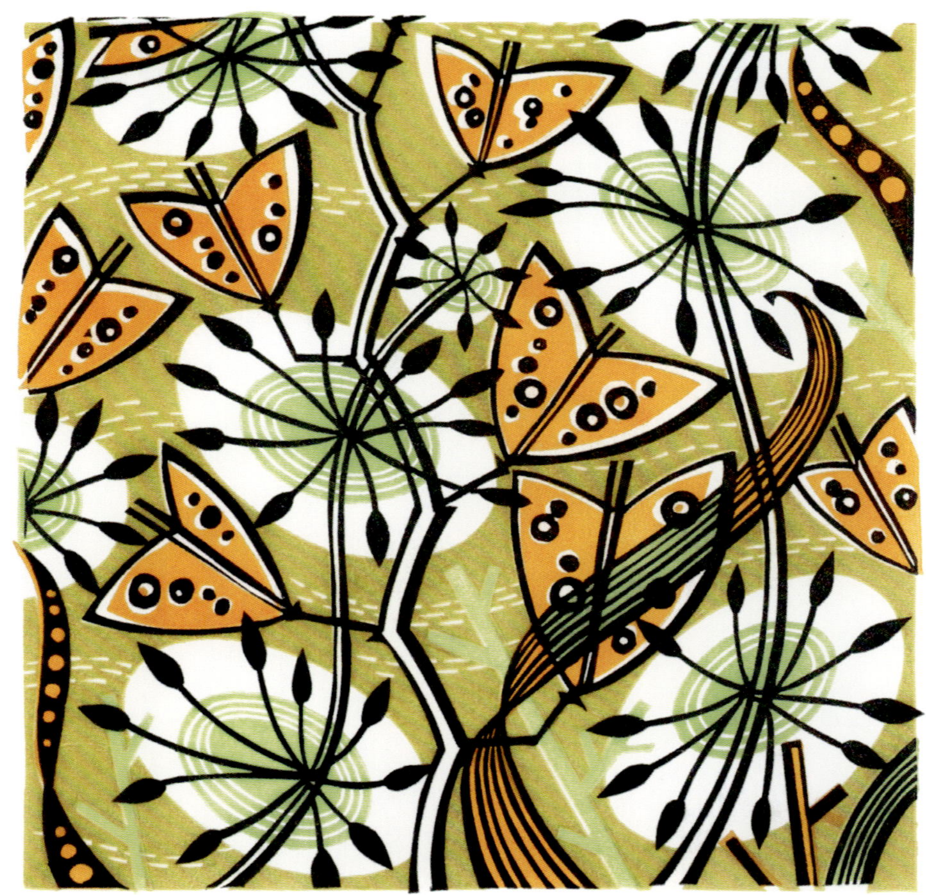

Shepherd's Purse

'Here I'm printing the final block
of Teasel (opposite): rolling ink on
to the woodblock, then transferring
the image on to Japanese paper by
burnishing with a wooden spoon.'

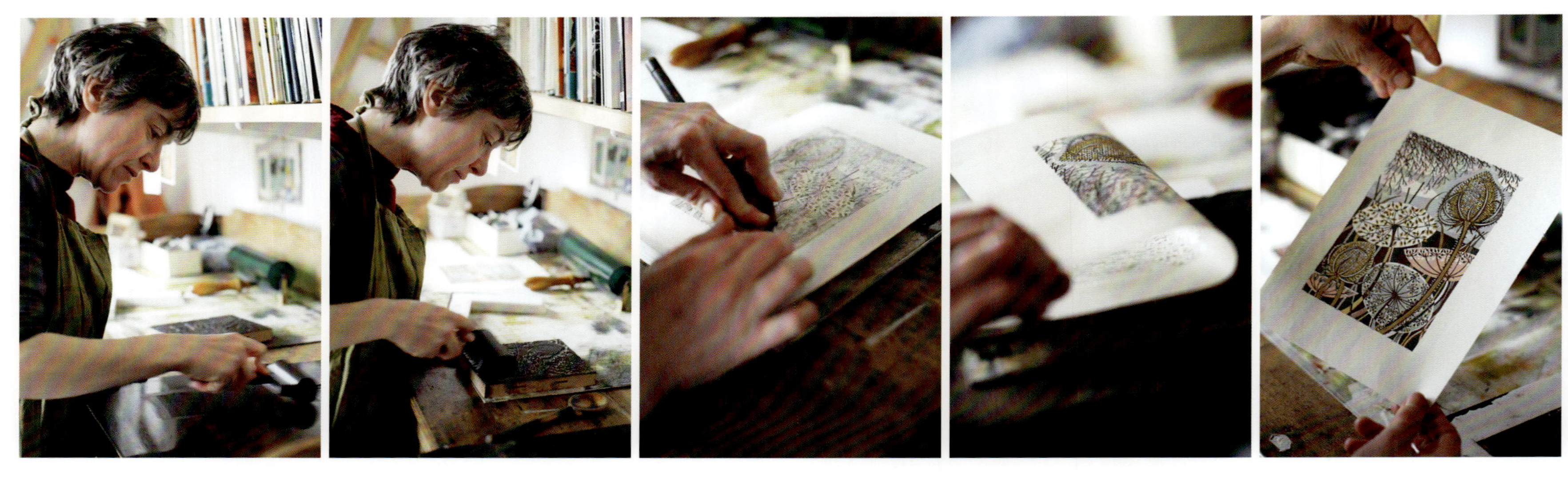

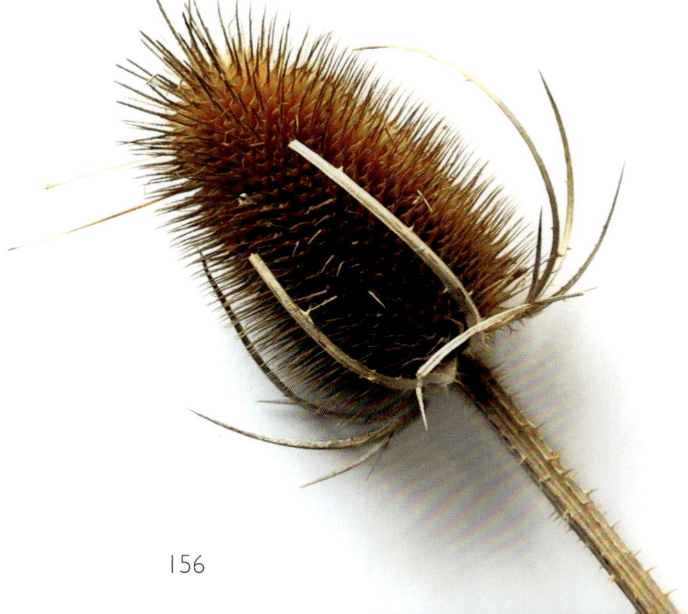

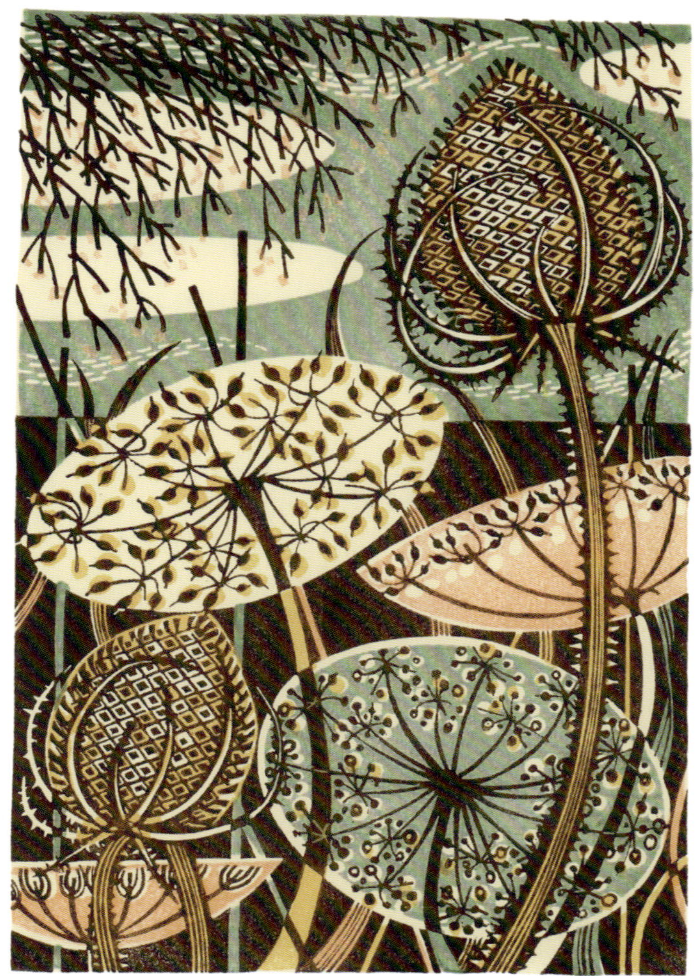

Teasel

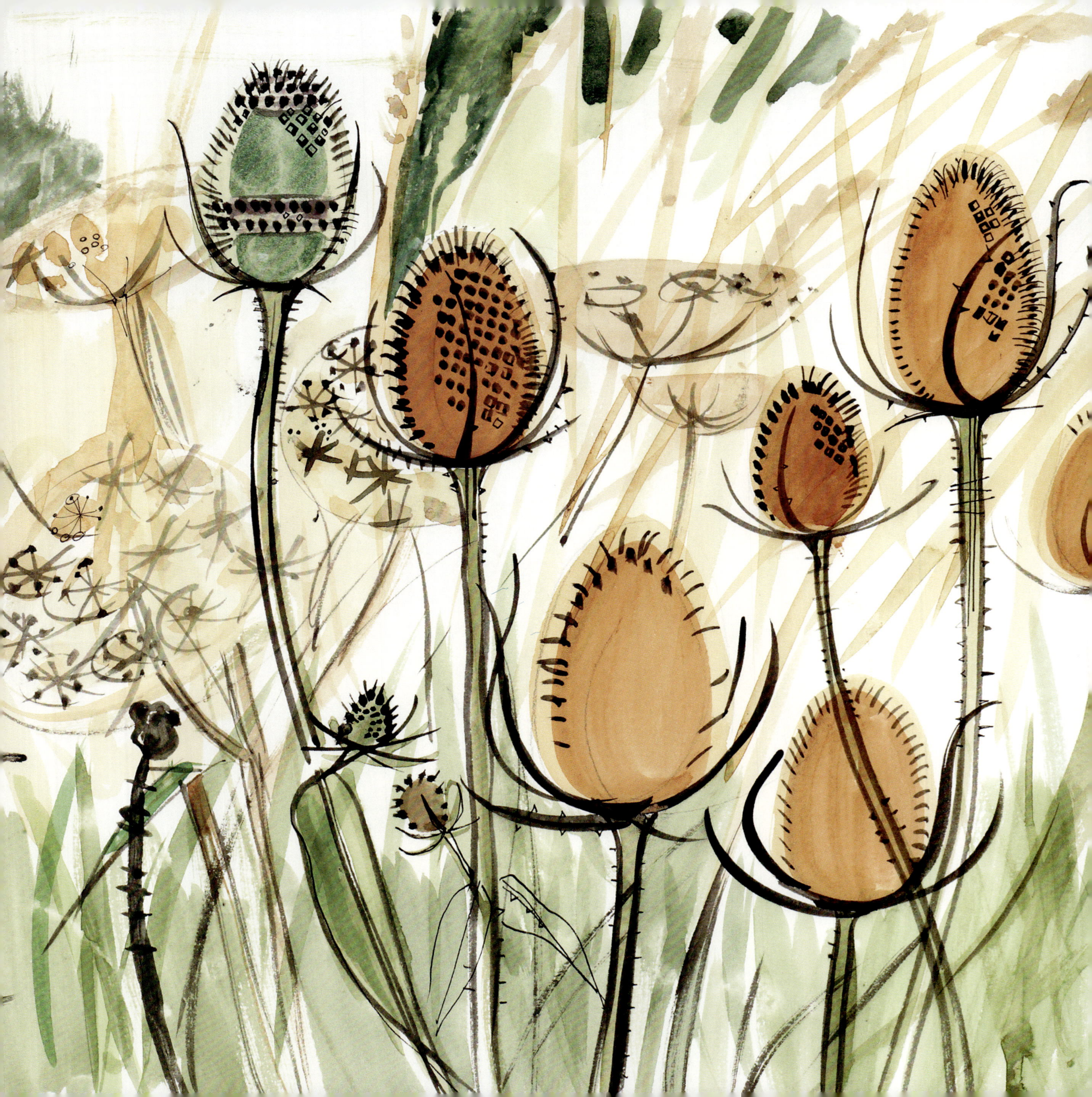

'I like the contrast between the
teasels' spiky egg-shaped flower heads
and strongly branching stems, and the
uncut grasses and poppies behind.'

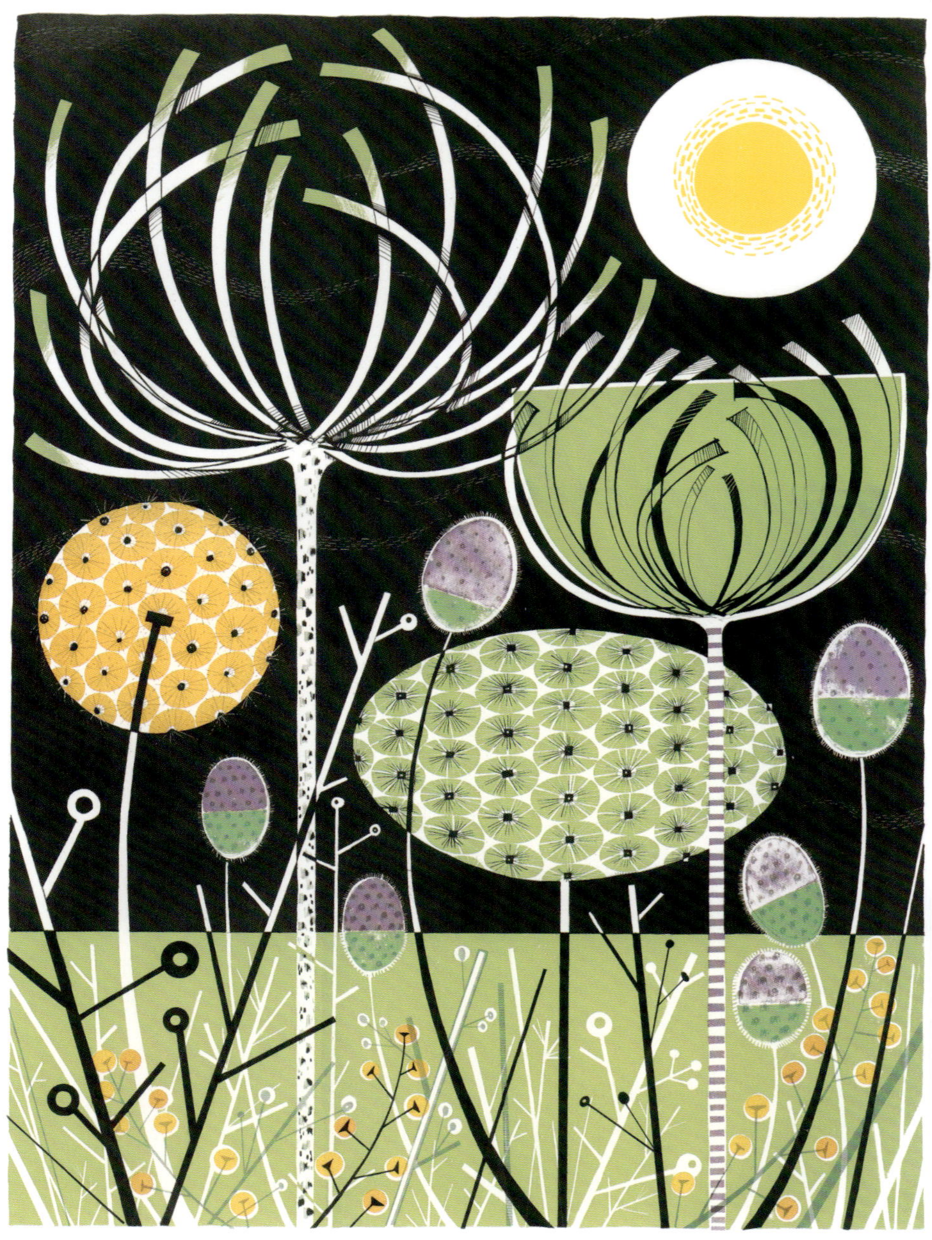

Wild Garden

'daisy-like shapes that spring
against a pale-yellow sky'

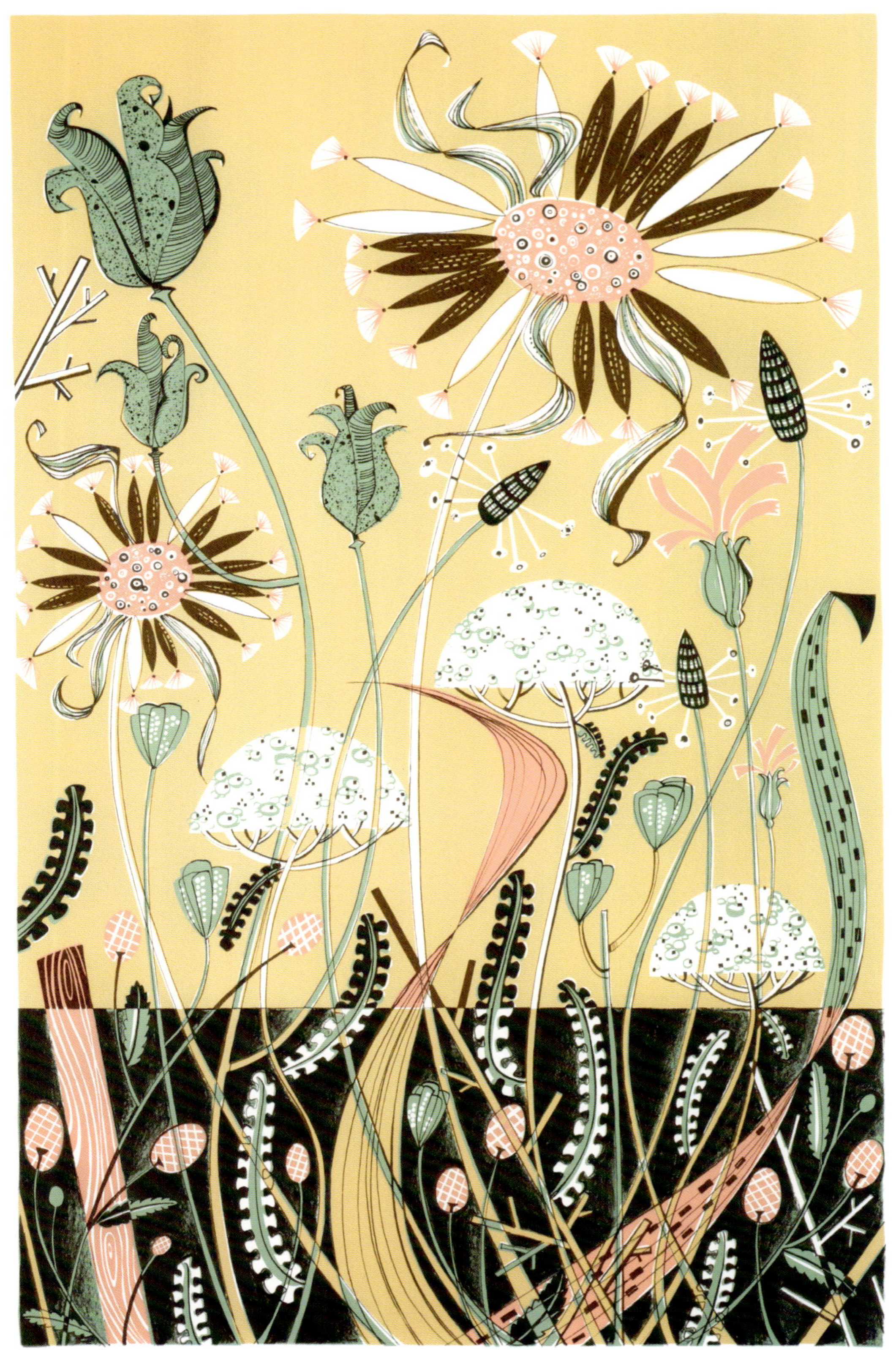

Wild Garden II

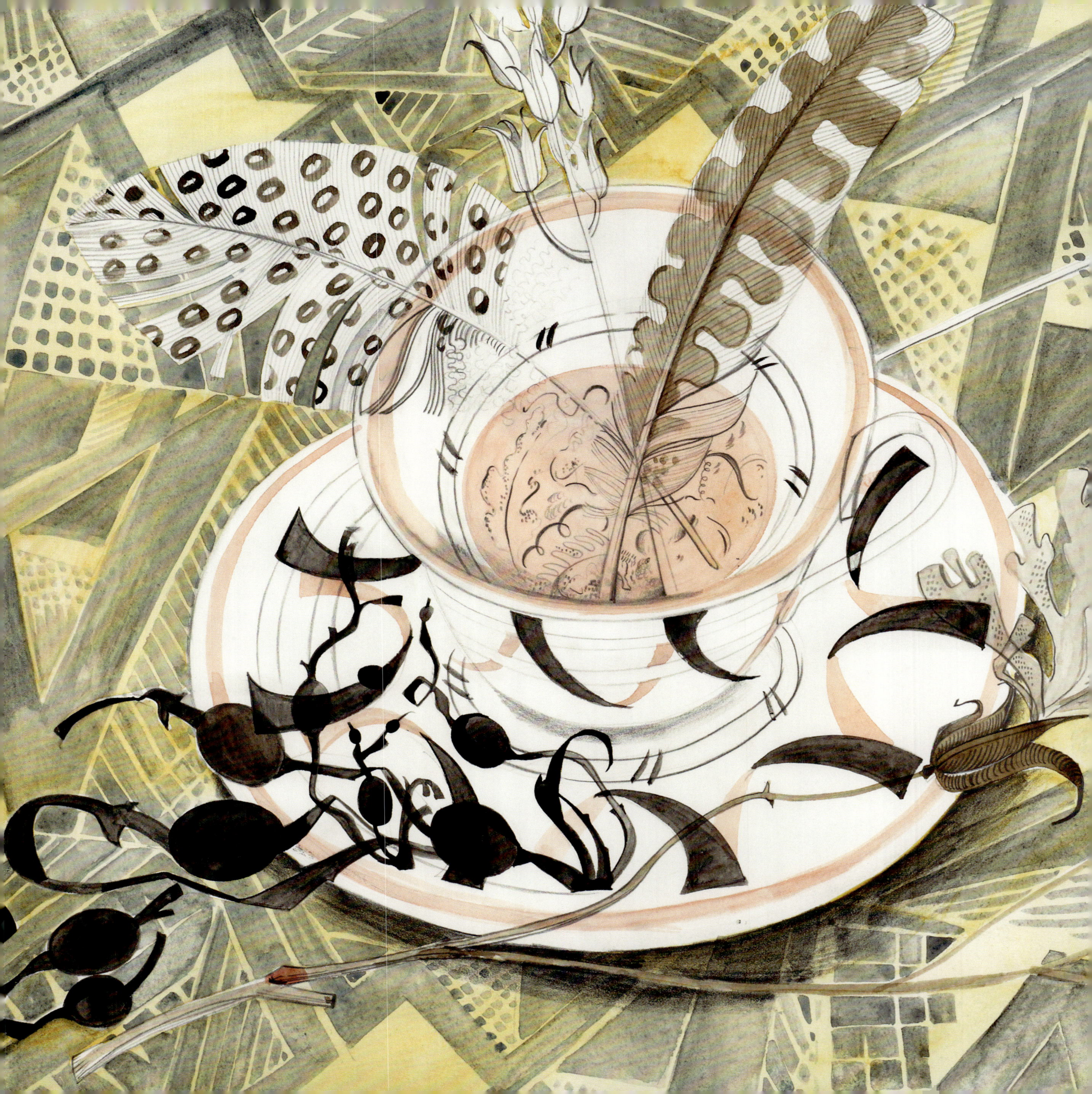

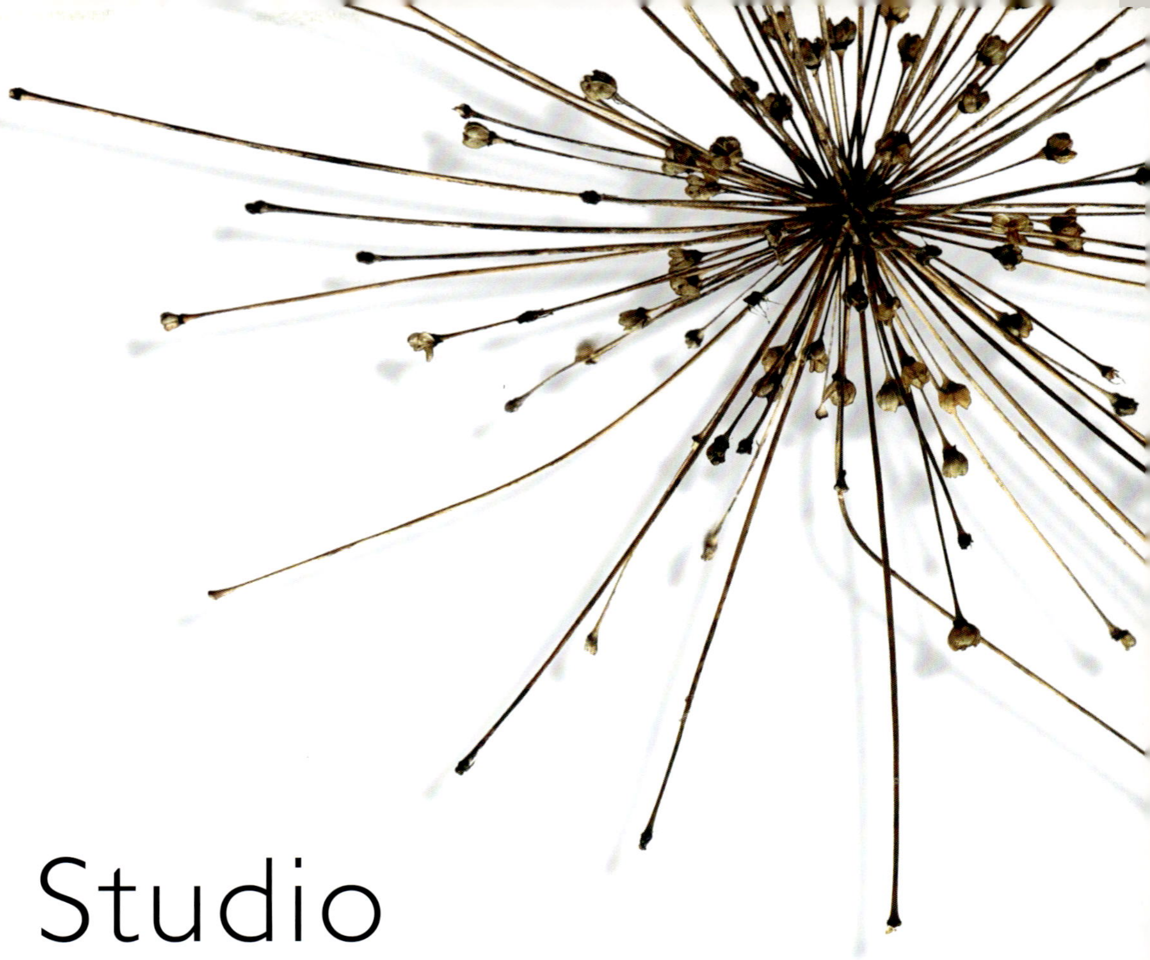

Studio

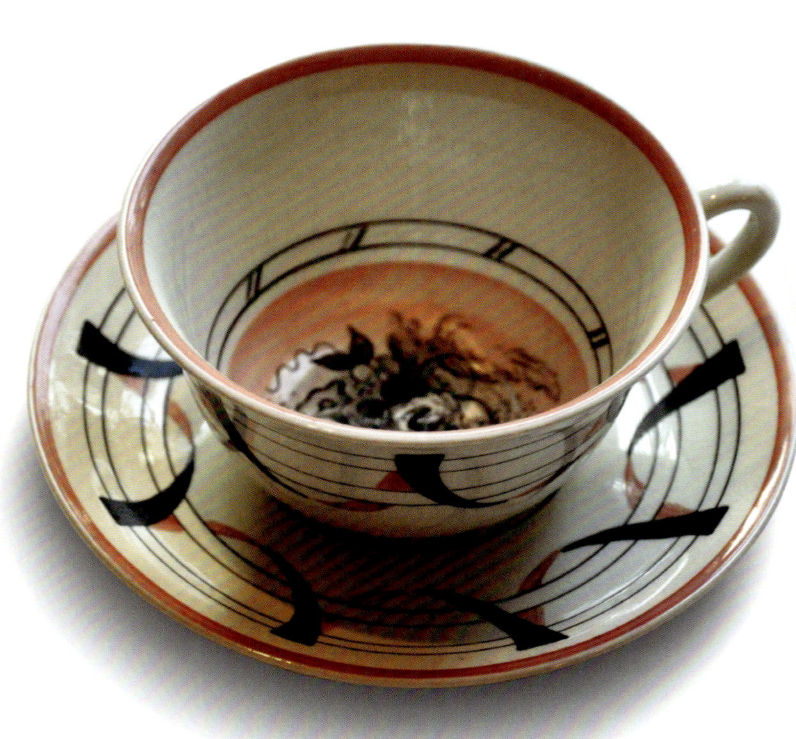

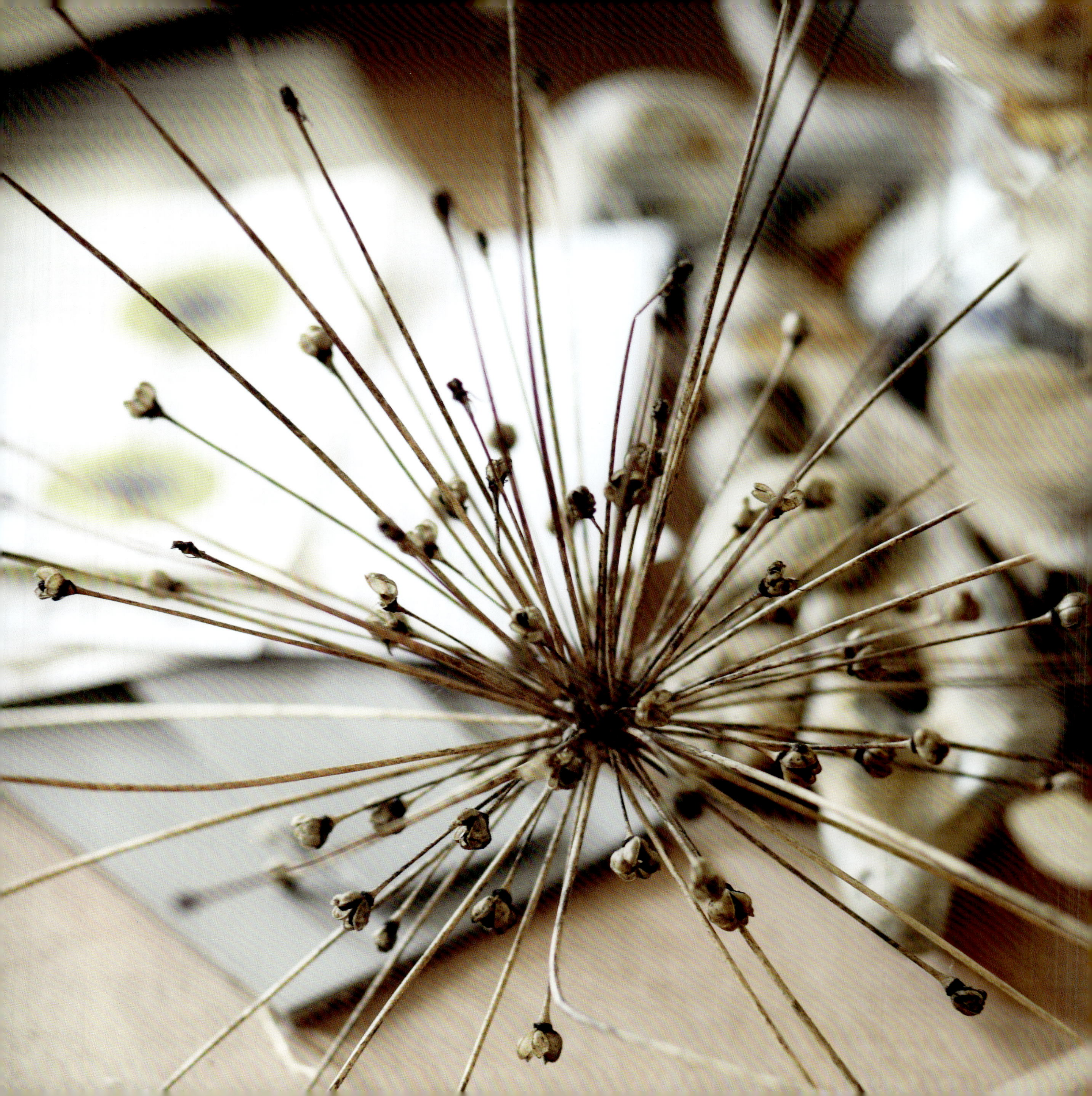

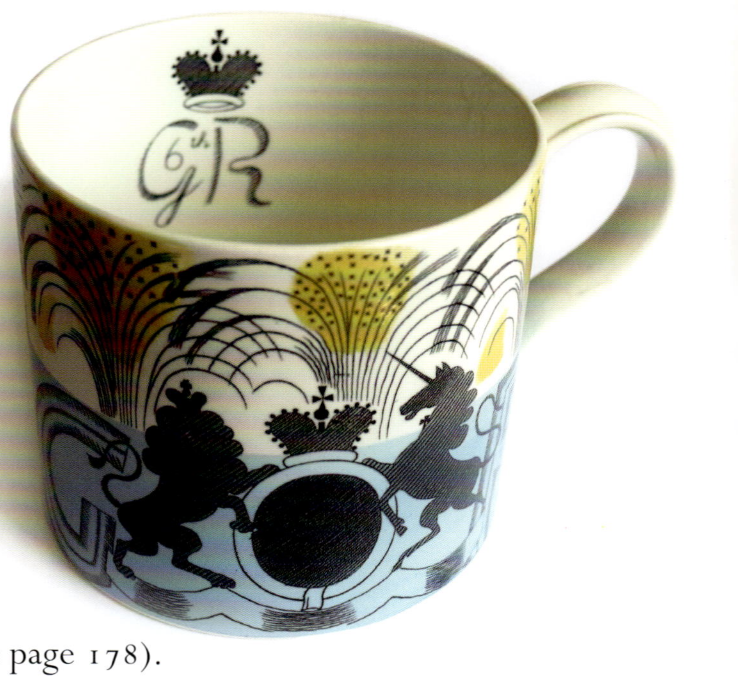

P rintmakers inspire other printmakers, and none has
inspired Lewin more than Eric Ravilious (1903–
1942), who designed dinner services, cups and mugs
for Wedgwood. Like Lewin, he also designed fabrics and
worked with the Curwen Studio. One of her favoured objects
is his coronation mug (originally designed for Edward VIII,
who was never crowned, and adapted by Wedgwood for
George VI in 1937 and again, in 1953, for Elizabeth II). It
appears, with dried seed heads, in an early Lewin print and
later, in *The 1953 Coronation Mug*, with an added pebble (see page 178).
Lewin has also portrayed a Ravilious cup with his 'Garden' design in *The Moonlit Cup* (see
page 167), and his 'Persephone' design in *Winter Persephone* (see page 187), with a guineafowl's
polka-dotted feather and a strand of the seaweed she picks up on her walks.

As Lewin explains, 'I collect seed heads, stones, flints, shells, broken pottery, wood,
driftwood, seaweeds, coral, lichen growing on branches and so on. Many of these objects relate
to very specific places and, when I'm composing still lifes in the studio, they carry memories
of where they were found. I also collect pots to store the seed heads in, and these are included
in still-life compositions – a "Totem" storage jar, jugs and chipped coffee pots, Rye pottery,
a perfect little pink-and-black Graham Sutherland teacup and saucer and, of course, Ravilious.
The still lifes can combine gathered elements from
many different places as I create a composition. I
sometimes take my favourite pieces with me
on my travels to Norfolk and Scotland.'

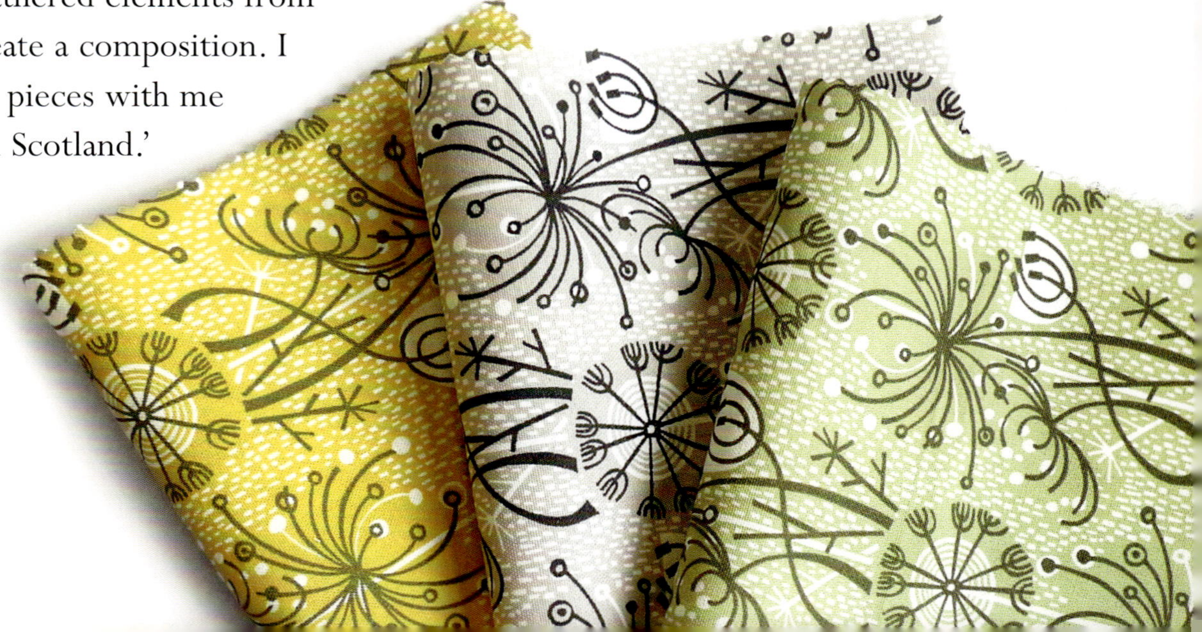

Opposite: Dried seed head of Allium
schubertii. *Above: Wedgwood 1937
coronation mug, with a design by
Eric Ravilious. Right: Swatches of Lewin's
'Dandelion 1' textile design (2005).*

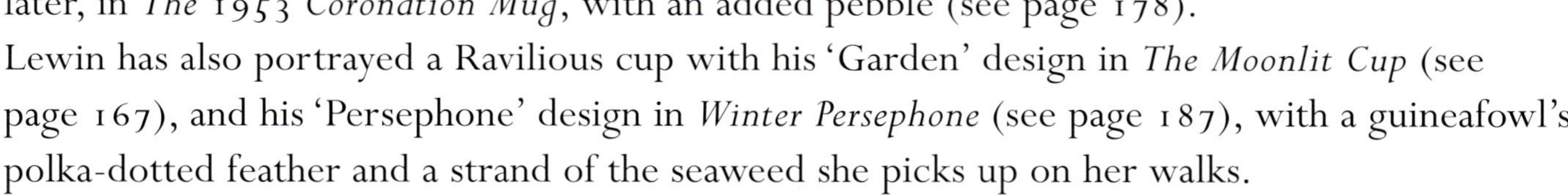

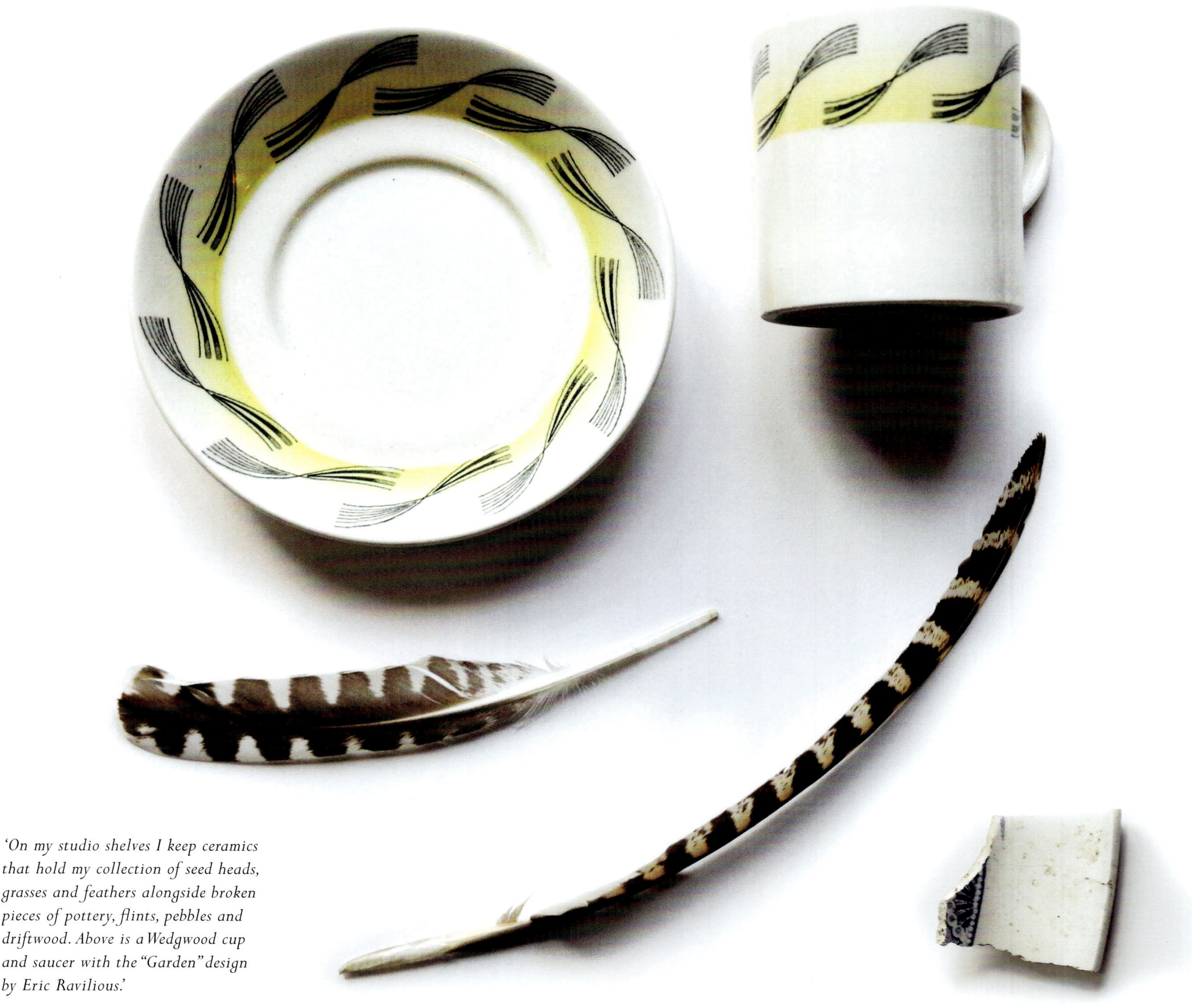

'On my studio shelves I keep ceramics
that hold my collection of seed heads,
grasses and feathers alongside broken
pieces of pottery, flints, pebbles and
driftwood. Above is a Wedgwood cup
and saucer with the "Garden" design
by Eric Ravilious.'

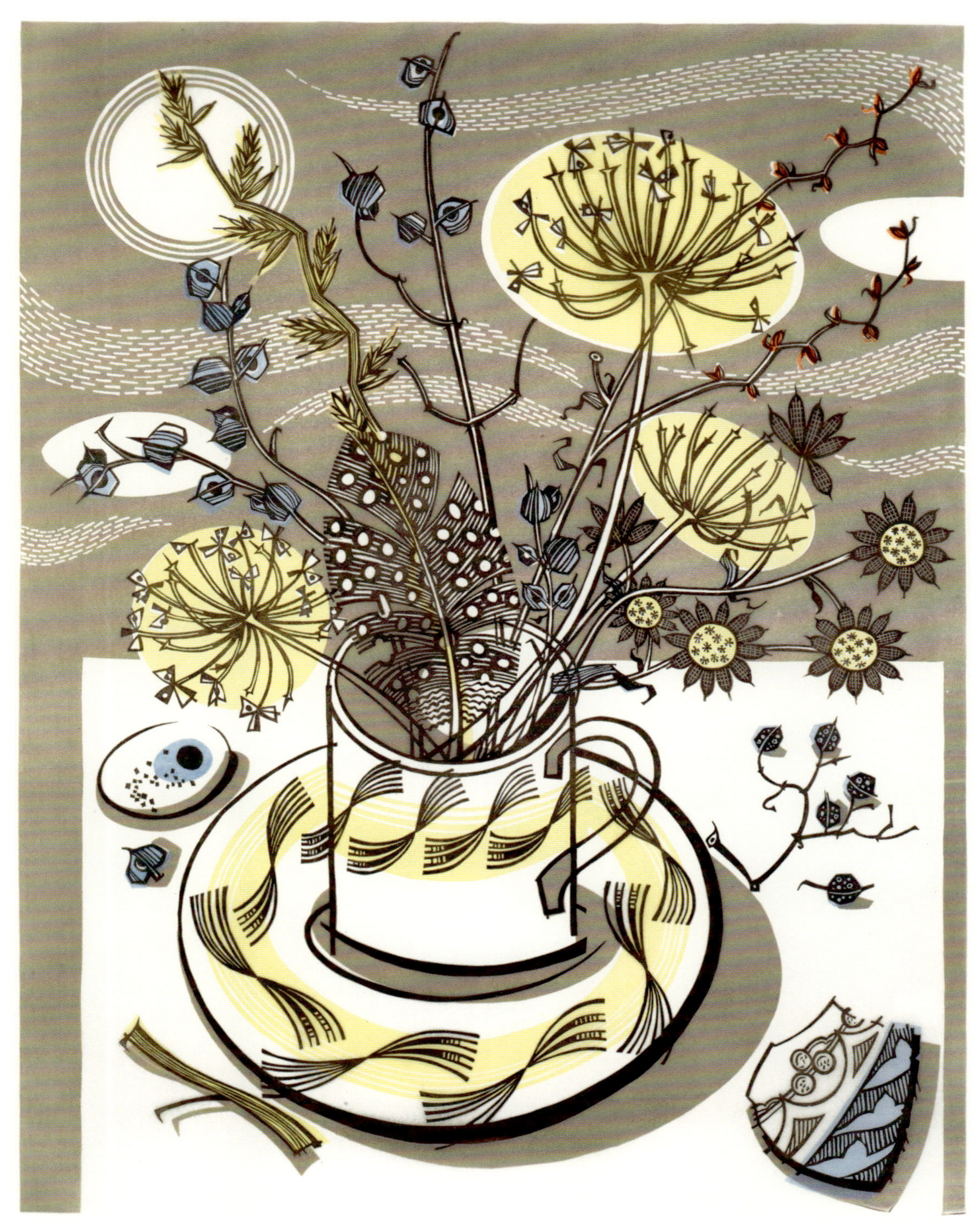

The Moonlit Cup

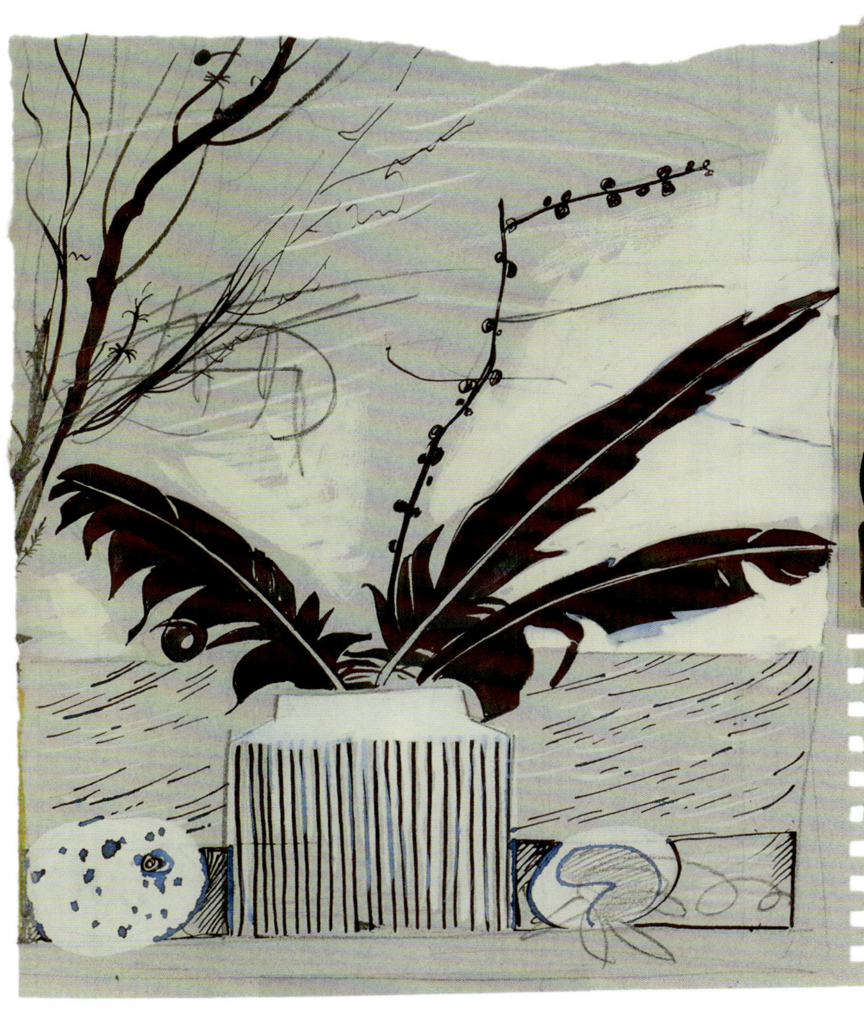

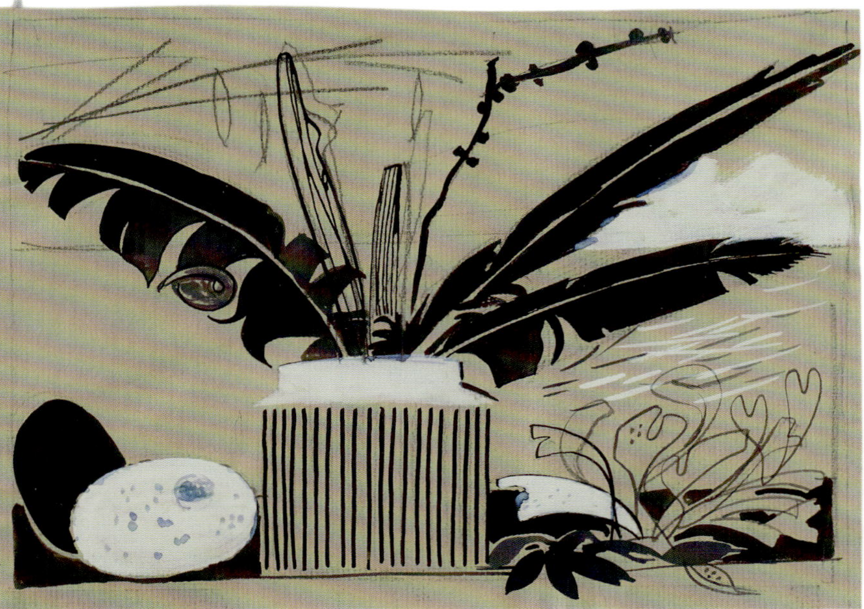

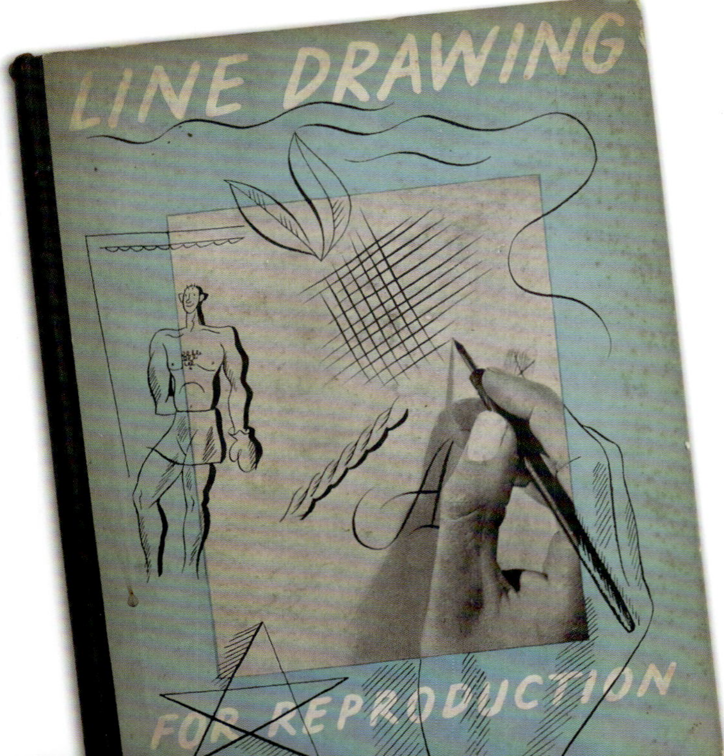
LINE DRAWING
FOR REPRODUCTION

'I made these two pen-and-ink sketches
in Aldeburgh in Suffolk. The same pot
now sits on a window sill in my cottage
in Scotland, holding dried plants that
I gathered on an autumn day.'

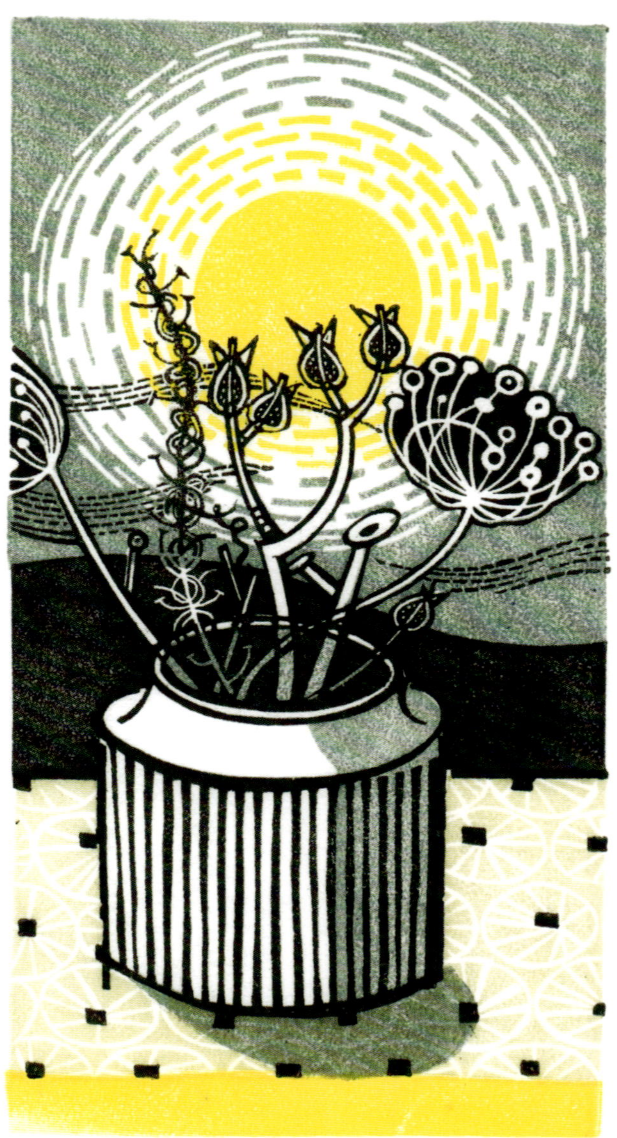

Rinour

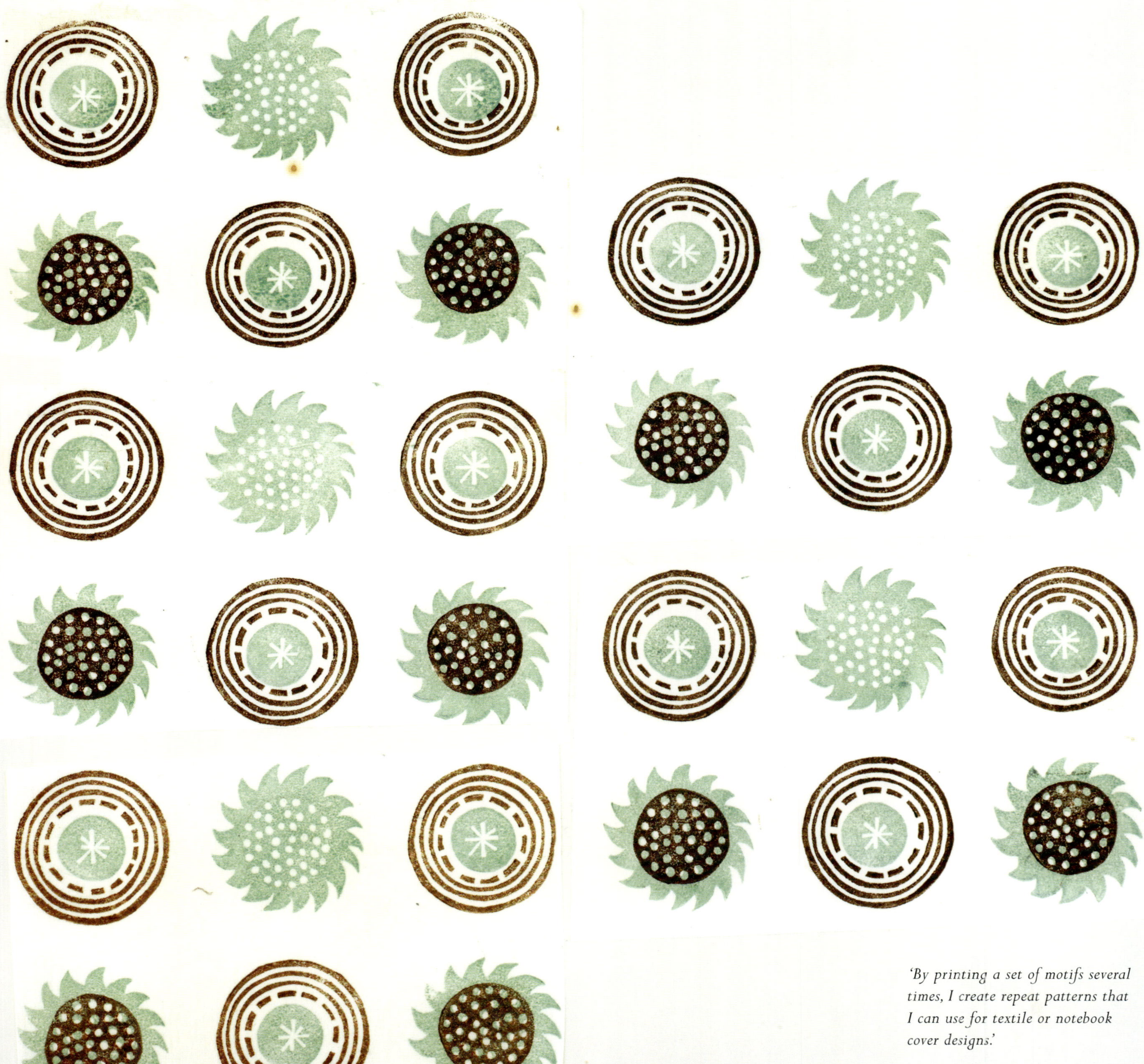

'By printing a set of motifs several
times, I create repeat patterns that
I can use for textile or notebook
cover designs.'

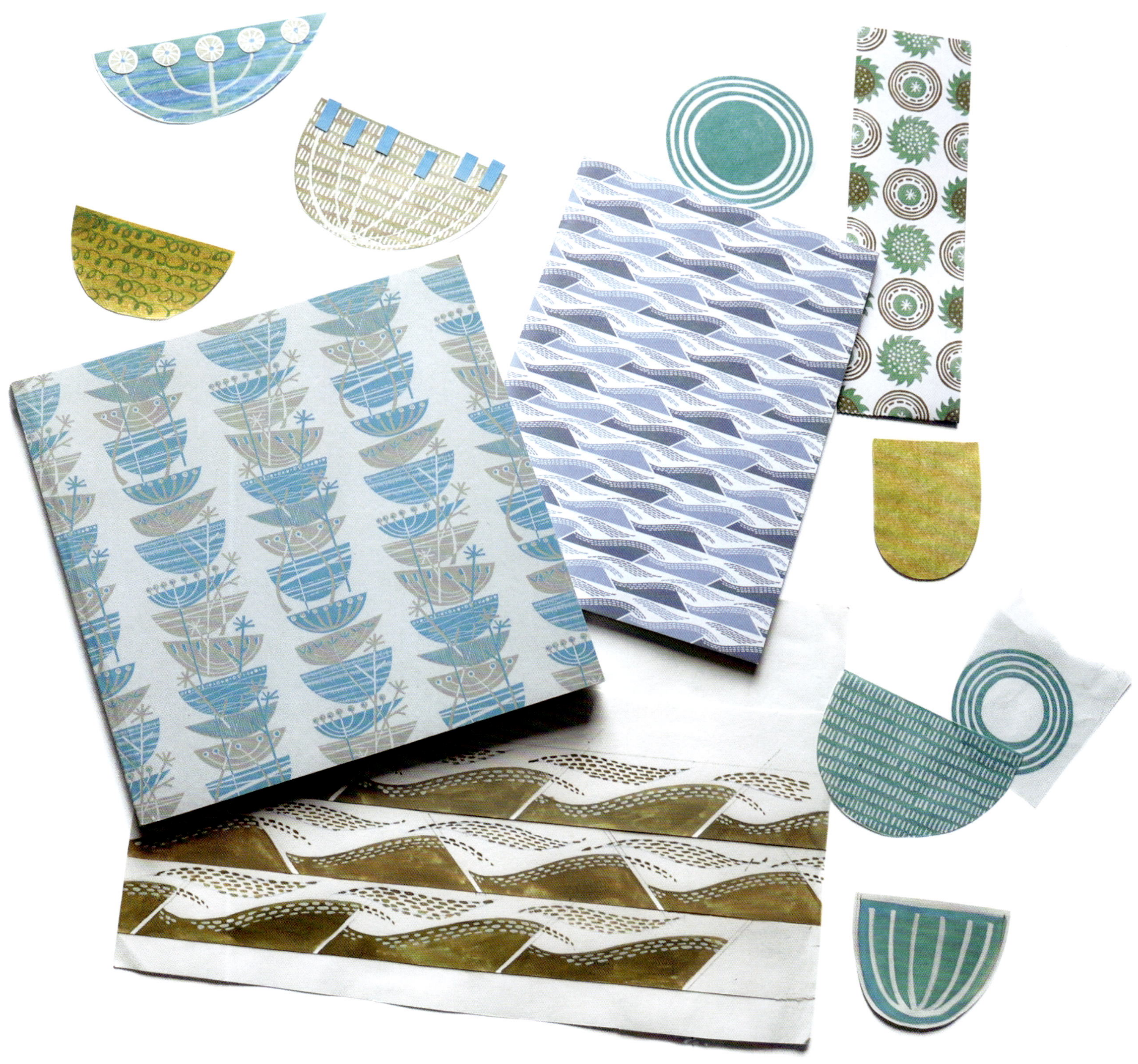

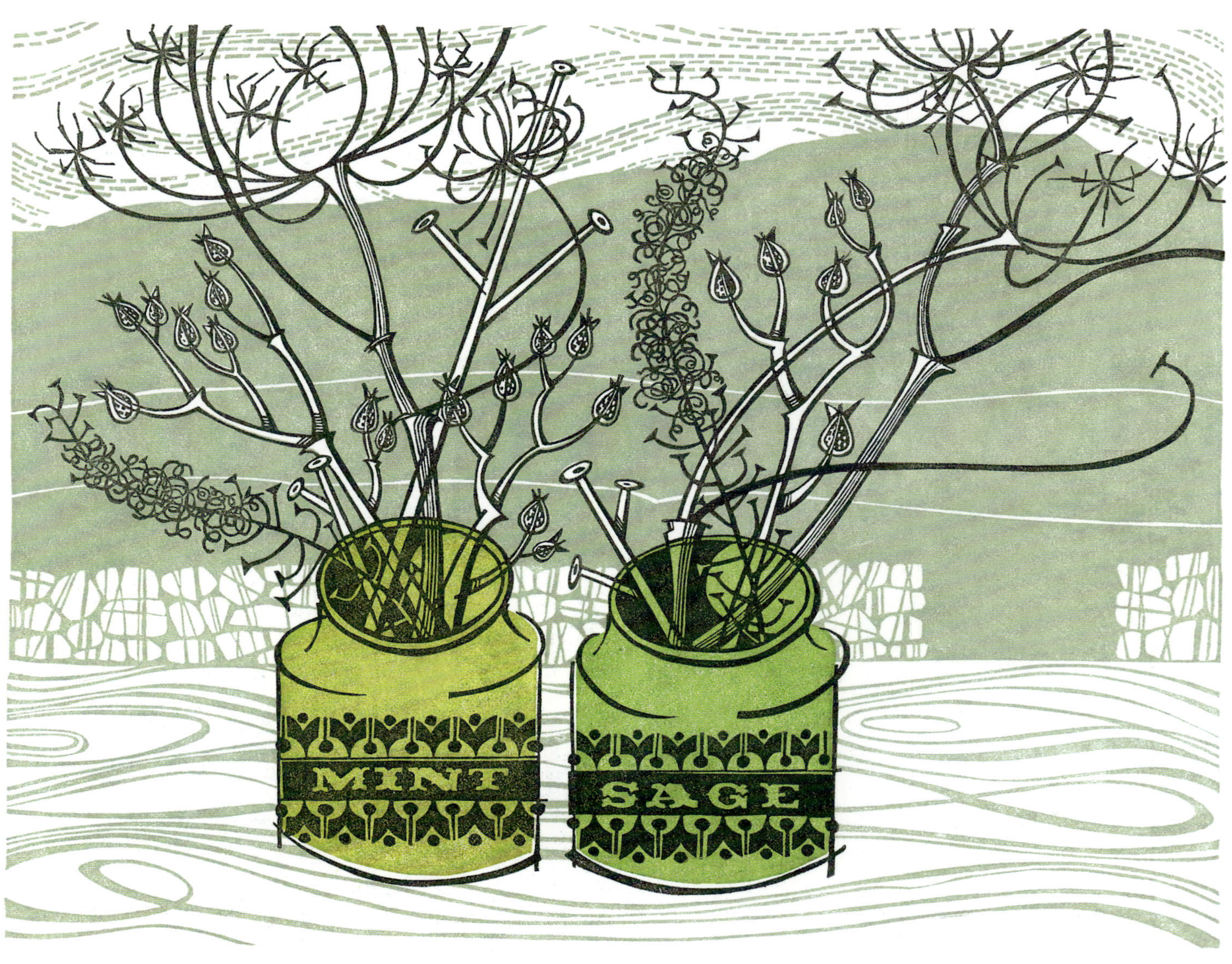

Two Green Jars

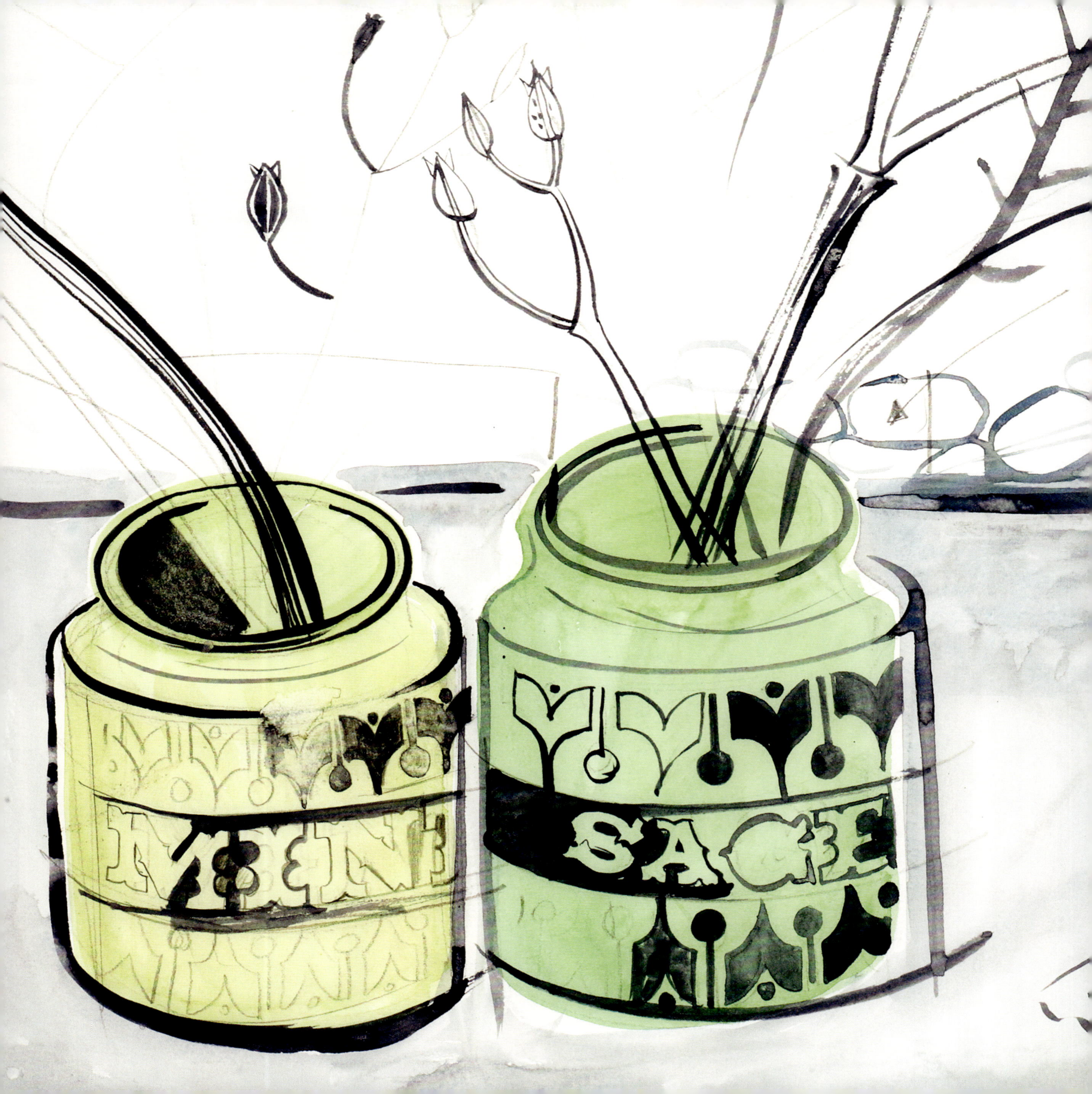

MINT
SAGE

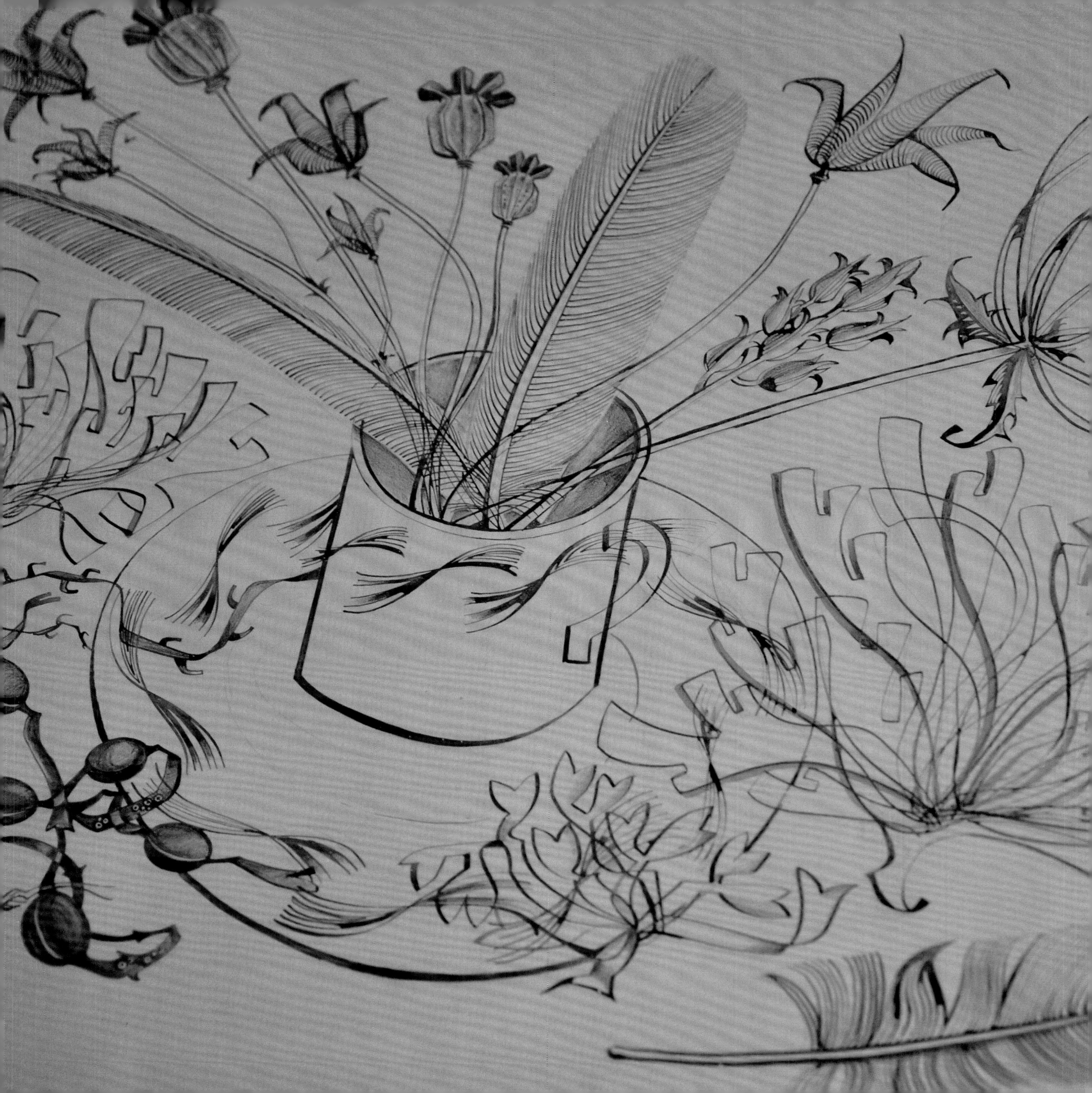

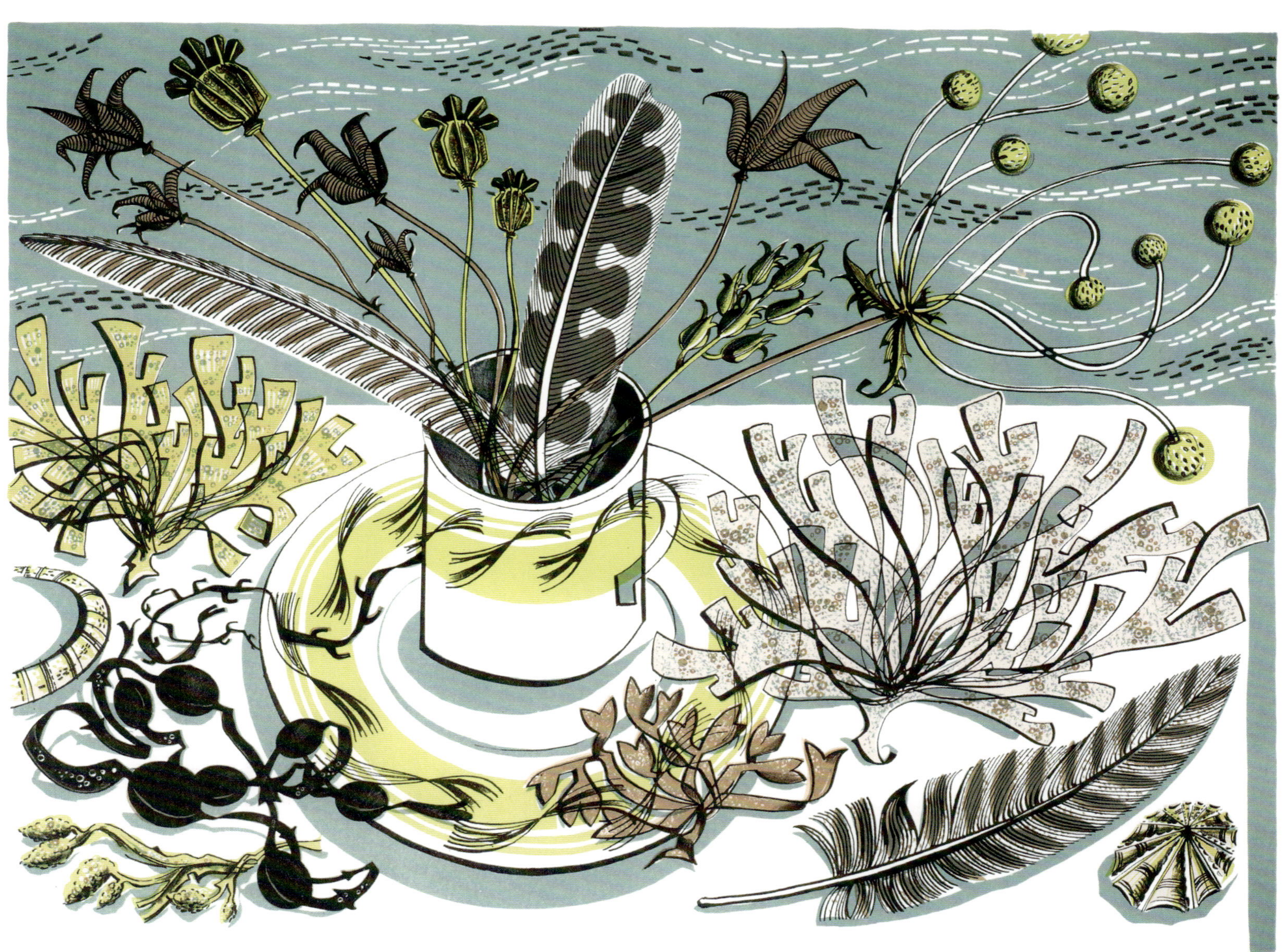

Cup, Feathers and Seaweed

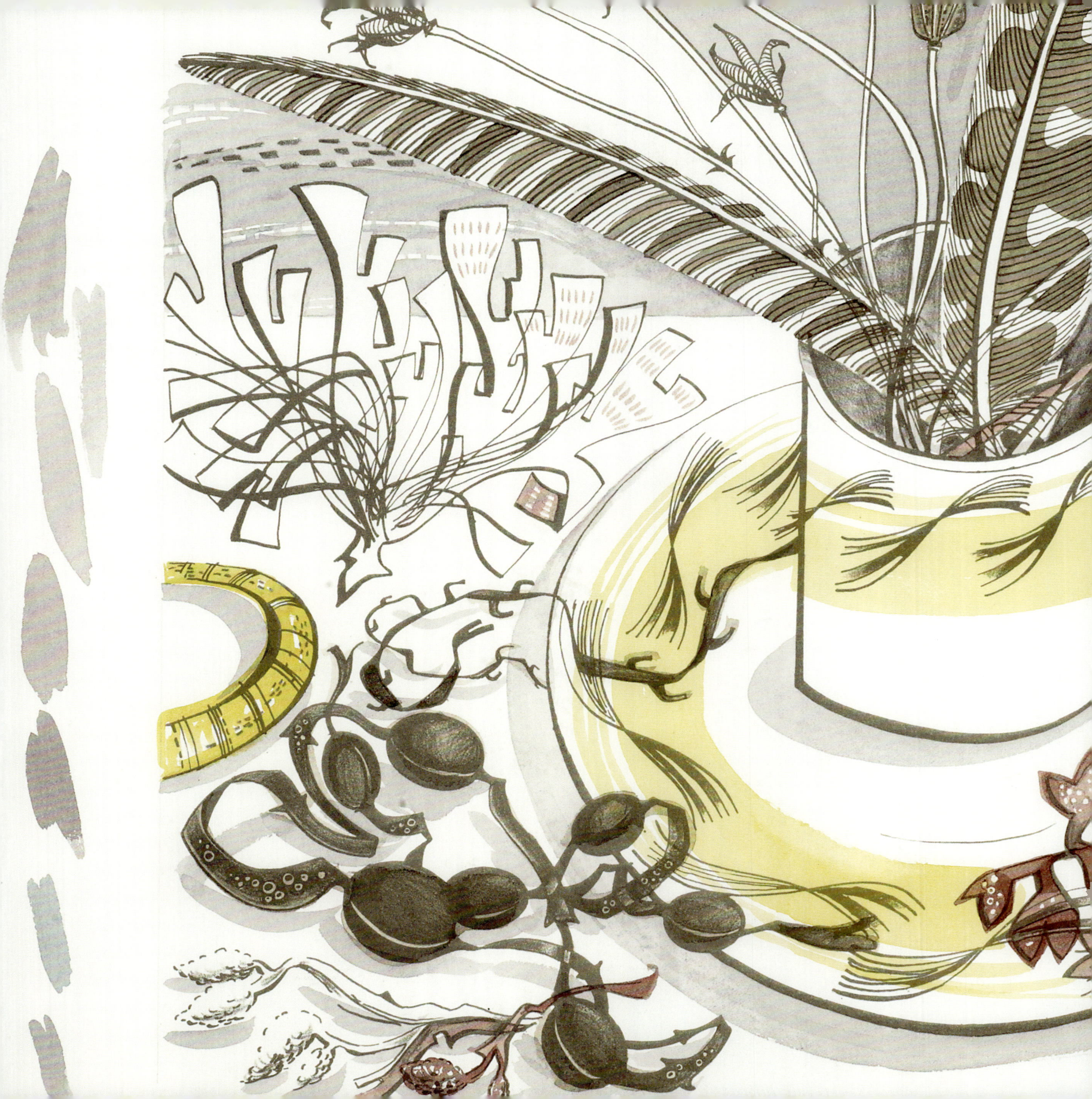

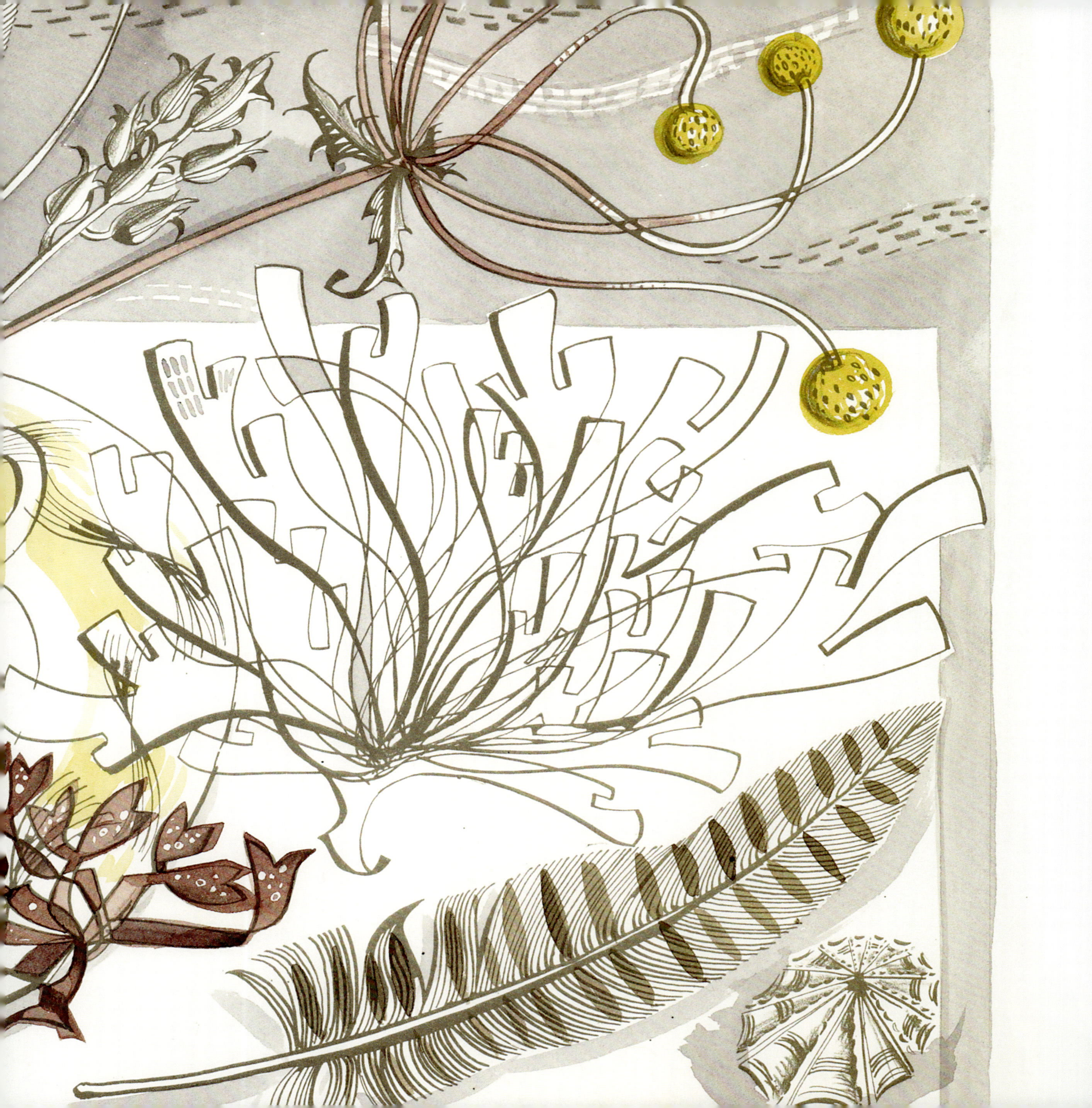

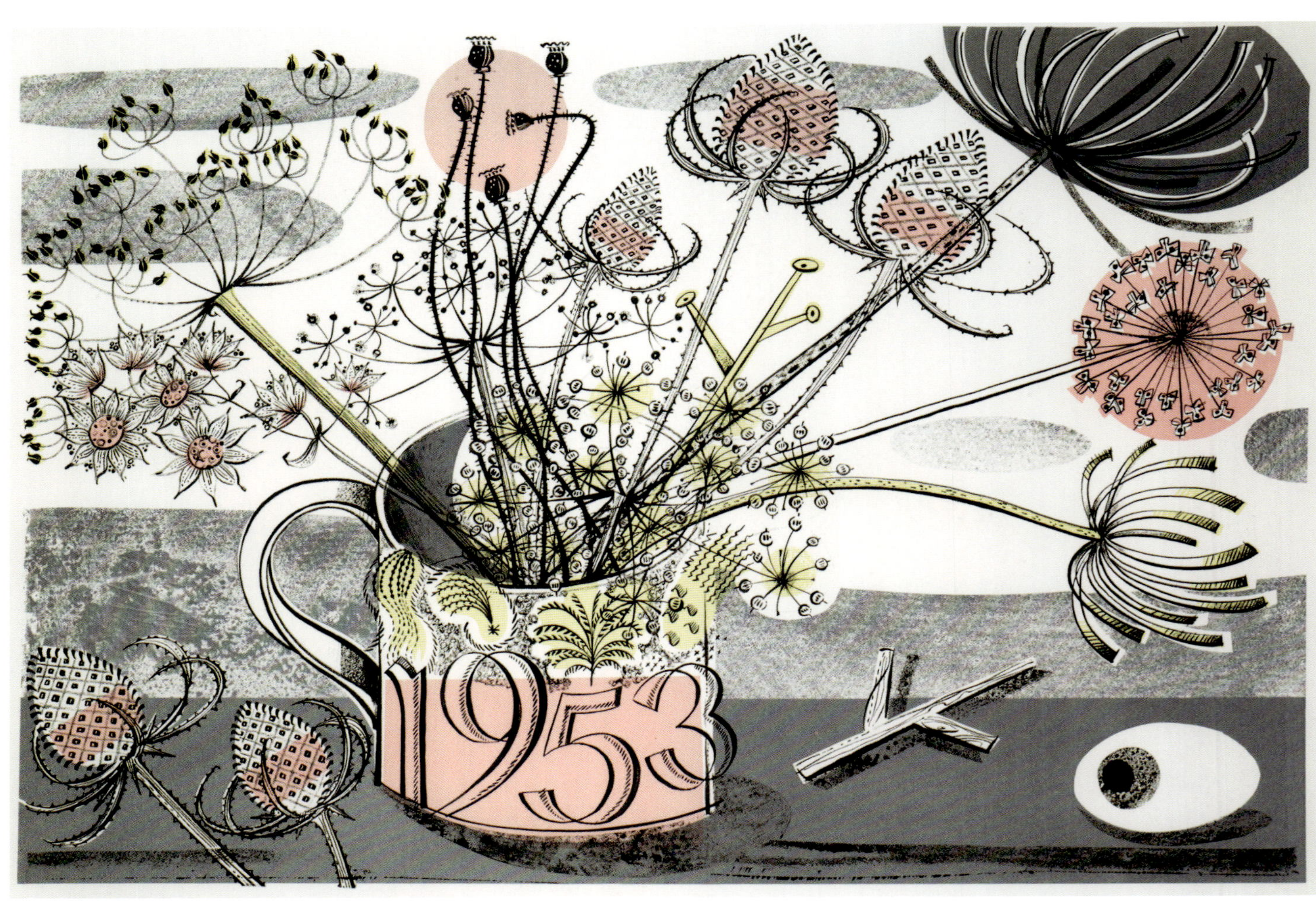

The 1953 Coronation Mug

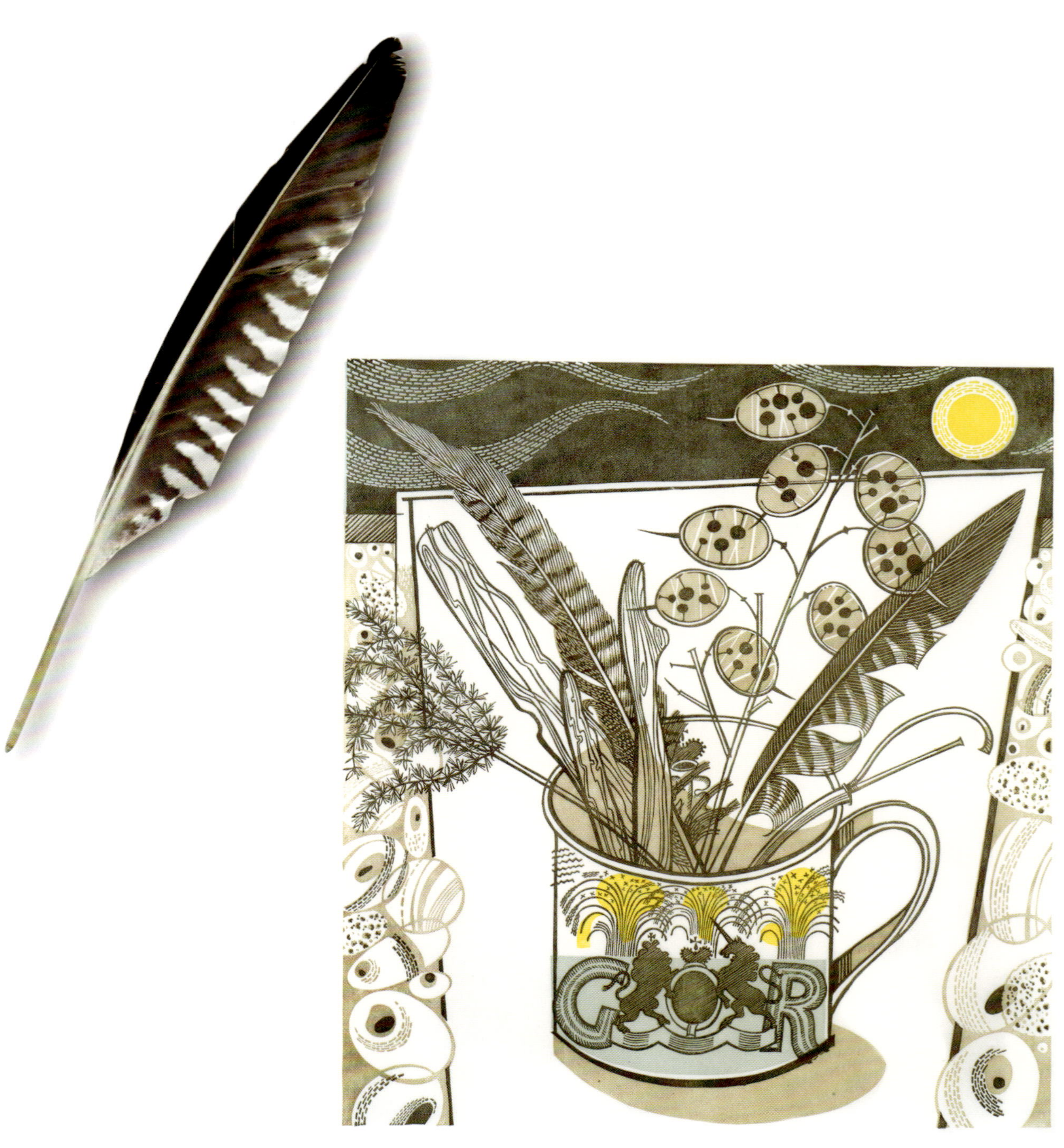

The 1937 Coronation Mug

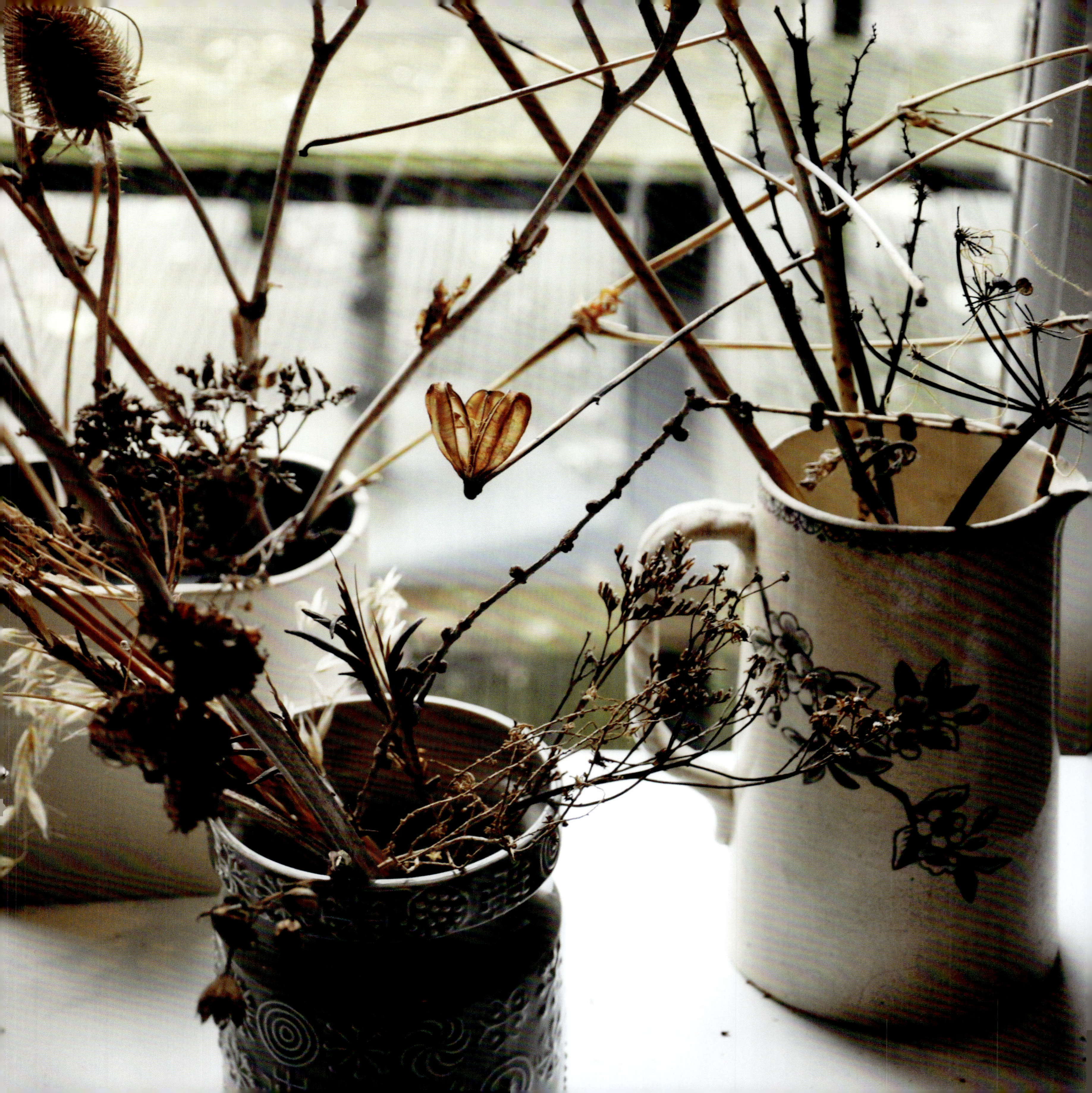

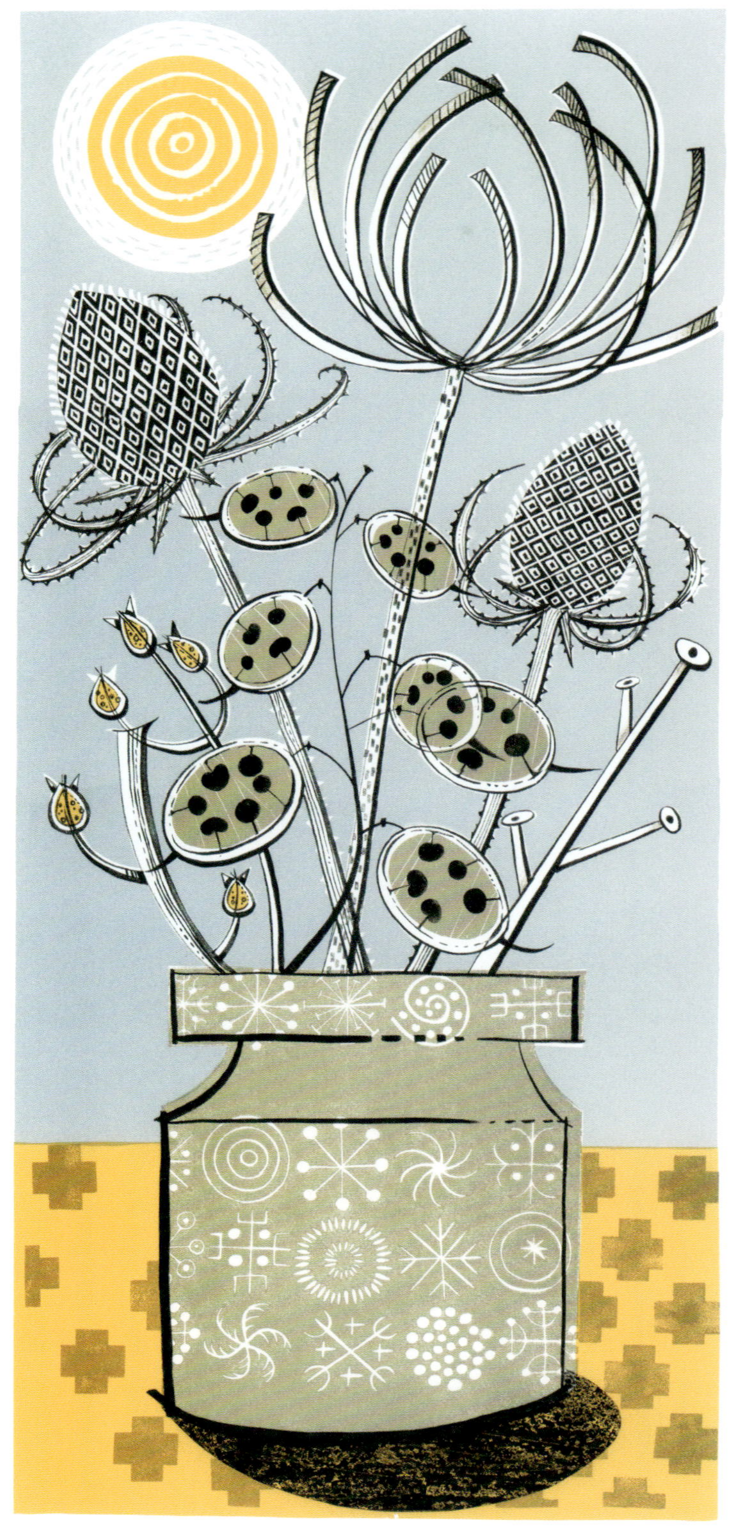

Totem

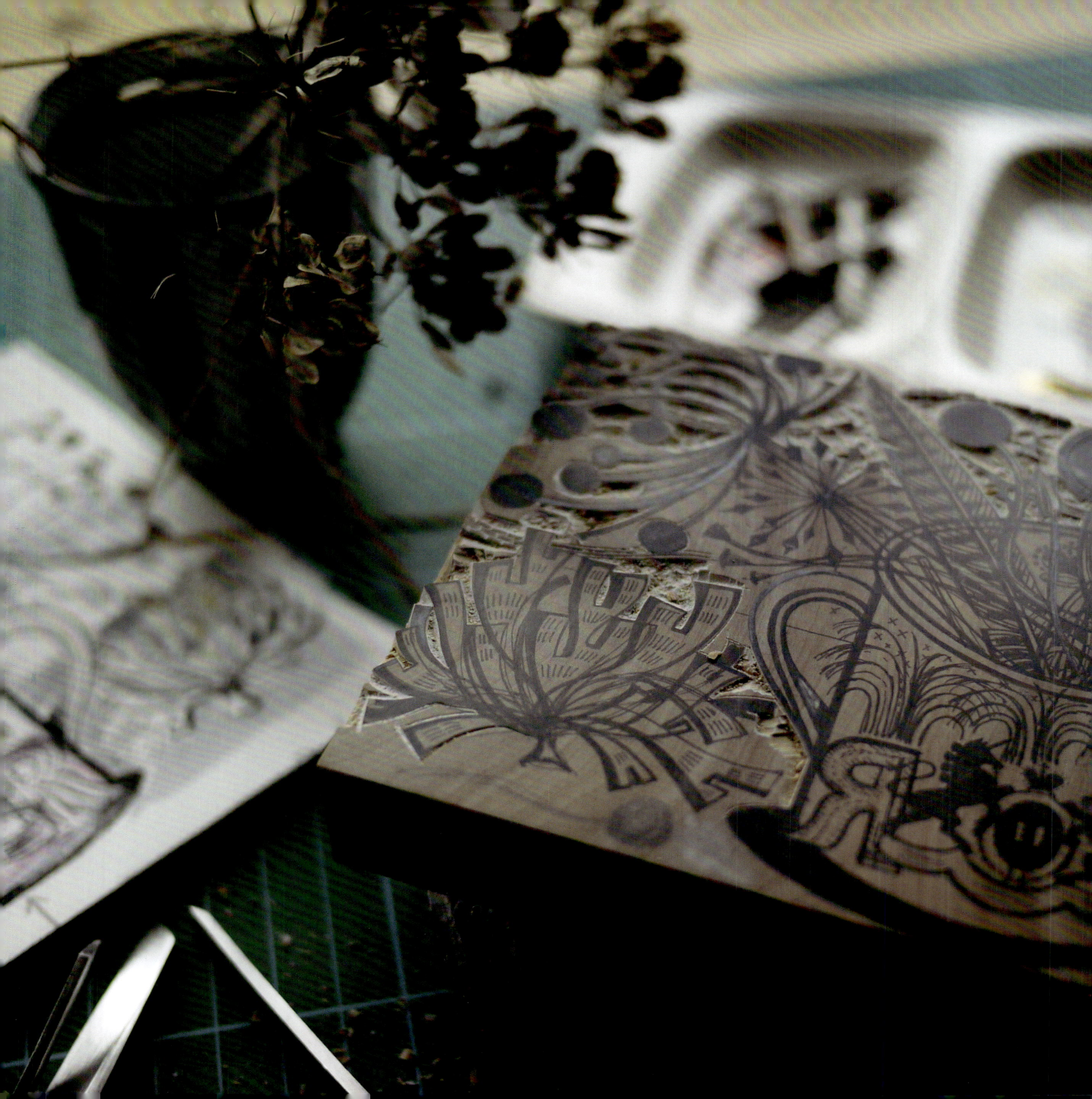

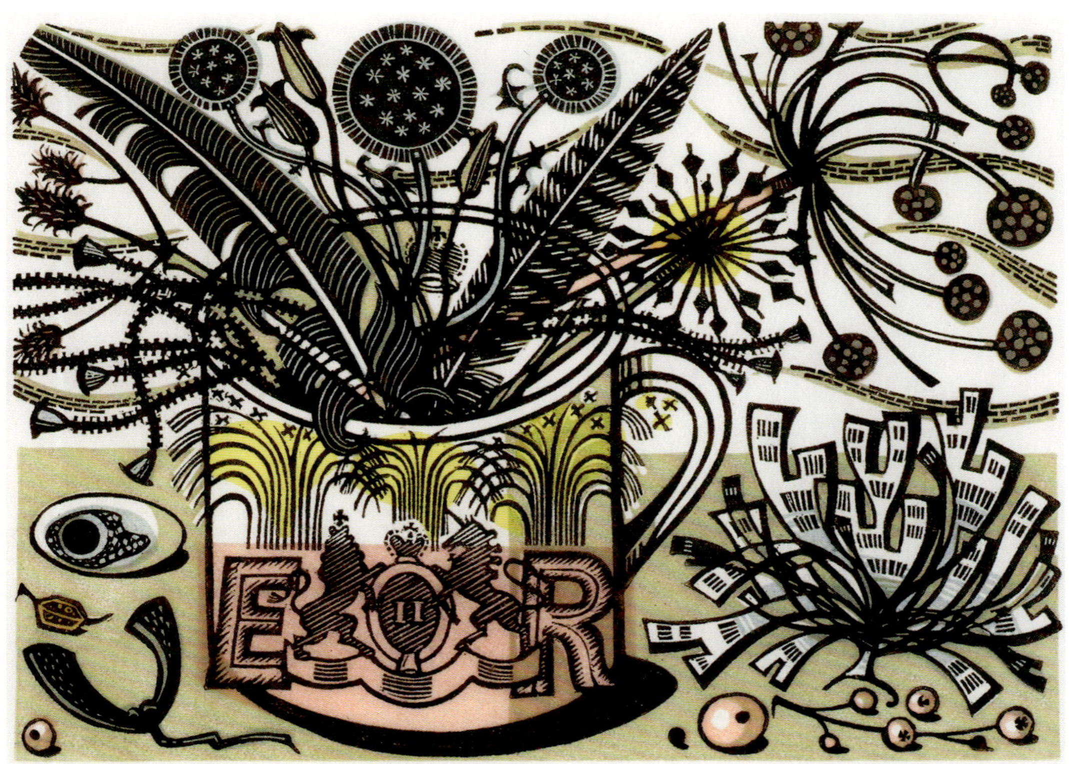

Mug with Feathers

'This lithograph is included, along
with the work of other artists who
worked at the Curwen Studio during
its fiftieth year (2008), in the
Curwen Anniversary Portfolio.'

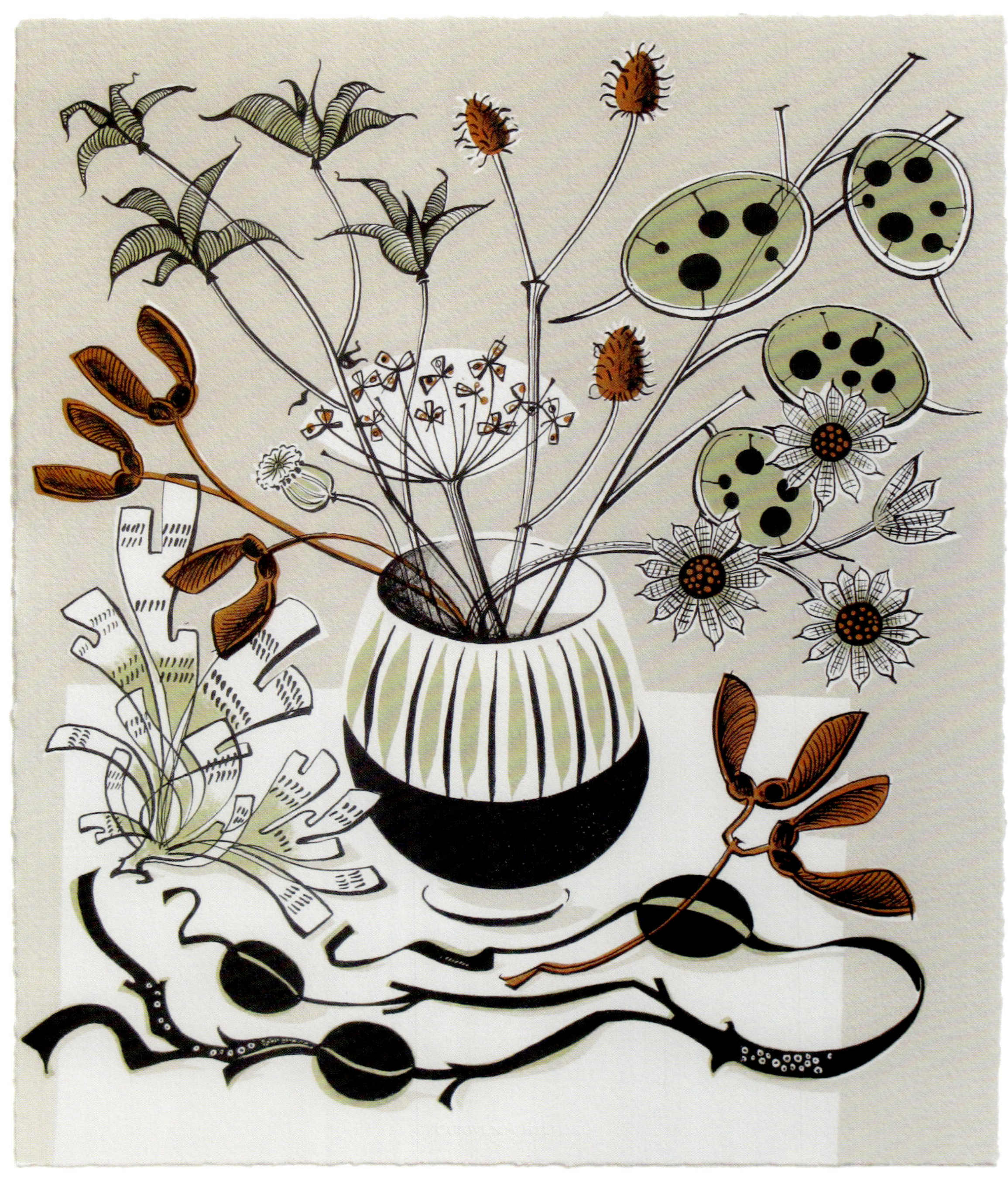

Autumn

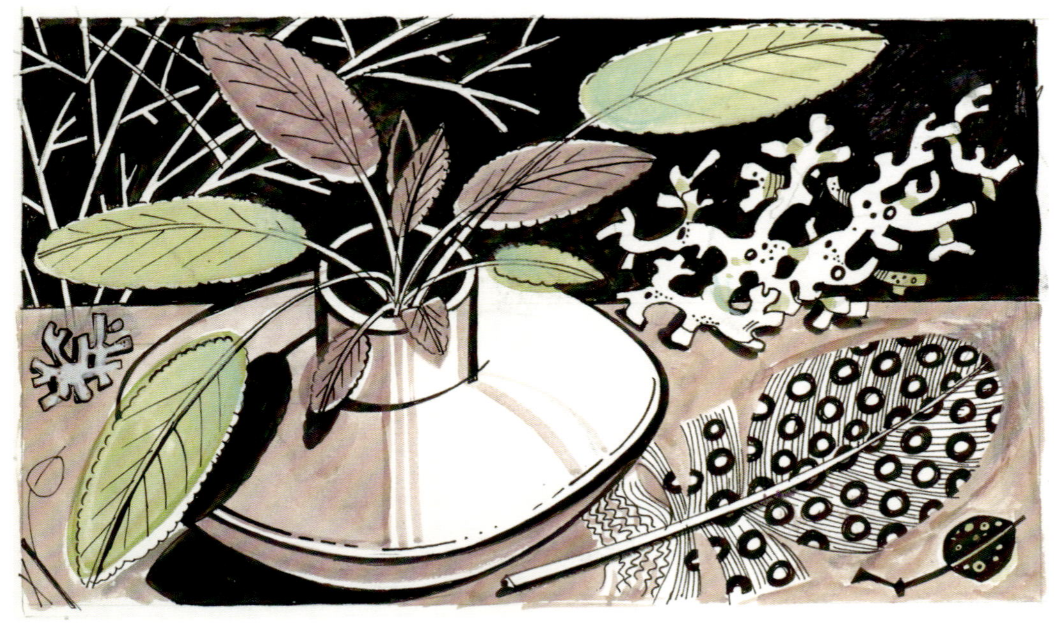

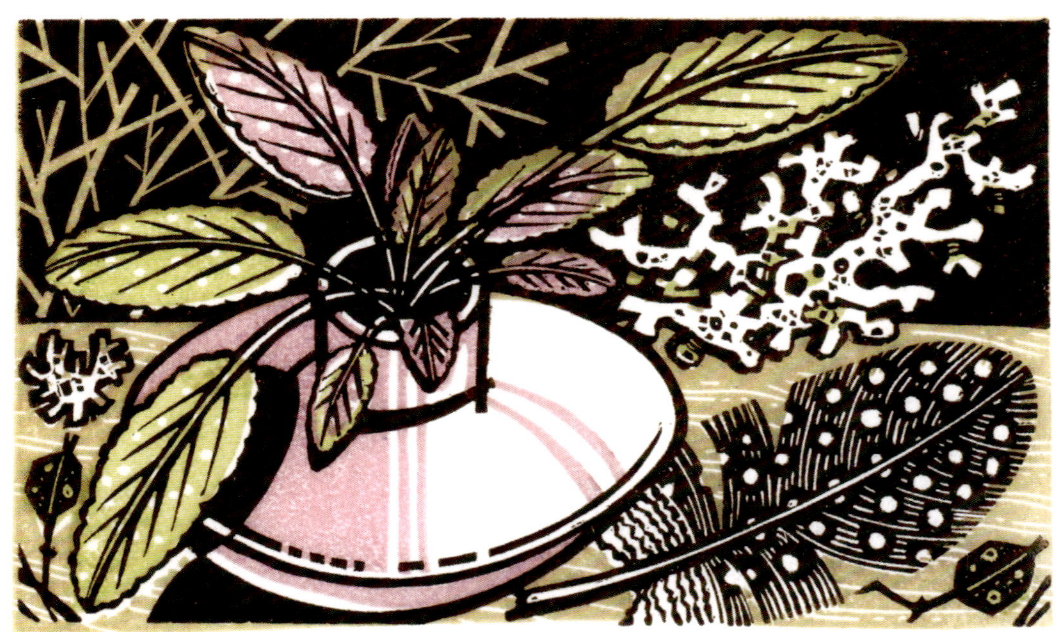

Coral and Sage

'a guineafowl's polka-dotted feather
and a strand of the seaweed
she picks up on her walks'

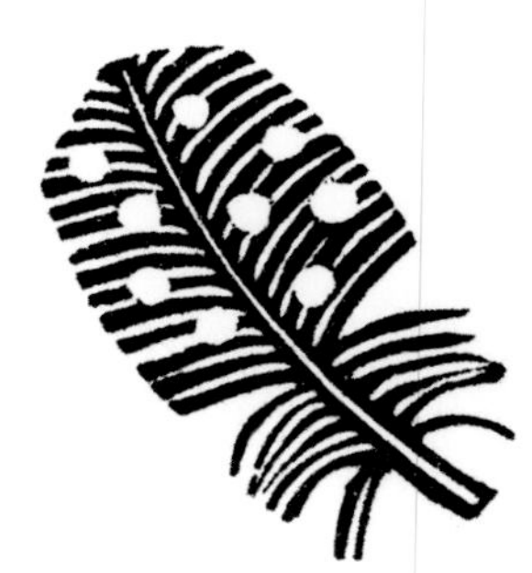

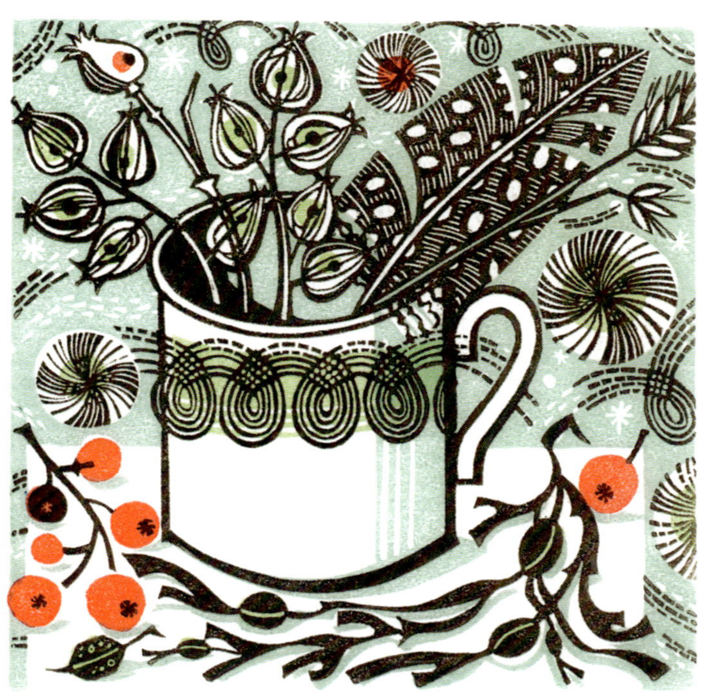

Winter Persephone

List of Works

Dimensions are given in centimetres (and inches), height preceding width.

PAGE 2: *Island with Teasels*, 2006, linocut, 29 × 21.5 cm (11⅜ × 8⅜ in.)

PAGE 21: *Coast*, 2008, collage (hand-printed papers), 9.2 × 8.9 cm (3⅝ × 3½ in.)

PAGE 27: *Winter Creek*, 2006, linocut, 24.5 × 36.5 cm (9⅝ × 14⅜ in.)

PAGE 29 top: *Black Island*, 2006, linocut, 8.2 × 14.5 cm (3¼ × 5⅝ in.)

PAGE 29 bottom: *Skye to Harris*, 2005, wood engraving and linocut, 4.4 × 8 cm (1¼ × 3⅛ in.)

PAGE 31: *Rain, Harris*, 2008, linocut, 30 × 43.5 cm (11¼ × 17⅛ in.)

PAGE 35: *Salthouse on the Scenic North Norfolk Coast* (poster), 2010, linocut, 70 × 50 cm (27½ × 19⅝ in.)

PAGE 36: *Agapanthus I*, 2003, screenprint, 45.5 × 24 cm (17¼ × 9 ½ in.)

PAGE 37: *Alexanders*, 2003, wood engraving and linocut, 11 × 7.4 cm (4⅜ × 3 in.)

PAGE 39: *Dandelion III*, 2004, wood engraving and linocut, 8.4 × 5 cm (3¼ × 2 in.)

PAGE 41: *Beach with Alexanders*, 2005, wood engraving and linocut, 12.5 × 10 cm (5 × 4 in.)

PAGE 42 bottom: *Clifftop*, 2003, wood engraving and linocut, 7.5 × 10 cm (2⅞ × 3⅞ in.)

PAGE 45 top: *Clifftop III*, 2004, wood engraving and linocut, 7.3 × 9.9 cm (2⅞ × 3⅞ in.)

PAGE 45 bottom: *Clifftop II*, 2003, wood engraving and linocut, 7.5 × 10.9 cm (2⅞ × 4¼ in.)

PAGE 49: *Scarista*, 2007, linocut, 28.5 × 21 cm (11¼ × 8¼ in.)

PAGE 51: *Seaweed, Buried Shell*, 2007, wood engraving and linocut, 6.7 × 9.8 cm (2⅝ × 3⅞ in.)

PAGE 53: *Salthouse*, 2003, linocut, 24.5 × 36.5 cm (9⅝ × 14⅜ in.)

PAGE 54: *Skye*, 2006, linocut, 10 × 6 cm (4 × 2⅜ in.)

PAGE 55: *The Beach, Aldeburgh*, 2005, linocut, 27.2 × 47.6 cm (10⅝ × 18¾ in.)

PAGE 57: *The Beach, Salthouse*, 2008, linocut, 24 × 42 cm (9⅜ × 16½ in.)

PAGE 59: *Weybourne to Sheringham*, 2003, linocut, 22.8 × 29.4 cm (9 × 11½ in.)

PAGE 61: *The Church, Salthouse*, 2008, linocut, 24 × 42 cm (9⅜ × 16¹¹⁄₁₆ in.)

PAGE 67: *Ballindalloch*, 2004, linocut, 28.3 × 38.3 cm (11⅛ × 15 in.)

PAGE 69: *5 Trees*, 2006, wood engraving and linocut, 12.2 × 4.5 cm (4¾ × 1¼ in.)

PAGE 70 bottom: *Birch*, 2004, wood engraving and linocut, 7.2 × 5 cm (2¾ × 2 in.)

PAGES 72–73: *Birches, Ballindalloch*, 2009, screenprint, 52.2 × 74 cm (20½ × 29⅛ in.)

PAGE 77: *Dandelion II*, 2003, wood engraving and linocut, 10.5 × 5 cm (4⅛ × 2 in.)

PAGE 79: *Ivy*, 2008, wood engraving and linocut, 5 × 5 cm (2 × 2 in.)

PAGE 83: *Ramsons*, 2009, wood engraving and linocut, 10 × 12.5 cm (4 × 5 in.)

PAGE 85: *Winter Birches*, 2010, screenprint, 55.5 × 22.8 cm (21⅞ × 9 in.)

PAGE 89 top: *Derelict Croft III*, 2009, collage (hand-printed papers and salvaged wallpaper), 11.5 × 11 cm (4½ × 4¼ in.)

PAGE 89 bottom: *Derelict Croft IV*, 2010, collage (hand-printed papers and salvaged wallpaper), 10.7 × 12.7 cm (4⅛ × 5 in.)

PAGE 91: *Autumn Spey*, 2008, lithograph, 30.3 × 55 cm (12 × 21⅝ in.)

PAGES 92–93: *By Green Bank*, 2009, screenprint, 45 × 74 cm (17⅝ × 29⅛ in.)

PAGE 96: *Loch with Dandelions*, 2005, linocut, 33.2 × 24.3 cm (13 × 9½ in.)

PAGE 99: *Late Summer Spey*, 2009, linocut, 24.6 × 57 cm (9⅝ × 22⅜ in.)

PAGE 101: *Moonlit Loch*, 2005, linocut, 26 × 19.3 cm (10¼ × 7⅝ in.)

PAGE 104 top: *Spey Path II*, 2006, linocut, 30.5 × 38.8 cm (12 × 15¼ in.)

PAGE 104 bottom: *Spey Path III*, 2007, linocut, 31 × 39.5 cm (12⅛ × 15½ in.)

PAGE 105: *Spey Path I*, 2004, linocut, 30.5 × 38.5 cm (12 × 15⅛ in.)

PAGE 107: *Spey Seedheads*, 2009, linocut, 16 × 16 cm (6¼ × 6¼ in.)

PAGE 110: *Winter Spey II*, 2008, wood engraving and linocut, 10 × 10 cm (3⅞ × 3⅞ in.)

PAGE 111: *Winter Spey III*, 2008, wood engraving and linocut, 10 × 10 cm (3⅞ × 3⅞ in.)

PAGE 113: *Winter Spey*, 2007, wood engraving and linocut, 10 × 12.5 cm (3⅞ × 4⅞ in.)

PAGES 116–17: *Yellow Rattle*, 2009, linocut, 23 × 51.9 cm (9⅛ × 20⅜ in.)

PAGE 123: *Agapanthus*, 2008, lithograph, 45 × 71 cm (17⅝ × 28 in.)

PAGE 125: *Alliums*, 2007, linocut, 26.5 × 22 cm (10⅜ × 8⅝ in.)

PAGE 127: *Alliums and Fennel*, 2008, lithograph, 30.8 × 54.9 cm (12⅛ × 21⅝ in.)

PAGE 129: *Anemone*, 2003, wood engraving and linocut, 7.2 × 4.5 cm (2¾ × 1¾ in.)

PAGE 131: *Blue Meadow*, 2004, linocut, 40.5 × 18.6 cm (16 × 7¼ in.)

PAGE 132 top: *Dandelion IV*, 2007, wood engraving and linocut, 4.8 × 4.8 cm (1⅞ × 1⅞ in.)

PAGE 132 bottom: *Dandelion I*, 2003, wood engraving and linocut, 5 × 7.6 cm (1⅞ × 3 in.)

PAGE 133: *Goat's Beard II*, 2003, linocut, 26 × 12.2 cm (10¼ × 4 ¾ in.)

PAGE 135: *Clocks II*, 2004, wood engraving and linocut, 10 × 7.7 cm (3⅞ × 3 in.)

PAGE 137: *Green Meadow*, 2008–2009, linocut, 35.5 × 35 cm (14 × 13¾ in.)

PAGE 139: *Hidden Fish*, 2008, wood engraving and linocut, 12.5 × 10 cm (5 × 4 in.)

Picture Credits

PAGES 140–41: *Meadow II*, 2008, lithograph, 30.8 × 54.9 cm (12⅛ × 21⅝ in.)

PAGE 143: *Meadow*, 2003, wood engraving and linocut, 10 × 7.6 cm (3⅞ × 3 in.)

PAGE 145: *Meadow's Edge*, 2006, wood engraving and linocut, 13 × 9.8 cm (5⅛ × 3⅞ in.)

PAGE 146: *Pale Day*, 2009, wood engraving and linocut, 7.5 × 4.8 cm (3 × 1⅞ in.)

PAGE 147: *Moonlit*, 2003, wood engraving and linocut, 15 × 10 cm (5⅞ × 4 in.)

PAGE 149: *Red Meadow*, 2004, wood engraving and linocut, 10.5 × 12.5 cm (4⅛ × 5 in.)

PAGE 153 left: *Ribwort Plantain*, 2003, linocut, 18.5 × 10.5 cm (7¼ × 4⅛ in.)

PAGE 153 right: *Plantain*, 2003, wood engraving and linocut, 5.7 × 4.5 cm (2¼ × 1¼ in.)

PAGE 154: *Spotted Leaf*, 2009, wood engraving and linocut, 9.8 × 7.2 cm (3⅞ × 2¼ in.)

PAGE 155: *Shepherd's Purse*, 2009, linocut, 16 × 16 cm (6¼ × 6¼ in.)

PAGE 157: *Teasel*, 2006, wood engraving and linocut, 17.2 × 11.7 cm (6¾ × 4⅝ in.)

PAGE 159: *Wild Garden*, 2006, lithograph, 60 × 43.8 cm (23⅝ × 17¼ in.)

PAGE 161: *Wild Garden II*, 2009, screenprint, 57 × 36 cm (22⅛ × 14⅛ in.)

PAGE 167: *The Moonlit Cup*, 2008, linocut, 56.5 × 43 cm (22¼ × 17 in.)

PAGE 169: *Rinour*, 2005, wood engraving and linocut, 13.3 × 6.9 cm (5¼ × 2⅝ in.)

PAGE 172: *Two Green Jars*, 2004, linocut, 30.5 × 38.5 cm (12 × 15⅛ in.)

PAGE 175: *Cup, Feathers and Seaweed*, 2010, lithograph, 36.7 × 48.9 cm (14⅜ × 19¼ in.)

PAGE 178: *The 1953 Coronation Mug*, 2007, lithograph, 39 × 57 cm (15⅜ × 22½ in.)

PAGE 179: *The 1937 Coronation Mug*, 2005, linocut, 46.5 × 41.5 cm (18⅜ × 16⅜ in.)

PAGE 181: *Totem*, 2007, lithograph, 54 × 24.5 cm (21¼ × 9⅝ in.)

PAGE 183: *Mug with Feathers*, 2010, wood engraving and linocut, 11 × 15 cm (4¼ × 5⅞ in.)

PAGE 184: *Autumn*, 2008, lithograph, 30 × 25 cm (11¼ × 9¾ in.)

PAGE 185 bottom: *Coral and Sage*, 2008, wood engraving and linocut, 6 × 10 cm (2⅜ × 4 in.)

PAGE 187: *Winter Persephone*, 2009, wood engraving and linocut, 10 × 10 cm (3⅞ × 3⅞ in.)

PAGE 192: *Applecross*, 2008, collage (printed Japanese papers on weathered Formica), 7.2 × 14.2 cm (2¼ × 5½ in.)

The photographs in this book have been reproduced courtesy of the following copyright holders:

Cristian Barnett: PAGES 10, 12, 13, 15, 43, 44, 156 (top row), 164

Simon Lewin: PAGES 9, 16, 22, 23, 24, 25, 34, 56, 62, 65, 80, 86, 88, 97, 103, 106, 118, 121 (top), 142, 152, 165 (top), 182

Additional photographs: Nicola Bailey

COVER: *Birches, Ballindalloch* (see pages 72–73)

PAGE 6: Preparatory drawing for *The Moonlit Cup* (see page 167)

PAGE 10: Angie Lewin in her Norfolk studio, checking a proof of *Teasel* (see page 157)

PAGE 22: Workbench in Lewin's Scottish studio

PAGE 62: Dried lichens and bracken in Lewin's Scottish studio

PAGES 86: Suilven, Sutherland, north-west Scotland

PAGE 100: Lewin's 'Dandelion 1' textile design, 2005, screenprinted on to heavyweight cotton

PAGE 103: The River Spey, north-east Scotland

PAGE 118: Knapweed and devil's-bit scabious in a Scottish meadow

PAGES 162–63: Pencil and watercolour sketch of a teacup and saucer with a design by Graham Sutherland, and the cup and saucer; dried seed head of *Allium schubertii*

PAGE 180: Dried seed heads in pots in Lewin's Norfolk studio

Bibliography

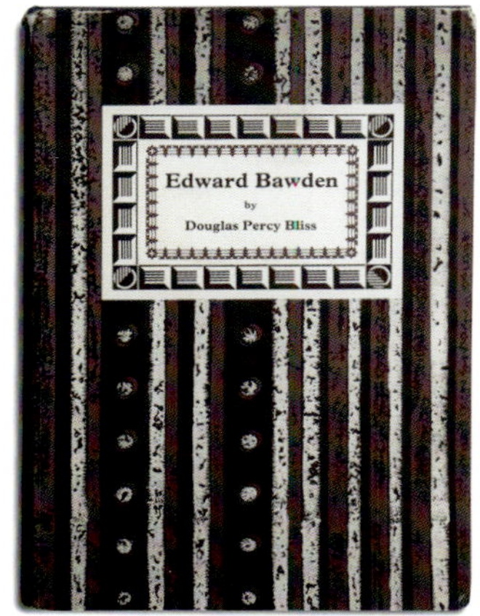

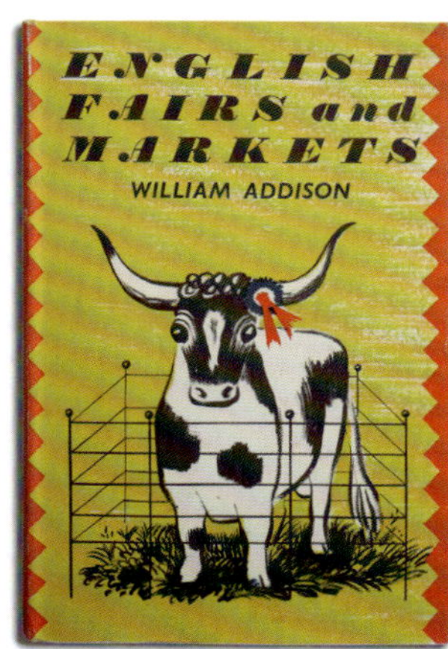

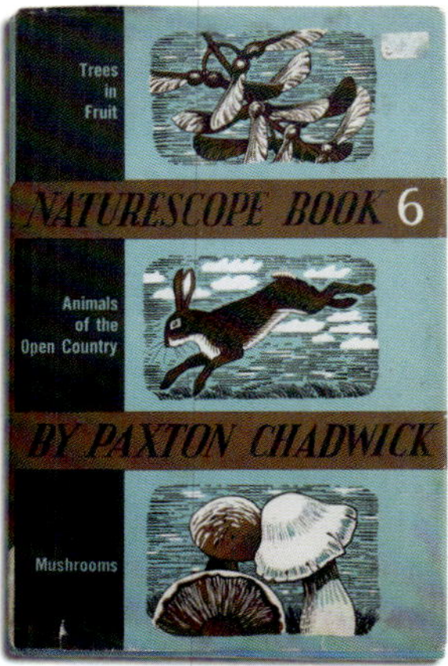

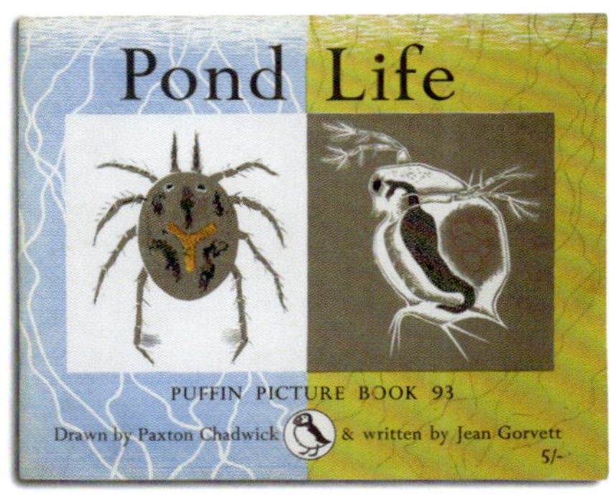

This list includes some of my favourite books. I spotted the Douglas Percy Bliss volume in a second-hand bookshop on Museum Street, London, just a few days after finishing my degree course at the Central School of Art and Design (now Central Saint Martins). I'd never come across Edward Bawden's work before, but was captivated by his witty and skilful illustrations and prints. This book led naturally to discovering more about him and his Bardfield contemporaries, including Eric Ravilious and Michael Rothenstein. Many of the artists who inspire me have also illustrated books and designed textiles and ceramics, so this list is an eclectic mix of 1940s natural history books and obscure titles collected for the artwork regardless of their subject. Wild-flower guides and gardening books are invaluable in helping me to identify the plants that I sketch.

Angie Lewin

William Addison, with illustrations by Barbara Jones, *English Fairs and Markets*, London (BT Batsford) 1953

Kenneth Allott, *The Penguin Book of Contemporary Verse*, Harmondsworth (Penguin) 1950

Alfred Alvarez, *The New Poetry*, Harmondsworth (Penguin) 1962

Ruth Artmonsky, *A Snapper Up of Unconsidered Trifles: A Tribute to Barbara Jones*, London (Artmonsky Arts) 2008

Mary Banham and Bevis Hillier (eds.), *A Tonic to the Nation*, London (Thames & Hudson) 1976

John H. Barrett, illustrated by Elspeth Yonge, *Pocket Guide to the Sea Shore*, London (Collins) 1964

Helen Binyon, *Eric Ravilious: Memoir of an Artist*, Cambridge (Lutterworth Press) 1983

Douglas Percy Bliss, *Edward Bawden*, Godalming (Pendomer Press) 1974

Paxton Chadwick, *Wild Flowers* [1949], Harmondsworth (Penguin) 1964

Paxton Chadwick, *Naturescope Book 6: Trees in Fruit, Animals of the Open Country and Mushrooms*, London (Cassell) 1962

Beth Chatto, *The Green Tapestry*, London (Harper Collins) 1995

Henry Cliffe, *Lithography*, London (Studio Vista) 1965

Philip Collins, *English Christmas*, Bedford (G. Fraser) 1956

Michael W. Davison (ed.), *Field Guide to the Wild Flowers of Britain*, London and New York (Reader's Digest) 1981

Roger Deakin, *Wildwood: A Journey Through Trees*, London (Penguin) 2008

Francis Martin Duncan, *British Shells*, London, Harmondsworth and New York (Penguin) 1943

Robert Elwall, *Evocations of Place: The Photography of Edwin Smith*, London and NY (Merrell) 2007

Fortnum & Mason Christmas 1955 catalogue, illustrated by Edward Bawden

Robert Gillmor, *Cutting Away: The Linocuts of Robert Gillmor*, Peterborough (Langford Press) 2006

Donal and Mabel Lindsay Glegg, *Ptarmigan Pie*, London (Golden Galley Press) 1946

Faye Godwin, *Land*, Boston (Little, Brown) 1985

Jean Gorvett, with illustrations by Paxton Chadwick, *Pond Life*, Harmondsworth (Penguin) 1952

Elliot L. Grant Watson, with illustrations by Charles F. Tunnicliffe, *What to Look for in Spring*, Loughborough (Wills & Hepworth) 1961

Jeremy Greenwood, *Edward Bawden: Editioned Prints*, Woodbridge (Wood Lea Press) 2005

Peter Hamilton, *An English Eye: The Photography of James Ravilious*, 2nd edn, Oxford (Bardwell Press) 2007

Robert Harling (ed.), *Ravilious and Wedgwood: The Complete Wedgwood Designs of Eric Ravilious*, Shepton Beauchamp (Richard Dennis) 1995

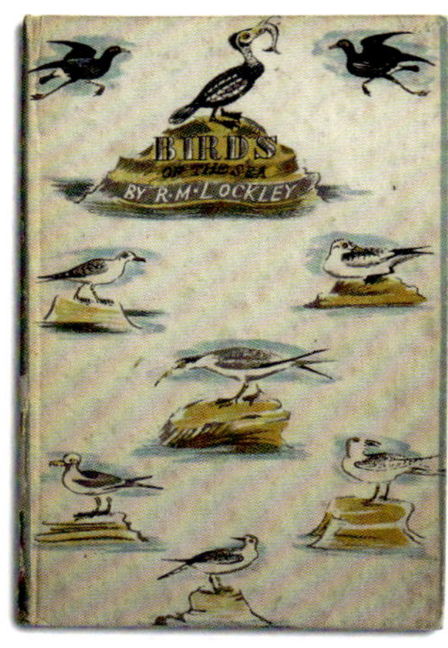 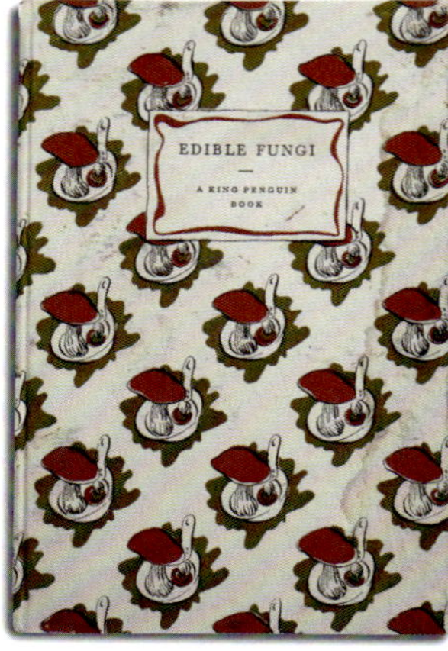 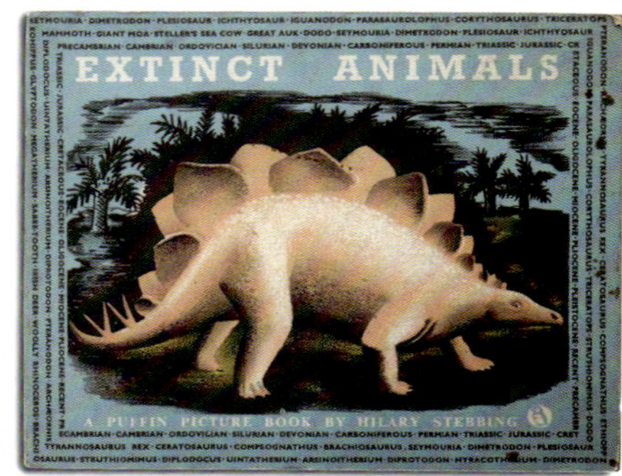

Wilhelmine Harrod (ed.),
John Betjeman (foreword),
*Norfolk Country Churches and the
Future*, Norwich (The Norfolk
Society) 1972

Ashley Havinden, *Line Drawing
for Reproduction*, London (The
Studio) and New York (The
Studio Publications) 1933

Lesley Jackson, *From Atoms to
Patterns*, Shepton Beauchamp
(Richard Dennis) 2008

Magda Joicey, with illustrations by
Edward Bawden, *Cook Book Note
Book*, London (Westhouse) 1946

Orde Levinson, *John Piper: The
Complete Graphic Works*, London
(Faber & Faber) 1987

Christopher Lloyd, *Meadows*, London
(Cassell) 2004

Ronald M. Lockley, *Birds of the Sea*,
London, Harmondsworth and
New York (Penguin) 1945

Linton Lynn, with illustrations by
Arthur Smith, *Whisker's Patch*,
London (Brown Watson) 1945

Norbert Lynton, *Ben Nicholson*,
London (Phaidon) 1993

Richard Mabey, *Flora Britannica*,
London (Sinclair Stevenson) 1996

Fiona MacCarthy, *Eric Gill*, London
(Faber & Faber) 1990

Robert Macfarlane, *The Wild Places*,
London (Granta) 2007

Gavin Maxwell, *Ring of Bright Water*
[1960], Wimborne Minster
(Little Toller) 2009

Roger Phillips, *Garden and Field
Weeds*, London (Elm Tree) 1986

Alan Powers, *Art and Print: The
Curwen Story*, London (Tate) 2008

Alan Powers and James Russell, *Eric
Ravilious: The Story of High Street*,
Norwich (Mainstone Press) 2008

John Ramsbottom, *Edible Fungi*,
revised edn, London
(Penguin) 1948

Ian Rogerson, *Barnett Freedman:
The Graphic Art*, Upper Denby
(Fleece Press) 2006

Judith Russell, *The Wood-engravings
of Gertrude Hermes*, Aldershot
(Scolar Press) 1993

Ludwig Schröter and Dr C.
Schröter, *Alpine Flora*, Zurich
(Albert Raustein) *c.* 1900

Tessa Sidey, *The Prints of Michael
Rothenstein*, Aldershot (Scolar
Press) 1993

Hilary Stebbing, *Extinct Animals*,
Harmondsworth and New York
(Penguin) 1946

Roberto Tassi, *Graham Sutherland:
Complete Graphic Work*, Barcelona
(Ediciones Poligrafa) 1988

Harry Ernest Towner-Coston,
The Swift Trout, 2nd edn, London
(Collins) 1946

Caroline Trant, *Art for Life: The Story
of Peggy Angus*, Oldham (Incline
Press) 2004

Visitor's London, with illustrations
by Edward Bawden and Eric
Ravilious, London (London
Transport) 1965

Charles White, *Country Walks*,
London (London Transport)
c. 1938

Malcolm Yorke, *Edward Bawden
and His Circle: The Inward Laugh*,
Woodbridge (Antique
Collectors' Club) 2007

BOOKS ILLUSTRATED BY ANGIE LEWIN

John Stewart Collis, *The Worm
Forgives the Plough* [1973],
London (Vintage) 2009

Carol Ann Duffy, *New Selected Poems*
[2004], London (Picador) 2009

Leslie Geddes-Brown (compiler),
Garden Wisdom, London and
New York (Merrell) 2009

Noël Kingsbury, with photography
by Nicola Browne, *Natural
Garden Style: Gardening Inspired
by Nature*, London and New York
(Merrell) 2009

Jenni Muir, *A Cook's Guide to
Grains* [2002], London (Conran
Octopus) 2008

Jeremy Page, *Salt* [2007], London
(Viking) 2008

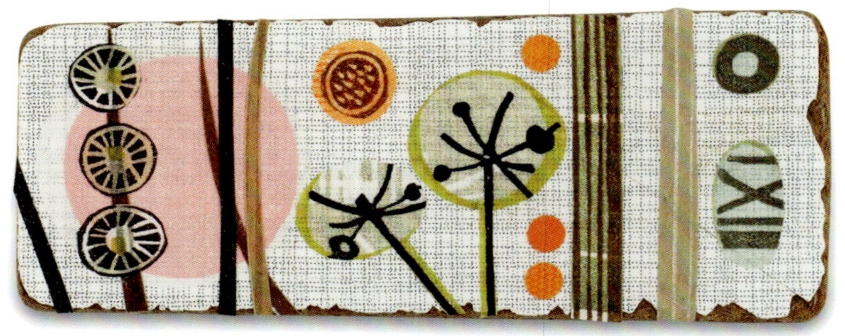

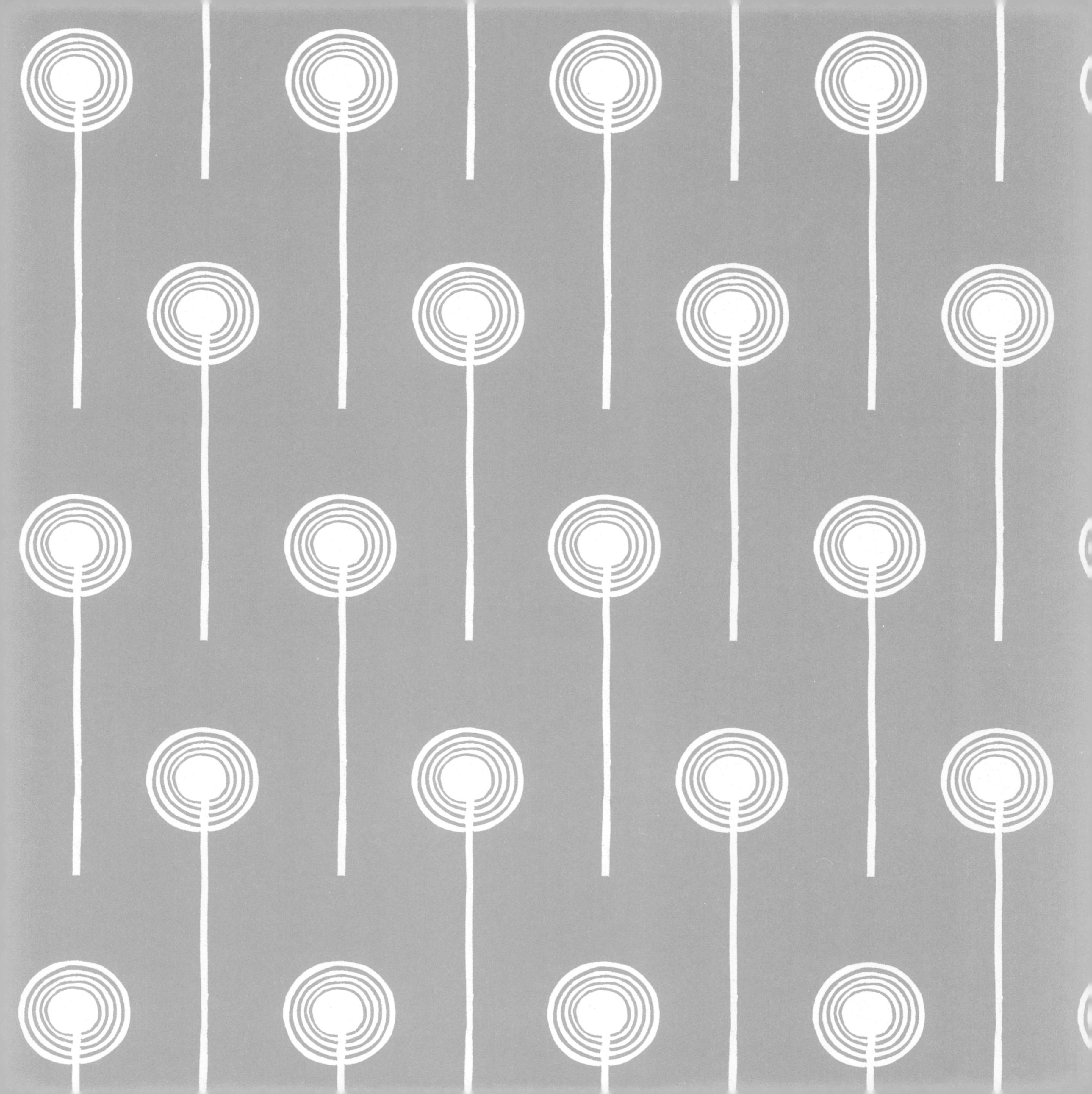

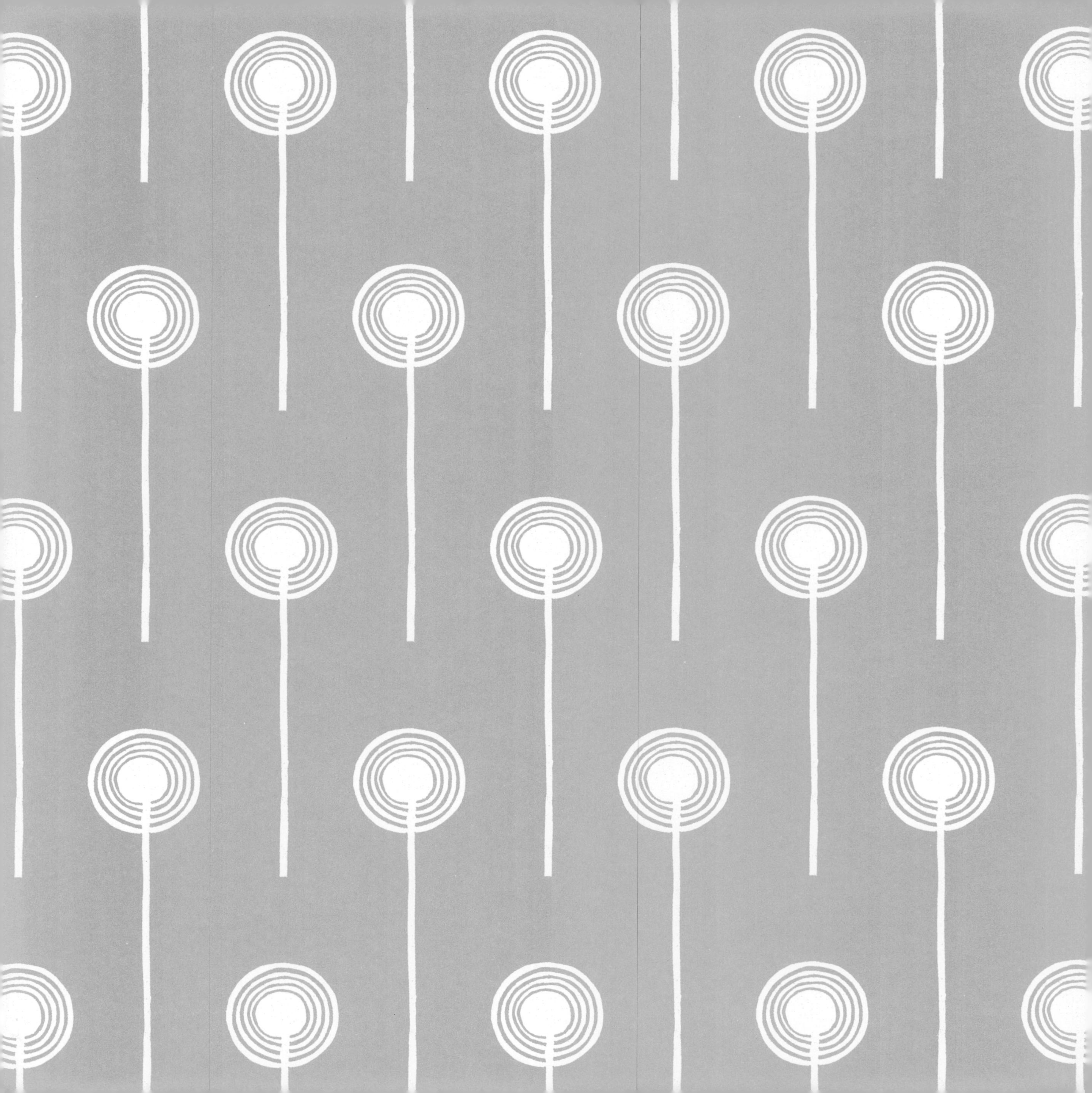